Schizophrenia, Culture, and Subj[ectivity]

Cambridge Studies in Medical Anthropology 11

This volume brings together a number of the foremost scholars – anthropologists, psychiatrists, psychologists, and historians – currently studying schizophrenia, its subjective dimensions, and the cultural processes through which these are experienced. Based on research undertaken in Australia, Bangladesh, Borneo, Canada, Colombia, India, Indonesia, Nigeria, the United States, and Zanzibar, it also incorporates a critical analysis of World Health Organization cross-cultural findings. Contributors share an interest in subjective and interpretive aspects of illness, but all work with a concept of schizophrenia that addresses its biological dimensions. The volume is of interest to scholars in the social and human sciences for the theoretical attention given to the relationship between culture and subjectivity. Multidisciplinary in design, it is written in a style accessible to a diverse readership, including undergraduate students. It is of practical relevance not only to psychiatrists, but also to all mental health professionals who encounter, day to day, the clinical problems arising at the interface of culture and psychosis.

Janis Hunter Jenkins, Professor of Anthropology and Psychiatry at Case Western Reserve University, is Principal Investigator for an NIMH-sponsored study of the subjective experiences of recovery among persons taking atypical antipsychotic medications. Professor Jenkins has published widely in the *British Journal of Psychiatry, American Journal of Psychiatry, Culture, Medicine and Psychiatry,* and *Transcultural Psychiatry,* as well as in anthropological journals such as *Ethos* and *Medical Anthropology Quarterly.*

Robert John Barrett is Professor of Psychiatry at the University of Adelaide and Clinical Advisor to the Psychiatric Services of the Royal Adelaide Hospital. Professor Barrett has published in cross-disciplinary journals such as *Culture, Medicine and Psychiatry,* and *Social Science and Medicine,* as well as in anthropological journals such as *Man.* His monograph, *The Psychiatric Team and the Social Definition of Schizophrenia* (1996), was published in the Cambridge University Press series Studies in Social and Community Psychiatry.

Cambridge Studies in Medical Anthropology

Editor
ALAN HARWOOD *University of Massachusetts, Boston*

Editorial Board
WILLIAM DRESSLER *University of Alabama*
RONALD FRANKENBERG *Brunel University, UK*
MARY JO GOOD *Harvard University*
SHARON KAUFMAN *University of California, San Francisco*
SHIRLEY LINDENBAUM *City University of New York*
MARGARET LOCK *McGill University*
CATHERINE PANTER-BRICK *University of Durham, UK*

Medical anthropology is the fastest growing specialist area within anthropology, in both North America and Europe. Beginning as an applied field serving public health specialists, medical anthropology now provides a significant forum for many of the most urgent debates in anthropology and the humanities. It includes the study of medical institutions and health care in a variety of rich and poor societies, the investigation of the cultural construction of illness, and the analysis of ideas about the body, birth, maturity, aging, and death.

This series includes theoretically innovative monographs and state-of-the-art collections of essays on current issues.

1 Lynn M. Morgan, *Community Participation in Health: The Politics of Primary Care in Costa Rica*
2 Thomas J. Csordas (ed.), *Embodiment and Experience: The Existential Ground of Culture and Health*
3 Paul Brodwin, *Medicine and Morality in Haiti: The Contest for Healing Power*
4 Susan Reynolds Whyte, *Questioning Misfortune: The Pragmatics of Uncertainty in Eastern Uganda*
5 Margaret Lock and Patricia Kaufert, *Pragmatic Women and Body Politics*
6 Vincanne Adams, *Doctors for Democracy*
7 Elizabeth Hsu, *The Transmission of Chinese Medicine*

Series information continues after the index.

Schizophrenia, Culture, and Subjectivity

The Edge of Experience

Edited by

Janis Hunter Jenkins
Case Western Reserve University

Robert John Barrett
University of Adelaide

PUBLISHED BY THE PRESS SYNDICATE OF THE UNIVERSITY OF CAMBRIDGE
The Pitt Building, Trumpington Street, Cambridge, United Kingdom

CAMBRIDGE UNIVERSITY PRESS
The Edinburgh Building, Cambridge CB2 2RU, UK
40 West 20th Street, New York, NY 10011-4211, USA
477 Williamstown Road, Port Melbourne, VIC 3207, Australia
Ruiz de Alarcón 13, 28014 Madrid, Spain
Dock House, The Waterfront, Cape Town 8001, South Africa

http://www.cambridge.org

First published 2004

Printed in the United States of America

Typeface Plantin 10/12 pt.   *System* LATEX 2$_\varepsilon$ [TB]

A catalog record for this book is available from the British Library.

Library of Congress Cataloging in Publication Data

Schizophrenia, culture, and subjectivity : the edge of experience /
edited by Janis Hunter Jenkins, Robert John Barrett.
    p. cm. – (Cambridge studies in medical anthropology ; 9)
Includes bibliographical references and index.
ISBN 0-521-82955-0 – ISBN 0-521-53641-3 (pb.)
1. Schizophrenia – Social aspects.   2. Schizophrenia – Cross-cultural
studies.   3. Subjectivity.   I. Jenkins, Janis H.   II. Barrett, Robert J.
III. Series.
RC514.S3349   2003
616.89′82–dc21   2003046125

ISBN 0 521 82955 0 hardback
ISBN 0 521 53641 3 paperback

Contents

Contributors

Robert John Barrett is a psychiatrist and anthropologist and Professor of Psychiatry at the University of Adelaide. His clinical training was in medicine and psychiatry. He received a Ph.D. from the University of Adelaide in anthropology and undertook postdoctoral studies at Harvard University. His earlier research was in the field of psychiatric hospital ethnography, and he is currently working on ethnographic and clinical studies conducted among the Iban in Borneo.

Ellen Corin is a psychologist and Professor of Anthropology and Psychiatry at McGill University and researcher at the Psychosocial Research Division, Douglas Hospital Research Centre. She received a Ph.D. in psychology from the Université de Louvain, Belgium. Her research in Central Africa, Quebec, and currently in India focuses on the interface between culture and subjectivity. Her current work deals with psychosis and culture. She is also a member of the Canadian Psychoanalytic Society and a clinical practitioner.

Esperanza Diaz is a psychiatrist and Associate Professor of Psychiatry and Medical Director of the Hispanic Clinic at the Yale University School of Medicine. She was educated at Javeriana University in Bogota, Colombia, and Yale University. She is working on a project following medication adherence for Latinos collecting quantitative and qualitative data. The purpose is to identify ethnic differences in medication adherence between Latinos and non-Latinos. She is interested in health services research.

Sue E. Estroff is an anthropologist and Professor of Social Medicine at the University of North Carolina at Chapel Hill. She did her undergraduate work at Duke University and her graduate studies in anthropology at the University of Wisconsin–Madison, where she was also a postdoctoral Fellow in psychiatry. She has studied people with schizophrenia and other severe psychiatric disorders in several settings in the United States over the past two decades. At present, she is conducting research on informed consent in experimental fetal surgery and an analytic review of antipsychiatric stigma programs in practice.

Alberto Fergusson, M.D., is a psychiatrist and Professor at the Colombian School of Rehabilitation as well as founder and president of FUNGRATA in Sopo, Colombia, and FAS in Washington, DC, institutions dedicated to the rehabilitation of mentally ill people. He is an advocate for the human rights of mentally and physically disabled people.

Marja K. Germans is a Ph.D. candidate at the University of California, Berkeley. She received her M.A. from Vanderbilt and her B.A. from Princeton University. Her research to date has investigated emotional responding in patients with schizophrenia and anhedonic college students. She is currently working on her dissertation research, which posits a link between impairments of emotional responding and deficits in attentional processing in patients with schizophrenia.

Byron J. Good is an anthropologist and Professor of Medical Anthropology in the Department of Social Medicine, Harvard Medical School, and the Department of Anthropology at Harvard. He studied comparative religion at Harvard Divinity School and social anthropology at the University of Chicago. He has conducted field research on social and cultural dimensions of mental illness and mental health care in Iran, Turkey, and the United States. He is currently conducting research on psychotic illness in Indonesia.

Kim Hopper is an anthropologist Research Scientist at the Nathan S. Kline Institute for Psychiatric Research and lecturer at Columbia University's Schools of Public Health and Law. He was educated at the University of Virginia and Columbia. For the past twenty years he has worked chiefly on the problem of urban homelessness in the United States (he has a book in press about New York), and issues in cross-cultural psychiatry. He is coediting the forthcoming volume on the WHO Collaborative Study on the Long-Term Course and Outcome in Schizophrenia.

Janis Hunter Jenkins is an anthropologist and Professor of Anthropology and Psychiatry at Case Western Reserve University. She received her doctoral degree in anthropology from the University of California at Los Angeles and undertook postdoctoral studies at Harvard Medical School. She has conducted research on culture and mental health over the past two decades. Currently, she is principal investigator for a NIMH-funded study of the experiences of recovery among persons taking atypical antipsychotic medications.

Arthur Kleinman is an anthropologist and psychiatrist and Professor of Social Anthropology in the Department of Anthropology and Maude and Lillian Presley Professor of Medical Anthropology and Psychiatry in the Department of Social Medicine at Harvard University. He has conducted research on illness (especially neurasthenia and depression) and suffering in Chinese society since 1968. Educated at Stanford and Harvard, he is currently engaged in the study of suicide in China.

Ann M. Kring is a psychologist and Associate Professor of Psychology and Director of the Clinical Science Program and the Psychology Clinic at the University of California, Berkeley. She received her Ph.D. from the State University of New York at Stony Brook. Her research is broadly focused on emotion and psychopathology, with a particular emphasis on emotion processes in schizophrenia, depression, and social anxiety.

Rod Lucas is an anthropologist and Lecturer in Anthropology in the School of Social Sciences at the University of Adelaide, where his Ph.D. research on the experiences of "deinstitutionalized" psychiatric culture was undertaken jointly in anthropology and medicine. He has worked in Island Melanesia, Aboriginal Australia, and suburban mental health settings. In addition to teaching medical anthropology and social theory, he works as a consultant to Aboriginal organizations on heritage, land, and native title matters.

Juli H. McGruder is an anthropologist and Professor of Occupational Therapy at the University of Puget Sound. She was educated at the University of Washington and Indiana University. She has studied persons diagnosed with mental illness both in the United States and in East Africa. She is currently working on an ethnography of three families with multigenerational histories of schizophrenia in Zanzibar.

Ramachandran Padmavati qualified in Psychiatry from the University of Bombay in India. She is a clinical psychiatrist and the deputy director at the Schizophrenia Research Foundation, Madras (now Chennai), India. Her research interests include epidemiology and community mental health.

Jonathan Sadowsky is a historian and the Theodore J. Castele Associate Professor of the History of Medicine at Case Western Reserve University. He received his Ph.D. in history from the Johns Hopkins University and studied psychiatric epidemiology at Columbia University. His 1999 monograph, *Imperial Bedlam: Institutions of Madness in Colonial Southwest Nigeria*, was published by the University of California Press. He is working on a cultural history of electroconvulsive therapy in America.

Louis A. Sass is a clinical psychologist and Professor and Chair of the Department of Clinical Psychology at Rutgers University, where he also serves on the faculties of the Program in Comparative Literature and the Center for Cognitive Science. He was educated at Harvard University and Berkeley. He has written extensively on phenomenological psychopathology, hermeneutics, and aspects of modernist and postmodernist culture. Recently he coedited a special issue of *Creativity Research Journal* on "Creativity and the Schizophrenia Spectrum" (2000/2001). He has also edited a forthcoming issue of the journal *Philosophy, Psychiatry, Psychology*, on the phenomenology of schizophrenia.

John S. Strauss is a psychiatrist and Professor Emeritus of Psychiatry at Yale Medical School. His background includes (the old) Gestalt psychology as a student of Kohler and others at Swarthmore College, an M.D. from Yale Medical School, studying with Jean Piaget, epidemiologic research on diagnosis and course of schizophrenia with WHO, and most recently, the role of subjectivity and the patient's own efforts in the origins, course, and improvement of severe mental disorders.

M. A. Subandi is Lecturer in the Department of Psychology at Gadjah Mada University, Yogyakarta, Indonesia. He received a masters degree from Queensland University of Technology and since 1996 has been working with Byron Good on a psychosis project in Java. He is currently undertaking doctoral research in the Department of Psychiatry at the University of Adelaide.

Rangaswami Thara is a psychiatrist by training who obtained her Ph.D. in psychiatry from Madras, India. She is the director of the Schizophrenia Research Foundation (SCARF), a voluntary organization committed to the cause of schizophrenia. SCARF is a WHO Collaborating Center for Mental Health. Her research interests include longitudinal studies and cultural and social issues of mental health.

James M. Wilce, Jr., is an anthropologist and Associate Professor of Anthropology at Northern Arizona University and received his Ph.D. in anthropology at UCLA. He has worked with Bangla speakers in Bangladesh, Los Angeles, New York, and London. He is currently preparing a monograph on modernity's impact on traditional genres of grief and grievance.

Preface

Schizophrenia is *the* defining problem for psychiatry. In the nineteenth century, American psychiatry first projected onto schizophrenia the images of treatment that it inherited from European medicine: strait-jackets, hydrotherapy, bloodletting, herbal compounds, and, of course, the asylum. Then it was moral therapy, which held up until the ethnic mix of American society changed so significantly that America could no longer project a single moral world, and contesting multicultural influences that challenged the presumptions of this "our crowd" therapeutic approach. Latterly, social Darwinism, eugenics, and social science reinvigorated a *fin de siecle* organic image of the deranged mind based in the brain tainted by degeneracy.

The twentieth century was the hothouse of psychological models, with Freudianism coming to dominate the image of what mental illness was. Side by side with psychodynamic projections, somatic treatments *evolved* – if we can call such a stop-and-go, recursive, and controversial process by this term – from insulin shock and electroconvulsive therapies through psychosurgery to what we now think of as modern psychopharmacology. The broken brain has become the dominant professional (and popular) image in America. Today's world of biological psychiatry claims schizophrenia as its own, even though the genetic contribution to the transmission of schizophrenia has gotten more and more complex and uncertain, and there is still no biological marker in everyday clinical practice that can be used to diagnose and follow the course of the disorder.

Much of the interest in social factors – class, community, family, networks, life events – has, if not diminished, then at least lost the excitement it held several decades ago, even though some of the findings (like the relation of expressed emotions in family members to vulnerability to exacerbation and rehospitalization) seem about as robust as biological evidence. This is not true of the interest of anthropologists in the relationship between culture, collective and subjective experience, and schizophrenia. Although anthropologists make up a relatively small percentage of schizophrenia researchers, they have built a remarkable, multifaceted colloquy on schizophrenia in society: a colloquy that has as much to say about the social world as about schizophrenia. Moreover, in an era of experience-distant causal models and remote-control research methods in psychiatry and even psychology, the work of anthropologists continues to emphasize the "experience-near" phenomenology of the illness and treatment experiences. By and large, this tradition of research is sequestered in specialist journals and conference proceedings. Although several full-scale ethnographies have received a wider audience, I think it is still fair to say that the field of culture and schizophrenia is not well understood among mental health professionals. Even within anthropology, this is the focus of a relatively small circle.

Schizophrenia, Culture, and Subjectivity is the most serious effort to date to present what is happening in the culture and schizophrenia field. It is a broad-ranging and ambitious collection that defines why schizophrenia is important to anthropologists (and others undertaking cultural studies) and illustrates what anthropologists contribute to the study of schizophrenia. Jenkins, Barrett, et al. explain the major changes that have occurred in the conceptual frameworks of social and cultural anthropology over the past decades and why these conceptual shifts hold salience for schizophrenia. Clearly, what most mental health professionals mean by *culture* is different from what most of the contributors to this collection mean. The current anthropological consensus, which emphasizes how culture is realized differently in particular interactions, processes, and interior worlds, leads to a very different set of ideas about how culture affects psychosis.

The ethnographic descriptions, of course, make the case for the context of local worlds shaping the experience of sufferers, family members, and professionals. But those descriptions do more than that. They challenge the core pathogenetic/pathoplastic ideology of psychiatry and psychology. They rethink the symptomology and classification of schizophrenia. They make the social course of the disease a powerful analytic alternative to the much better known natural history model of prognosis. They tell us about personal, family, and community responses to schizophrenia that convince the reader that treatment and prevention include much more than professional interventions. And in so doing, a number of the chapters show how schizophrenia and its study alter how we think of inner life and intersubjective connections.

Illness experience, for the ethnographer, is a moral phenomenon because, like all forms of experience, particular things are most at stake for sufferers and their families. Schizophrenia, seen in this ethnographic angle of vision, not only has a political economy but a moral economy as well. Values are embodied and have a presence in the symptoms and course of psychosis, but they are also alive in the experience of caregivers and

researchers, so that the entire enterprise of understanding and managing schizophrenia is inseparable from the pull and push of different and
contested values and the political economy that supports them. Thus,
the subject matter of ethnography is not schizophrenia as some kind of
stripped-down biomedical disease entity, but schizophrenia as a nexus of
the medical, the moral, the economic, and the political. The chapters in
this collection differ in how they conceptualize and analyze this nexus,
but they share this crucial framing. They also do what anthropology routinely does by bringing a broad comparative framework to bear in which
national, regional, and local differences are prominent. This assures that
important cultural and ethnic differences in how schizophrenia is lived
and engaged receive the attention they deserve.

The result is a different agenda for future research and an original
and iconoclastic rethinking of how schizophrenia should be studied. I
don't believe the subject will ever quite be the same again for readers
new to this perspective; and for those who are already initiates, their
interest will be revivified, as mine was. Will social theory and ethnography
make a difference to patients and families? I, for one, think they could
if these ideas can be translated into policies and programs. However,
that is still an area of uncertainty. Can the study of schizophrenia alter
anthropological approaches by, for example, making the study of inner
worlds, interpersonal processes, and experiences that resist being only
about difference, more central to a discipline that has become fixated on
cultural representations and social constructions? The challenge is there,
and it should be one of the more unsettling issues for anthropologists
who read this collection. But just demonstrating that schizophrenia has
as much to do with society as it has to do with biology should be seen in
our biologized times as one of the book's more serious achievements.

Arthur Kleinman
Harvard University

Acknowledgments

We wish to express our gratitude to Eric Wanner and the Russell Sage Foundation for generous funding of the international conference convened in New York City. The papers presented at that conference served as the starting point for this volume. From Alan Harwood, editor of the medical anthropology series for Cambridge University Press, we have enjoyed sustained support and a steady editorial vision. From Case Western Reserve University, we thank several research assistants and students who assisted in the preparation of the volume: Meredith Holmes, Dawn Miller, Sarah Adler, Jean Berggren, Maureen Williams, Elizabeth Carpenter, and Holly Augusta. We are also grateful to Sue Sullivan at the University of Adelaide Department of Psychiatry for her assistance throughout. The volume as a whole was considerably enhanced by the thoughtful critique that was provided by three anonymous referees.

We wish to reciprocally acknowledge our editorial appreciation of one another in relation to the spark, stamina, and grace involved in seeing this volume through to completion. Likewise, this volume has benefited from the steady involvement of a number of close colleagues including Mary Jo DelVecchio Good, Arthur Kleinman, Marvin Karno, and Byron Good. For the loving indulgence of our families throughout this process, JHJ thanks her children, Vanessa and Graham, and husband, Thomas Csordas. RJB expresses his gratitude to daughter, Githie, and wife, Mitra, his most perspicacious critic of all. To the several hundred persons among whom ethnographic and clinical research was conducted globally to gain understanding of the ordinary and extraordinary courage mustered in the face of suffering and recovery from schizophrenia, we wish this book to honor you.

Schizophrenia, Culture, and Subjectivity

Introduction

Janis Hunter Jenkins and *Robert John Barrett*

The fact of the psychoses is a puzzle to us. They are the unsolved problem of human life as such. The fact that they exist is the concern of
everyone. Jaspers 1964 [1923].

Background to the Collection

In the fall of 1986, as postdoctoral fellows together in the Department
of Social Medicine at Harvard Medical School, Janis Jenkins and Robert
Barrett, the editors of this volume, began a conversation about culture
and schizophrenia. By the fall of 1996 when Rob visited Janis, then a
scholar-in-residence at the Russell Sage Foundation in New York City,
it was time to do something about this conversation. We began by organizing a panel that developed into an invited session at the 1997 meeting
of the American Anthropological Association in Washington, DC. The
session was entitled, "The Edge of Experience: Schizophrenia, Culture,
and Subjectivity."

After this meeting, we submitted a proposal to the Russell Sage Foundation to fund a symposium that would assemble an even larger group
of scholars working at the interface of culture and schizophrenia. The
foundation generously supported this project under its mandate to generate scholarship concerned with the "improvement of social and living
conditions." The three-day symposium that took place brought together
twenty-two scholars of diverse academic and professional backgrounds –
anthropologists, psychiatrists, psychologists, and historians – to report
on research that had been carried out in North America, Latin America,
Africa, South and Southeast Asia, and Australia, as well as on the international studies of the World Health Organization. As our aim was to
foster research in culture and schizophrenia, we deliberately invited a mix
of scholars, from senior, well-established figures to young researchers reporting on their doctoral work. Students rubbed shoulders with doyens.
In the 1930s, the psychiatrist, Harry Stack Sullivan lived just half a block
from where the Russell Sage Foundation now stands on East 64th Street,

1

and it was during this era that his collaboration with the anthropologist, Edward Sapir flourished, generating a body of scholarship oriented to the dynamics of social interaction as the locus of both schizophrenia and culture. Our project continued this rich heritage of studies in culture and mental health associated with this particular New York City neighborhood.

It is from these origins that this volume emerged.

Framework for the Volume: Conceptualizing Schizophrenia, Culture, and Subjective Experience

Disorders of Schizophrenia

It has become commonplace to observe that schizophrenia is probably not a single disorder but more likely a number of disorders that are, for the time being, classified under one rubric. As Bleuler (1950) was the first to emphasize, "the Group of Schizophrenias" is fundamentally heterogeneous. The origins of this heterogeneity may be similarly biological and cultural (Lin 1996). While this volume selects cultural analysis for primary consideration, it is axiomatic that biological investigations are no less critical to an understanding of schizophrenia. This being said, the role of culture has been regarded in many quarters as secondary at best. In seeking to redress the situation, this volume is perhaps the first systematic effort to advance a cultural approach to the study of schizophrenia that takes the complex phenomenal reality of subjective experience as a starting point. We anticipate that the material presented here will therefore be of practical value to mental health professionals, not only for the insights into schizophrenia that are offered by contributing authors, but also for the interpretive approaches that are developed herein – approaches that health professionals themselves can adopt to understand their patients better.

Schizophrenia is one of the most severe psychiatric disorders. It carries serious implications for those who suffer from it and those who care for them because it is associated with significant disability and a substantial mortality rate. The widespread distribution of this disorder and its remarkable variability are two of its striking characteristics. It affects people from all class backgrounds, though persons of lower socioeconomic status are particularly at risk (Cohen 1993). Whether this is due to "social causation" or "downward drift," the association between schizophrenia and social class is one of the most consistent findings in psychiatric epidemiology (Fox 1990). Schizophrenia has been recognized in a wide range of cultures. Contemporary epidemiological evidence indicates that its prevalence varies from 1.4 to 4.6 per 1,000, and incidence rates range from 0.16 to 0.42 per 1,000 population (Jablensky 2000). Germane to many of the contributions to this volume are the well-established, cross-cultural differences in the clinical features of schizophrenia, particularly in relation to its course.

With regard to the conceptualization of the disorder, we have adopted a strategy that employs contemporary research diagnostic criteria as a productive starting point for cross-cultural studies, notably those of the International Classification of Diseases (World Health Organization 1994), and the Diagnostic and Statistical Manual IV (DSM-IV) (American Psychiatric Association 1994, 2000). Given that, we are broadly concerned with a pattern of symptoms characterized by positive symptoms (disordered thinking, disorganized speech, hallucinations, and delusions), negative symptoms (such as withdrawal or blunting of emotional expression), and disorders of motor behavior that may include catatonia. And we are concerned with a pattern of illness that is of sufficient duration and severity that it leads to a loss of social function in those who suffer from it.

The DSM-IV diagnostic criteria were, for the first time, developed in consultation with a working group of anthropologists and psychiatrists charged with the task of providing cultural perspectives for particular disorders (Mezzich, Kleinman, Fabrega, and Parron 1996). One of the editors (Jenkins) served as the anthropologist charged with summarizing available cultural materials on schizophrenia and supplying text for incorporation into DSM-IV that could provide clinical guidance for an understanding of the ways in which culture should be taken into consideration in diagnostic assessments. Cultural evidence in relation to the symptom criteria for schizophrenia and related psychotic disorders are summarized in a review by Karno and Jenkins (1997). Given the depth and breadth of the ways in which culture mediates nearly every aspect of schizophrenia, it was a significant milestone when "culture" was incorporated into DSM-IV. Nevertheless, publication of DSM-IV fell considerably short of the mark by virtue of a limited representation, in light of available evidence, of the relevance of culture to diagnostic formulation (Jenkins 1998). Moreover, we are mindful that schizophrenia as a clinical concept has arisen within a European and North American intellectual milieu (Barrett 1998). For this reason alone, it is necessary to pursue the study of schizophrenia from a historically and cross-culturally informed point of view. Thus, a number of the contributions pursue a reflexive analysis of contemporary diagnostic criteria and concepts, raising questions about their western cultural underpinnings and their validity in other settings (Good 1992). It is this Janus-faced approach – working with schizophrenia, as currently defined, while at the same time subjecting it to cultural critique – that characterizes this volume.

Cultural Orientations

The likelihood of a mutual interaction between culture and psychotic illness has been recognized since dementia praecox and its successor, schizophrenia, were first formulated as a category of illness. With the publication of this volume, we mark the centenary of Kraepelin's 1903 voyage to the psychiatric institutions of Singapore and Java, a voyage sometimes taken to be the ancestral journey that founded transcultural psychiatry. For a number of reasons, at the intersection of culture and schizophrenia, much remains to be charted nearly a century later. Anthropologists who have worked with a sophisticated and deeply contextualized approach to culture have only rarely brought clinical or research diagnostic skills to the task, while psychiatrists who have developed well-honed, operationalized definitions of schizophrenia have tended to employ lay versions of culture that look more like superficial national stereotypes than anything else. Furthermore, schizophrenia has long been regarded as the core conundrum of psychiatry, and it could well be argued that the concept of culture has occupied a similar position in anthropology, in which case it is not surprising that the question of how the two influence each other has been difficult to specify.

One aim of the present volume is to break this impasse, first, as we have seen, by treating contemporary definitions of schizophrenia seriously, either as research tools or as a body of knowledge deserving thoughtful cultural critique, and second, by bringing more expressly articulated and rigorously theorized concepts of culture to the equation. Whereas schizophrenia is defined from the top down – the WHO (1994) The International Statistical Classification of Diseases and Related Health Problems, tenth revision (ICD) – 10 symptom criteria or the American Psychiatric Association's (1994) DSM-IV definition – culture is defined here from the bottom up, a strategy that reflects the ethnographic spirit of this volume. It is important that the clinical definition of schizophrenia be operationalized in order to achieve agreement among researchers in diverse field sites that they are talking about more or less the same thing. In contrast, culture is an emergent property of context-bound human interaction, and cannot be operationalized in the same way. Attempts to do so reduce it to something it is not, a quantifiable "cultural factor" or a "cultural variable."

The papers in this collection are based on research carried out in a range of cultural settings. And while there are as many approaches to

culture as there are chapters, the commonalities among them lend coherence to the collection. All the authors recognize culture, in its broad-
est dimensions, as shared symbols and meanings that people create
in the process of social interaction. They see it as shaping experience
(including the experience of schizophrenia), interpretation, and action.
It thereby orients people in their ways of feeling, thinking, and being in
the world. Throughout the volume contributors express an interest in
culture as the basic moral and ideational domain from which individuals
may deviate. Schizophrenia is an instance of transgression situated at the
margins of culture, at the very edge of meaningful experience. There is
also agreement that while culture can be regarded as an object (a corpus
of shared knowledge, a body of routine practice, a set of values), it is important to recognize that it is more fundamentally a process including the
production and reification of knowledge, the transformation of practice,
and the reproduction of values. This is best captured in Obeyesekere's
(1990:xix) expression "the work of culture," by which he means the subjective process of formation and transformation "whereby symbolic forms
existing on the cultural level get created and recreated through the minds
of people." Culture theory has come to incorporate distinctions between
disciplinary or discursive knowledge in relation to institutional forms of
power, on the one hand, and situated, local knowledge in relation to personal forms of power and resistance, on the other. Conceptualization of
the relation between these two forms of cultural knowledge and power
is best formulated not as mutually exclusive, but rather as reciprocally
produced (Bourgois 1995; Ortner, 1996; Floersch 2002).

It is noteworthy that much of the research for this collection has been
done across cultural divides, whether it be cross-cultural research in
a classical sense, or the exploration of meaning structures within the
researcher's own context that are nonetheless foreign to him or her. Where
this is so the authors have brought with them a strong sense of culture
as a reflexive process. They have viewed their research as an interaction
between cultures, that of the researcher and that of the people with whom
she or he is working.

As an analytic and pragmatic strategy, all the authors work with specific concepts of culture; they toil at the microscopic level or in medium
focus, not with broad brush. The collection as a whole argues that
it is no longer useful in this field of research to equate culture with
nation-state or society at large as pursued in much of the initial international multisite research. Instead, analytic attention must be focused
in specific domains such as family interaction, gender, religion, ethnicity, or personhood, and each of these, in turn, specified ethnographically.
At this analytic level, it is possible to see that culture may be contradictory, fragmented, contested, and politicized rather than necessarily

coherent or uniform. Cultural meanings attributed to schizophrenia are very often embedded in conflict between "tradition" and modernity, for example, between witchcraft and medicine, between patient advocacy groups and psychiatric orthodoxy, or between competing religions and sects. Thus, what unites the authors in this volume is an approach to culture that works between shared and conflicting meanings, between overarching structures and specific contexts, between macroscopic and microscopic.

There is a point at which the microinteractional approach to culture merges with the concept of intersubjectivity, for both are concerned with the meaning structures and interpretive processes through which individuals together make sense of each other. Working on schizophrenia demands such a merger for it is these interactions that are often so fraught for people who have the disorder, as well as for those around them. It is for these reasons that in this volume Jenkins builds a framework for research in this field from the work of social theorists like Sapir, whose concept of culture is interactional and meaning centered, and psychiatrists like Sullivan, whose concept of schizophrenia is located in the everyday details of lived experience.

intercultural & intersubjective

A number of the chapters raise important theoretical issues for debate. The so-called pathoplastic model has provided a conventional framework to understand the relationship between culture and mental illness. It proposes that symptoms are invariant in form, but that their content is shaped by culture (McHugh and Slavney 1986). Several chapters (Jenkins, Barrett, Hopper, Corin and colleagues, Good and Subandi, and Sadowsky) critique this model, raising questions about the validity of distinguishing between form and content that has been identified by Kleinman (1988). Alternative models are examined that accord a more fundamental role to cultural processes in constructing the experience of illness. Culture may provide stable frameworks of meaning that enable a person to make sense of experiences that may be bizarre and anomalous. They may enable that person to build intersubjective understandings of the illness with others. Alternatively, some people with schizophrenia may draw on cultural resources to obfuscate and conceal experience from themselves and others, creating a barrier to understanding which serves to establishing social distance.

In sum, what we know about culture and schizophrenia at the outset of the twenty-first century is the following: Culture is critical in nearly *every* aspect of schizophrenic illness experience: the identification, definition and meaning of the illness during the prodromal, acute, and residual phases; the timing and type of onset; symptom formation in terms of content, form, and constellation; clinical diagnosis; gender and ethnic differences; the personal experience of schizophrenic illness; social response, support, and stigma; and, perhaps most important, the course and outcome of disorders with respect to symptomatology, work, and social functioning (Jenkins 1998:357).

Subjective Experience

Clinical psychiatry has long been intrigued by the subjective dimension of psychotic experience. It has been a particular focus of attention for psychiatrists who work from a phenomenological perspective, or those who practice within a psychoanalytic framework. Yet with few exceptions (Chapman 1966; Cutting and Dunne 1989; Strauss 1994; Jenkins 1997), the subjective experience of schizophrenia has been a neglected area of research in the latter part of the twentieth century. Some people with schizophrenia say that it affects their sense of who they are, their body, their thoughts and feelings, their day-to-day activities, and the people around them. The illness seems to pervade their world. Yet this is by no means the only pathway leading from a psychotic episode. Many of those with schizophrenia experience periods of recovery between episodes, with or without residual symptoms, while still others enjoy sustained improvement. Substantial recovery is possible in relation to favorable living conditions and medication response (particularly for many patients taking the newer, atypical antipsychotic drugs); moreover, such patients are not likely to characterize their lives as dominated by the illness (Jenkins and Miller 2002).

Conventional approaches to subjective experience flowing from descriptive psychopathology and classificatory psychiatry have not provided an adequate basis to understand the pervasive, alternating, or transformative aspects of schizophrenia. A number of studies in this volume break new ground in this area. Grounded in an empirical tradition of ethnographic research and a theoretical tradition of social phenomenology, they investigate the triadic relationship between an illness, a person, and that person's lived world. By these means, they provide new insights into the subjective experience of schizophrenia, how the illness may influence a person's sense of self, its impact on immediate social relationships, and the distinctive ways in which it may shape that person's lifeworld.

A theoretical move toward *subjectivity* has taken hold in anthropology at a time when retreat from this domain of inquiry has largely taken place in psychiatry and psychology. As this volume is guided by the rise of anthropological thinking about subjective experience, it is useful to provide a brief summation of recent ideas in culture theory that have led to this development: (1) the primacy of lived experience over analytic categories imposed by anthropological theory (Kleinman 1988); ②the active engagement of subjects in processes of cultural construction; and ③ the irrepressibility of subjectivity as embedded in intersubjectively created realms of meaning and significance.

First is the primacy of lived experience. This is reflected in the movement away from what Geertz (1984:124), borrowing from Kohut, has called "experience-distant" concepts and toward "experience-near" concepts. As applied to anthropology, the differentiation is as follows:

An experience-near concept is, roughly, one which someone – a patient, a subject, in our case an informant – might himself naturally and effortlessly use to define what he or his fellows see, feel, think, imagine, and so on, and which he would readily understand when similarly applied by others. An experience-distant concept is one which specialists of one sort or another – an analyst, an experimenter, an ethnographer, even a priest or an ideologist – employ to forward their scientific, philosophical, or practical aims. 'Love' is an experience-near concept, 'object cathexis' is an experience-distant one. 'Social stratification,' or perhaps for most peoples in the world even 'religion' (and certainly 'religious system'), are experience-distant; 'caste' or 'nirvana' are experience-near, at least for Hindus and Buddhists. (Geertz 1984:124)

The theoretical movement in anthropology toward experience has led to person-centered ethnographies and the development of culture theory to incorporate subjectivity (Devereux 1980; Rosaldo 1984; Estroff 1989; Desjarlais 1992; Csordas 1994a; Good 1994; Pandolfo 1999, 2000; Scheper-Hughes 2001). Evidence from such ethnographies called into question the generalizabilty of European-derived categories for experience. Thus, what is "medicine" in one cultural context may be indistinguishable from "religion" in other contexts, as LeVine (1984) has shown, for example, among the Gusi of East Africa.

Exemplary among contemporary studies of experience is Lovell's (1997) narrative analysis of schizophrenia and homelessness in New York City. Her work provides an ethnographic cautionary tale for the consequences of the denial of subjectivity of persons experiencing schizophrenia that diminishes the "range of communication in clinical settings as well as everyday relations" (356). Likewise, an incisive ethnographic analysis of personal experience, narrative, and institutional structures in Ireland has been elegantly set forth by A. Jamie Saris (1995).

No one has raised these questions with more perspicacity than Desjarlais (1997:10–27), who dissects layer upon layer of assumptions (most of them stemming from romantic and postromantic thought) that attach to contemporary anthropological uses of the term "experience" – its so-called primacy, supreme authenticity, facticity, fundamental constancy, interiority and reflexivity, and proximity to the sensate. His argument, that experience itself is historically and culturally constituted, is by no means new, but what is remarkable about *Shelter Blues* is the way it is worked out ethnographically, in this instance among Boston shelter residents, for whom experience was a matter of "'struggling along,' a journey, a series of movements through a landscape at once physical and metaphoric" (20).

One cannot follow Desjarlais' injunction to take history and culture seriously without assigning a critical role to linguistic processes in constituting lived experience, a central concern of this volume. As Gergen (1990:576) has observed, "when we use language of other peoples to access their subjectivities, it is essentially their category or conceptual systems that are at stake." Sapir (1924) summarized this vital issue of language with his statement that "the worlds in which different societies live are distinct worlds, not merely the same world with different labels attached." Sapir was no less tenacious in his insistence on the importance of individual variability in the creation of psychocultural dimensions of subjectivity. Such variability, really what we can call a "constrained idiosyncrasy," defies neat classification on the basis of the psychological and cultural categories for experience.

Second, an emphasis on experience has meant an emphasis on the active engagement of subjects in processes of cultural construction. This has been premised to a great extent on philosophical notions of agency and intentionality, with the intended subject moving toward, as Kleinman and Kleinman (1995) would have it, whatever is "at stake" for an individual. As Ortner (1996:2) argues, contemporary ethnographies that "omit, exclude, or bid farewell to the intentional subject" are no longer viable in light of recent developments in culture theory. These developments include the cultural "making" of forms of subjectivity "from the actor's point of view" – where the "question is how actors 'enact,' 'resist,' or 'negotiate' the world as given, and in so doing, 'make' the world."

Third, the notion of intersubjectivity is increasingly important as a bridge between individual experience and social reality, between a subjectivity too often criticized as implicitly isolated and solipsistic and the material conditions of life that are generated in collective processes of production and reproduction. Indeed, part of the discomfort with granting the notion of experience a central place in social theory has been failure on the part of its proponents to theorize experience as thoroughly interpersonal and intersubjective. This step has been decisively and eloquently taken by Arthur Kleinman:

Experience is thoroughly *intersubjective*. It involves practices, negotiations, and contestations among others with whom we are connected. It is a medium in which collective and subjective processes interfuse. We are born into the flow of palpable experience. Within its symbolic meanings and social interactions our senses form into a patterned sensibility, our movements meet resistance and find directions, and our subjectivity emerges, takes shape, and reflexively shapes our local world. (Kleinman 1999:358–9)

Kleinman shows that such a conception allows a theoretical and empirical appreciation of the "interpenetration of the moral and the emotional, the social and the subjective" (1999:378), and consequently a more precise understanding of the interactions among cultural representations, collective processes, and subjectivity. Such an approach is essential for understanding schizophrenia, not only as the biologically conditioned affliction of an isolated individual, but, in Kleinman's term, as a form of *social suffering* conditioned by the moral coloring of practical activity that occurs "under the impress of large-scale transformations in politics and economics that define an era or a place" (1999:381). To borrow a contrast framed by Kleinman, it is essential to regard schizophrenia not as a disordered modulation of "human nature," but as a function of a particular configuration (not excluding the biological) of "human conditions."

Introduction to the Three Parts: Themes and Cross-Currents

This volume is intended to bring the puzzle of schizophrenia under scrutiny from the standpoint of the social sciences; that is, those disciplines that take as their central concern the problem of human life as such. And while the chapters represent perspectives that combine social and medical sciences broadly, the overarching conceptual framework for the volume hinges largely on culture theory from contemporary anthropology. The volume is organized in three parts that elaborate cultural analyses of the problem, each of which constitutes a piece of the puzzle of the psychoses. In the first part, authors outline state-of-the-art understandings of culture, self, and experience that are critical to a cross-culturally comparative and global understanding. Each of the four chapters in the second part sets out a methodological strategy, in turn developing the ethnographic, sociolinguistic, clinical, and historical dimensions of schizophrenia and related psychotic disorders. The third part plumbs the depths of subjectivity and emotion, without an understanding of which the daily lived experience of schizophrenia must remain unnecessarily incomprehensible.

We will summarize each of the parts in turn, and conclude our introduction by reflecting on the clinical implications of the work collected here.

Culture, Self, and Experience

The first part deals with a number of critical issues that confront all studies of human experience, and culture and schizophrenia in particular. One is the relationship between the ordinary and the extraordinary; another is the nexus between subjectivity and culture; and a third is the tension between general and specific concepts of culture. These problematics, elaborated through studies of schizophrenia, define the broader terms for analysis that are developed more fully in the ensuing parts. Jenkins (Chapter 1) argues that schizophrenia itself offers a paradigm case for understandings of culturally fundamental and ordinary processes and capacities of the self, the emotions, and social engagement. She also shows how the experiences of people with schizophrenia can be quintessentially extraordinary just as they can be exquisitely ordinary. As a consequence, people who suffer from the disorder have a unique capacity to teach us about human processes that are fundamental to living in a world shared with others. A single-minded focus on the similarities between those who have schizophrenia and those who do not carries the risk of negating what is so extraordinary about this illness, underestimating the intensity of suffering it entails, and overlooking the resilience of those who grapple with it. But if the focus is restricted to understanding differences between abnormal and normal, the risk is one of devaluing the person with schizophrenia. Difference may lead to diminution and decomposition of the person into an object. Jenkins embraces the extraordinary and the ordinary in schizophrenia, the abnormal and the normal, and gives no quarter to those who would play down the insights that people with the illness offer, nor to those who would characterize them as flawed or emotionally empty humans.

Lucas (Chapter 5), in exploring some of the cultural processes at work around this ordinary/extraordinary interface, carries this analysis further. Drawing on ethnographic work in Australia among people with schizophrenia and juxtaposing these data with classical formulations of the disorder within the psychiatric literature, he locates schizophrenia both outside and inside the bounds of culture. Psychiatric discourse identifies the source of this illness in the body and in nature, thereby placing it beyond culture. On the other hand, schizophrenia itself is a cultural category, replete with cultural tropes. It is sometimes construed as a primitive state in which archaic sources of violent energy erupt through surface layers of control; or a state of confusion and alienation that mirrors the complex modern society in which we live; or a form of creative power akin to artistic genius. Such images are not only invoked by psychiatrists, but also by people so diagnosed when representing schizophrenia to themselves.

Jenkins

Lucas

Lucas's analysis goes further than this, beneath the crust of objectified culture to a more fluid, praxiological sense of culture as a context-bound activity. At this level, he found the participants in his study harnessing elements of popular culture – film, rock music, popular literature – as the medium through which they comprehended experiences that were extraordinary, anomalous, and transgressive. It was through these cultural forms that they conveyed such experiences to others, including the ethnographer. Whether we approach schizophrenia as an objective category of psychiatry, argues Lucas, or engage with people as they negotiate the experience of schizophrenia, we are working both inside and outside culture, across the interface between the "un-understandable" and the familiar.

This focus on the experience of schizophrenia leads directly to the question of how best to approach the nexus between subjectivity and culture. Jenkins makes the case that the "self" is of central analytic importance, for it draws in subjective experience, emotion, intersubjective engagement, and cultural orientation. Her approach is worked out by Corin, Thara, and Padmavati (Chapter 4) in a South Indian context, based on narratives of patients recently diagnosed with schizophrenia. The authors draw on phenomenological psychiatry to grasp the nuances of altered experiences and feelings, especially patients' distinctive voicing of fear, confusion, and the increasing porosity of personal boundaries. Their analysis is grounded in an understanding of the Indian self as highly sensitive to interpersonal context. Both positive and negative consequences of this kind of interpersonal environment are explored. There is the anguish of failure, the quest for significance that is less a search for etiological understanding than "a general inquiry about the meaning of one's existence," and the struggle for a solution that can lead to intensified religious involvement and strategic social withdrawal. The authors provide insightful reflections on the difference between schizophrenic withdrawal and Hindu renunciation. They conclude with a call for longitudinal studies that will even more firmly situate the phenomenology of schizophrenia within the pragmatics of culture.

The third issue is a question of culture and scale. It is addressed first by Hopper (Chapter 2) through a critical interrogation of the corpus of WHO collaborative studies: the International Pilot Study of Schizophrenia, the Determinants of Outcome Study, and the International Study of Schizophrenia. Hopper first demonstrates that no matter what confounding variables are taken into account (gender, age, loss to follow-up, diagnostic imprecision, insensitivity of outcome measures), the conclusions of these studies do hold true – the course of schizophrenia is more benign in the developing world, both in the short term or the long term.

But it is far from clear what bearing culture might have on this differential outcome. Indeed the status assigned to culture in these WHO collaborative studies is even less clear. Sometimes the term "culture" stands for a specific location, sometimes a mixture of ill-defined variables (beliefs, practices, poverty, inadequate treatment). Mostly it means "developing" versus "industrial," and implicitly, he suggests, "there" versus "here." However when culture was taken more seriously, notably in a WHO substudy comparing families in Denmark and India, suggestive evidence emerged that lower levels of expressed emotion among relatives in India helped to explain the more favorable short-term outcome there, a finding that is explored ethnographically by McGruder later in this volume. Hopper cautions against the use of uniform, societywide concepts of culture, and especially against precipitous attempts to operationalize such concepts to generate "cultural factors." Instead, his chapter persuasively argues that to move forward, we would be best advised to equip ourselves with a definition of culture as local, grounded in ethnography and, as Lucas has shown, embedded in context-bound activities. It should be able to encompass intracultural contradiction and variation, with the capacity to elucidate "microecologies" that may hinder or facilitate the process of recovery from schizophrenia. This is not an injunction to ignore macroscopic cultural forces that influence peoples and epochs. But in this field of research, "culture" writ large can become disconnected from the clinical context. Culture must be conceptualized in a way that is specific enough to connect with notions of self and lived experience of illness.

Barrett (Chapter 3) shows the importance of using such a highly specified understanding of culture in a clinical and ethnographic study that compares psychosis in the Iban people of Malaysia and in Australians. He demonstrates the cultural specificity of perception and thought that must be taken into account in understanding the subjective experience of psychosis by focusing on the process of translating the Present State Examination (PSE) diagnostic interview, particularly those parts of it concerned with Schneider's First Rank Symptoms. He shows how questions concerning auditory hallucinations translate with ease from English to Iban. However, problems with thinking (thought insertion, withdrawal, broadcast) make little cultural sense in an Iban context, for Iban construe thinking partly as a bodily process, a matter of the heart, and partly as an interactional process, a matter of conversation. It is not surprising, therefore, that he identifies auditory hallucinations with approximately the same frequency in the two populations, but finds different rates of subjective thought disorder. The latter occurs at expected levels in Australian patients but is virtually absent in Iban patients. Perhaps it is simply not possible to identify such experiences among Iban people due to the problems of translation, but it is more likely, argues Barrett, that subjective symptoms of thought disorder are configured differently in Australian and Iban experience. By demonstrating the utility of ethnography attuned to phenomenological detail, this chapter offers a strategy by which the Western psychiatric category of schizophrenia might be refined rather than simply reproduced.

The chapters in the first part, therefore, set conceptual parameters for the subsequent contributions, arguing for an approach to culture that can be specified and contextualized, an approach to subjectivity that takes the culturally constituted self as central, and an approach to experience that has the capacity to explore and move between the ordinary and the extraordinary.

Four Approaches for Investigating the Experience of Schizophrenia

The second part presents four approaches to understanding schizophrenia: ethnographic, sociolinguistic, clinical, and historical. The ethnographic approach is represented by Good and Subandi's (Chapter 6) exploration of temporal patterns of psychoses in Java, a classic site for anthropological theorizing about culture and experience. The study is framed by a set of enquiries that arise in relation to the tendency in Indonesia, and elsewhere in the developing world, for psychotic experience to be characterized by acute, brief episodes of positive symptoms (auditory hallucinations, confusion, thought disorder) that resolve relatively quickly with no apparent residual symptoms, and that may or may not recur. The method of analysis is by a single case study of a thirty-six-year-old Javanese woman, Yani, and her mother, who we follow as they grapple with Yani's episodic psychosis. The authors take the reader into a crowded neighborhood in Yogjakarta to Yani's house, where their ethnography focuses on everyday modes of being in the world, revealing the day-to-day interactions of Yani and her mother around this illness. Good and Subandi show how self processes are constituted by Javanese and Islamic themes, where contestations over power and potency, danger and protection, are part of the everyday experience. These themes of Javanese cultural psychology mediate psychological and social adaptation to psychotic experience, including ascetic withdrawal, but also remarkable periods of apparently full recovery. The chapter underlines the value of longitudinal research that is based on an enduring relationship between ethnographer and patient. Another strength is its close attention to family interaction. One feels Yani's irritation and frustration and her mother's abiding sense of disappointment. It is the specificity of these interactions that is accounted for in the light of locally constructed emotions and ideas.

Wilce (Chapter 7) uses a high-powered lens, that of sociolinguistics, or the ethnography of communication, to achieve a more microscopic analysis still. His fieldwork was undertaken in a village not far from the city of Chandpur, situated in a low-lying delta region of Bangladesh. The case is that of Rani, a young Hindu woman. Wilce uses videotape and audiotape recordings of interviews and family conversations, that enable him to provide the reader with transcripts as well as detailed descriptions of posture and gesture, as family members interact with one another. In Rani's house you hear her speaking out of turn, and you follow her frustrated sister imploring her, in the end, to "Speak beautifully!" What is unique is the way the author focuses on the minute details of turn taking in conversational interchange, or the use of the passive versus active voice in response to an interview question. If Good and Subandi demonstrate the importance of following patients over months and years, Wilce's work reveals the value of observing interactions second by second, frame by frame. At the same time, like Good and Subandi, he embeds his analysis within a wider cultural context, here, a deeply gendered but rapidly modernizing Bangladeshi culture. By these means, Wilce leads the reader to an understanding of *pāgalāmi* (madness) and the rupture of intersubjectivity that it entails. He demonstrates that this rupture, and the continual attempts that are made to mend it, cannot be fully grasped without an understanding of the language, gesture, and aesthetics of interaction.

The work of Diaz, Fergusson, and Strauss (Chapter 8) is set within a rehabilitation psychiatry framework, and is written in a more clinical style. Yet certain features of this chapter resonate with the previous two chapters. The first is the richly textured clinical descriptions that take you into the lifeworld of those undergoing rehabilitation in a way that is rarely achieved in the conventional psychiatric literature. The second is the attention that is continually paid to the location of the rehabilitation program, its ethos and methods, within its South American context. Established to help the homeless mentally ill in Colombia, the program combines rural and urban facilities that provide systematic opportunities for work, artistic, and cultural activities. Because allowance is made for unlimited length of stay, the authors can provide a long-term perspective on people with schizophrenia. Whereas Wilce works in a timeframe of seconds and minutes, and Good and Subandi in months and years, this study draws on data that often exceed a decade. Diaz and colleagues describe six patients who find various degrees of relief and stability through the program, and across these cases they develop an understanding of the subjective experience of recovery as a life trajectory, characterized at some times by fragility and at other times by resilience. They examine a series of articulated experiential themes concerning illness and its symptoms, spiritual forces, and religion. The authors describe activities such as begging, stealing, scouting for food, adopting a guarded manner, walking, and wandering, as strategies that transcend the weight of the poverty and violence that surrounds these patients. The program places emphasis on these street skills, and discovers innovative ways to harness them in the rehabilitation process. The chapter provides a model of how to develop a psychiatric service in a way that is responsive to local socio-economic conditions and cultural meanings, while at the same time being cognizant of its own institutional ideology – here, one of autonomy and independence.

Sadowsky's (Chapter 9) analysis of psychosis in southwest Nigeria is starkly different from the other three contributions in this section because it employs quite different methods. What light can be thrown on psychotic illness without interview data, ethnographic description, videotape recording, or clinical interaction? By comparison, the data with which Sadowsky works might appear fragmentary and distanced, yet he shows how the incisive use of several complementary historical methods can reveal insights into illness and its symptoms. His data are drawn from the National Archives in Ibadan and two mental hospitals, and include letters written by asylum inmates. The strength of this contribution derives from the historian's capacity to reveal how the symptomatic expressions of individuals are embedded within, and informed by epochs, political relationships, and social movements, and, in this instance, colonialism and independence. Like the other contributors, Sadowsky is interested in the reciprocal relationship between content and context although, for him, context is conceived on a vaster timescale. His textual analysis of letters reveals the extent to which the experience of inmates was immersed in the ethos of resistance and revolution that characterized the period of Nigeria's imminent independence, symbolized by the cry of "*Irapada!*" (Redemption!). The content of illness experience was for many Nigerian patients characterized by what Sadowsky calls "the political construction of delusion." He demonstrates how delusional talk becomes a vehicle to caricature, for example, the "paternalism" of the culture of colonialism. The analysis emphasizes the subjective experience of "persecutory delusions" as "over-determined by the persecutory nature of colonialism itself."

By juxtaposing these chapters, we are highlighting different perspectives that ethnographers, linguists, clinicians, and historians bring to the study of schizophrenia, and the different time structures of their analysis. Their common project is to understand the lived experience of schizophrenia by placing this experience within broader temporal, political, and cultural contexts.

Subjectivity and Emotion

Jenkins, we have seen, proposed that the study of emotion is critical to understanding the nexus between subjectivity and culture. This third group of chapters explores a variety of emotional dimensions of schizophrenia. As in the previous part, they exemplify radically different approaches to the study of emotion. McGruder's contribution (Chapter 10) represents an ethnographic working out of the "expressed emotion" (EE) construct that was identified by Hopper as one of the most promising directions in which to explore links between culture and schizophrenia. The study of EE across cultures has raised problems concerning the cultural norms and social processes applicable to its component dimensions, hostility, criticism, and emotional overinvolvement. McGruder's work, which took place in Zanzibar, tackles these problems by means of some of the classical techniques available to the ethnographer: long-term engagement with people, detailed observational studies of individual families, attention to narrative, and sensitivity to her own contribution to the interactions she observes. This enables her to highlight the interplay of local norms for familial emotional expression and understandings of illness constructed against the background of both psychiatric care and traditional etiologies. McGruder describes, for example, the gendered norms pertaining to the concealment of hatred, anger, grief, and love, and her case material highlights contrasting emotional styles characterizing families of patients with schizophrenia in Zanzibar. Concealment of hatred was found in families where indirectness in conflict resolution was valued, and tolerance for idiosyncratic family members was notable. It was intertwined with the conviction that "all adversity is sent from Allah for a purpose one cannot know, and that preternatural spirits are active in producing deranged behavior." Concealment of anger was premised less upon religious constructs and more around the shame that could encompass both patient and family. By describing day-to-day household scenes, McGruder helps us see with immediacy and clarity the ways in which these emotional styles are legitimately praiseworthy, though certainly not to be romanticized. Against the background of studies showing that the familial emotional milieu predicts clinical course, this chapter is compelling because it concerns arguably the most critical question: How does culture make a difference for who recovers and who remains ill?

A sheer emotional chasm separates the concealment and indirectness of expression described by McGruder in Zanzibar from the open anguish and rage that bursts onto the pages in Chapter 11. Here Estroff explores a body of literature from North America written by those who suffer schizophrenia and those who care for them. These are works that most often appear in publications such as *The Lighthouse, Altered State,* and *Dendron,* in newsletters put out by local self-advocacy groups, and collections privately published, or they may be found in a series devoted to first-person accounts in *Schizophrenia Bulletin.* This genre has hitherto remained marginalized because it critiques current psychiatric treatment practices in a way that is difficult to read and absorb, and even harder to respond to, given the feelings that it provokes. A personalized and politicized literature of extremes, it speaks out in anger and loathing to themes of danger, fear, personal damage, invalidation, and sensate torture, but also in gracious tones of thankfulness about healing and survival. Estroff is able to usher in these works since she herself has been the subject of a maelstrom of personal criticism and is honest enough to expose the sense of hurt and confusion it evoked in her. Furthermore, she is punctilious in ensuring that the authors represented in the chapter speak for themselves. The analytical structure of the chapter brings these first-person narratives (written and told by individuals with a diagnosis of schizophrenia) and second-person narratives (by people who have been close to them) into confrontation with third-person narratives (by clinicians, advocates, academics). This enables Estroff to explore the fiercely contested field of mutual misunderstanding that, for some North American patients and their families, saturates the experience of schizophrenia. Like Sadowsky, who explicates the relationships between expressions of illness and colonialism, Estroff emphasizes the salience of sociopolitical context. Her work shows the extent to which the emotional texture of schizophrenia may be embedded within that vigorously contested arena that characterizes the political landscape of mental health in North America.

The two final chapters in this volume are both concerned with negative symptoms of schizophrenia. Sass (Chapter 12) brings a cultural and historical analysis to bear on the problem while Kring and Germans (Chapter 13) bring experimental psychology to task. Sass shows how negative symptoms have long been represented in the psychiatric literature as a diminution of higher mental faculties stemming directly from a brain deficit, a model of psychopathology that can be traced back at least as far as Hughlings Jackson. Sass's counterthesis is that they represent a heightened, not diminished, form of conscious activity, characterized by a combination of hyperreflexivity and disengagement. He argues that the essence of schizophrenia, though not necessarily its cause, is a distinctive way of being in the world in which the individual focuses intensely on what is normally taken for granted. What is obvious or axiomatic may become a source of fascination for the person with schizophrenia. What is tacit becomes explicit; background becomes foreground. Bodily processes and sensations that are normally unnoticed are subject to focused attention and this leads to heightened levels of self-consciousness. With such effort and concentration focused on the commonplace, the individual is not able to engage with day-to-day reality in a pragmatic way. Instead, he or she becomes estranged from it and unable to cope with the mundane practical tasks of daily life. Attenuation of emotional expression is one of the principal negative symptoms. Sometimes termed "flattening," sometimes "blunting," it is associated with apathy, paucity of speech, social withdrawal, and other negative symptoms. As such, it is a cardinal diagnostic feature of schizophrenia. But what emotions are subjectively experienced by those who outwardly manifest this clinical sign? A commonplace clinical assumption is that beneath the exterior expression lies a similar flattening and impoverishment of emotional life, as inwardly experienced by the patient. This is not a universal assumption however. A notable exception, for example, comes from Sullivan, who cautioned that "alleged indifference, apathy, and emotional disharmony . . . is more a matter of impression than correct evaluation of the inner experience." Like Corin, Thara, and Padmavati, and the links they trace between social withdrawal and Hindu renunciation, Sass's analysis is subtle. He does not argue for a simplistic causal relationship between culture and psychopathology, but for more subtle forms of resonance and amplification.

The work of Kring and Germans is predicated on a psychological definition that divides emotion into a behavioral or expressive component, a subjective or experiential component, and a physiological component. The authors describe a series of elegant experiments among unmedicated patients, to demonstrate empirically that these patients are indeed not without feeling. While they find a "lack of coordinated engagement of emotion response components" among persons with schizophrenia, these patients may actually experience as much (and sometimes more) emotion than their "normal" counterparts. Furthermore, there is evidence to suggest a lack of congruity between facial expression and physiological arousal. While their work lies clearly in the domain of laboratory studies, Kring and Germans recognize the utility of complementing their approach with naturalistic studies, ethnography, and interpretive analysis. Indeed their chapter can be read as working through at an experimental and clinical level the themes that Sass's interpretive work has identified.

Put together, the contributions in this section argue that culture modulates the expression of emotions that surround schizophrenia, and that family interactions appear to be central to this process. But the political and institutional landscape in which schizophrenia is diagnosed and treated also gives force, and a particular accent, to these emotions. At the same time, cultural images, transmitted through conventional psychiatric theories and assumptions, and reinforced by patients' withdrawal, may also serve to limit our appreciation of the emotional intensity that characterizes the inner, lived experience of schizophrenia.

Clinical Implications

A principal objective of this volume is to bring the findings of social science research to a clinical readership because many of the questions it tackles are questions that confront mental health professionals in their day-to-day work. Clinicians, in the main, are alert to the possibility of interactions between culture and schizophrenia, but very often encounter difficulties thinking through these interactions at a practical level. The works represented here suggest a number of strategies.

There is a dynamic tension within this collection between the broad-scale, societywide, and historically continuous dimensions of culture, and the dimensions of culture that, as Hopper emphasizes, are local, context-bound, and emergent in interpersonal interaction. The influence of colonial rule and the independence movement in Nigeria, or of modernity in Europe and North America are examples of the former. A telling instance of the latter is the description by Diaz, Fergusson, and Strauss of the woman who loved begging, in which they develop a personalized understanding of her begging as a compromise between the submissiveness that typifies Colombian womanhood and the rebellion and sense of freedom that it allowed her. To achieve an understanding of psychosis that is culturally informed, it is necessary to work clinically with this same dynamic tension. The clinical question becomes, "What large-scale cultural influences could be at play?" and in the same breath, "How do these influences affect this person in this setting?" To ask only the first part of the question can leave the clinician with a working definition of culture that is spuriously homogenous, and often based on dubious dichotomies (such as, modern versus traditional, West versus non-West). This lends itself to stereotypes and may even serve as an indirect way of saying, "Not like me." It may be relevant for clinicians, therefore, to read the contributions to this volume with the following question foremost in their mind: "What is the distinctive configuration of cultural influences at play in the patient's context?" Wilce, for example, not only raises the issue of gender in Bangladesh, but shows how gendered norms of conversation and behavior are transgressed by Rani and responded to by her family, along with the intersubjective rupture that this entails. Likewise, Good and Subandi address the importance of Islam in Java, but also show how Yani invokes particular Islamic ideas of purity to frame her understanding of psychosis, an interpretive frame that is vehemently contested by her mother who has other views altogether. By moving between the general and the specific, culture can be brought into the clinic as a working construct that can deal with nuances, competing influences, and internal contradictions. This strategy also enables the clinician to approach and understand the conflict and mutual misunderstandings that can surround schizophrenia, as Estroff, more than any other, demonstrates so well.

Many of the chapters in this collection make the case that culture interacts with schizophrenia by means of its influence on patients' families. Here again, they are concerned with the cross-cutting interplay of norms that provide for certain types of interaction between family members, rather than a more generalized notion of "the family in such-and-such a culture." Thus McGruder's work in Zanzibar examines norms for the expression of emotion by exploring variations that depend on the particular emotion concerned, on a person's gender, or on their status within the family. And she is concerned with a range of family responses to schizophrenia that are possible within this culture. For clinicians who are already sensitive to the role of family emotional dynamics in psychotic illness, it is a short step to sharpen this sensitivity through an awareness of the cultural underpinnings of these dynamics.

Also evident throughout this collection is the inestimable clinical advantage that derives from working with patients and families in their homes, their suburbs, and their villages. It enables direct observation of interactions that take place during scenes of family life: welcoming visitors, eating meals, cooking. Familiarity with the domestic space within which the patient moves when ill, or when well, provides privileged entrée into the lived experience of schizophrenia, enabling one to understand the relationship between symptom and lifeworld. The advantages, too, that accrue from a long-term relationship with the patient and their family are readily apparent throughout. Shared space and shared time, this volume argues, enable depth of understanding. This comes as no surprise to community mental health workers who have long recognized the potential for a rich therapeutic relationship that flows from working with patients over time and in their own setting. Institutional and practical constraints dictate that for many this ideal cannot be achieved. Even within these constraints, however, clinicians who foster within themselves an attitude of ethnographic curiosity can, at the very least, allow themselves to be taken by narrative means into their patients' lived world, where their schizophrenic illness is experienced in space and in time.

The clinical reader will be drawn to discussions of the relationship between culture and self. Usually tacit and subtle, the cultural assumptions that constitute the self are easily overlooked. But by studying in an Indian setting where a permeable, context-bound notion of self prevails, Corin, Thara, and Padmavati provide the clinician with a method of working that brings a patient's sense of self into the foreground, explores its cultural location, and pursues the consequences for the way schizophrenia is experienced by that patient. Barrett's discussion, too, reminds clinicians that there may be considerable variation in the way people account for core self-processes of thinking and feeling, their location, their relation to the body, and their accompanying sense of privacy. All of these, he suggests, may influence patients' subjective experience of schizophrenia. One way to appreciate these variations is to be sensitive to language, and the cultural idioms through which patients construct their sense of self, thought, and emotion.

Day-to-day clinical work with schizophrenia requires the agility to tack back and forth between the normal and the abnormal, between the ordinary and the extraordinary. Jenkins puts a fine point on this by showing that it is a matter of grasping patients' extraordinary experience without dehumanizing them, while at the same time appreciating their normal experience without ignoring their uniqueness. How does one work at this multiple interface? Lucas's analysis is invaluable for clinicians because he teases out the cultural resources that they and their patients rely on for this task, whether they do so wittingly or unwittingly. His chapter alerts the clinician to some core cultural themes that patients invoke when attempting to capture and convey experiences that are so unusual, inchoate, or evanescent that they are almost impossible to grasp. It stresses how intersubjective understandings of these experiences are very often developed between patient and clinician on the basis of their respective participation in this shared culture.

Clinicians for whom cultural psychiatry implies working with people whose country of origin, ethnic background, or first language differs markedly from their own will find within this volume a way of thinking about the cultural aspects of schizophrenia that can be useful for patients whose background is closer to home. This is because it moves beyond an equation of "culture" with "other" to a view of culture as a process of creating shared understandings in a way that always confronts similarities and differences. In addition, there is a strong reflexive theme throughout, whereby an interest in the patient's culture is matched by an equal measure of interest in the culture of the clinician. Diaz, Fergusson, and Strauss show the value of being aware of the ideological underpinnings of the institution in which one works, in their case, a rehabilitation program, and how this affects the way patients are perceived and treated. It is equally necessary to be aware of the cultural tropes that saturate conventional psychiatric constructions of schizophrenia, or the cultural assumptions that lie beneath standardized psychiatric interview questions. Sass and Kring and Germans show these cultural constructs may not tally with patients' inner experience of schizophrenia. It can be uncomfortable for clinicians to turn the cultural gaze back on themselves and their institutional location, but no more so than examining countertransference feelings. Perhaps there is a common process at work. It could be argued that Estroff is able to consider patients' expressions of anguish with such poignancy only because she herself has been the subject of hostile controversy.

It is anticipated that this volume will reinvigorate an interest in culture among mental health professionals by opening them to new ways of thinking about culture and context, and their relevance to lived experience, emotional expression, sense of self, family milieu, and the unspoken assumptions that they themselves bring to the clinical interaction. It is hoped, thereby, to generate a strong awareness among clinicians of the many ways, obvious and subtle, in which culture and schizophrenia mutually influence each other.

REFERENCES

American Psychiatric Association. 1994. *Diagnostic and Statistical Manual of Mental Disorders: DSM-IV*, 4th Edition. Washington, DC: American Psychiatric Association.

American Psychiatric Association. 2000. *Diagnostic and Statistical Manual of Mental Disorders: DSM-IV TR*, 4th Edition, text revision. Washington, DC: American Psychiatric Association.

Barrett, Robert J. 1997. "*Sakit Gila* in an Iban Longhouse: Chronic Schizophrenia." *Culture, Medicine and Psychiatry* 21(3): 365–79.

Barrett, Robert J. 1998. "Conceptual Foundations of Schizophrenia, I: Degeneration." *Australian and New Zealand Journal of Psychiatry* 32: 617–26.

Bleuler, Eugen. 1950. *Dementia Praecox or the Group of Schizophrenias*. New York: International Universities Press.

Bourgois, Philippe. 1995. *In Search of Respect: Selling Crack in El Barrio*. Cambridge: Cambridge University Press.

Chapman, James. 1966. "The Early Symptoms of Schizophrenia." *British Journal of Psychiatry* 112: 225–51.

Cohen, Carl I. 1993. "Poverty and the Course of Schizophrenia: Implications for Research and Policy." *Hospital and Community Psychiatry* 44(10): 951–8.

Csordas, Thomas. 1994a. *Embodiment and Experience: The Existential Ground of Culture and Self*. Cambridge and New York: Cambridge University Press.

Cutting, John and Francis Dunne. 1989. "Subjective Experience of Schizophrenia." *Schizophrenia Bulletin* 15(2): 217–31.

Davidson, Arnold I., ed. 1997. *Foucault and his Interlocutors*. Chicago: University of Chicago Press.

Desjarlais, Robert. 1992. *Body and Emotion: The Aesthetics of Illness and Healing in the Nepal Himalayas*. Philadelphia: University of Pennsylvania Press.

Desjarlais, Robert. 1997. *Shelter Blues: Sanity and Selfhood among the Homeless*. Philadelphia: University of Pennsylvania Press.

Devereux, George. 1980. *Basic Problems of Ethnopsychiatry*. Chicago: University of Chicago Press.

Estroff, Sue E. 1989. "Self, Identity, and Subjective Experiences of Schizophrenia: In Search of the Subject." *Schizophrenia Bulletin* 15: 189–97.

Floersch, Jerry. 2002. *Meds, Money, and Manners: The Case Management of Severe Mental Illness*. New York: Columbia University Press.

Fox, John W. 1990. "Social Class, Mental Illness, and Social Mobility: The Social Selection-drift Hypothesis for Serious Mental Illness." *Journal of Health and Social Behaviour* 31: 344–53.

Geertz, Clifford. 1984. "From the Native's Point of View." In R.A. Shweder and R.A. LeVine, eds., pp. 123–35, *Culture Theory*. Cambridge: Cambridge University Press.

Gergen, Kenneth J. 1990. "Social Understanding and the Inscription of Self." In J. W. Stigler, R.A. Shweder, and G. Herdt, eds., pp. 569–607, *Cultural Psychology: Essays on Comparative Human Development*. Cambridge: Cambridge University Press.

Good, Byron J. 1992. "Culture and Psychopathology: Directions for Psychiatric Anthropology." In T. Schwartz, G.M. White, and C.A. Lutz, eds., pp. 181–205, *The Social Life of Self: New Directions in Psychological Anthropology*. Cambridge: Cambridge University Press.

Good, Byron J. 1994. *Medicine, Rationality, and Experience: An Anthropological Perspective*. Cambridge: Cambridge University Press.

Jablensky, Assen. 2000. "Epidemiology of Schizophrenia: the Global Burden of Disease and Disability." *European Archives of Psychiatry and Clinical Neuroscience* 250 (6): 274–85.

Jaspers, Karl. 1964 (1923). *General Psychopathology*. Chicago: University of Chicago Press.

Jenkins, Janis Hunter. 1997. "Subjective Experience of Persistent Psychiatric Disorder: Schizophrenia and Depression among U.S. Latinos and Euro-Americans." *British Journal of Psychiatry* 170: 20–5.

Jenkins, Janis Hunter. 1998. "Diagnostic Criteria for Schizophrenia and Related Psychotic Disorders: Integration and Suppression of Cultural Evidence in DSM-IV." *Transcultural Psychiatry* 35: 357–76.

Jenkins, Janis Hunter and Dawn Miller. 2002. "A New Kind of Evidence for Mental Health Services and Interventions: Subjective Experience of Atypical Antipsychotic Medications." Fifteenth International Conference on Services Research. Washington, DC: National Institute of Mental Health.

Karno, Marvin and Janis Hunter Jenkins. 1997. "Culture and the Diagnosis of Schizophrenia and Related Disorders and Psychotic Disorders Not Otherwise

Classified." In T. Widiger, A. Frances, H. Pincus, R. Ross, M. First, and W. Davis, eds., *DSM-IV: Sourcebook*, Volume 3. Washington, DC: American Psychiatric Association.

Kleinman, Arthur. 1988. *Rethinking Psychiatry: From Cultural Category to Personal Experience*. New York: The Free Press.

Kleinman, Arthur. 1999. "Experience and Its Moral Modes: Culture, Human Conditions, and Disorder." In Grethe B. Peterson, ed., pp. 357–420, *The Tanner Lectures on Human Values*. Salt Lake City: University of Utah Press.

Kleinman, Arthur and Joan Kleinman. 1995. "Suffering and its Transformations." In A. Kleinman, ed., pp. 95–119, *Writing at the Margin: Discourse between Anthropology and Medicine*. Berkeley: University of California Press.

LeVine, Robert A. 1984. "Properties of Culture: an Ethnographic View." In R.A. Shweder and R.A. LeVine, eds., pp. 67–87, *Culture Theory: Essays on Mind, Self, and Emotion*. Cambridge: Cambridge University Press.

Lin, Keh-Ming. 1996. "Psychopharmacology in Cross-cultural Psychiatry." *Mount Sinai Journal of Medicine* 63: 283–4.

Lovell, Anne. M. 1997. "'The City is My Mother': Narratives of Schizophrenia and Homelessness." *American Anthropologist* 99(2): 355–68.

McHugh, P. and A. Slavney. 1986. *The Perspectives of Psychiatry*. Baltimore, MD: Johns Hopkins University Press.

Mezzich, Juan E., Arthur Kleinman, Horacio Fabrega, and Delores Parron. 1996. *Culture and Psychiatric Diagnosis: A DSM-IV Perspective*. Washington, DC: American Psychiatric Press, Inc.

Obeyesekere, Gananath. 1990. *The Work of Culture: Symbolic Transformation in Psychoanalysis and Anthropology*. Chicago: University of Chicago Press.

Ortner, Sherry B. 1996. *Making Gender : The Politics and Erotics of Culture*. Boston, MA: Beacon Press.

Pandolfo, Stefania. 1999. Le noeud de l'ame. In Rue Descartes, Number 25. "A Partir de Michel de Certeau." Paris: College International de Philosophie.

Pandolfo, Stefania. 2000. "The Thin Line of Modernity: Some Moroccan Debates on Subjectivity." In T. Mitchell, ed., pp. 115–47, *Questions of Modernity*. Minneapolis and London: University of Minnesota Press.

Rosaldo, Michelle A. 1984. "Toward an Anthropology of Self and Feeling." In R.A. Shweder and R.A. LeVine, eds., pp. 137–57, *Culture Theory: Essays on Mind, Self, and Emotion*. Cambridge: Cambridge University Press.

Sapir, Edward. 1924. "Culture, Genuine and Spurious." *American Journal of Sociology* 29: 401–29.

Saris, A. Jamie. 1995. "Life Histories, Illness Narratives, and Institutional Landscapes." *Culture, Medicine and Psychiatry* 19: 39–72.

Scheper-Hughes, Nancy. 2001. *Saints, Scholars, and Schizophrenics: Mental Illness in Rural Ireland*, 2nd Edition. Berkeley: University of California Press.

Strauss, John S. 1994. "The Person with Schizophrenia as a Person II: Approaches to the Subjective and Complex." *British Journal of Psychiatry* 164 (suppl. 23): 103–7.

World Health Organization. 1994. *Pocket Guide to the ICD-10 Classification of Mental and Behavioural Disorders*. Washington, DC: American Psychiatric Press.

Part 1

Culture, Self, and Experience

1   Schizophrenia as a Paradigm Case for Understanding Fundamental Human Processes*

Janis Hunter Jenkins

> We have found in the most disorganized group of people – I believe the psychiatrist would agree that the schizophrenic is the most disorganized of the functional mental illnesses – a continuation of very much that is simply human. Harry Stack Sullivan, *Schizophrenia as a Human Process* (1962: 224).[1]

> In psychotics we see more spectacularly the process of personal affective evaluation as a common symbol ... even the private world of meaning of a psychotic patient has its roots in culture. Edward Sapir, "The Symbol" (1933), in *The Psychology of Culture* (edited by Irvine 1994: 224).[2]

From the standpoint of an anthropology concerned with the nature and meaning of subjective experience, it would appear to be commonplace to argue that a theoretically grounded understanding of cultural orientation, self, emotion, and social relations is vital to the analysis of a complex pathological phenomenon such as schizophrenia.[3] At the same time, the study of schizophrenia illuminates the nexus between culture and fundamental human processes and capacities for experience. Although the latter idea may appear novel or undue both in an anthropology that typically bypasses schizophrenia and in a psychiatry dominated by neuroscience and psychopharmacology, in this chapter I seek to demonstrate that it is neither.[4]

My argument cuts both ways – not only does the anthropological commonplace hold for the study of schizophrenia, but schizophrenia itself offers a paradigm case for scientific understandings of culturally fundamental and ordinary processes and capacities of the self, the emotions, and social engagement.[5] This position stands in contrast to the presumption in medical and social sciences that schizophrenia is immaterial to theorizing the configuration of human experience and development because it is utterly foreign to normal experience and subversive of normal development. This is because it is thought to dislodge fundamental capacities for subjective experience. Degenerative and irreversible physiological processes are deemed to render such persons quite unlike their "normal" counterparts, no longer having the capacity to be active within, or responsive to, culturally created worlds.[6] This is not the case (see Kring this volume).

Moreover, people who suffer from this disorder can offer insights into human processes that are fundamental to living in a world shared with others. This is the case because the construction of shared meaning, usually taken for granted, can become fraught in schizophrenia (see Corin, Good, Lucas, Estroff, Diaz, and colleagues this volume). Their attempts to create shared meanings often entail a tremendous struggle, whereas for those who do not have schizophrenia, this is so often taken for granted (see also Jenkins 1988a, 1991).

In this chapter, then, I argue that (1) the subjective experience of persons with schizophrenia is forged at the nexus of culture and agency, desire and attachment, none of which are annulled by disease process; and (2) the study of schizophrenia casts a bright light on our understanding of culture and subjectivity more generally. Thus, the "extreme case" of schizophrenia poses a challenge for the human sciences. The challenge is to specify the conditions of erosion, retention, or transformation of subjective faculties. The challenge is, furthermore, to take into consideration the complicated tangle of motive, strategy, and stance that persons inhabit not only as a consequence of, but also in spite of, their schizophrenic illness. Finally, these subjective processes figure most significantly in the mediation of the course of illness, that is, along pathways to recovery and improved functioning or sustained states of psychosis with impaired functioning.

Thus the "edge of experience" is cut in ways that are at once ordinary and extraordinary, conventional and inverted, lucid and distorted, making schizophrenia a paradigm case for the broader elucidation of fundamental human processes. In other words, in certain ways that can be specified, people afflicted with schizophrenia are just like everyone else, only more so.[7]

I wish to make clear the terms of my approach to the study of *fundamental* and *ordinary* human processes and capacities. First, in examining fundamental processes I presume the dialectical constitution of culture and psyche, intentional persons and intentional worlds, in the sense outlined by Richard Shweder (1990). This approach proceeds "without the presumption of fixity, necessity, universality, and abstract-formalism" (24). It represents a shift away from an *a priori* expectation of psychic unity based on invariant central-processing mechanisms. Instead, it conceptualizes fundamental processes in terms of domains (such as self or emotion) that are viewed, from the outset, as invariably mediated by culture and context.

The relationship between schizophrenia and fundamental human processes is also usefully understood in terms of the particular perspectives or "situated standpoints" that actors adopt (Haraway 1991; Harding 1991). From such standpoints, culture can be understood as shared and patterned in some respects, while particularized, contested, and fragmented in others (Lutz and Abu-Lughod 1990). Awareness of the particularization of experience leads to a cautionary note that what is often taken to be "fundamental" about human processes may not be their universally invariant form but rather their culturally constituted form at the most basic level of organization.

Second, through examination of ordinary processes and capacities I mean to call attention, not only to the extraordinary, but also to the everyday dimensions of schizophrenic experience. This shift in attention is critical to apprehend schizophrenia in its own right and as a means for understanding ways in which subjective experience is routinized. For example, Corin (1990) shows how structured, predictable, and sometimes solitary activities such as taking a daily walk to a favored coffee shop or bus stop can be a kind of positive withdrawal that constitutes a social "stance" and "buffer" against emotional upset. Moreover, such strategies and routines appear to be critical to recovery and stabilization. In addition, the ordinariness of schizophrenia is revealed through attention to patients' most vexing personal issues, arguably little different than those of their non-afflicted counterparts. How can anyone love me? Why would I love anyone when all it means is torture? What can I do in this life? Where is my hope that relief is in sight, that my pain and suffering will end? These questions become particularly pressing for those who have experienced substantial recovery from their illness, for example, those who have responded to medication with "atypical antipsychotics" (Jenkins and Miller 2002). Examining the factors contributing to the success or failure of the afflicted in answering these questions adds to our understanding of how those same questions are addressed in more mundane lives with less complex challenges.

Conceptualizations of the normal and the abnormal are implicated in the study of both fundamental and ordinary processes. In the study of psychopathology we have yet to resolve the problem of what Georges Canguilhem (1989) defined as the ontological versus positivist conceptions of disease. Is there, as the ontological view would have it, a distinct qualitative difference between anxiety as a normal emotion and anxiety as a pathological state? Or, as the positivist view would hold, is there only one anxiety, the intensity of which can vary quantitatively from total absence to a degree that becomes so great as to be pathological? In this view, abnormality is defined as "more" of what otherwise might be considered within the bounds of normal human experience (Jenkins 1994b:104).

Canguilhem (1989:45) invokes Nietzsche to underscore that "the value of all morbid states [is] that they show us under a magnifying glass certain states that are normal – but not easily visible when normal." In this chapter, I argue that in the case of schizophrenia, strict differentiation between the normal and abnormal is not possible to sustain epistemologically or empirically.

Culture Theory, Schizophrenia, and Human Processes

As noted in the Introduction, the inception of the line of thinking I advance here took place in the 1920s at the interface of psychiatry and social science among a circle of scholars working on culture, normality, and psychopathology (Sapir 1924; Mead 1928; Lasswell 1930; Benedict 1934; Sullivan 1937; Powdermaker 1939; Bateson and Mead 1942). This interdisciplinary alliance was sparked particularly by the collaboration of psychiatrist Harry Stack Sullivan and anthropologist Edward Sapir. In an essay entitled "Cultural Anthropology and Psychiatry" that first appeared in 1932, Sapir (1932:151) theorized that the "true locus of culture is in the interactions of specific individuals and, on the subjective side, in the world of meanings which each one of these individuals may unconsciously abstract for himself from his participation in these interactions." Sapir's dynamic formulation of culture as created and recreated among persons in the process of social interaction paralleled Sullivan's (1953:10) conception of psychiatry as the study of interpersonal relations under any and all circumstances in which these relations exist. Their colleague Ruth Benedict (1934) argued for the cultural specification of such circumstances to include gender; only recently has this theoretical proviso been accorded empirical attention in studies of schizophrenia (Goldstein and Tsuang 1990; Haas, Glick, Clarkin, Spencer, and Lewis 1990; Kulkarni 1997; Lewine 1994).[8]

Sullivan (1962:12) located schizophrenia in everyday social and cultural situations and as such implied "nothing of deterioration" but rather of a "disorder in which the total experience of the individual is reorganized" especially in the domain "of thinking in complex images, to use Levy-Bruhl's excellent expression." Sullivan's point was not to pathologize everyday experience but to emphasize the continuity between the ordinary and the pathological in contrast to a too-rigid, categorical distinction between them.

For Sapir, thinking about schizophrenia was a productive route for anthropological theorizing about subjective experience. Take, for example, the concomitant requirements to orient consistently to cultural and social circumstances, on the one hand, and to protect the self from such circumstances when potentially self-injurious, on the other. One strategy for resolving the conflict between the self and the powerful socioemotional milieu is "to blot out the external world by realizing one's weakness in the midst of strong forces" (Sapir 1994:155). Opting for the solution of "blotting out" or denying the external environment over which one has control was for Sapir, "(i)n its morbid extreme" nothing less than *dementia praecox*"(Sapir 1994:155).

Taken together, these early conceptualizations serve as forerunners of contemporary anthropological theory of lived experience (Turner 1992; Corin and Lauzon 1994; Csordas 1994a; Good 1994; Kleinman 1995). Arthur Kleinman and Joan Kleinman (1995:95–6) have identified accomplishments and challenges for the study of lived experience within the field of medical anthropology. On the one hand, the interpretive method of these studies invariably reveals illness as a socially constructed reality. On the other hand, we are faced with an "interpretive dilemma" when, having established the myriad facets of illness "as social role, social strategy, or social symbol," illness is reinscribed "*as anything but* human experience" (Kleinman and Kleinman 1995:96, emphasis added). To transcend this paradox, Kleinman and Kleinman (97) call for "experience-near" ethnographic categories that concern "processes and forms of experience," in which "something is at stake for all of us in the daily round of happenings and transactions." This proviso is critical, not only to the present analysis but also for the broader field of anthropology insofar as it is concerned with the contours of human experience.

Byron Good's (1994) review of theoretical developments in medical anthropology offers a critique of notions of culture reduced to observable but unmotivated behavior or the cognitive contents imagined to reside "in one's head." He describes the recent theoretical movement away from "a medical social science focused on belief and behavior" and toward "meanings and experience" (Good 1994:5; see also Good 1977; Good and DelVecchio Good 1981). Good's (1994) analysis is illuminating for awareness of the ways in which the central analytic category of "belief" has been deployed historically and culturally in European and North American scientific and popular thinking. Going beyond culture characterized as "belief," this formulation includes the daily trafficking in paradoxes, puzzles, and fluidity characteristic of a "subjunctive mood" (Good 1994:153–8).

Sherry Ortner (1996:1–2) has argued that the cultural "making" of subaltern subjects – women, minorities, and, for my purpose here, the mentally ill – is accomplished in two ways. In the first, "cultural categories, historical subjects or forms of subjectivity are – passive voice – made (in that they are) constructed by, and subjected to, the cultural and historical discourses within which they operate." The second arises (as introduced above) "from the actor's point of view" – where the "question is how actors 'enact,' 'resist,' or 'negotiate' the world as given, and in so doing, 'make' the world." This sort of "making" may amount to reproduction of "the same old cultural and social thing" or, "it may turn out to produce something new, although not necessarily what the actors intended. Indeed, intention plays a complex role in the process, for while intention is central to what the actor seeks to accomplish – and therefore must be understood very carefully – its relationship to the outcome is often quite oblique" (Ortner 1996:1–2).

To make known the theoretical erasures of the subject and agency char-acteristic of social and cultural theory of the past, Ortner convincingly argues two forms of analysis must constitute the anthropological project "in its fullest sense." She argues (1996:2) that, on the one hand, cul-ture theory must include "practice theory" to reveal the ways in which "human action is constrained by the given social and cultural order (of-ten condensed in the term 'structure')." On the other hand, in culture theory "there is also an insistence that human action makes 'structure' – reproduces or transforms it, or both" (Ortner 1996:2). This clarification of ethnographic and historical method, with the injunction against posi-tions that "omit, exclude, or bid farewell to the intentional subject," is critical for the development of theories that do not make it a central the-oretical point of organization to relegate the "abnormal" to a subordinate analytic status. Studies that begin to make this clarification with reference to depression and anxiety include the examination of state control of emo-tional discourse in Iran by Good and DelVecchio Good (1988) and my own examination of the Salvadoran political ethos as "the organization of feeling and sentiment pertaining to social domains of power and inter-est" (Jenkins 1991:140). With specific reference to schizophrenia, Warner (1985) has found a correlation between poor clinical outcome and eco-nomic downturns within nation-states; much more research along these lines is required.

Against the background of the tradition launched by Sullivan and Sapir, in the following sections I elaborate the assertion that psychotic-related symptoms and processes are not so distinctly and categorically differ-ent from the fundamental and ordinary processes of everyday life. I will take up this task with respect to self, emotion, social engagement, and cultural orientations. As a matter of subjectivity these are theo-retically and experientially inseparable, indeed, even for Emil Kraeplin "loss of inner unity"[9] is central, and need not be construed as presum-ing that the self is an unchanging, bounded entity free of contradiction.

Nevertheless, for purposes of analytic clarity I will treat each of these domains successively.

The Self and Self-Processes

The position that the self is a basic phenomenon in all psychic life is argued by Karl Jaspers (1963:57) in terms of a "confrontation of a subject with an object," such that "*awareness of an object* may be contrasted with *self-awareness.*" Irving Hallowell (1955) was among the earliest ethnographers to make his interest explicit by developing a notion of culture in relation to self-awareness. In the history of psychiatric inquiry into schizophrenia, the location of the self has shifted over time. Disorders of the self have been thought to be central to the psychoses in which, as suggested by Eugen Bleuler (1950), experience becomes constructed self-referentially in a world where fantasy and symbolization are continuously invoked.

Sullivan's theory of the "self-system" was conceptualized as a constellation of interpersonal mechanisms in service of emotional protection against a noxious emotional milieu (Sullivan 1953). Here the self is not a discrete and fixed entity but instead an intersubjective creation, a constellation of interpersonal processes developed during childhood and adolescence. However, though once regarded as the centerpiece of theoretical formulations, the self has receded to the periphery of contemporary psychological and psychiatric discourse concerning schizophrenia. The relative lack of attention to the continuity of self-processes in schizophrenia has been consistent with a focus on psychopathology and the way these processes are sustained. This shift, coterminous with the ascent of neuroscience and brain studies mentioned previously (see also Luhrmann 2001), has resulted in a most startling assertion regarding the self in schizophrenic process. The customary mental capacities and strategies we presume all humans to possess are often viewed as diminished or absent in people with schizophrenia.

The turning of American psychiatric attention away from psychological processes in schizophrenia is evident in their erasure from Diagnostic and Statistical Manual-IV (DSM-IV). While the previous edition of the diagnostic manual included "characteristic symptoms involving multiple psychological processes" such as alterations in "sense of self," these were entirely deleted from DSM-IV. New sections include "associated laboratory findings" and "associated physical examination findings and general medical conditions" (Jenkins 1998).

As a corrective to this theoretical retreat from the self, the core of my argument is that if we take the definition of the self as a set of processes and capacities for orientation and awareness, then we may learn something about the self by observing the manner in which experience becomes disoriented and by observing the struggle of those afflicted with schizophrenia to remain oriented in the world. Consider the ordinarily common experience of schizophrenia as "hearing voices" in relation to fundamental self-process. In culturally sanctioned settings such as religious communication with spirits or ancestors,[10] or the ingestion of hallucinogenic drugs, the hearing of voices is generally transient and not experientially at odds with the self (Karno and Jenkins 1997). In schizophrenia, voices tend to be habitual (though not continuous at all times), and the self-process of orientation in the world is undermined by both the lack of an appropriate setting and the absence of volition, such that the self is experienced as distinctly and profoundly different. In this respect, a sense of being at odds with intrusive auditory experience is the basis for an embattled self with whom the voices wreak havoc with respect to power, desire, and control.

There has been a swell of anthropological writings specifically concerned with the self during the last three decades (Gaines 1982; Shweder and Bourne 1984; Ewing 1990; Csordas 1994b; Battaglia 1995). On the basis of ethnographic evidence, the idea of the self as standardized in terms of psychologized, internal experience has been shown as an instance of how a European-derived ethnopsychological[11] category may become reified in social scientific thinking (Shweder and LeVine 1984; Lutz 1988). Such understandings of the self have been supplanted in cultural and psychological anthropology by a notion that among many peoples the self is constituted more fluidly and with far from determinate boundaries.

If we take culture to be an orienting axis for interaction with others, a useful formulation is Thomas Csordas's recent definition of the self as "an indeterminate capacity for orientation, characterized by effort and reflexivity" (1994b:5). Csordas's (1994b) argument for a new paradigm of embodiment in anthropology is critical in requiring studies of the self to be conceptualized not "from the neck up" but rather from the starting point of bodily experience. Such a strategy aims to avoid the methodological error of conceptualizing the self as a cultural category that refers primarily to "mental" phenomena.

Consider the following interchange between interviewer Ira Glass and Patricia Deegan (1997).[12] Deegan is a psychologist and a self-avowed "voice hearer," and is both reflective and articulate with respect to the phenomenology of her illness. At the outset, Glass mistakes the common experience of hearing songs in one's head for the hearing of voices in schizophrenia. Deegan tries to correct this error, describing voices as a "primordially, profoundly auditory experience, to the point where you can actually startle if a voice starts up suddenly." She asserts that this auditory phenomenon is not "on a continuum" of what everyone hears in auditory imagination – one does not "really" hear a song in one's head. Yet despite this experiential discontinuity with ordinary experience, Deegan does not count them as discontinuous with self:

IG: How do you conceive of the voices that you hear? As *separate* from your self, or do you conceive of them as *part of* your self that you can recognize?

PD: I think that for me it's a goal to eventually say these voices are a part of me, and that's actually one of the self-help coping strategies that I do use sometimes. . . . So, for instance, if I have a particularly derogatory or awful voice, that I might say, as a coping strategy, 'today *I am feeling like* I am no good, today *I am feeling like* I'm a worthless person, these are *my* thoughts, these are *my* feelings.

IG: Is that because when the voice is saying that, literally you are *not* having the feeling 'oh, I'm feeling bad today.'

PD: That's right.

In this excerpt, the reflexivity that characterizes our capacity for orientation cannot be taken for granted by the self, and is crystallized, or rendered experientially opaque, in the voices. Yet Deegan's trained capacity for self-awareness allows her to reappropriate her own reflexivity by insisting that the voices are part of herself. Deegan's account also shows that orientation is not an effortless outcome, for resistance is encountered at the interface of subject and world. As with reflexivity, this effort, which is the taking up of a stance in the world, cannot be taken for granted by the patient. It appears as a moral uncertainty that is amplified in the voices' accusation that the self is "bad." Assertion of moral goodness, literally the right to be in the world, is the surplus effort required for Deegan to become oriented in spite of her affliction.

Deegan's experience leads me to another dimension of subjective experience at issue for the self, a dimension in which intentionality, agency, and meaning coincide in schizophrenic process. Here I use the term "intentionality" in its general existential sense of an implicit tending toward and taking up of aspects of our world. It is the condition of possibility for the kinds of self-processes of orientation that speak, linking us to everything in our world, constituting the texture of relationship to it. In this sense the "voices" can be understood as intentional without being intended. Deegan describes a phenomenon in which agency catches up with intentionality in a remarkable form of intervention.

IG: You say that some people have found that putting an earplug in an ear can greatly reduce or eliminate distressing voices.

PD: Yes, this is an interesting finding. And empirically what they have found is that, putting the wax in both ears does not work. You have to try, through trial and error work with your right ear, then your left ear. For some people, for instance, putting it in the right ear, leaving it there for fifteen minutes will interrupt the voices and in some cases make them go away. For other people, you leave it in the right ear for fifteen minutes, and it's only when you take the plug out that the voices are interrupted and/or stopped...

IG: Is it just as simple as 'well, let's just change the situation' and just any change, like any sort of physical change might help?

PD: I think frankly, after my studies and also through a lot of personal trial and error and learning experiences myself, that there really is enormous truth that (it's) anything that promotes a sense of personal efficacy and power. That seems to be the key that, these voices which present themselves as these all-knowing, all-powerful, 'we know everything,' 'we see everything you do,' and on and on and on. To find that I can interrupt that powerful a force, really creates a space for me to have some power. And of course, this flies in the face of much of what modern psychiatry is saying. That people who are experiencing major mental illness are having 'broken brains' and can't possibly take a stand towards what's ailing them except to take medications. I feel we're doing an enormous disservice in the United States in particular by saying that medications are the only answer.

What is critical about the use of earplugs as a bodily practice is that plugging two ears doesn't work, an embodied recognition that the voices are not from outside the self and they can be blocked from entering through the ears. The same conclusion can be drawn, perhaps even more vividly, from the observation that the voices are in some cases affected only by *removing* the plugs. Finally, the indeterminacy of the self-processes is implicit in that the voices are often interrupted or suspended, but not necessarily eliminated in a definitive way. Deegan and her patients carry the earplugs for use when necessary rather than leaving them in as a permanent measure.

I would also take Deegan's own understanding in terms of agency/power/control one step further to include meaning. It will hardly be lost on readers that the use of earplugs can be interpreted as a kind of placebo intervention. However, this is only helpful insofar as we follow Daniel Moerman's (2002) recent reconceptualization of the placebo effect as a "meaning response." There is an error in a truncated conception of placebo as in all respects inert and nonspecific in effect, for the placebo often creates meaning that carries a highly specific efficacy. In this respect the technique of the earplugs is not just an exertion of power against power, but also a meaningful metaphor of reappropriating one's own intentionality. It thus embodies self-process aimed at resecuring the capacity for orientation in the world and hence the very possibility of having a self.

The possibility has been raised that a discursive model of human experience may be useful in helping someone who experiences verbal hallucinations. In a case study of a woman's personal narrative, Davies, Thomas, and Leudar (1999) explicated verbal hallucinations as a variety of inner speech in which a supportive voice created a dialogic space of response to distressing and dangerous voices. In this instance, the inner dialogue was a singularized self process that created personal efficacy and power.

Neuroimaging studies have shown that when patients actually hear voices their speech perception and production network is activated in a way that suggests that hallucinations result from the "misattribution" of inner speech as coming from an external source (Hoffman 1999; Stein and Richardson 1999). While psychological attribution theory may be a narrow cognitive model for human experience, Anthony Morrison (1999:298) has suggested that "auditory hallucinations are normal phenomena and that it is the misinterpretation of such phenomena that cause the distress and disability" commonly experienced by patients. In a comparison of three groups of patients with schizophrenia, patients with dissociative disorder, and nonpatient voice hearers, Saeed Wahass and Gerry Kent (1997) found that the nonpatient group, unlike the patient groups, perceived their voices as predominantly positive: They were not alarmed or upset by their voices and felt in control of the experience. For most patients, the onset of auditory hallucinations was preceded by either a traumatic event or an event that activated the memory of earlier trauma. This study presents evidence that the form of the hallucinations experienced by both patient and nonpatient subjects is similar, irrespective of diagnosis. Differences between groups were predominantly related to the content, emotional quality, and locus of control of the voices.

These newer interpretations of voices are critical to my argument here in supporting the role of agency and intentionality of the auditory hallucinating self-based on neuroscientific, discursive, and cognitive studies of these particular forms of subjectivity (Carter, MacKinnon, and Copolov 1996; Leudar, McNally, and Glinski 1997; Rojcewicz and Rojcewicz 1997; Behrendt 1998; Close and Garety 1998). Analysis of the cultural specificity of these processes has barely begun,[13] although Wahass and Kent (1997) have identified differences in coping strategies among Saudi and British patients. The strategies differ since the former invokes religion to account for voices and the latter invents techniques for distracting themselves or physiologically self-stimulating.

Against the background of these considerations, I encourage a research agenda aimed at exploring how people with schizophrenia think, have awareness, feel desire, self-protect, make social attachments, negotiate a gendered identity, deploy psychological defenses, enact personally encrusted transference dynamics, and act with agency and intentionality in the pursuit of goals that are considered reflectively. Such an agenda allows for a rereading of classic texts in a new light as in Silvano Arieti's (1955) rereading of Freud's 1896 study of projection and repression in relation to hallucinatory experience in schizophrenia. As is also the case among persons without schizophrenia, repression of self-reproach, for example, can be projected on to others who thus become the persecutors (Arieti 1955:23). For Arieti, Freud's greatest contribution in this area was his recognition of the importance of symbolization in the formation of schizophrenic symptoms. Other psychoanalytic concepts, including the unconscious, repression, and transference, are equally valuable for understanding the subjective experience of schizophrenia. "For instance, the unconscious decreases in extension in schizophrenia, as a consequence of a partial return to consciousness of what is generally repressed in psychoneuroses and normal conditions" (Arieti 1955:26).

Finally, it is worth pointing to the manner in which themes of selfhood can be identified by offering examples from my own explorations of the subjectivities of Latino and Euro-American patients with long-term schizophrenia or depression (Jenkins 1997:24). First, there was a subjective sense of engagement in what can be termed the *rhythm of life*. Often there appeared to be a moral struggle represented in narrative themes of "good" or "bad" self-perceptions as in relation to maintaining an embodied sense of rhythm and involvement in the flow of everyday activities. Second was the self-experience of temporality. The phenomenology of feeling ill may take the temporal form of flashes, moments, or waves that come and go and are not objectified as enduring identities. For example, Julia, a person who steadfastly discarded the notion that she was "ill," described her problems as "just part of my personality." She conveyed that she was "obsessed with the passage of time." She wondered what she might do the rest of the day and said that she is always thinking of time and how to fill it. Third was the strategic attempt to represent to self and others that one was not marked by the stigma of mental disorder: Euro-American patients often invoked the category of physical illness to achieve this end, while Latinos described their illness in terms of *nervios* to achieve the same end. The fourth theme of self-hood was the implicit or explicit hope for recovery. In Byron Good's (1994:153) formulation, illness stories portray a "subjunctive world, one in which healing was an open possibility even if miracles were necessary." The subjunctive state of distress, misfortune, and illness is particularly impressive in the illness stories of our Latino respondents, for whom cure, recovery, and miracles were distinct possibilities (Jenkins 1997). The play of such themes across everyday life need not entail coherence of self or identity, and may play their own role in the perpetuation as well as the amelioration of suffering.

The Feel of Schizophrenia

Problems with emotion have long been considered an important aspect of the schizophrenic disorders (Sullivan 1927; Flack and Laird 1998). Yet there are a number of apparently contradictory formulations of what these problems might be,[14] and the repertoire of emotions and distortions of emotion are not well described in the literature. Perhaps the most critical issue with respect to emotion in schizophrenia is a pervasive clinical expectation that illness entails a flattening or blunting of affect. This expectation of flattened affect can be traced to the observations of Kraeplin (1919) in relation to the syndrome he termed *dementia praecox*. Bleuler (1950) sought to modify this characterization by emphasizing that affectivity is not absent in schizophrenia, but a complex and defining feature of the illness itself. Bleuler identified ambivalence – by which he meant the noteworthy simultaneous occurrence of opposing feelings for the same subject-object – as central to schizophrenia. Sullivan's formulation of the problem highlighted the exquisite sensitivity of emotional life.

We find that the schizophrenic is an extremely shy individual, extremely sensitive, possessed of a singular ability to get his feelings hurt, who has rather naturally erected an enormous defensive machinery between himself and intimate contact with other people. (Sullivan 1962:223)

Over time, however, Kraeplin's formulation (1919:32–5) of an "emotional dullness," "ataxia of the feelings," and "blunting of emotions" dominated psychiatric characterization of a distinct absence of emotion in schizophrenia.

Contemporary psychiatric researchers conceptualize the claim of difference in schizophrenia patients' emotionality relative to their normal counterparts, as well as to patients with other disorders, as a deficit (Andreasen 1994) that is classified among "negative symptoms" according to the DSM-IV criteria (American Psychiatric Association 1994). This scientific conceptualization – along with the popular notion that having emotion qualifies as the *sine qua non* of being human – provides challenges for anyone diagnosed with schizophrenia. That is, the perception that such persons do not have emotions may compromise their claim to human status. In this respect, a convergence of popular and professional construction of persons with schizophrenia as something "other" than human transpires. This lack of emotionality, then, serves to construct people with schizophrenia as less than fully human. The counterpoint to the argument that the lack of emotion is irrational, and hence inhuman, is that schizophrenic emotion is intensely disorganized. This leads ironically to the same cultural conclusion, that "the schizophrenic" is irrational, and hence, less than human.

To compound the irony, when emotionality *is* recognized within schizophrenia, it is often to amplify the imputation of irrationality. This is the case, for example, when instances of "schizophrenic rage" are sensationalized in the popular media. To grant a diversified emotional life to patients from the outset would be to recognize that rage is hardly unique to schizophrenia, and that such outbursts must be considered along with instances described as "road rage" or "hockey rage."[15] It is as unacceptable to regard a specific emotion as a symptom of schizophrenia as it is to diagnose the individual erupting in "road rage" with schizophrenia.

A stance that emphasizes what schizophrenia can teach us about fundamental human processes might foster research that encompasses *disorganization* while at the same time, moving beyond it to apprehend the *complexity* of emotion and thought in this illness. Forrest (1965:9) has analyzed language use of persons with schizophrenia to find that "(i)t would seem that in a real sense the schizophrenic is forced into an act of poiesis, and that in using language he is *making* something, not merely describing something, or performing, or communicating, or giving vent to something." Although much of schizophrenic speech is poetic, clearly there is no such thing as "schizophrenic language:"

Many of the peculiarities of the schizophrenic's speech may indicate, not that he is incapable of 'using words like somebody else,' but that his inventions and aberrations are purposive. That the poets in their mastery may have used words similarly is evidence of this, when it is shown that the poets and the schizophrenics have in common the search for an external order in language to lend authority to similar wishes. The wishes of schizophrenics have been assumed to be like those of other men, including poets. (Forrest 1965:18)

The final sentence of this quote perhaps begs the question of whether poets are like other persons, and whether poetic language is like everyday language. The issue is not whether to place the poet on the side of the normal or the abnormal person, or to set up poetry as a bridge or transitional form between normal and abnormal speech. It is rather to remind us that the figurative use of metonymy, synecdoche, and other devices in their language use are part of normal speech. Take, for example, Renee's narrative from *Autobiography of a Schizophrenic Girl* (Sechehaye 1951):

I saw things mocking me. I cannot say that I really saw images; they did not represent anything. Rather I felt them. It seemed that my mouth was full of birds, which I crunched between my teeth, their feathers, their blood and broken bones were choking me.

Here we have an embodied first-person account of an exceptionally threatening situation that experientially melds image and emotion. While it could be argued that not all persons with schizophrenia are similarly verbal, it remains that the methodological challenge to observing and interpreting diverse linguistic devices for affective communication should not dissuade us from attempting to apprehend subjective experience (see Saris 1995).

That humanity is precisely what is at stake is well known among those who live with schizophrenia as a matter of first-person subjectivity and intersubjectivity in family contexts or clinical and research encounters. The ironic fact that the suffering of persons with schizophrenia is substantially constituted by others' (healthcare providers, employers, kin, neighbors, strangers in the community) cultural ambivalence and reluctance to grant them full "human" status was made explicit in a recent field encounter by one of the members of our research team. After a series of informal interviews and numerous weekly trips to a fast-food restaurant, one of the ethnographers for our research team witnessed a moment of spontaneous relief experienced by a patient named Mark who announced quite abruptly: "Sarah, you see me as *human*."[16]

The foregoing considerations reveal a paradox in the research and clinical representation of the subjective experience of emotion among persons with schizophrenia. They are represented as "vacant," without emotional register, dull, flat – yet they are exquisitely sensitive to socioemotional communications. This paradox can in part be resolved with reference to a series of studies by Ann Kring and colleagues (Chapter 13 this volume; Kring and Neale 1996), who carefully insist that emotion phenomena must be specified with respect to behavioral and bodily manifestation, on the one hand, and subjective self-experience, on the other. Kring's work shows that although the experiential realities of schizophrenia patients are suffused by as much or more emotion than their "normal" counter-parts, an apparent emotional "discontinuity" may indeed exist between behavioral expression and subjective experience, particularly insofar as customary facial expression cues are (not) necessarily displayed. Thus, while an emotion may not be "readable" to an observer, it can nonetheless be experienced and reported upon by the person, and may also be ac-companied by "readable" physiological indicators such as muscle activity (Tarrier, Vaughn, Lader, and Leff 1979). In this light, the characteriza-tion of persons with schizophrenia as having "flat affect" appears related to two analytic errors:

1. Conflation of experience with expression of emotion – certainly the failure or inability to draw upon the cultural repertoire of what Hildred Geertz (1959) referred to as the "vocabulary of emotion" can result in doubt or accusation regarding one's social competence and moral status as "human."
2. Clash of perspectives between observer and subject – this is in fact a failure of intersubjectivity. Here, the arrogation by the observer (whether clinician, researcher, family member, or partner in casual social interaction) to represent the subjectivity of the afflicted casts doubt on the legitimacy and veracity of patients' claims regarding their own emotional experience.

The World Health Organization's (WHO 1979) International Pilot Study of Schizophrenia (IPSS) was a longitudinal investigation of schizophrenic symptomatology and course of illness for 1,202 patients in nine coun-tries (United Kingdom, former Union of Soviet Socialist Republics, United States, Czechoslovakia, Denmark, China, Colombia, Nigeria, and India). Two-year, follow-up data provide a striking range in the presence of flat affect: from 8 (Ibadan, Nigeria) to 50 percent (Moscow, Russia) of patients were so rated.[17] Whatever the methodological difficulties, these IPSS follow-up data for flat affect were reported as the second most common symptom present for the sample overall.[18]

Given the problematic status of flat affect, it is all the more important to observe that the repertoire of strong emotions characteristic of sub-jectivity under conditions of schizophrenia is not well described in the literature. In the domain of painful and upsetting emotions, perhaps anx-iety, fear, and terror are the most common. These affects, attached to specific or generalized sources, may be extraordinary in intensity and du-ration. Margaret Sherman, a thirty-two-year-old Euro-American woman, explained to me that she nearly always felt anxious, particularly at night before going to sleep. When I asked her what happened when going to sleep she said, "I worry. What if I forget something, like my brush, or my purse, or the birds, or the *sky*?" This sweeping array of world-constituting objects – at once personal and mundane, small and grand – cannot be taken for granted by her as ordinary and stable objects in her world. The objects and the attendant worry she attaches to them are arguably ordinary, yet her anxiety is extraordinary in frequency and scope. This means that the routinization of her daily experience cannot be taken for granted.

Beyond anxiety, the subjective feel of schizophrenia is frequently shaped by fears and abject terror (Corin this volume). The source of fear or terror may be threatening or horrifying voices, visions, and ideas as some of the foregoing examples have indicated. These frightening emotional forays lead to another dimension of the illness experience that is not sufficiently appreciated, that is, that psychotic experience – occurring transiently and unpredictably – is traumatizing (Shaw, McFarlane, Bookless 1997). Sergio Sanchez, a young Mexican man, explained that he felt in a state of fear. At the time, his new neuroleptic medication (Haldol) had not made as much of an improvement as he and his doctor and family had hoped. An exceptionally bright student, his plans to continue his studies at a local institute of technology were shattered since his cruel and oppressive voices ruled the roost when it came to his daily schedule. He would arise in the morning to make plans for studies and attendance of classes only to be thwarted by his voices that informed him otherwise:

Now, let's lie down on the bed and think about all the bad things you've done. You're worse than a child molester. You'll be lucky if you burn in hell. Imagine how it will feel to have your flesh burn. You think you're something? You're nothing and we'll show you.

Sergio knew not to ignore the voices since, after much thought, he had concluded that indeed this was the voice of God. He did not understand why God tortured him with these thoughts, which left him stunned and shaking. The trauma of such enforced rituals can, of course, become unbearable. This is likely why some 10 percent of persons with schizophrenia commit suicide: It is simply beyond endurance. Yet the fact that most do not, in spite of horrific and unspeakable suffering, points to the deep wellspring of human endurance and resilience when confronted with arguably the most painful and horrifying of human experience imaginable.

The occurrence and form in schizophrenia of positive emotions such as hope, contentment, joy, and humor, has received little attention. The relative eclipse of more positive emotions may be due to the intensity and prevalence of hard affects commonly noted. While less dramatic than the horror and the fear engendered by psychosis, positive emotions may well be part of everyday emotional experience. This was remarkable, for example, among a group of long-term and severely ill Latino and

Euro-American persons diagnosed with schizophrenia and depression for whom the subjunctive mood (Good 1994) of hope nonetheless colored the course of their lives and illness experience (Jenkins 1997). While some patients claimed they were unable to remember or imagine their lives in so-called "normal" terms (that is, when they were not ill), they had lost neither the desire nor the hope that somehow things might change for the better. Although this sense of hope and faith was articulated (implicitly or explicitly) among both ethnic groups, it was more apparent among the Latino (predominantly Puerto Rican) group. Latinos invoked their religious hopes as the basis for assuming that anything was possible, be it a medical cure or a miraculous divine intervention.

With the advent of the newer antipsychotic drugs (such as Clozapine, Risperidone, and Olanzapine) over the last decade, there have been some remarkable improvements described as "awakenings" (Sacks 1990) as occurred in people with postencephalitic Parkinsonism treated with L-DOPA. Significant recovery from psychosis often involves self-processes of newfound joy and satisfaction, on the one hand, alternating with recrimination and humiliation, on the other (Weiden, Aquila, and Standard 1996). According to Duckworth, Nair, Patel, and Goldfinger (1997:227):

When a patient experiences a significant reduction in psychotic symptoms... (t)he challenges inherent in such improvement often involve a fundamental re-assessment of one's identity, relationships, and purpose in being. When the hallucinations, tangential thinking, or delusions are quieted, patients are 'free' to reassess their status in life. During this period, many of them have reported periods of emptiness, disillusionment, sadness, loss and anger. The psychological reaction to dramatic pharmacological response is largely uncharted territory.

Duckworth and colleagues (228) found that "patients experienced a process of psychological redefinition and confronted developmental tasks that were dormant prior to their improvement... including three issues that challenge this population: sense of self, sense of connectedness, and sense of purpose." Difficult affects, such as anger and loneliness, joy and contentment, are also likely to surface. Social relations, once distant or broken, may be renewed with relative success or failure. These claims of dramatic changes in the subjective reactions and social relations of patients present major challenges in the clinical management and scientific understanding of schizophrenia (Weiden and Havens 1994; Weiden, Scheifler, Diamond, and Ross 1999). In our current research project on schizophrenia (N = 90) with persons treated with atypical antipsychotic medications, we find that the process of recovery – while substantial and discernable both objectively and subjectively – is better characterized as *incremental* rather than *dramatic* through reference to the metaphor of "awakenings" (Jenkins and Miller 2002).

Spontaneous laughter and joke telling are also part of the more recent emotional landscape of subjective experience among persons who have experienced improvement in their condition. In one of the community clinic settings where our research team is conducting research, the waiting room has become a site for ritual performances of joke telling: "Hey: when you talk to God it's called prayer, but when he talks *back* it's schizophrenia," among a myriad of others. Although analysis of these ethnographic (and other interview) data is ongoing, it is clear to us that poking fun at "the illness" and "medications" is highly relished.[19]

Social Engagement, Cultural Orientation

Sullivan conceived of mental disorder as an interactive process. As a starting point for cultural investigation, it requires that mental disorder be examined within the arena of everyday social life rather than in the brain scan or clinic (Scheper-Hughes 2001). The early theoretical formulations by Sullivan provide a bridge between the subjective experience of the afflicted self and the world of everyday social interaction. A more recent consideration of this issue has been set forth in Jessica Benjamin's (1995) *Like Subjects, Love Objects: Essays on Recognition and Sexual Difference*. Benjamin notes that, in the strict sense, no subject ever constitutes herself in the absence of other subjects and objects. In this sense, I would suggest, when we speak of subjectivity we actually mean to invoke the notion of intersubjectivity. Indeed, Benjamin supplants classic formulations of "object relations" with the notion of intersubjectivity in asserting "where objects were, subjects must be." The idea of intersubjectivity has been formulated in deliberate contrast to the logic of subject and object through entry into the interactive zone of lived experience in which the self is processually, dynamically, and multiply constituted.

The theoretical reformulation of differences between subject and object, self and other, entails finding a way to account for the difficulty each subject has in recognizing the other as an equivalent center of experience. In the case of schizophrenia, potential failures of recognition can be two-edged: There may be a staunch cultural refusal of others to grant the ontological status of subjects to "schizophrenics"; and, among persons with schizophrenia there can likewise be a strained ability to grant the legitimacy of subject status to others. The tension of sustaining the contradiction of intersubjective structure, which includes mutuality, simultaneity, and paradox, can lead to a common fact of mental life: the breakdown in the relation between self and others in favor of relating as subject and object. Even so, a developmental formulation of this problem underscores the fundamental need humans have for *recognition* and a *capacity* to recognize others in return (Benjamin 1995).

If the understandings of subjectivity and social engagement as formulated by Sullivan and Benjamin are valid where schizophrenia is concerned, the clinical and popular assumption that psychotic persons do not respond emotionally to their social surroundings cannot be tenable. This assumption may stem from the idea that psychotic experience is so self-consuming that persons experiencing psychotic symptoms (hallucinations, delusions) are not capable of taking note of or responding to features of their setting (a variation on the "nobody's home" model of flat affect as characteristic of subjective experience described previously). That this conceptualization of persons with schizophrenia is mistaken is clear from empirical studies illustrating that they are not only fully aware of their socioemotional surroundings but are particularly responsive to them. This is not only a matter of daily life experience; even more significantly, these processes of social engagement mediate the clinical course of illness defined in terms of improvement and recovery. Clearly, the understanding of these processes is of primary importance.

There are several areas of empirical research that are critical in demonstrating the significance of social relations and engagement for persons with schizophrenia: (1) family "expressed emotion" in cross-cultural perspective; (2) the relationship of "expressed emotion" to cultural interpretations of the "problem" conceived by researchers/clinicians as "schizophrenia"; (3) the type of emotional style adopted by patients toward their social world; (4) the relationship between gender and recovery; and (5) the importance of social ecology (as type of residential setting) as a mediator for treatment response.

First, there has been extensive research to demonstrate that the empirically derived construct of "expressed emotion" (that is, subjective data on criticism, hostility, and overinvolvement insofar as they constitute a particularly familial emotional ambiance) is significantly predictive of clinical relapse (Brown, Birley, and Wing 1972; Vaughn and Leff 1976; Vaughn, Snyder, Jones, Freeman, and Falloon 1984). Paul Bebbington and Liz Kuipers (1994) summarize a total of twenty-five methodologically comparable studies completed from around the world to produce an aggregate analysis confirming this relationship. Marvin Karno and colleagues (1987) extended this research beyond British and Anglo-American English speakers to determine that in a sample of seventy Spanish-speaking Mexican-descent families in California these emotion factors (1) also significantly predicted the course of schizophrenic illness; and (2) were found to be cross-culturally variable, with significantly lower levels of criticism and hostility relative to their Anglo-American counter-parts. Because much of this empirical research tradition had proceeded apace on the basis of statistical "prediction without meaning," we also took it upon ourselves to examine the theoretical nature and meaning of what was inside the empirical "black box" of expressed emotion, to conclude that this research construct taps a variety of culturally variable kin responses to the problem of schizophrenic illness in the family, in addition to features of social ecology and historically specific political processes (Jenkins and Karno 1992).

Second, our research on the meaning of indigenous conceptions of schizophrenia produced the finding that such conceptions substantially determine the emotional response ("expressed emotion" as above) to the problem (Jenkins 1988a). That socially transacted (kin and commu-nity) cultural orientations "make" reality by specifying the conceptual-emotional parameters of "schizophrenia" (*nervios* or laziness, for exam-ple) such that they mediate the emotional response (warmth/sympathy or anger/hostility, for example) and thereby shape the actual course and outcome of the illness is powerful cultural evidence that there is no such object as a "natural" course of schizophrenia (Jenkins 1988b, 1991). Rather, the course of illness is inherently social and cultural, and a mat-ter of intersubjective engagement. Thus, the import of culturally specific conceptions of schizophrenic illness extends beyond the question that came to dominate psychiatric anthropology during the 1960s and 1970s. At that time anthropologists wanted to know, in effect, whether "what was crazy for us was also crazy for them" (Edgerton 1966). They investi-gated the issue by analyzing indigenous conceptualizations of what would, by "Western" standards, be diagnosed as psychiatric disorder (Kennedy 1974; Waxler 1974; Janzen 1978; White 1982; Scheper-Hughes 2001). Taking into account the kind of concerns I have raised here promises to help make sense of the array of disturbances in body, mood, thought, and behavior that so perplexes families of afflicted individuals. Family mem-bers' attempt to arrive at any understanding of the problem, however tentative or imperfect it might be, is invariably guided by sociocultural models of illness (Jenkins 1988a). These models, along with their asso-ciated emotional response, mediate the course and outcome of mental disorder (Jenkins 1988a; Jenkins and Karno 1992). Specifying the cul-tural variation in the course of schizophrenia (WHO 1979; Kleinman 1988; Hopper this volume) thus goes to the heart of a critical feature of illness experience: recovery.

A third area of empirical research in which social engagement has been observed as key to the course of illness concerns the type of emo-tional style patients adopt toward their social world, again in many cases prominently including kin (in this case, siblings). In her study of male patients in Montreal, Ellen Corin (1990) found that men with schizophrenia developed two styles of social distancing. The first type remains voluntarily and purposively "detached" from others as a protective strategy; the second pattern is experienced as being involuntarily "excluded" by others.[20] More men who employed the "excluded" style were rehospitalized than those who remained voluntarily more detached. Thus George Devereaux's (1939) characterization of schizophrenia as an adaptation to loneliness was found to vary according to personal style of organization. Based on available scientific literature, we might also expect this to vary in relation to gender.

Fourth, in the last decade there has been increasing recognition of the role of sex and gender in schizophrenia.[21] Women have been found to have later onset of illness, more affective-type symptoms, better response to treatment, and superior course and outcome (Goldstein and Tsuang 1990). In a study comparing schizophrenia and depression among eighty Latino and Euro-American households, we found that the only statistical main effect in the area of social and household functioning is accounted for by sex, with women doing far better in this domain than their male counterparts (Jenkins and Schumacher 1999). We also observed that in these family settings, women with schizophrenia – like their normal counterparts – carry out the lion's share of household work and management relative to men. Kaplan's (1991) analysis of sex and gender differences in psychopathology invokes the notion of variations in psychological strategies that require a performance of socially enacted gender stereotypes.

Finally, the significance of social engagement for persons with schizophrenia has been empirically specified in relation to subjective response to personal therapy and residential setting (Hogarty, Kornblith, Greenwald, and DiBarry 1995). In this American study, patients living with family and receiving personal therapy treatments have a significantly better course and outcome compared with patients living independently. For the latter group, a reverse effect was noted: Patients who received personal therapy but lived alone or in group-home settings experienced significantly more psychotic decompensation. The particular technique developed for "personal therapy" here entails patients learning to identify their subjective states – particular their affective states – and the development of appropriate social perception – that is, learning to gauge one's own and another's "emotional temperature" and selecting a likely successful response before initiating an interpersonal encounter. While patients living with family were able to benefit from this therapeutic method, the authors suggest that patients living apart from family may have experienced personal therapy as a cognitive overload. In addition, these patients were forced to cope with subsistence issues on an everyday basis. They suffered with greater difficulty securing food and clothing, and suitable, stable, and conflict-free housing. The critical importance of household conditions and social relations had already been empirically demonstrated as etiologically predictive for depression (Brown and Harris 1978). This research shows not only that these factors are likewise significant for persons with schizophrenia but also that such conditions mediate their ability to engage positively in particularly types of therapeutic interventions where monitoring of their own subjectivity is concerned.

Conclusion

In *A Beautiful Mind*, Sylvia Nasar (1998) examines the life of mathematical genius John Forbes Nash, afflicted with intermittent bouts of florid schizophrenia since the age of thirty. While eventually awarded the Nobel Prize for his contribution to economic game theory, committee deliberations about Nash were constituted in large part by a fierce, if often subterranean, antipathy toward a "schizophrenic" as recipient since, as framed by one committee member, "(h)e's sick . . . you can't have a person like that." After all, "[W]hat would happen at the ceremony: Would he come? Could he handle it? It's a big show" (366). In the end, other committee members prevailed with the view that "on the whole, Nash (was) no more eccentric, irrational, or paranoid than many other academics" (362). Be that as it may, Nash's personal experience of psychosis, no less his intuitive flights of mathematical genius, renders him *just like us but very much more so.*

In this chapter, I have examined the cultural grounding of subjective experience in schizophrenia as a paradigm case for understanding fundamental human processes, drawing on Sapir's interactional, meaning-centered theory of culture and on Sullivan's theory of schizophrenia as grounded firmly in the everyday world. With the added insights of a number of contemporary cultural theorists, I have examined particular processes of self, emotion, social engagement, and cultural orientation, all vital for the analysis of a complex phenomenon such as schizophrenia. The discussion is intended as evocative rather than definitive, and points toward further substantive research in each of the three domains.

First, in the domain of the self, the intersection of culture, subjectivity, and schizophrenia is perhaps most intense, most problematic, and most fundamentally human. In the experience of "voices," for example, the nuances of intentionality, agency, and meaning are intertwined in the service of appropriating experiences that are profoundly discontinuous with normality into an ordinary self that is singularly continuous with normality. This analysis points toward power, resistance, and identity, each of them fruitful areas for further research.

Second, in the domain of emotion, schizophrenia has long been construed as a state of affective deficit. This could scarcely be further from the truth, for a groundswell of contemporary research is now beginning to show that it is emotional intensity and complexity that epitomizes this disorder, even for those whose emotional expression appears to others to be flattened out. Further studies are needed, with the breadth to encompass the extremes (abject terror) and the ordinary (hopes and disappointments). They will enrich our understanding, not only of schizophrenia, but also of human emotional processes per se.

Third, in the domain of social engagement, we have seen that persons with schizophrenia, like their counterparts, are exquisitely tuned to social relations and cultural orientations for their lives and illness experience. In particular, cultural conceptions of the illness are associated with particular emotions that affect significantly the clinical course of illness. This association, initially established for schizophrenia, has subsequently been found for other stress-related conditions, psychiatric and nonpsychiatric alike (Jenkins and Karno 1992). In addition, cultural orientations for gender and type of household affect the capacity to monitor personal subjective states.

In this chapter, then, I have maintained that the subjective experience of persons with schizophrenia invariably involves culture and agency. That their subjective experience is hardly voided by illness process runs contrary to many scientific and popular representations. In addition, I have argued that the study of schizophrenia illumines our understanding of culture and subjectivity more generally. Thinking with schizophrenia – perhaps ironically considered the "most" biogenetic and "least" cultural of psychiatric disorders – provides a compelling case for the necessity of conceptualizing fundamental processes and capacities as invariably mediated by culture and context. Moreover, because the experiences of people with schizophrenia can be quintessentially extraordinary just as they can be exquisitely ordinary, people who suffer from the disorder have a unique capacity to teach us about human processes that are fundamental to living in a world that is shared with others.

NOTES

* This chapter was completed through support of funding by the National Institute of Health (MH 60232) to the author as Principle Investigator of "Culture, Schizophrenia and Atypical Antipsychotics."

1 In this chapter, we prefer usage of "person with schizophrenia" rather than "the schizophrenic."

2 This quote is taken from Sapir's reconstructed lectures (1994:224, 237) on "The Psychology of Culture" edited by Judith Irvine. Irvine's footnote for this quote has been incorporated in specific reference to psychosis.

3 Over the past few decades, there has been a proliferation of studies by anthropologists on culture and emotion (Geertz 1973; Rosaldo 1984; Shweder and LeVine 1984; Lutz 1988; Jenkins 1994a), notably Michelle Rosaldo's formulation of emotions as "not only self-concerning, partly physical responses" but also "aspects of moral or ideological attitudes" that are "of strategic importance to analysts concerned with the ordering of action and the ways that people shape and are shaped by their world" (Rosaldo in Levy 1983:128).

4 While there are various psychiatric views of schizophrenia – from the biological, psychosocial, cognitive-behavioral, to the psychodynamic (see Barrett 1996), this rich variety of theories and approaches is frequently eclipsed in relation to the lack of adequate funding when state and local mental health services provide services. Thus, providers often fall back on the biological perspective as the default option, feeling that it is the least, and perhaps the only, treatment option they can provide. In addition, over the last two decades we have witnessed the paradigmatic ascendancy of biological psychiatry across many academic schools and departments (Luhrmann 2001).

5 In this chapter, I rely on my ethnographic and clinical research experience over the past two decades, through a series of research projects funded by the U.S. National Institute of Mental Health on culture and schizophrenia: "The Course of Schizophrenia among Mexican-Descent Immigrants" (MH 30911), "Schizophrenia and Depression among Latinos and Euro-Americans," (MH 47920), and "Schizophrenia Experience and the Culture of Recovery through Atypical Antipsychotics" (MH-60232). Examples and illustrations for this chapter are taken from the data of these studies.

6 This assumption regarding an inevitable neurodevelopmental degeneration in the course of schizophrenia has been shown not to be true by virtue of international and cross-cultural evidence (Hopper this volume), neuroscientific (Lieberman 1994), or longitudinal (Harding 1987).

7 The notion of being "just like us only more so" has been invoked in a variety of contexts; see Jenkins (1988a) for the application of this point in relation to the fluidly applied concept of *nervios* as applied to schizophrenia illness among Mexican immigrants.

8 As more women theorists and researchers have become involved in the study of schizophrenia, and the National Institutes of Health have implemented the requirement to include women and minorities in scientific protocols, studies of schizophrenia have begun to include women.

9 The emphasis on "lack of inner unity" appears in Kraepelin's seventh edition of *Psychiatrie* (1903).

10 Hearing the voice of a deceased love one is not uncommon among many cultural groups (Karno and Jenkins 1997).

11 The term "ethnopsychology" refers to cultural assumptions about the mind, emotion, and the self (Shweder and LeVine 1984). Jenkins (1994b:100) has summarized ethnopsychological themes as "the relative egocentricity of

the self; indigenous categories of emotion; the predominance of particular emotions within societies; the interrelation of various emotions; identification of those situations in which emotions are said to occur; and ethnophysiological accounts of bodily experience of emotions. This constellation of sociocultural features will mediate how persons experience and express emotion."

12 Excerpts taken from an interview conducted by Ira Glass (1997) with Patricia Degan in a radio program on "The Edge of Sanity," for "This American Life," Public Radio International.

13 A general theory to account for the presence of positive symptoms such as auditory hallucinations has been that overstimulation (although understimulation may also be a trigger) is likely to provoke symptoms (Vaughn and Leff 1976).

14 The problem of emotion in schizophrenia is complicated in cross-cultural perspective, given recent anthropological formulations of emotion as culturally constituted (Geertz 1973; Rosaldo 1984; Lutz 1988).

15 "Road rage" is periodically reported on the highways of the United States, involving apparently unwarranted violent acts by one motorist toward another. "Hockey rage" refers to the episode widely reported in January 2002 of the manslaughter trial of the parent of a youth hockey player in Boston, Massachusetts, who killed his son's coach, and can be generalized to violent outbreaks on the part of parents of youth athletes in other sports.

16 This example is excerpted directly from field notes from NIMH-funded study MH-60232, "Schizophrenia Experience and the Culture of Recovery through Atypical Antipsychotics" (SEACORA).

17 Methodological questions regarding cultural validity linger since precisely how flat affect was assessed is not part of the published record. Part of the methodological challenge is to rate "flat affect" in terms of a quantitative continuum between flatness (pathological) and expressiveness (normal).

18 The most frequently reported symptoms, across sites, was "lack of insight," conceived as a failure to recognize the presence of illness. However, another cultural possibility exists: The IPSS data may indicate that what may have been apparent from an observer's point of view may not have been experientially true for the subject. The idea that the psychiatric interpretation of the presence of illness wherein the patient might claim otherwise seems evidence that there likely were instances of a clash of perspectives regarding the rating of symptoms.

19 This observation was noted by members of the research team for NIMH-funded study MH-60232.

20 In this study, patients attached a particular importance to their sense of being "excluded" from social participation with their siblings.

21 This has served to advance what Sandra Harding (1991) would term feminist empiricist "corrections" of the scientific record in "getting it (more) right" by virtue of analyzing data to include the dichotomously coded variable of "sex." However, studies in this area have yet to address the more challenging question that, again from Harding's (1991) point of view, would be termed feminist standpoint theory insofar as research is undertaken with a set of critical epistemological assumptions regarding the more complicated

question of gender. Thus far in the medical, psychiatric, and psychological literatures attention to gender as a cultural orientation has been largely ignored, but is the subject of the current NIMH-funded study MH-60232 (SEACORA).

REFERENCES

American Psychiatric Association. 1994. *Diagnostic and Statistical Manual-IV.* Washington, DC: American Psychiatric Association.

Andreasen, Nancy C. 1994. *Schizophrenia: From Mind to Molecule.* Washington DC: American Psychiatric Press.

Arieti, Silvano. 1955. *Interpretation of Schizophrenia.* New York: R. Brunner.

Barrett, Robert J. 1996. *The Psychiatric Team and the Social Definition of Schizophrenia: An Anthropological Study of Person and Illness.* Cambridge: Cambridge University Press.

Bateson, Gregory and Margaret Mead. 1942. *Balinese Character, a Photographic Analysis.* New York: The New York Academy of Sciences.

Battaglia, Debbora. 1995. *Rhetorics of Self-Making.* Berkeley: University of California Press.

Bebbington, Paul and Liz Kuipers. 1994. "The Predictive Utility of Expressed Emotion in Schizophrenia: An Aggregate Analysis." *Psychological Medicine* 24: 1–11.

Behrendt, Ralf-Peter. 1998. "Underconstrained Perception: A Theoretical Approach to the Nature and Function of Verbal Hallucinations." *Journal of Comprehensive Psychiatry* 39(4): 236–48.

Benedict, Ruth. 2001 [1934]. "Anthropology and the Abnormal." In P. K. Moser and T. L. Carson, eds., pp. 80–9, *Moral Relativism: A Reader.* New York: Oxford University Press.

Benjamin, Jessica. 1995. *Like Subjects, Love Objects: Essays on Recognition and Sexual Difference.* New Haven, CT: Yale University Press.

Bleuler, Eugen. 1950 [1911]. *Dementia Praecox or The Group of Schizophrenias.* New York: International Universities Press.

Brown, G. W., J. L. Birley, and J. K. Wing. 1972. "Influence of Family Life on the Course of Schizophrenic Disorders: A Replication." *British Journal of Psychiatry* 121(562): 241–58.

Brown, George W. and Tirril Harris. 1978. *Social Origins of Depression: A Study of Psychiatric Disorder in Women.* London: Tavistock.

Brown, George W., Tirril Harris, and John R. Copeland. 1978. "Depression and Loss." *British Journal of Psychiatry* 130(1): 8.

Canguilhem, Georges. 1989. *The Normal and the Pathological.* New York: Zone Books.

Carter, Dorothy, Andrew MacKinnon, and David L. Copolov. 1996. "Patients' Strategies for Coping with Auditory Hallucinations." *Journal of Nervous and Mental Disease* 184(3): 159–64.

Close, Hele and Philippa Garety. 1998. "Cognitive Assessment of Voices: Further Developments in Understanding the Emotional Impact of Voices." *British Journal of Clinical Psychology* 37(2): 173–88.

Corin, Ellen. 1990. "Facts and Meaning in Psychiatry: An Anthropological Approach to the Lifeworld of Schizophrenics." *Culture, Medicine and Psychiatry* 14(2): 153–88.

Corin, Ellen and Gilles Lauzon. 1994. "From Symptoms to Phenomena: The Articulation of Experience in Schizophrenia." *Journal of Phenomenological Psychology* 25(1): 3–50.

Csordas, Thomas. 1994a. *Embodiment and Experience: The Existential Ground of Culture and Self.* Cambridge and New York: Cambridge University Press.

———. 1994b. *The Sacred Self: A Cultural Phenomenology of Charismatic Healing.* Berkeley: University of California Press.

Davies, Peggy, Philip Thomas, and Ivan Leudar. 1999. "Dialogical Engagement with Voices: A Single Case Study." *British Journal of Medical Psychology* 72 (pt. 2): 179–87.

Devereux, George. 1980 [1939]. "A Sociological Theory of Schizophrenia." In *Basic Problems of Ethnopsychiatry.* Basia M. Gulati and George Devereaux, trans. Chicago: University of Chicago Press.

Duckworth K., V. Nair, J. Patel, and S. M. Goldfinger. 1997. "Lost Time, Found Hope and Sorrow: The Search for Self, Connection, and Purpose During 'Awakenings' on the New Antipsychotics." *Harvard Review of Psychiatry* 5: 227–33.

Edgerton, Robert B. 1966. Conceptions of Psychosis in Four East African Societies. *American Anthropologist* 68: 408–25.

Ewing, Katherine P. 1990. "The Illusion of Wholeness: Culture, Self, and the Experience of Inconsistency." *Ethos* 18: 251–78.

Flack, William F. and James D. Laird. 1998. *Emotions in Psychopathology. Theory and Research.* New York and Oxford: Oxford University Press.

Forrest, David. 1965. "Poiesis and the Language of Schizophrenia." *Psychiatry: Journal for the Study of Interpersonal Processes* 28(1): 1–18.

Gaines, Atwood. 1982. "Cultural Definitions, Behavior and the Person in American Psychiatry." In A. Marsella and G. White, eds., pp. 167–92, *Cultural Conceptions of Mental Health and Therapy.* Dordrecht, Holland: D. Reidel Publishing Company.

Geertz, Clifford. 1973. *The Interpretation of Cultures.* New York: Basic Books.

Geertz, Hildred. 1959. "The Vocabulary of Emotion: A Study of Javanese Socialization Processes." *Psychiatry* 22(3): 225–37.

Glass, Ira. 2000. [1997]. "The Edge of Sanity," for Program on "This American Life," Public Radio International.

Goldstein, Jill M. and M.T. Tsuang. 1990. "Gender and Schizophrenia: An Introduction and Synthesis of Findings." *Schizophrenia Bulletin* 16: 263–75.

Good, Byron J. 1977. "The Heart of What's the Matter: The Semantics of Illness in Iran." *Culture, Medicine and Psychiatry* 1: 25–58.

———. 1994. *Medicine, Rationality and Experience: An Anthropological Perspective.* New York: Cambridge University Press.

Good, Byron J. and Mary-Jo DelVecchio Good. 1981. "The Meaning of Symptoms: A Cultural Hermeneutic Model for Clinical Practice." In L. Eisenberg and A. Kleinman, eds., pp. 165–96, *The Relevance of Social Science for Medicine.* Dordrecht, Holland: D. Reidel Publishing Company.

———. 1988. "Ritual, the State, and the Transformation of Emotional Discourse in Iranian Society." *Culture, Medicine and Psychiatry* 12(1): 43–63.

Haas, Gretchen L., I. D. Glick, J. F. Clarkin, J. H. Spencer, and A. B. Lewis. 1990. "Gender and Schizophrenia Outcome: A Clinical Trial of an Inpatient Family Intervention." *Schizophrenia Bulletin* 16: 277–92.

Hallowell, Irving. 1955. "The Self in its Behavioral Environment." In I. Hallowell, ed., pp. 75–110, *Culture and Experience*. Philadelphia: University of Pennsylvania Press.

Haraway, Donna J. 1991. *Simians, Cyborgs, and Women: The Reinvention of Nature.* New York: Routledge.

Harding, Courtenay M. 1987. "Chronicity in Schizophrenia: Fact, Partial Fact, or Artifact?" *Hospital and Community Psychiatry* 38: 477–91.

Harding, Sandra. 1991. *Whose Science? Whose Knowledge? Thinking from Women's Lives.* Ithaca, NY: Cornell University Press.

Hoffman, Ralf E. 1999. "New Methods for Studying Hallucinated 'Voices' in Schizophrenia." *Acta Psychiatrica Scandinavica Supplementum* 99(suppl. 395): 89–94.

Hogarty, Gerard E., Sander J. Kornblith, Deborah Greenwald, and Ann Louise DiBarry. 1995. "Personal Therapy: A Disorder-Relevant Psychotherapy for Schizophrenia." *Schizophrenia Bulletin* 21(3): 379–93.

Janzen, John. 1978. *The Quest for Therapy in Lower Zaire.* Berkeley: University of California Press.

Jaspers, Karl. 1963 [1923]. *General Psychopathology.* John Hoenig and Marian W. Hamilton, trans. Chicago: University of Chicago Press.

Jenkins, Janis Hunter. 1988a. "Ethnopsychiatric Interpretations of Schizophrenic Illness: The Problem of Nervios within Mexican-American Families." *Culture, Medicine and Psychiatry* 12(3): 303–31.

———. 1988b. "Conceptions of Schizophrenic Illness as a Problem of Nerves: A Comparative Analysis of Mexican-Americans and Anglo-Americans." *Social Science and Medicine* 26(12): 1233–43.

———. 1991. "The 1990 Stirling Award Essay. Anthropology, Expressed Emotion, Schizophrenia." *Ethos: The Journal of the Society for Psychological Anthropology* 19: 387–431.

———. 1994a. "Culture, Emotion, and Psychopathology." In S. Kitayama and H. Markus, eds., pp. 307–38, *Emotion and Culture: Empirical Studies of Mutual Influence.* Washington, DC: American Psychological Association.

———. 1994b. "The Psychocultural Study of Emotion and Mental Disorder." In P. Bock, ed., pp. 97–120. *Handbook of Psychological Anthropology.* Westport, CT: Greenwood Publishers.

———. 1997. "Subjective Experience of Persistent Psychiatric Disorder: Schizophrenia and Depression among U.S. Latinos and Euro-Americans." *British Journal of Psychiatry* 170: 20–5.

———. 1998. "Diagnostic Criteria for Schizophrenia and Related Psychotic Disorders: Integration and Suppression of Cultural Evidence in DSM-IV." *Transcultural Psychiatry* 35: 357–76.

Jenkins, Janis Hunter and Marvin Karno. 1992. "The Meaning of 'Expressed Emotion': Theoretical Issues Raised by Cross-Cultural Research." Special article in *American Journal of Psychiatry* 149: 9–21.

Jenkins, Janis Hunter and Dawn M. Miller. 2002. "A New Kind of Evidence for Mental Health Interventions: Subjective Experience of Atypical Antipsychotic Medications." Washington, DC: National Institute of Mental Health, Fifteenth International Conference on Services Research.

Jenkins, Janis Hunter and John Schumacher. 1999. "Sociocultural Dimensions of the 'Family Burden' of Chronic Mental Disorder: Specifying Ethnic, Gender and Diagnostic Effects." *British Journal of Psychiatry* 174: 31–8.

Kaplan, Louise J. 1991. *Female Perversions: The Temptations of Emma Bovary.* New York: Doubleday.

Karno, Marvin, Janis Hunter Jenkins, Aurova de la Selva, Felipe Santana, Cynthia Telles, Steven Lopez, and Jim Mintz. 1987. "Expressed Emotion and Schizophrenic Outcome among Mexican-American Families." *Journal of Nervous and Mental Disease* 175(3): 143–51.

Karno, Marvin and Janis Hunter Jenkins. 1997. "Culture and the Diagnosis of Schizophrenia and Related Disorders and Psychotic Disorders Not Otherwise Classified." In T. Widiger, A. Frances, H. Pincus, R. Ross, M. First, and W. Davis, eds., pp. 901–8, *DSM-IV: Sourcebook. Volume.* Washington, DC: American Psychiatric Association.

Kennedy, John. 1974. "Cultural Psychiatry." In J. Honigmann, ed., pp. 1119–98, *Handbook of Social and Cultural Anthropology.* New York: Rand-McNally.

Kleinman, Arthur. 1988. *Rethinking Psychiatry: From Cultural Category to Personal Experience.* New York and London: Free Press; Collier Macmillan.

———. 1995. *Writing at the Margin: Discourse between Anthropology and Medicine.* Berkeley: University of California Press.

Kleinman, Arthur and Joan Kleinman. 1995. "Suffering and its Transformations." In A. Kleinman, ed., pp. 95–119. *Writing at the Margin: Discourse between Anthropology and Medicine.* Berkeley: University of California Press.

Kraepelin, Emil. 1903. *Psychiatrie,* 7th edition. Barth: Leipzig.

———. 1919 [1971]. *Dementia Praecox and Paraphrenia.* R. Mary Barclay, trans. Edinburgh: E and S Livingstone.

Kring, Ann M. and John M. Neale. 1996. "Do Schizophrenic Patients Show a Disjunctive Relationship among Expressive, Experiential, and Psychophysiological Components of Emotion?" *Journal of Abnormal Psychology* 105: 249–57.

Kulkarni, J. 1997. "Women and Schizophrenia: A Review." *Australian and New Zealand Journal of Psychiatry* 31: 46–56.

Lasswell, Harold D. 1930 [1951]. "Psychopathology and Politics." In *The Political Writings of Harold D. Lasswell.* Glencoe, IL: Free Press.

Levy, Robert I. 1983. Introduction: Self and Emotion. *Ethos: Journal of Society for Psychological Anthropology* 11: 128–34.

Leudar, Ivan, Philip Thomas, D. McNally, and A. Glinski. 1997. "What Voices Can Do with Words: Pragmatics of Verbal Hallucinations." *Psychological Medicine* 27(4): 885–989.

Lewine, R. J. 1994. "Sex: An Imperfect Marker of Gender." *Schizophrenia Bulletin* 20: 777–9.

Lieberman, Jeffrey A. 1994. "Predictors of Outcome in Schizophrenia: The Concept of Time." In W. Gaebel and A. G. Awad, eds., pp. 43–9, *Prediction of*

Neuroleptic Treatment Outcome in Schizophrenia: Concepts and Methods. New York: Springer-Verlag.

Luhrmann, Tanya M. 2001. *Of Two Minds: An Anthropologist Looks at American Psychiatry.* New York: Vintage Books.

Lutz, Catherine. 1988. *Unnatural Emotions: Everyday Sentiments on a Micronesian Atoll and their Challenge to Western Theory.* Chicago: University of Chicago Press.

Lutz, Catherine and Lila Abu-Lughod, eds. 1990. *Language and the Politics of Emotion.* New York: Cambridge University Press.

Mead, Margaret. 1928. *Coming of Age in Samoa.* New York: William Morrow.

Moerman, Daniel. 2002. "Deconstructing the Placebo Effect and Finding the Meaning Response." *Annals of Internal Medicine* 136: 471–6.

Morrison, Anthony P. 1999. "A Cognitive Analysis of the Maintenance of Auditory Hallucinations: Are Voices to Schizophrenia What Bodily Sensations Are to Panic?" *Behavioural & Cognitive Psychotherapy* 26(4): 289–302.

Nasar, Sylvia. 1998. *A Beautiful Mind: A Biography of John Forbes Nash, Jr., Winner of the Nobel Prize in Economics, 1994.* New York: Simon & Schuster.

Ortner, Sherry B. 1996. *Making Gender: The Politics and Erotics of Culture.* Boston, MA: Beacon Press.

Powdermaker, Hortense. 1939. *After Freedom: A Cultural Study in the Deep South.* New York: Viking Press.

Rojcewicz, Stephen J. and Richard Rojcewicz. 1997. "The 'Human' Voices in Hallucinations." *Journal of Phenomenological Psychology* 28(1): 1–41.

Rosaldo, Michelle. 1984. "Toward an Anthropology of Self and Feeling." In R.A. Shweder and R.A. LeVine, eds., pp. 137–57, *Culture Theory: Essays on Mind, Self, and Emotion.* Cambridge: Cambridge University Press.

Sacks, Oliver. 1990. *Awakenings.* New York: Harper Perennial.

Sapir, Edward. 1924. "Culture, Genuine and Spurious." *American Journal of Sociology* 29: 401–29.

_____. 1932. "Cultural Anthropology and Psychiatry." *Journal of Abnormal and Social Psychology* 27: 229–42.

_____. 1994. *The Psychology of Culture.* Edited and reconstructed by Judith T. Irvine. Berlin and New York: Mouton de Gruyter.

Saris, A. Jamie. 1995. "Telling Stories: Life Histories, Illness Narratives, and Institutional Landscapes." *Culture, Medicine and Psychiatry* 19: 39–72.

Scheper-Hughes, Nancy. 2001. *Saint, Scholars, and Schizophrenics: Mental Illness in Rural Ireland,* 2nd edition. Berkeley: University of California Press.

Sechehaye, Marguerite. 1994 [1951]. *Autobiography of a Schizophrenic Girl: The True Story of 'Renee'.* New York: Meridian.

Shaw, K., A. McFarlane, and C. Bookless. 1997. "The Phenomenology of Traumatic Reactions to Psychotic Illness." *Journal of Nervous and Mental Disease* 185: 434–41.

Shweder, Richard. 1990. "Cultural Psychology: What Is It?" In J. W. Stigler, R. A. Shweder, and G. Herdt, eds., pp. 1–43, *Cultural Psychology: Essays on Comparative Human Development.* Cambridge and New York: Cambridge University Press.

Shweder, Richard and Edmund J. Bourne. 1984. "Does the Concept of the Person Vary Cross-Culturally?" In. R. A. Shweder and Richard A. LeVine, eds., pp. 158–99, *Culture Theory: Essays on Mind, Self, and Emotion.* New York and London: Cambridge University Press.

Shweder, Richard A. and Robert A. LeVine. 1984. *Culture Theory: Essays on Mind, Self, and Emotion.* New York and London: Cambridge University Press.

Stein, John and Alexandra Richardson. 1999. "Cognitive Disorders: A Question of Misattribution." *Current Biology* 9(10): R374–R6.

Strauss, John. 1994. "The Person with Schizophrenia as a Person II: Approaches to the Subjective and Complex." *British Journal of Psychiatry* 164 (suppl. 23): 103–7.

Sullivan, Harry Stack. 1927. "Affective Experience in Early Schizophrenia." *American Journal of Psychiatry* 6: 467–83.

———. 1937. "A Note on the Implications of Psychiatry, the Study of Interpersonal Relations, for Investigations in the Social Sciences." *American Journal of Sociology* 42: 848–61.

———. 1953. *Basic Conceptions of Modern Psychiatry.* New York: W.W. Norton & Co.

———. 1962. *Schizophrenia as a Human Process.* New York: W.W. Norton & Co.

Tarrier, Nicholas, Christine Vaughn, Malcolm H. Lader, and Julian P. Leff. 1979. "Bodily Reactions to People and Events in Schizophrenics." *Archives of General Psychiatry* 36(3): 311–15.

Turner, Edith. 1992. *Experiencing Ritual: A New Interpretation of African Healing.* Philadelphia: University of Pennsylvania Press.

Vaughn, Christine E. and Julian P. Leff. 1976. "The Influence of Family and Social Factors on the Course of Psychiatric Illness: A Comparison of Schizophrenic and Depressed Neurotic Patients." *British Journal of Psychiatry* 129: 125–37.

Vaughn, Christine, Karen Snyder, S. Jones, W. Freeman, and I. Falloon. 1984. "Family Factors in Schizophrenic Relapse: A California Replication of the British Research on Expressed Emotion." *Archives of General Psychiatry* 41: 1169–77.

Wahass, Saeed and Gerry Kent. 1997. "Coping with Auditory Hallucinations: A Cross-Cultural Comparison between Western (British) and Non-Western (Saudi Arabian) Patients." *Journal of Nervous and Mental Disease* 185(11): 664–8.

Warner, Richard. 1985. *Recovery from Schizophrenia: Psychiatry and Political Economy.* London and Boston: Routledge & Kegan Paul.

Waxler, Nancy. 1974. "Culture and Mental Illness: A Social Labeling Perspective." *Journal of Nervous and Mental Disorders* 159: 379–95.

Weiden, Peter and Leston Havens. 1994. "Psychotherapeutic Management Techniques in the Treatment of Outpatients with Schizophrenia." *Hospital & Community Psychiatry* 45(6): 549–55.

Weiden, Peter, Ralph Aquila, and Janet Standard. 1996. "Atypical Antipsychotic Drugs and Long-term Outcome of Schizophrenia." *Journal of Clinical Psychiatry* 57(suppl. 11): 53–60.

Weiden, Peter J., Patricia L. Scheifler, Ronald J. Diamond, and Ruth Ross. 1999. *Breakthroughs in Antipsychotic Medications: A Guide for Consumers, Families, and Clinicians.* New York: W.W. Norton & Co.

White, Geoffrey. 1982. "The Ethnographic Study of Cultural Knowledge of 'Mental Disorder.'" In A. Marsella and G. White, eds., pp. 167–92, *Cultural Conceptions of Mental Health and Therapy*. Dordrecht, Holland: D. Reidel Publishing Company.

World Health Organization. 1979. *Schizophrenia: An International Follow-up Study*. New York: John Wiley & Sons.

2   Interrogating the Meaning of "Culture" in the WHO International Studies of Schizophrenia

Kim Hopper

An Epidemiological Provocation

Field studies of mental disorders date from the 1920s; discussion of the difficulties inherent in such comparative work, from the late 1950s (Hammer and Leacock 1961). In 1967, the WHO initiated a set of studies investigating the manifestation, consequences, and course of schizophrenia and related disorders. Since then, nearly thirty research sites, spanning nineteen countries, have participated in one or more of them. The two main studies – the International Pilot Study of Schizophrenia (IPSS, beginning 1967) and the Determinants of Outcome of Severe Mental Disorder (DOSMeD, beginning 1978), with initial follow-up periods ranging from two to five (and, in several sites, ten) years – have consistently found persons clinically diagnosed with schizophrenia and related disorders in the industrialized West to have less favorable outcomes than counterparts in developing countries. Although the number of distinctive "cultures" was small,[1] the resiliency of this finding, extensively documented and assessed with increasingly sophisticated instruments, is noteworthy[2] – arguably the more so for emerging from such anthropologically suspect ground. (When within-group variation is so extensive and changes over time, contrast effects between groups are likely to be muted and the probability of Type II error – missing real difference when it is there – rises.)

But it was far from clear that the pronounced differences seen in short-term follow-up would hold up over time. Nor was this the only problem. The analytic adequacy (let alone empirical fidelity) of such labels as "developed" and "developing" were questioned (Hopper 1991; Edgerton and Cohen 1994).[3] When so many investigators take part, some hailing from distinctive psychiatric traditions,[4] and assessments take place over as much as a quarter-century, diagnostic ambiguities invariably intrude (Gureje 1996:128). Most relevant here, what accounts for the apparent "benefits" of underdevelopment remained mysterious, though speculation has ranged widely. Cultural signposts signifying expectations of

62

recovery, idioms of illness attribution that exempt the self, the therapeutic benefits of accommodating work, extensive kin-based stores of support, the anonymity of life in industrialized centers, were variously proposed (Cooper and Sartorius 1977; WHO 1979:371; Warner 1994).

The recently completed International Study of Schizophrenia (ISoS), the latest of the WHO-Collaborative Projects, promised to address at least the question of outcome over time. Whether it could plumb the developmental determinants of outcome – and, especially, their cultural configurations and coloring – was less assured. In early 1997, investigators completed data collection in follow-up interviews of both the original IPSS cohort (twenty-four years after the episode of inclusion) and the DOSMeD cohort (thirteen to fifteen years after initial episode), as well as two other groups of subjects – an incidence cohort from three centers of the Reduction and Assessment of Psychiatric Disability Study (RAPyD, beginning 1978), and a mixed set of subjects (two treated incidence cohorts, one prevalence) from three additional centers.

This chapter examines, as closely as the available data permit, the durability of that provocative finding of a distinct advantage in course and outcome for the developing countries, and poses two questions: Has it survived the thirteen years since last reported for (some of) these same subjects? If so, how sound (that is, not merely artifactual) is the result? To put it bluntly: Before we undertake more of the arduous work of reanalysis and further interpretation of this much-plundered epidemiological preserve, how good is the evidence that this finding is *not* something (to steal and tweak a phrase from Orwell) *only* an anthropologist could believe?

I focus here on course and outcome for the combined *incidence* cohort of ISoS – that is, for the 809 subjects followed since "first (treated) episode" of psychosis (Table 2.1), only some of whom appeared in earlier WHO analyses of IPSS and DOSMeD cohorts.[5] I first review the consistency of the finding of a "developed versus developing" differential in course and outcome in the three WHO studies. Drawing upon a recent analysis of these data (Hopper and Wanderling 2000), I examine a variety of course and outcome measures that illustrate differences in illness trajectory for the two groups, and analyze the likely impact of seven potential sources of bias. I conclude by limning an especially dense area of cultural analysis – marriage – for further study.

Briefly, then, this chapter addresses two questions: To what extent do the results of WHO-Collaborative Studies of schizophrenia support the case for *taking culture seriously* in assessing course and outcome in schizophrenia? And, assuming they do so, what *guidance do they offer to investigators seeking to take the measure of cultural influence and identify likely vehicles of its effects?* To anticipate somewhat: I hope to show that the

Table 2.1. *WHO ISoS – Treated incidence cohorts*

	Original N	Follow-up N*	Lost to follow-up	Deaths
"Developing" centers				
Chandigarh				
urban	155	80	61	14
rural	55	38	7	10
Hong Kong	100	70	19	11
Madras	100	77	14	9
Total	410	265	101	44
		(65%)	(25%)	(11%)
"Developed" centers				
Dublin	67	37	22	8
Groningen	83	63	11	9
Honolulu	71	26	41	4
Mannheim	70	56	7	7
Moscow	72	52	10	10
Nagasaki	115	57	51	7
Nottingham	99	86	4	9
Prague	118	79	28	11
Rochester	58	33	25	0
Sofia	60	55	3	2
Total	813	544	202	67
		(67%)	(25%)	(8%)

Note: Follow-up time ranged from fourteen to eighteen years.

answer to the first is very much so, while to the second, a more hedged, if hopeful, response is necessary.

Uses of Culture in the WHO-Collaborative Studies of Schizophrenia

To an anthropologist's eye, culture is conspicuous both for its salience and for its imprecision in the WHO research corpus. Not that architects of the studies were unmindful of either the difficulties in conceptualizing it or the problems of measuring it (see WHO 1973:25ff.; or 86–93 on translation problems); they simply had other priorities to attend to – that is to say, the task of mounting an international cross-cultural psychiatric research project and legitimizing its conduct to a primarily clinical audience.

This has not, however, impeded the occasional speculative effort at hypothesis development. In a 1977 article, Cooper and Sartorius argue that what are by now historical curiosities in the West – large extended families in relatively self-sufficient communities, flexible and accommodating work roles unchecked by educational or skill requirements, undifferentiated notions of mental illness that overlap with religious and magical beliefs – are still vital parts of third-world cultures and may help explain the favorable picture of schizophrenia seen there.

Such large-scale conjectures aside, for the most part when the term "culture" is referred to in the WHO studies, it usually seems to be serving as a synonym for specific place (as in the commonly employed phrase "sociocultural setting"). This, in turn, is typically treated as a black box of variables: the exotic stuff of beliefs, practices, and accountings enveloped by ruder exigencies of poverty, environmental degradation, resource scarcity, and badly stretched treatment facilities. Traces of recent anthropological rethinking of the question of culture are strikingly absent from most of the contemporary psychiatric epidemiology literature, as is apparent from a glance at recent reviews of the "environment" and schizophrenia. One such review reduces the role of "culture" in explaining the more favorable outcomes seen in "developing" countries to features of "the agrarian community" found in "peasant societies" (Freeman 1989:96). This isn't simply inelegant nomenclature; it's resonant, and misleading, archaism.

Some may put this down to the cultural naiveté of psychiatrically based researchers. But, apart from its casual attitude toward history and change, it may also attest to the unsettled state of our own deliberations on cultures and histories, parts and wholes, processes and taxonomies (Roseberry 1989). Culture, it seems clear, is more than an assemblage of "variables" – echoes of the late "shreds and patches" school notwithstanding – if something less than a seamless whole (Geertz 1983). How it should be *measured*, to no one's surprise, is still a vexing question (for example, Brumann 1999).

Not to put too fine a point on it, throughout the WHO literature – with the notable exception of the DOSMeD substudies examined as follows and some latter-day defensive commentaries – "culture" has been a mock-elegant way of referring to "there" as opposed to "here." With one exception (Nagasaki), "there" has meant the research centers located in Africa, Asia, and Latin America, while "here" has meant centers in Europe and the United States.[6] This division, in turn, has been formalized in the now routine used (and ritually criticized)[7] convention of "developing" versus "developed" centers. Although this may recall an earlier era in anthropology in which the tenets of unilinear evolution held sway, I think the usage here is more benign if no less exasperating when examined closely.

There's simply no gainsaying that such practices drive fastidious anthropologists mad. They, of course, do have a professional stake in seeing culture as an extraordinarily complex phenomenon, something requiring great skill and care to document properly. Indeed, the animus one detects in some anthropological critiques may be owing in part to what is (mis)perceived as the substitution of geographical place (a location) for cultural space (a toolkit of beliefs, practices, notions, and things held dear). Such a sin, were it to have been committed, would indeed grate upon anthropological sensibilities: It would suggest, however inadvertently or indirectly, that taking context into account may not be that difficult an undertaking after all.

But the picture is rather more complex when one examines how culture actually makes its appearance in the WHO studies. True, when it comes to describing – let alone testing – the evidence for cultural influence, the studies themselves tend to be uneven and disappointingly thin, as Edgerton and Cohen (1994:225), among others, complain. Take, for example, the material included in the WHO two-year follow-up report on the original IPSS cohort (which contains by far the most detailed descriptions of local study contexts). In this 400-plus page volume (WHO 1979), there is little in the way of documentary evidence for local setting. The profiles of Field Research Centers (FRCs) during the follow-up period are uneven, following no prescribed format or apparent method.

Consider the descriptions of Agra and Ibadan, two centers with highly favorable outcomes (over half the subjects experienced only the episode of inclusion, followed by full remission thereafter):

• *In Agra:* "Nearly all patients were found to be engaged in some form of work" (WHO 1979:104), usually of low-skilled or domestic order. "[F]amily acceptance of the sick person" is also notable, the authors assert, while at the same time complaining that "ignorance about the nature of mental illness" can deprive patients of needed treatment, adding for good measure (and as a critical observation) that "misconceptions and superstitious beliefs about mental illness" coupled with widespread belief in possession drive them to resort to "faith-healers."

• *In Ibadan:* The high mobility of the cohort is a problem. Because they are working (at jobs obtained through and supported by kin), or attending festivals far away, this results in extended "visits" out of the catchment area, making relocation difficult. (Even within the city proper, the absence of house numbers in some precincts [shantytowns?] makes tracing "a very irksome duty.") The costs and distance associated with formal psychiatric treatment mean that patients "often end up in a residential facility of a traditional healer." Here again, this sounds like a complaint – yet another of the "factors related to general underdevelopment" (poor hygiene, illiteracy, ignorance, malnutrition, and so on), which "may reinforce psychological symptoms" – *except* that the authors go on to note that those treated in university-affiliated hospitals do *worse* than those seen by traditional village-based healers. Similarly, work is easy to find in rural areas, but impossible to obtain in urban precincts. Relatives assume the burden of purchasing medications and supporting the patient, a situation that causes a good deal of guilt about being a burden and no little implicit pressure: "A relapse," they note ominously, "is not always taken kindly by the relatives" who have invested time and money in the patient's recovery (WHO 1979:107).

Aside from their color and specificity, these passages are convincingly (if puzzlingly) filled with internal tensions. The reports are impressionistic, variable in coverage, and not always pitched or inflected in the expected direction of effect or with the anticipated dynamic. But such mild muddle is as it should be, and reassures an anthropologist: Cultures are not seamless, hypercoherent wholes, but assemblages of relatively distinctive tools and strategies for meeting the essential tasks of life. That documented variation occurs within a research site is testament to the fidelity of its fieldworkers, even as it complicates the task of characterizing – at the ecological level of "center" – how local culture works. Such reassuring inconsistencies are not much help, however, as the IPSS authors clearly recognized, in ferreting out those contextual features that might shed light on differential course and outcome.

The later DOSMeD was designed to further inquiry into the "effect of culture on the course of schizophrenic disorders" (Jablensky, Sartorius, Ernberg, Anker, Korten, Cooper, Day, and Bertelsen 1992:3). Once again, subjects in "developing" centers did better than their counterparts in "developed" centers. And although early on the term "culture" tends to recede, in favor of the linguistically boring but noncommittal "geographic area," it reemerges tellingly in the final discussion of differential outcome between the two groups. The authors reject selection bias, the inclusion of anomalous diagnostic groups ("atypical transient psychotic illnesses"), and mode of onset as sufficient to explain the observed prognostic difference. The admittedly poor proxies for social practice showed little predictive value in log-linear analyses, even as they reinforced suspicions about the feasibility of measuring such variables. In the end, the authors argue that "a strong case can be made for a real pervasive influence of a powerful factor which can be referred to as 'culture'" (Jablensky et al. 1992:89). "*Unfortunately,*" they go on pointedly to note, neither IPSS nor DOSMeD was designed to "penetrate in sufficient depth below the surface on which the impact of this unknown factor was established" (Jablensky et al. 1992, emphasis added).[8]

For the most part, then, culture is everywhere in the WHO studies – hovering in the wings of project design and implementation, boldly (if briefly) assuming center stage in the text, and loitering in the margins of the reports, where it may sometimes be glimpsed. But *how* its presence is registered ranges from the frankly mysterious to the subtly substantial. Take, for example, the largely unremarked bias that creeps into a prevalence study of schizophrenia owing simply to local treatment resources. Irregularities in sampling in IPSS, Murphy (1982) has argued, resulted in the inclusion of more patients with longer histories of schizophrenia (even with the five-year limit on onset) in the developed centers.[9] But given huge differences in local resources for treatment and custodial care – easily accessible clinics and state-supported institutions chiefly[10] – the *converse* bias would seem to be all but inevitable in a study like this. That is, to the extent that ease of access affects the threshold at which families, significant others, or the police resort to psychiatric facilities, there should be profound differences in the mix of cases brought to clinical attention. Where thresholds of accessibility are high (owing to transportation difficulties, costs, suspicion of unfamiliar clinics, and so on) and local alternatives exist, "therapy-managing groups" (Janzen 1978) may decide it makes practical sense to triage informally all but the most recalcitrant cases (cf. Edgerton and Cohen 1994).[11] This not only biases *entry* into the study but logically – to the extent that difficult early courses predict continued difficulties later – should affect illness *course* as well. In this way, an artifact of the logistics of help seeking could later turn up as an epidemiological finding – an eventuality that makes the more favorable outcome in the developing centers the more remarkable.

But culture isn't always merely unappreciated stagecraft at the locale. Nor is it the case, in the understandably annoyed phrasing of two anthropological critics, that it is always and only "a synonym for unexplained variance" (Edgerton and Cohen 1994:228).

When Attention Was Paid: Explicit Attempts To Take Culture into Account

Three substudies of DOSMeD attempted to take culture seriously in specific domains of "risk" that had earlier been identified (for example, WHO 1979:371) as potentially productive lines of research: the role of expressed emotion among relatives of people diagnosed with schizophrenia; the role of stressful life events in precipitating psychoses; and the cultural shaping of the expression of psychoses. Despite difficulties in translation (for example, "over-involvement," "stressful" events, what counts as "warmth" in family interaction), measurement (for example, adjusting thresholds), and substantive limitations (no attention to work, little to specifically rural settings, and limited participation of research centers), some intriguing results turned up.

Take the example of expressed emotion (EE) in Chandigarh and Aarhus (Leff, Wig, Ghosh, Bedi, Menin, Kuipers, Korten, Ernberg, Day, Sartorius, and Jablensky 1987; Wig et al. 1987a; Wig et al. 1987b). (1) Researchers found some cross-cultural differences in the distribution and covariance of the elements of EE (even – and, again, reassuringly – within western cohorts of Danish and British relatives, *and* between rural and urban Indian families); (2) documented lower EE overall in the Indian relatives; and (3) concluded that the "differential effect of culture on the various components is puzzling and needs further exploration" (Wig et al. 1987b:164). They did suggest, however, that lower EE among Indian families might help explain the more favorable short-term outcome seen there.

These are promising leads, and hold real potential for spanning the macro-micro gap that an ecological analysis of culture otherwise leaves yawning. But the documentation of such variables is labor intensive in the extreme, requires regular updating and (probably) successive retraining, and can be very challenging analytically. Needless to say, such features hardly recommend them for longitudinal study. And, indeed, the impact of these substudies on ISoS was modest, in part because none of their primary architects was recruited as part of the international collaborative team that hammered out the later design. (The one anthropologist on the earlier team [Richard Day] had since defected and joined the ranks of the biostatisticians.)

ISoS – Promise and Limits

I turn now to the study with which I am most familiar, the latest in a thirty-year lineage of WHO-coordinated multinational investigations: the "International Study of Schizophrenia" (or ISoS). My strategy here, as before, is to try to take the measure of the studies as conducted, critically assess what might be legitimately concluded from them (given their deficiencies), and ask what feasible next steps might be planned. As a strategy ("weed it and reap"?), this doubtless will strike truly *critical* readers as breathtakingly generous. But again, my objective here is not to rehabilitate the WHO studies as unwittingly *anthropological* all along; rather it is to take stock of what, warts and all, they suggest might be anthropologically worth a closer look.

With respect to limits, the first and in some ways most critical thing to note is that, as a follow-up study, ISoS is heir to the faults and hostage to the blindspots of its germinal studies, besides being subject to unforeseen logistical difficulties.[12] To some extent, we might have hoped that retrospective reconstructions could assist in the project of tapping cultural dimensions missed the first time around. Aside from the methodological problems such a strategy presents,[13] however, there were other more practical considerations at stake.

Some limitations, for example, have as much to do with the microsociology of knowledge production on an international collaborative research project, as with inherited conceptual or methodological deficiencies. I had joined the project, late in the game, as its most junior member, sole anthropologist (in the data organizing and analysis group), and one of only three or four social scientists in the group of investigators overall. The Nathan Kline Institute team had developed a social inventory instrument to investigate (if only retrospectively) the roles of safe havens and receptive public spaces (Corin 1990), or accommodating work alternatives, of social support and reciprocity, and of more detailed illness accountings. For all the limitations imposed by a semistructured (if narratively enhanced) format, the verdict on its inclusion was driven not by data quality considerations but by the length of the interview, and the instrument was dropped. A fallback effort to collect information on social factors, family participation in treatment, stigma, and attitudes (the Family Interview Schedule) was the final instrument added, and the one least consistently used (with most missing data on it).[14]

In the end, a simplistic template tapping investigators' notions was resorted to (sometimes supported, sometimes surmised) of how things work locally (with respect to women and work, attitudes toward mental illness, sources of instability, notions of suffering – the sorts of things any "native" ought to be able to comment upon). There are, of course, obvious dangers in relying uncritically on self-appointed experts on custom and belief – that they are reliable informants in the first place, or that local cultures are relatively coherent and uniform on the dimensions queried.[15] Without solid ethnographic data about local moral and practical worlds, complemented by detailed observations over time of subjects' households and social rounds, one can't know whether these afflicted families fall within the range of acceptable variation by local cultural standards, or lie well outside of it along some crucial dimensions of behavior, history, or belief.

A note on diagnostic terminology is also in order. How was schizophrenia defined and operationalized in this study? Briefly, the diagnoses were assigned by local clinicians, most of whom had undergone a training regimen in the use of a common psychopathology assessment tool (the Present State Examination [PSE-9], supplemented in most cases by the Psychiatric and Personal History Schedule [PPHS]). The PSE was translated into indigenous languages as needed. (The diagnoses of the

DOSMeD centers were also reviewed by a WHO-convened group of experts.) Both before and during the study, investigators were required to demonstrate reliability (within centers and across centers) by rating videotaped clinical interviews of subjects. The diagnoses rendered can, I believe, legitimately claim to be local psychiatric "ethnographic reality" (as it appeared fifteen years ago).[16] In order to minimize the risk of classification artifact, in the analyses below I present findings by several different diagnostic conventions.

Still, to a skeptical, nonclinical audience (one made up, say, of professionally contrary anthropologists) what kind of validity can the term "schizophrenia" be said to have? Operationally, the answer (just outlined) is fairly clear. But conceptually, how "objective" can this term – promiscuously deployed in a striking variety of cultural settings, over a decade and a half – claim to be? In Megill's terms (1994), the WHO diagnostic claim is the rather limited one of "disciplinary objectivity": It "emphasizes not universal criteria of validity but particular, yet still authoritative, disciplinary criteria . . . not the eventual convergence of all inquirers of good will, but the proximate convergence of accredited inquirers [here, trained clinicians using the same diagnostic instruments] within a given field" (Megill 1994:5). For that cranky audience of anthropologists, of course, analytic acceptance of this assertion of "authoritative jurisdiction over its area of competence" requires a "bracketing" (Rhodes 1993) of the prior question of the constitutive power of the instruments and training themselves.[17] It brackets, that is, the "knowledge production" activities of the clinical diagnostic endeavor (Fabian 1994; Barrett 1996). In the analyses that follow, such knowledge production activities are an *a priori* "given," and potentially distinctive variations in such activities are ignored.

Three Findings

*The Developed Versus Developing Differential
in Course and Outcome Is Consistent*

As Table 2.2 illustrates, the finding of a consistent outcome differential favoring the "developing" centers is remarkably robust. It extends across all three WHO-Collaborative projects. It holds for brief and long-term follow-up periods, for various diagnostic groupings (ICD-9, converted ICD-10, and all psychoses), and for different country groupings (note the changes in the makeup of developing and developed groupings from DOSMeD to ISoS). It even appears to be relatively constant, as indicated by the odds ratios of recovery calculated in the right column.

Table 2.2. *WHO outcome studies – a synopsis (percentages "best" versus "worst"[1])*

	"Developed"[2]	"Developing"	Relative odds of recovery*
IPSS (1967–)			
2-yr.	35 v. 33	52 v. 19	1.5
5-yr.	23 v. 24	38 v. 14	1.7
DOSMeD (1976–)			
2-yr.			
all Ss	33 v. 17	49 v. 11	1.5
ICD-9 Sz[†]	32 v. 19	49 v. 13	1.5
ISoS 15-yr. F-U			
(incidence only) [% never psychotic in last two years versus continuously psychotic]			
ICD-10 Sz	37 v. 38	53 v. 27	1.5
ICD-9 Sz	40 v. 33	58 v. 23	1.5
all psychoses	45 v. 30	58 v. 22	1.3

* Percent recovered in developing centers versus percent recovered in developed.
† Sz = Schizophrenia.
1 Various measures of patterns of course and recovery were used in the earlier studies; for details, see Hopper 1991: Table 1, note a.
2 Assignment of centers to categories of developed versus developing as per individual studies.

The Differential Holds for a Variety of Course and Outcome Indicators in the ISoS

The late course differential shown in Table 2.2 for percentage of subjects with no psychotic episodes versus percentage with continuous illness in the most recent two years of follow up, also applies to a variety of other outcome indicators. As Table 2.3 shows, it holds for general clinical state (Bleuler scale [Bleuler 1978]), symptomatology (scores on the Global Assessment of Functioning-Symptoms scale), disability (scores on the Global Assessment of Functioning-Disability and Disability Assessment scales), and social functioning (at least for paid work or housework). Nor is it erased if a narrow or broad ("spectrum") classification of schizophrenia is used, or if the diagnostic net is expanded to take in all psychoses. The odds ratios consistently favor the developing centers, ranging from 1.57 to 3.51 for ICD-10 diagnosis of schizophrenia, and from 1.59 to 3.61 for the broad-spectrum diagnosis.

Potential Sources of Bias and Confounding Can't Explain the ISoS Findings

Such findings could be artifactual if it were the case that unobtrusive differences between the two groups obtained in a way worked to the

Table 2.3. *Outcome measures, odds ratios, developed versus developing**

Ns	Developed		Developing		Odds ratio** (confidence interval)
	319	**388**	183	**114**	

A. ICD-10 Schizophrenia

	Developed		Developing		Odds ratio** (confidence interval)
Bleuler scale recovered	44	**46**	55	**56**	1.57 (1.09–2.27) / **1.52 (1.00–2.32)**
GAF-S (>60)	43	**49**	70	**69**	3.15 (2.12–4.70) / **2.32 (1.48–3.65)**
GAF – D (>60)	41	**46**	65	**66**	2.64 (1.79–3.90) / **2.25 (1.45–3.51)**
Global DAS excellent/ good	24	**28**	53	**49**	3.51 (2.27–5.41) / **2.47 (1.57–3.89)**
Last 2-year course; never psychotic	37	**38**	53	**59**	1.97 (1.36–2.86) / **2.33 (1.52–3.57)**
Working most of last 2 years	46	**49**	73	**82**	3.13 (2.09–4.70) / **4.71 (2.78–8.00)**

Ns	Developed		Developing		Odds ratio** (confidence interval)
	410	**480**	230	**160**	

B. Broad spectrum (ICD-10 Sz. + schizoaffective + schizophrenia-like)

	Developed		Developing		Odds ratio** (confidence interval)
Bleuler scale recovered	49	**49**	60	**63**	1.59 (1.15–2.21) / **1.77 (1.23–2.56)**
GAF-S (>60)	48	**52**	73	**74**	3.05 (2.13–4.38) / **2.71 (1.81–4.05)**
GAF-D (>60)	44	**47**	69	**71**	2.74 (1.93–3.89) / **2.73 (1.84–4.04)**
Global DAS excellent/ good	28	**31**	57	**56**	3.48 (2.38–5.08) / **2.87 (1.94–4.26)**
Last 2-year course; never psychotic	40	**40**	58	**64**	2.07 (1.49–2.88) / **2.62 (1.80–3.79)**
Working most of last 2 years	49	**50**	77	**85**	3.61 (2.48–5.25) / **5.70 (3.52–9.23)**

* Note: Hong Kong classified as "developing" in shaded columns; otherwise in "developed."
** Odds of good outcome in developing centers versus comparable odds in developed centers.
Note: For diagnoses: Sz = schizophrenia; S/A = schizoaffective disorder; Sz-like = schizophrenia-like disorder. For instruments: DAS = Disability Assessment Schedule; GAF-S = Global Assessment of Functioning – Symptoms; GAF-D = Global Assessment of Functioning.

advantage of a finding of relative benefit in the developing group. We examined a number of candidates and concluded that their effects were either small or worked in favor of the developed group (Hopper and Wanderling 2000).

- *Attrition:* Loss to follow-up rates were comparable for the two groups, and differences in mortality were small. Still, if systematic differences entered in *who* was followed up, this could skew the comparative picture of outcome. Analyzed several ways, however, the chances of being retained in the study were better for those subjects in the *developed* world with favorable early illness course (perhaps the best predictor of later outcome) than for their counterparts in the developing centers.

- *Questionable groupings:* The developed versus developing grouping has been rightly criticized and the passage of fifteen years compounds its difficulties. Hong Kong's placement in the developing group seems especially open to question. Table 2.3, however, shows that moving Hong Kong to the developed world column, or excluding it altogether, only modestly affects the differences between the two groups.[18] (Without Hong Kong, the three other developing centers are all Indian, simplifying the cultural question but restricting its application.)

- *Diagnostic ambiguities:* In anthropological circles, "schizophrenia" is seen less as a label for a poorly understood and only partially mapped neurobiological entity, than as a part of a powerful discursive practice that not only authoritatively names, but in the process invariably shapes the objects of its attention.[19] In any event, there is a serviceable utility, so long as the ways and means employed in its provenance are understood, to be exploited in continuing to use it as a marker of difference and disorder. The more pointed challenge posed by "non-affective acute remitting psychosis" (or NARP; see Susser and Wanderling 1994) – a *mis*diagnosis of schizophrenia with a markedly better prognosis (built into the definition) that could explain the "developing" advantage – also failed to pan out. NARP was more common among cases labeled schizophrenia in the *developing* world, but the difference NARP made in improving chances of recovery was greater in the *developed* world. "Corrected for" its possible contaminating effects, recovery rates for non-NARP subjects in the developing centers are 52 percent, compared with 38 percent in the developed world (55 percent versus 42 percent for broad spectrum schizophrenia). The difference is only slightly affected, moreover, if we drop all "suspect" cases of single-episode psychoses (Stevens 1987) from the analyses: Recovery rates decline to 50 percent and 40 percent, but still favor the developing centers.

- *Inappropriate outcome measures:* Certain measures of outcome – like hospitalization: an "administrative outcome" reflecting policy and resources, not an elastic indicator of need met (Harrison, Mason, Glazebrook, Medley, Croudace, and Docherty 1994) – could conceivably skew findings. The outcome indicators used here avoid most such "institutional effects" (Obeyesekere 1985:149), but not all. Where welfare states provide disability payments, the spur of necessity for those recipients is blunted, and motivation to work may suffer. (Work rates do differ substantially between the two groups of centers.) Rather than an artifact of context, however, might not this be better read as a trace feature of culture? As noted earlier, others have argued that tightly strapped circumstances of livelihood and flexible means of addressing them may produce therapeutic benefits unavailable under circumstances that virtually enforce dependency (Warner 1994; Wikan 1996).[20]

• *Gender and age:* Women enjoy a small advantage over men in recovery rates, though the effect is larger in the developed world and gender representation is nearly identical in the two groups. Even when differential loss to follow-up by gender is accounted for, the rates hardly change. Similarly, within each grouping (developed, developing) long-term recovery rates slightly favor subjects over 40 at the time of follow-up, and the ranks of the developing centers are disproportionately younger.

In summary, none of these potential sources or bias and/or confounding suffices to explain the consistent finding that the long-term course differential favors subjects in the developing world. Further, with respect to the longitudinal findings, the latter term enjoys at least a modicum of cultural homogeneity, as all three "developing" centers (when the analysis was pared of Hong Kong) are Indian.

Time, too, plays a role. If the staging of the outcome differential is examined, the picture that emerges is one of an early and delayed effect combined. With respect to the early phase, the prospects that the disorder will be characterized by a remitting course (two-thirds of which will show long-term recovery at fifteen years) are much better in the developing world: nearly half of those subjects versus less than a third in the developed world. But a secondary, delayed advantage is also apparent among those subjects whose early illness course was unfavorable: 42 percent of those cases in the developing world go on to recover, as opposed to 33 percent in the developed centers. Put differently, roughly one-fifth of all ISoS subjects display those "slow-uphill returns to health" predicted earlier by Harding and her colleagues (1992).

Reclaiming Culture

As noted earlier, logistical difficulties and local turmoil prevented two of the original cast of "developing" countries from participating in the ISoS 15-year follow-up. Of the two added cohorts, Hong Kong and

Madras/Chennai, only the latter fits easily into the "developing" category. The upshot is that ISoS is a long-term study of course and outcome – not in "the developing world" but in that great, teeming, postcolonial, sectarian-riven complicated place that is India. More specifically, it concerns one rural area, one modernist-planned city and one ancient metropolis of that subcontinent – *versus* the rest, mostly west (mostly, for that matter, western Europe). In principle, this should simplify matters greatly. Comparative analysis is stymied, however, because we lack even the limited cultural data collected in the early years of DOSMeD by the substudies.[21] Too, we are still largely flummoxed when it comes to dealing with cultures as active – sometimes heaving, sometimes quiet – presences. To add that its members are invariably adept at fashioning fresh variations on convention, and that such variations are crucial sources of corrective tacks and accommodating tendencies in their cultures, merely confirms suspicions in some quarters that anthropology not only studies sorcery but practices it as well.

Despite the occasional flare of pessimism, the argument assembled here is not meant to suggest that cultural signposts – toolkits may be the better trope – are too diffuse, unstable, or variable to be described. Rather, following the examples of others (Rosaldo 1989; Bourdieu and Wacquant 1992; Kleinman 1992; Ortner 1999), its intent is to urge researchers to seek the vital signs of living culture locally, at the level of documented practice, rather than ecologically, at the level of reputed habitat. Take for example, the different roles that the "same" variable, *family*, may play in mediating course and outcome in ISoS (following up on Jenkins and Karno 1992):

• *In Chandigarh:* very favorable outcome results, which some have attributed (at least in part) to the lack of emotional overinvolvement and paucity of critical comments, coupled with steady support, in family environs (Leff et al. 1987);
• *In Sofia:* generally poor results – high symptoms, high levels of social disability coupled with low hospitalization, with family serving as surrogate for custodial care: for at least 39 percent of subjects at some time in the last two years; some attribute this to high level of family involvement in ongoing care, a pattern which reflects (unspecified) "cultural" factors (Ganev, Onchev, and Ivanov 1998);
• *In Moscow:* the principal investigator on the other hand, suspects that his follow-up cohort may be biased in the direction of better outcome because those who experienced early relapse and hospitalization left the city soon thereafter – having no long-term ties or prospects for support once they lost jobs – and returned to family homes in the provinces (Tsirkin, in press).

Were we able to document closely the practices that embody these variant expressions of family – accepting emotional atmosphere, residential respite, ancestral home – it would thicken the epidemiological story recounted here. But the leavening in that case would still be a matter of specificity with respect to how something works. Culture in the anthropological telling is larger still, a matter of constitutive reason as well as moral frame. If we consider how psychosis affects *marriage*, we can mount a more persuasive case for dealing with culture as both constitutive reason and moral frame for sorting out those daily reckonings that make for viable compounds of inherited ideal and workable real – forgivable failures that nonetheless ratify a certain perfection (Geertz 1983:181).

The long-term marital prospects of subjects in the developing centers of ISoS offer a striking contrast to the conventional wisdom on the impact of psychotic disorder on marriage (for example, Saugstad 1989) and, indeed, to the situation of their developed center counterparts as well. The odds of marriage for members of the ISoS Indian cohort at follow-up were 3:1 (73 percent; 71 percent male, 74 percent female); for the developed centers, they were 3:5 (38 percent; 28 percent male, 48 percent female) – making for an odds ratio of 5. More telling still, this marriage differential holds when unfavorable early illness course is taken into account. The odds of marriage for an Indian woman with a poor two-year course decline somewhat, but are still 2:1; for her developed world counterpart, they are 2:3. For men, the comparable figures are 3:2 versus 1:4.[22]

Anthropologists have come to appreciate both the stubborn particularities of the local and its sometimes surprising degree of interconnectedness with nonlocal elsewhere. Sustained documentary work, trademark of classical ethnography, commonly reveals beliefs and practices to be highly variable, often internally inconsistent, situation-dependent, and split by class, gender, ethnic, religious, and other structural divisions (Ortner 1995). At the same time, salience is a relative matter in comparative work, and the durable, duty-based social ethic of traditional Hindu India – the *dharma*-governed world its members live and thrive in – has long drawn anthropological curiosity and commentary (for example, Srinivas 1966; Singer 1972; Dumont 1980; Shweder 1991). Indigenous psychiatrists in Madras have recently remarked upon the high degree of marital success in persons diagnosed with schizophrenia, attributing it to the importance of *dharma*, children, and the continuity of lineage (including, even, women whose household management skills are impaired) (Thara and Srinivasan 1997, 2000). Throughout India, marital rates of 90–95 percent among middle-aged adults are the norm. The evidence here suggests that they apply as well, if perhaps not quite so forcefully, to persons with adult histories of psychotic break.

Again the old story, no less remarkable for being so often and so variously told: The institution adapts and endures, accommodating even those whose nuptial capital would seem to be seriously devalued, given the persistent stigma attached to mental illness in India with respect to marriage especially (Thara and Srinivasan 2000; Weiss, Jadhav, Raguram, Vounatsou, and Littlewood 2001). The puzzle is how this remarkable elasticity in both the pragmatic and moral carrying capacity of the institution is actually achieved. The marital inclusion/extension to disabled members is a gesture of both support and cultural consonance. Not so incidentally, that practice seems to be associated with decidedly favorable outcomes, especially when measures of "social recovery" are taken into account. As with diagnosis – which anthropological inquiry treats as a powerful discursive practice that not only authoritatively names but materially shapes the objects of its attention (Barrett 1996)[23] – so with affliction: We need to examine, at key transition points and over time, the social construction of the person with schizophrenia.

Our ethnographic ignorance is all too plain: How, precisely, with respect to this most central of sociocentric institutions, does "a great tradition modernize" conventional practice? Jablensky and Cole (1997) have recently argued that the DOSMeD baseline data offer convincing evidence for the protective effect of marriage in delaying the onset of psychosis. (Because early unions are more common for women, this explains the gender difference in age of onset.) But if marriage is to endure, it is the adaptive capacity of the established relationship, the kinship capital and practical/emotional support invested by the families, and the commitment of the afflicted spouse to an ordained duty that will determine its resiliency. And that resiliency, in turn, may bear upon prospects of recovery. If the first issue is endurance, the second and equally pressing one – more so for men because it affects proportionately more first-break schizophrenics – is hope. Most marriages in India are still, after all, arranged, for the simple reason that (as one of Shweder's informants put it) with "something that affects so many relatives and friends, [h]ow can you leave it up to one person, blinded by lust or passion, to make the decision?" (1991:163). How do prospective marital negotiations – already a complex, strategic undertaking involving multiple players that must weigh fine-grained caste, income, education, region, religion, birthchart compatibility, personal appearance, and price (dowry) – factor in this new concern? How are goodness of fit requirements, or readings of the "auspiciousness" (Harlan and Cartwright 1995) of the match, relaxed or reworked? Are particular efforts or offers made to counter or neutralize the psychiatric cargo? Phillips (1993) has reported that Chinese families in Beijing make calculated offers of matrimony on behalf of schizophrenic sons or daughters to prospective mates (military personnel, rural dwellers) for whom established urban residence would represent a huge advance in station and standing. The parents "make the selection . . . and undertake the negotiations," contravening trends in declining parental authority and freer choice in marriages (294).

A more recent and remarkable instance of family-mediated elective affinities is recounted in *Disability India Journal,* in which a Bangalore mother writes of her good fortune in locating a match for her daughter, newly stabilized on clozapine. Through the agency of a local family self-help group (AMEND), she found:

> another affected family, who were caregivers of their son [and] keen on getting a girl to marry him. When they saw my daughter and her paintings, they proposed an alliance with their son in that very first meeting. We, with our daughter's consent, arranged the marriage. The pace at which things progressed seems like a dream but within three months, my daughter was married to their son. (Anonymous 2001)

How such "cultural lessons" could be *applied* elsewhere is anything but clear. Cultural practice is not an intervention whose fidelity characteristics can be inventoried, carefully described, and then converted into training manuals for dissemination. One can't very well, as the title of a recent article appeared to do (Salokangas, Honkonen, Stengard, and Koivisto 2001), simply *prescribe* marriage as adjunctive therapy. In any event, to extract and apply elsewhere would amount to counsel not simply to go and *do* likewise, but to yearn, fear, desire, and aspire in ways, and with like-minded others, that make this doing – this social practice – come naturally. Or, a more modest proposal, it might suggest reexamining the circumstances under which persons with psychiatric histories are encouraged to seek life partners (Shanks and Arkins 1985).

More ethnography is needed, if only to elucidate those aspects of everyday practice that remain obscure. And if the times are hardly propitious for pitching large-scale, special-purpose anthropological ventures, an alternative suggestion seems both warranted and prudent: that community studies of various stripes routinely take stock of local theories of misfortune and the everyday means – especially ones that go-without-saying – for managing it.

An anthropology of suffering has much to learn from epidemiology, not the least of which is the litany of pressing issues its rates and measures are ill equipped to tackle. Improvisation upon received ways of thinking and doing – what Scott (1998) calls practical knowledge or *metis* – may also be a vital aspect of the work of recovery as practiced by troubled selves and supported by well-placed others. Ethnographic tradecraft would seem well poised to ask new questions and follow fresh lines of inquiry.

NOTES

1 The "developing" world was represented by samples from Ibadan (Nigeria), Cali (Colombia), and Agra (India) in IPSS; by Agra, Chandigarh (India), Cali, and Ibadan in DOSMeD, and by Agra, Cali, Chandigarh, Madras/Chennai (India), Beijing (China), and Hong Kong in ISoS. If one combines the three studies, the category takes in a single Latin American and African example, two from Asia, and three from the Indian subcontinent.

2 Excepting a few anomalies: Early on, for example, it was apparent that short-term pattern of course for IPSS subjects in Cali "approximated centres in developed countries" (WHO 1979:369n). Conversely, in a recent recursive partitioning analysis of short-term outcome in DOSMeD (Craig, Siegel, Hopper, Lin, and Sartorius 1997), Prague and Nottingham tended to align with the developing centers.

3 A point implicitly illustrated by the anomalous failure (cited in footnote 2) of a few centers to group with their assigned class.

4 See the intriguing comment by Wiersma, Nienhuis, Slooff, and Giel (1998) in discussing the usually small proportion of Groningen subjects initially assigned the diagnosis of schizophrenia: This anomaly, they suggest, reflects the "somewhat arbitrary" assignment of cases to either ICD-9 schizophrenia or reactive psychosis, as well as "a certain reluctance to make the diagnosis of schizophrenia in the late 1970s" (Wiersma et al. 1998:82). When the initial baseline diagnoses were later reclassified, using only information available at the time of study entry, a much higher percentage of subjects was diagnosed as schizophrenic.

5 Focusing on the treated incidence cohorts only minimizes differences in length of illness and treatment received prior to study, both of which can affect course.

6 An example from the first of three papers on the EE substudy of DOSMeD: "Danish culture is similar to that in England, both being industrialized western countries with a well-developed welfare system, whereas India provides a marked contrast" (Wig, Menon, Bedi, Ghosh, Kuipers, Leff, Korten, Day, Sartorius, Ernberg, and Jablensky 1987a:157). The next installment in this series, however, finds a difference in mean criticism scores between the British and Danish samples, and wonders whether this "may indicate a genuine cultural difference" (Wig et al. 1987b:163).

7 For good reasons: Hughes and Hunter 1970; Waxler 1974:393; Hahn 1978; Eaton 1985; Edgerton and Cooper 1994.

8 With a nod to the EE studies, they conclude that no one variable will likely suffice to account for culture's impact. Deja vu: Thirteen years earlier, the authors of the IPSS follow-up study had concluded similarly: "At this point we can only speculate that 'culture' in a global sense has an effect on the course of schizophrenia" (WHO 1979:393). They repeat the qualification (*pace* Edgerton and Cohen) in a later response to criticism (Jablensky et al. 1992).

9 In fact, what Murphy's analysis shows is that acute onset is more common among the developing centers; his second indicator – prior psychiatric
   contact – is, I would argue, better read (as I go on to try to do in the text) as an
   indicator of the availability and accessibility of local treatment resources. Had
   he used other data from the original IPSS table he raided – say, percentages
   of present episode less than six months in duration – the pattern he claims to
   detect is much more ambiguous. Recall too, that continuous illness of over
   three years standing was an exclusion criterion – and for this reason, a "dis-
   proportionate number of patients in Agra, Ibadan, and Taipei" were excluded
   (WHO 1973:148). In truth, the study had no solid indicator of severity of
   disorder at time of entry.

10 At the time of the IPSS Agra, for example, had one psychiatric facility of 718
   beds for a catchment area of 17 million people (WHO 1973:54f).

11 Such a "culturally determined sampling artifact" may explain the higher percentage of DOSMeD subjects in the developing world with a "history of as-
   sault," and the fact that their pathway to help more often involves the police,
   as acknowledged in a recent analysis (see Volavka, Laska, Baker, Meisner,
   Czobar, and Krivelevich 1997:13). Specifically, those authors suggest that
   "...it may be that less dramatic indicators of an individual's distress are responded to, by lay people and professionals alike, earlier and/or more effectively in developed countries."

12 Lack of funding (in Cali) and civil unrest (in Ibandan) prevented two of the
   "developing" nations from participating in the long-term follow-up study,
   greatly reducing the already slim spread of "cultures" represented.

13 To cite only a few: the continued presence, willingness to participate, and
   goodness of recall of relevant informants; the irritating tendency that settings have of changing over time (for five centers, their national boundaries were redrawn or central governments reconstituted since the study
   began); the use of measures woefully unequal to the task of capturing a dynamic situation; danger of confounding mediating variables with effects; and
   so on.

14 An attempt to fund a parallel project, that would have made use of indigenous interviewers querying a subset of subjects using a semistructured format,
   never got off the ground. The proposal to NIMH failed, owing both to misgiv-
   ings about the feasibility of the major project and methodological skepticism
   about the proposed study – "How does Hopper plan to handle the problem
   of phenocopies [sic] of schizophrenia?" asked one reviewer.

15 The limited data we were able to collect on experienced stigma from family
   members, for example, suggests a great deal of variation across households in
   the same locale.

16 The official WHO analyses (Hopper, Harrison, Janca, and Sartorius, forthcoming) use the nomenclature of the most recent ICD-10 standard, obtained
   by using an algorithmic conversion from the original ICD-9 diagnoses (WHO
   1994). See also Craig, Wanderling, and Janca (forthcoming), for a discussion
   of diagnostic stability over time in ISoS.

17 For an illuminating study of how that process works on a single psychiatric
   unit, see Barrett (1996).

18 Generally, the addition of Hong Kong tends to boost the group's ratings with respect to symptomatology and worsen those relating to functioning.

19 Whether this radically distinguishes it from other "disease entities" in the psychiatric (or biomedical) canon is, some observers argue, a less sophistic objection that might have been allowed a few years ago (Sedgwick 1976; Baruch and Treacher 1978; Good 1994).

20 In the treated incidence group, the percentage of ICD-10 schizophrenia subjects working for most of the past two years in the developing centers was 73 percent versus 46 percent for the developed centers; for broad spectrum schizophrenia, the figures were 77 percent versus 49 percent, respectively. Intriguingly, when looking only at subjects who were rated as having substantial symptoms and/or significant disability, the developed centers actually reported slightly more (ICD-10 schizophrenia) subjects working (21.3 percent versus 15.4 percent), or doing housework (39.5 percent versus 34.6 percent) (see Hopper et al. forthcoming).

21 Although we have baseline EE data on the relatives of seventy-eight subjects in Chandigarh, we have no data more recent and none at all for any other participating research center (Aarhus, too, was unable to participate in the follow up).

22 Analysis currently underway confirms that the differences hold whether one examines the impact of psychotic disorder on established marriages (disruption) or prospective ones (prevention). See Hopper, Wanderling, and Narayanan (in preparation).

23 Whether this radically distinguishes it from other "disease entities" in the psychiatric (or biomedical) canon is, some observers argue, a less sophistic objection that might have been allowed a few years ago (Sedgwick 1976; Baruch and Treacher 1978; Good 1994).

REFERENCES

Anonymous. 2001. "A Painful Experience of a Helpless Mother." *Disability India Journal.* http://www.webcottage.net/dij/march2001/article6.cfm.

Barrett, Robert. 1996. *The Psychiatric Team and the Social Definition of Schizophrenia.* New York: Cambridge University Press.

Baruch, Geoff and Andrew Treacher. 1978. *Psychiatry Observed.* Boston: Routledge and Kegan Paul.

Bleuler, Manfred. 1978. *The Schizophrenic Disorders. Patient Long-Term and Family Studies.* New Haven, CT: Yale University Press.

Bourdieu, Pierre and Loïc J. D. Wacquant. 1992. *An Invitation to Reflexive Sociology.* Chicago: University of Chicago Press.

Brumann, Christoph. 1999. "Writing for Culture: Why a Successful Concept Should not be Discarded." *Current Anthropology* (suppl.) 40: S1–S28.

Cooper, John and Norman Sartorius. 1977. "Cultural and Temporal Variations in Schizophrenia: A Speculation on the Importance of Industrialization." *British Journal of Psychiatry* 130: 50–5.

Corin, Ellen E. 1990. "Facts and Meaning in Psychiatry: An Anthropological Approach to the Life-World of Schizophrenics." *Culture, Medicine and Psychiatry* 14: 153–88.

Craig, Thomas, Carole Siegel, Kim Hopper, Shang Lin, and Norman Sartorius. 1997. "Outcome in Schizophrenia and Related Disorders Compared between Developed and Developing Countries: A Recursive Partitioning Re-analysis of the WHO DOSMD Data." *British Journal of Psychiatry* 170: 229–33.

Craig, Thomas J., J. Wanderling, and A. Janca. In press. "Long-term Diagnostic Stability in International Cohorts of Persons with Schizophrenia and Related Psychoses." In K. Hopper, G. Harrison, A. Janca, and N. Sartorius, eds., *Recovery from Schizophrenia: An International Perspective*. Westport, CT: Psychosocial Press.

Dumont, Louis. 1980. *Homo Hierarchicus: The Caste System and its Implications*. Chicago: University of Chicago Press.

Eaton, William. 1985. "Epidemiology of Schizophrenia." *Epidemiologic Reviews* 7: 105–26.

Edgerton, Robert B. and Alex Cohen. 1994. "Culture and Schizophrenia: The DOSMD Challenge." *British Journal of Psychiatry* 164: 222–31.

Fabian, Johannes. 1994. "Ethnographic Objectivity Revisited: From Rigor to Vigor." In A. Megill, ed., pp. 81–108. *Rethinking Objectivity*. Durham, NC: Duke University Press.

Freeman, Hugh. 1989. "Relationship of Schizophrenia to the Environment." *British Journal of Psychiatry* (suppl. 5) 155: 90–9.

Ganev, Kostadin, G. Onchev, and P. Ivanov. 1998. "A 16-year Follow-up Study of Schizophrenia and Related Disorders in Sofia, Bulgaria." *Acta Psychiatrica Scandinavica* 98: 200–7.

Geertz, Clifford. 1983. *Local Knowledge*. New York: Basic Books.

Good, Byron J. 1994. *Medicine, Rationality, and Experience*. New York: Cambridge University Press.

Gureje, Oye. 1996. "Schizophrenia." In D. Tantam, L. Appleby, and A. Duncan, eds., pp. 111–31. *Psychiatry in the Developing World*. London: Gaskell.

Hahn, Robert A. 1978. Abstract of N. Waxler, "Is Mental Illness Cured in Traditional Societies?" and "Culture and Mental Illness." *Transcultural Psychiatric Research* 15: 157–63.

Hammer, Muriel and Eleanor Leacock. 1961. "Source Material on the Epidemiology of Mental Illness." In J. Zubin, ed., pp. 418–86. *Field Studies in the Mental Disorders*. New York: Grune & Stratton.

Harding, Courtenay M., Joseph Zubin, and John S. Strauss. 1992. "Chronicity in Schizophrenia: Revisited." *British Journal of Psychiatry* (suppl. 18) 161: 27–37.

Harlan, Lindsey and Paul B. Courtright. 1995. "Introduction: On Hindu Marriage and its Margins." In L. Harlan and D. B. Courtright, eds., pp. 3–18. *From the Margins of Hindu Marriage*. New York: Oxford University Press.

Harrison Glynn, Peter Mason, Cristine Glazebrook, Ian Medley, Tim Croudace, and Sarah Docherty. 1994. "Residence of Incident Cohort of Psychotic Patients after 13 Years of Follow up." *British Medical Journal* 308: 813–16.

Hopper, Kim. 1991. "Some Old Questions for the New Cross-cultural Psychiatry." *Medical Anthropology Quarterly* (new series) 5: 299–330.

Hopper, Kim, G. Harrison, A. Janca, and Norman Sartorius, eds. In press. *Recovery from Schizophrenia: An International Perspective. A Report from the*

WHO-Collaborative Project, The International Study of Schizophrenia. Westport, CT: Psychosocial Press.

Hopper, Kim and J. Wanderling. 2000. "Revisiting the Developed vs. Developing Country Distinction in Course and Outcome in Schizophrenia: Results from ISoS, the WHO-Collaborative Follow-up Project." *Schizophrenia Bulletin* 26: 835–46.

Hughes, Charles C. and John M. Hunter. 1970. "Disease and Development in Africa." *Social Science and Medicine* 3: 443–93.

Jablensky, Assen and Steven W. Cole. 1997. "Is the Earlier Age at Onset of Schizophrenia in Males a Confounded Finding?" *British Journal of Psychiatry* 178: 234–40.

Jablensky, Assen, Norman Sartorius, G. Ernberg, M. Anker, Ailsa Korten, J. E. Cooper, Robert Day, and Aksel Bertelsen. 1992. "Schizophrenia: Manifestations, Incidence and Course in Different Cultures. A World Health Organization Ten-Country Study." *Psychological Medicine* (monograph supplement) 20: 1–97.

Janzen, John M. 1978. *The Quest for Therapy in Lower Zaire.* Berkeley: University of California Press.

Jenkins, Janis Hunter and Marvin Karno. 1992. "The Meaning of 'Expressed Emotion': Theoretical Issues Raised by Cross-cultural Research." *American Journal of Psychiatry* 149: 9–21.

Kleinman, Arthur. 1992. "Pain and Resistance." In M. J. DelVecchio Good, P. E. Brodwin, B. J. Good, and A. Kleinman, eds., pp. 169–97. *Pain as Human Experience.* Berkeley: University of California Press.

Leff, J., N. N. Wig, A. Ghosh, H. Bedi, D. K. Menin, L. Kuipers, Ailsa Korten, G. Ernberg, Robert Day, Norman Sartorius, and Assen Jablensky. 1987. "Influence of Relatives' Expressed Emotion on the Course of Schizophrenia in Chandigarh." *British Journal of Psychiatry* 151: 166–73.

Megill, Allan. 1994. "Introduction: Four Senses of Objectivity." In A. Megill, ed., pp. 1–20. *Rethinking Objectivity.* Durham, NC: Duke University Press.

Murphy, Henry B. M. 1982. "[Review of] Schizophrenia: An International Follow-up Study." *Transcultural Psychiatric Research Review* 17: 158–61.

Obeyesekere, Gananath. 1985. "Depression, Buddhism, and the Work of Culture in Sri Lanka." In A. Kleinman and B. Good, eds., pp. 134–52. *Culture and Depression.* Berkeley: University of California Press.

Ortner, Sherry B. 1995. "Resistance and the Problem of Ethnographic Refusal." *Comparative Studies in Society and History* 77: 173–93.

Ortner, Sherry B., ed. 1999. *The Fate of "Culture" – Geertz and Beyond.* Berkeley: University of California Press.

Phillips, Michael R. 1993. "Strategies Used by Chinese Families Coping with Schizophrenia." In D. Davis and S. Harrell, eds., pp. 277–306. *Chinese Families in the Post-Mao Era.* Berkeley: University of California Press.

Rhodes, Lorna A. 1993. "The Shape of Action: Practice in Public Psychiatry." In S. Lindenbaum and M. Lock, eds., pp. 129–44. *Knowledge, Power & Practice.* Berkeley: University of California Press.

Rosaldo, Renato. 1989. *Culture and Truth.* Boston: Beacon Press.

Roseberry, William. 1989. *Anthropologies and Histories.* New York: Routledge.

Salokangas, R. K. R., T. Honkonen, E. Stengard, and A. M. Koivisto. 2001. "To Be or Not To Be Married: That is the Question of Quality of Life in Men with Schizophrenia." *Social Psychiatry and Psychiatric Epidemiology* 36: 381–90.

Saugstad, Letten F. 1989. "Social Class, Marriage, and Fertility in Schizophrenia." *Schizophrenia Bulletin* 15: 9–42.

Scott, James C. 1998. *Seeing Like a State*. New Haven, CT: Yale University Press.

Sedgwick, Peter. 1976. *Psychopolitics*. New York: Harper & Row.

Shanks, John and Paul Atkins. 1985. "Psychiatric Patients Who Marry Each Other." *Psychological Medicine* 15: 377–82.

Shweder, Richard. 1991. *Thinking Through Cultures*. Cambridge, MA: Harvard University Press.

Singer, Milton. 1972. *When A Great Tradition Modernizes*. New York: Praeger.

Srinivas, Mysore N. 1966. *Social Change in Modern India*. Oxford: Clarendon.

Srinivasan, T. N. and R. Thara. 1999. "The Long-term Home-making Functioning of Women with Schizophrenia." *Schizophrenia Research* 35: 97–8.

Stevens, Janice. 1987. "Brief Psychoses: Do They Contribute to the Good Prognosis and Equal Prevalence of Schizophrenia in Developing Countries?" *British Journal of Psychiatry* 151: 393–6.

Susser, Ezra and Joseph Wanderling. 1994. "Epidemiology of Nonaffective Remitting Psychosis vs. Schizophrenia, Sex and Sociocultural Setting." *Archives of General Psychiatry* 51: 294–301.

Thara, R. and T. N. Srinivasan. 1997. "Outcome of Marriage in Schizophrenia." *Social Psychiatry and Psychiatric Epidemiology* 32: 416–20.

_____. 2000. "How Stigmatizing is Schizophrenia in India?" *International Journal of Social Psychiatry* 46: 135–41.

Tsirkin, S. In press. "Moscow." In K. Hopper, G. Harrison, A. Janca, and N. Sartorius, eds. *Prospects for Recovery from Schizophrenia – An International Investigation: Report from the WHO-Collaborative Project, The International Study of Schizophrenia*. Westport, CT: Psychosocial Press.

Volavka, Jan, Eugene Laska, Sherryl Baker, Morris Meisner, Pal Czobar, and Ilya Krivelevich. 1997. "History of Violent Behaviour and Schizophrenia in Different Cultures." *British Journal of Psychiatry* 171: 9–14.

Warner, Richard. 1994 [1985]. *Recovery from Schizophrenia*. New York: Routledge and Kegan Paul.

Waxler, Nancy. 1974. "Culture and Mental Illness: A Social Labeling Perspective." *Journal of Nervous and Mental Disease* 159: 379–95.

Weiss, Mitchell G., Sushrut Jadhav, R. Raguram, Penelope Vounatsou, and Roland Littlewood. 2001. "Psychiatric Stigma Across Cultures: Local Validation in Bangalore and London." *Anthropology and Medicine* 8: 71–87.

Wiersma, Durk, Fokko J. Nienhuis, Cees J. Sloof, and Robert Giel. 1998. "Natural Course of Schizophrenic Disorders: A 15-year Followup of a Dutch Incidence Cohort." *Schizophrenia Bulletin* 24: 75–85.

Wiersma, Durk, Fokko J. Nienhuis, Cees J. Slooff, Robert Giel, and A. de Jong. In press. "Moscow." In K. Hopper, G. Harrison, A. Janca, and N. Sartorius, eds., *Recovery from Schizophrenia: An International Perspective. A: Report from the WHO-Collaborative Project, The International Study of Schizophrenia*. Westport, CT: Psychosocial Press.

Wig N. N., D. K. Menon, H. Bedi, A. Ghosh, L. Kuipers, J. Leff, Ailsa Korten, Robert Day, Norman Sartorius, G. Ernberg, and Assen Jablensky. 1987a. "Expressed Emotion and Schizophrenia in North India. Cross-cultural Transfer of Ratings of Relatives' Expressed Emotion." *British Journal of Psychiatry* 151: 156–60.

Wig N. N., D. K. Menon, H. Bedi, J. Leff, L. Kuipers, A. Ghosh, Robert Day, A. Korten, G. Ernberg, Norman Sartorius, and Assen Jablensky. 1987b. "Expressed Emotion and Schizophrenia in North India. 2. Distribution of Expressed Emotion Components Among Relatives of Schizophrenia Patients in Aarhus and Chandigarh." *British Journal of Psychiatry* 151: 160–5.

Wikan, Unni. 1996. "The Nun's Story: Reflections on an Age-old, Postmodern Dilemma." *American Anthropologist* 98(2): 279–89.

Wolf, Eric. 1990. "Facing Power – Old Insights, New Questions." *American Anthropologist* 92: 586–96.

World Health Organization. 1973. *The International Pilot Study of Schizophrenia.* New York: John Wiley & Sons.

———. 1979. *Schizophrenia: An International Follow-up Study.* New York: John Wiley & Sons.

———. 1994. *The ICD-10 Classification of Mental and Behavioral Disorders: Conversion Tables between ICD-8, ICD-9 and ICD-10, Revision 1* (WHO/MNH/92.16.Rev.1). Geneva: World Health Organization.

3   Kurt Schneider in Borneo: Do First Rank Symptoms Apply to the Iban?

Robert John Barrett

Introduction

This chapter reports on an ethnographic and clinical inquiry into the experience of psychotic illness among the Iban, an indigenous people of Sarawak, Malaysia. Its starting point is a problem of translation, for in the course of this study, considerable difficulties arose in translating the Present State Examination (PSE), a standardized psychiatric diagnostic interview, from English into the Iban language. I critically examine these difficulties in order to raise more fundamental questions concerning the way schizophrenia is experienced, defined, and studied cross-culturally. Some of these questions are concerned with the nexus between language and social relationships and with cultural variations in the way people talk about their subjective experiences. Others are concerned with variations in the way particular subjective experiences – notably perceptions and thoughts – are themselves signified and interpreted within different cultural settings. These issues have a bearing on the so-called First Rank Symptoms (FRS), symptoms that have long been regarded as important to the diagnosis of schizophrenia. They carry implications, therefore, for the way schizophrenia itself is defined and conceptualized. I will argue that future cultural and biological research might fruitfully focus on patients who suffer from long-term auditory hallucinations, irrespective of diagnosis, rather than on patients who fall within the category of schizophrenia as it is currently defined. In sum, this chapter is a record of an encounter between a psychiatry that has its roots in European phenomenological psychopathology and Iban ways of knowing and experiencing psychotic illness.

First-Rank Symptoms in Cross-Cultural Context

Schneider's (1959) First Rank Symptoms (FRS) emerged from the tradition of German academic psychopathology, a cultural and intellectual tradition within Europe that was central to the evolving definition of

Table 3.1. *First rank symptoms**

Audible thoughts: The patient experiences auditory hallucinations with voices speaking his thoughts aloud.

Voices arguing: There are two or more hallucinatory voices in disagreement or in discussion.

Voices commenting on one's action: The content of the auditory hallucinations is a description of the patient's activities as they occur.

Thought insertion or thoughts ascribed to others: The patient experiences thoughts that do not have the quality of being his own.

Thought withdrawal: The patient describes his thoughts being taken from his mind. As his thoughts cease, he simultaneously experiences them being withdrawn by some external force.

Diffusion or broadcasting of thoughts: The patient, during the process of thinking, has the experience that his thoughts are not contained within his own mind. The thoughts escape from the confines of the self into the external world, where they may be experienced by all around.

Made impulses (drives): A powerful impulse overcomes the patient to which he almost invariably gives way. The impulse to carry out this action is not felt to be his own, but the actual performance of the act is.

Made volitional acts: The patient experiences his actions as being completely under the control of an external influence.

Influences playing on the body; somatic passivity: The patient is a passive and invariably a reluctant recipient of bodily sensations imposed upon him by some external agency.

Delusional perception: Schneider described the delusional perception as a two-stage phenomenon. The delusion arises from a perception, which to the patient, possesses all the properties of a normal perception and which he acknowledges would be regarded as such by anyone else. This perception however has a private meaning for him, and the second stage, which is the development of the delusion, follows almost immediately. The crystallization of an elaborate delusional system following upon the percept is often very sudden.

---

* After Mellor 1970.

dementia praecox in the nineteenth century, and of schizophrenia in the twentieth century. A well-known English translation of the FRS (see Table 3.1) has been provided by Mellor (1970). The progressive acceptance of FRS within clinical and research psychiatry has been documented by Andreasen and Carpenter (1993:201). Although no longer regarded as pathognomonic of schizophrenia (Carpenter and Strauss 1974), FRS nonetheless appear as diagnostic criteria in the DSM-IV (American Psychiatric Association 1994:285), and even more prominently so in the ICD-10 Classification of Mental and Behavioral Disorders (World Health Organization 1994:93) where they carry special weight for the diagnosis of schizophrenia. As such, questions relating to

FRS are prominent within standardized sets of diagnostic questions (or diagnostic "instruments," as these are called, in reference to the ideal of scientific objectivity) that are used to determine patients' diagnoses for research purposes. They form an important component, for example, of the schizophrenia section of the Present State Examination (Wing, Cooper, and Sartorius 1974) that is used to ascertain diagnoses in terms of ICD-10 criteria.

Remarkable cross-cultural variation in the frequency of FRS has been observed in patients with schizophrenia (Malic, Ahmed, Bashir, and Choudhury 1990; Ndetei and Vadher 1993), varying from 76 percent of a sample of patients in London (Carpenter and Strauss 1974) to 25 percent of patients included in a study in Sri Lanka (Chandrasena and Rodrigo 1979). Within the literature a limited number of explanations are invoked to account for these differences. One such explanation is that diagnostic practices are not the same from one setting to the next. Differences in the frequency of FRS are therefore attributed to the groups of patients being, strictly speaking, incomparable. Another explanation focuses on possible differences in the illness itself. It proposes that schizophrenia varies cross-culturally, either in its fundamental nature, or in its symptomatic expression. A third explanation looks at the degree of fit between culture and schizophrenia, proposing, for example, that FRS are more commonly reported in Western than non-Western settings because the experience of FRS, though bizarre to the Westerner, may be normative in non-Western contexts (see Chandrasena and Rodrigo 1979; Zarrouk 1978). Rather than providing a culturally grounded accounting for difference, however, these latter explanations reproduce a form of primitivism identified by Lucas and Barrett (1995:303), which proposes a correspondence or sympathy between "native" mentality and psychosis, the tacit premise being that they are both examples of a more rudimentary or primitive level of human functioning.

Others have raised issues of translation and language in seeking to understand cross-cultural variation. Koehler (1979) has noted fundamental differences between the several translations of Schneider's work into English, while Gharagozlou and Behin (1998) have demonstrated that the frequency with which FRS are observed depends on which translation is being used (see also Hoenig 1984; Tandon and Greden 1987). Coffey, Mackinnon, and Minas (1983), in a study comparing English-speaking people with those who speak other languages, showed an association between English proficiency and rates of reported FRS. It was their impression that among non-English-speaking patients it was difficult to elicit FRS clinically because the "culturally derived psychological categories used to express the subjective experience of FRS by non-English speaking patients may not be readily translatable into English" (Coffey et al. 1983).

Most accounts within the literature, however, rest on the assumption that schizophrenia, given one or two pathoplastic cultural modifications, is the same the world over, and that any observed variations in its clinical features are not sufficient to justify a reexamination of the category itself. In this chapter, issues of translation, language, and culture are addressed not so much to preserve the construct of schizophrenia as it is currently defined, but in order to subject it to a more critical cross-cultural examination.

The Iban

The Iban are a people of north-western coastal Borneo, the great majority of whom (over 400,000) live in Sarawak. They are celebrated in the ethnographic literature for their history of migration and head-hunting (Padoch 1982) as well as their rich oral tradition and corpus of ritual practices, notably those concerned with shamanic healing (Graham 1987). Freeman's (1970) account of the Iban remains a modern classic, one of the first descriptions of a small-scale acephalous society. Iban live in longhouses that comprise separate family apartments, or *bilik*, aligned side by side to form a single dwelling, each bilik facing onto an enclosed gallery, the *ruai*, that runs along the front of the structure. The architecture of the longhouse reflects a balance between the autonomy of the family unit and its engagement with the community as a whole. A traditional religion distinctive to the Iban people underpins every aspect of their society (Jensen 1974). Over the past century and a half there has been a steady conversion to Christianity, although Iban Christians remain aware of the world of spirits, preserve a strong underlying sense of *adat* (traditional law), and continue to observe many ritual prohibitions, all these practices and beliefs being rooted in the traditional Iban religion.

Since entering the Federation of Malaysia in 1963, Sarawak has undergone steady economic development, and this has influenced all areas of Iban life: the shift from subsistence hill-padi farming to cash crops; the growth of a ramifying network of roads; the rapidly expanding hospital and medical system, including a mental health service; the availability of state education for all children. A standardized system of spelling using the Roman alphabet has been arrived at. This enables the Iban language, formerly an oral tradition, to be written. Migration to towns and cities is gaining pace as Iban school graduates increasingly undergo further training to enter professions and occupations, notably those within the government sectors of health and education. Nevertheless, the majority remain agriculturists who live in longhouse communities along the rivers that flow down from the highlands across the coastal plains.

I conducted ethnographic and clinical studies of psychiatric illness among the Iban, the ethnographic phase being undertaken over a fifteen-month period at Ulu Bayur, a longhouse community in the Saribas district of the Second Division of Sarawak. It focused on Iban shamanic healing (Barrett 1993), personhood and illness (Barrett and Lucas 1994), and *sakit gila* (Barrett 1997). Best translated as mad sickness, *sakit gila* is a broad category approximately coterminous with the psychiatric category of chronic psychosis, for it is reserved for those who remain severely and persistently ill.

The clinical phase of the research was carried out in two periods of field work, each of three-months' duration. Using psychiatric hospital records as a starting point, I located fifty Iban people who were identified by their own communities as suffering from *sakit gila* and who also fulfilled broad diagnostic criteria for schizophrenia (including schizo-affective disorder and schizophreniform psychosis). Diagnostic and family assessments were carried out in their home setting, using ethnographically specific questions pertaining to *sakit gila*, as well as the ninth edition of the Present State Examination (Wing et al. 1974), or PSE-9 as it is known. These data were subsequently compared with data derived from fifty patients who lived in Adelaide, Australia. The two samples were comparable in terms of their diagnosis, as well as their age (Iban mean 34, Australian 36) and their length of illness (Iban mean 13, Australian 12). However, the Iban sample contained more females than males (28 F: 22 M) whereas for the Australian sample it was the reverse (20 F: 30 M).

Translating the PSE: Sociolinguistic Considerations

I arranged for a translation of the PSE-9 to be undertaken by an experienced Iban mental health professional. The back-translation was carried out by an Iban educationalist and author. For the most part, the back-translation resembled the original English version indicating that the translation had been accurate. While undertaking field tests of this translation at Ulu Bayur, initially on those who had never suffered psychiatric disorder, I found that Iban people had considerable difficulty grasping the questions.

In response to this problem, I involved Aru anak Gundi, my mentor, informant, and language tutor at Ulu Bayur, to work on the translation with me in an effort to render it more "longhouse friendly." At the same time, in order to keep abreast of contemporary developments in research, I changed from the ninth to the tenth modification of the Present State Examination, or PSE-10 (World Health Organization 1990). Aru was a wordsmith, recognized in the district as a orator of repute. He spoke little English. Once, while working with me at this task, he paused and asked ruefully, "I know this is a great work of your culture, and perhaps the meaning is very deep, but we find its questions *bebalut* (convoluted). Why ask two or three questions in one – why not one at a time?" With customary verbal facility, he rearranged parts of the PSE-10 and rendered them into rhyming stanzas after the style of the great Iban invocatory chants that call ancestors and Gods to join Iban mortals in ritual celebration:

Kala nuan ngasai ka diri balat rindu ati nadai tuju?	Have you ever felt extremely happy for no reason?
Kala nuan ngasai ka diri ringat nadai menuku?	Have you ever become unaccountably angry?
Bisi nuan rindu ati begulai enggau sulu?	Do you like to go out with friends a lot?
Kala nuan bejalai betemu enggau antux?	Have you met up with spirits?
Kala nuan dani pagi hari kelalu tumu?	Are you waking up too early in the morning?

This wry, perceptive, satirist had made his point. Though not Mozart's requiem or Hamlet, the PSE is an exemplar of the culture of Western psychiatric science, a product of the clinical-academic institutions in which it was developed. In English, the style is formal to the point of being slightly stiff, the language is abstract, the grammar is correct:

Question 17:2: What about other unusual experiences that some people have, such as seeing things that others cannot see, having second sight, or being aware of strange presences? (World Health Organization 1990:85)

PSE-10 questions are indeed convoluted, with variations on the main theme of each question added on, one clause after another. Although intended to be spoken aloud as if making conversation, they do not resemble spoken English as much as carefully crafted written compositions. They bear the hallmarks of an elaborated code (Bernstein 1973:93) that is associated with professional communication. This is a language code that displays the abstract precision of systematic inquiry, while tacitly conveying the power relations implicit in such inquiry. Psychiatric research instruments such as the PSE are imprinted with the stamp of the men and women who produce them, their professional location, their language, their class background, cultural environment, tacit assumptions – all of these standing apart from, yet influencing, the ostensible purpose for which the instrument is designed. The consequences for psychiatric research have not been explored. For example, although there is an extensive literature on social class and schizophrenia (Fox 1990), it does not address class relationships between psychiatrist/diagnoser and patient/diagnosed, the way these relationships are signaled in spoken clinical interaction, and their potential diagnostic implications.

The first translation into Iban had been written in the language repertoire (Hymes 1972:38) of an educated Iban middle class. This repertoire is associated with people who were schooled in colonial times and fluent in English, with its use of direct expression, the active voice, and complex extended sentences replete with subordinate clauses. The first Iban version had been faithful to these grammatical features and, like the English, was couched in a formal style associated with written Iban, rather than the more informal style of day-to-day speech.

There is another repertoire – that of the longhouse hill-padi farmer who has had little formal schooling. It is characterized by brevity, clarity, and elegance. Iban pay careful attention to language. Verbal finesse is an important element within longhouse life, both in the ceremonial domain, with its ritual chants, rhyming prayers, and skilled oratory, and in everyday conversation, where word play abounds and riddles are a favorite game. Under Aru's direction, the second Iban translation divided the lengthy convoluted questions into discrete component questions and rendered each into the style of the more elegant, oral, "longhouse" repertoire. Asking questions in this way clearly influenced the relationship between researcher and patient, generating a sympathetic conversational atmosphere that enabled a more subtle degree of intersubjective attunement.

Nowhere was this more evident than in Aru's use of *jako nyindir*. An important exception to the customary directness and clarity of expression, *jako nyindir* is a form of indirect speech or allusion used to convey politeness, especially when transacting important business or broaching sensitive issues. Respect, for example, is conveyed by being careful not to use a person's name, either when addressing that person or, in some instances, when referring to them. Sensitive to this, Aru produced translations that sometimes hinted at the point. When making reference to spirits (in order, for example, to enquire about strange visual or auditory experiences) it is polite and prudent not to refer to them directly as *antu* (spirits) but indirectly as *utai* (things) or *orang* (an ambiguous term that encompasses humans and spirits). It is said that spirits can overhear what humans say. Direct reference to them can risk attracting their attention. Worse still, spirits may regard such talk as disrespectful; retribution might ensue. Thus, attention to the way in which words signify relationships of respect, not only between interviewer and interviewee, but also between both them and spirits, is critical in the production of a sensitive diagnostic instrument. Within this social domain of respect, attention to the ritual danger that attends particular Iban words is the paramount consideration.

It is widely agreed that the translation of psychiatric instruments raises complex problems having to do with the extent to which it is possible to render concepts that were generated in one language into another. These problems are usually conceptualized in terms of a tension between literal and conceptual, or between emic and etic. Insufficient scholarly attention, however, has been devoted within the literature to the sociolinguistic dimensions of this enterprise, which are equally as critical in producing a body of questions that make sense to those being questioned, especially social sense. The status of an interviewee vis-à-vis the interviewer may determine, for example, whether one uses *tu* or *vous*, or their equivalents. Within many Indian languages, the caste relationship between interviewer and interviewee will have a crucial bearing on the language used. The type of difficulties encountered with the first translation of the Iban PSE, and the way they were smoothed out in the second, indicate that this is more than a matter of appropriate grammar or dictionary meaning. It has to do with the social stance adopted by the interviewer in relation to the person being interviewed and how this is signified through language. Relationships of power that are encoded in language require particularly close attention when moving, as in this instance, from a Western context in which professional language is a means of articulating social class, to a small-scale society in which language can be imbued with ritual danger and spiritual power. Such sociolinguistic parameters exert a decisive influence over how one frames psychiatric questions, what subjective experiences may be properly enquired into, and hence, what data a researcher and patient can generate together.

In cross-cultural psychiatric research, a back translation that resembles the original has long stood as the guarantor of accuracy and validity. In this instance, however, the questions in the second Iban translation differed in style and sentence structure from the English original and were, at times, quite indirect. The back translation looked markedly different. A faithful back translation, I would argue, is more likely to guarantee that the translator has captured the core concept of each question as this is constructed in English, and rendered this concept into a format that remains faithful to English syntax and style. On the other hand, if one is to achieve a set of questions that make sense to the person who is expected to respond to them, it is necessary to pay attention to issues of respect, decorum, power, and danger, and the way these are signified and negotiated linguistically. Translation of a psychiatric instrument entails developing an appreciation of its sociolinguistic dimensions, including its repertoire, style, and code, in order to decide how such parameters are best carried into the new cultural context.

Translating the PSE: Hearing versus Thinking

Having developed an Iban PSE-10 that was more elegant and accessible, yet appropriately indirect where necessary, it remained to tackle a specific group of FRS questions that resisted easy translation. Several subgroups may be discerned within the FRS, of which I am concerned with two. The first encompasses auditory hallucinations, including voices heard arguing, and voices heard commenting on one's actions. The second subgroup is concerned with the subjective experience of disordered thinking. It includes thought withdrawal, thought insertion (or thoughts ascribed to others), and diffusion (or broadcasting) of thoughts.

Schneider recognized that these latter had to do with the relationship between self and other, for he conceptualized "thought withdrawal, thought control, thought diffusion, and everything that the patient experiences as imposed on him in the spheres of feeling, drive, and volition" in terms of "permeability of the ego-world boundary" (Koehler 1979:236). Support for this proposed division between symptoms related to auditory perception and those related to thinking came from an empirical study carried out by Mellor (1970) who found that the symptom of *voices arguing* tended to occur in patients who also heard *voices commenting*, whereas the symptoms of *thought insertion* and *thought withdrawal* were found in close association.

In the process of translation, little difficulty was encountered in rendering questions about auditory hallucinations into Iban. There were minor differences between the two languages. The idea of a depersonalized voice was foreign to the Iban and so hearing "voices" was translated as *ninga munyi nyawa orang* or hearing the voices of people (or spirits). Nonetheless, "hearing voices" in English was more or less the same as "hearing people talking" in Iban.

By contrast, questions related to the subjective experience of thought disorder were difficult to translate. Introduced to writing only this century, Iban found the idea of thoughts being "read" nonsensical. And by what stretch of imagination could thoughts be taken from the head? Was the question some sort of riddle? Given that FRS are, in themselves, quite strange experiences, I wondered if the questions made more sense to people who might be expected to have experienced them. The questions were equally puzzling, however, to people who had been treated for psychotic illness.

Iban cultural concepts of thinking differ substantially from the concepts of thinking that may be found in a Western, English-speaking context, such as in Australia. In Australia, thinking is regarded as a mental activity that occurs within the brain inside the head. Distinguished from emotion, desire, and will (though seen as closely related to them), it is a silent, solipsistic activity, which differs from talking. The very possibility of subjective thought disorder is predicated on this view of thinking. Building on Schneider's original observations, Fabrega has made the point that certain FRS are embedded within a set of western, psychologistic cultural assumptions:

These symptoms imply to a large extent persons are independent beings whose bodies and minds are separated from each other and function autonomously. In particular, they imply that under ordinary conditions external influences do not operate on and influence an individual: that thoughts are recurring inner happenings that the self "has"; that thoughts, feelings, and actions are separable sorts of things which together account for self-identity; that thoughts and feelings are silent and exquisitely private . . . and it is based on this psychology (i.e., a Western cultural perspective) that schizophrenic symptoms have been articulated. (Fabrega 1982:56–7)

Within Western culture, there are a number of counterexamples to the ideals of mental autonomy and privacy. They include telepathy and hypnotism. A more pervasive, and therefore important, counterexample is the Christian belief in an omniscient God who knows our inner thoughts without us speaking them. In societies that evolved from the Christian tradition, individuals can be punished, or feel guilty and ashamed of thoughts, even if these thoughts are not verbalized. This direct communicative relationship between the individual and the personal God serves, perhaps, as a cultural model for disorders of the privacy of thinking.

The Iban have a more embodied and interactional notion of thinking. Cleverness and calculative ability are located in the brain, as in the expression *tajam untak*, sharp brain. But the closest equivalent to the Western notion of thinking is experienced as arising from the heart-liver region, and it is intimately tied up with emotion, desire, and will. The term *ati* refers to this anatomical region:

Tusah ati aku dalam nyin, could be translated literally as "My heart was sad in there," or idiomatically as "I felt sad."
Ati aku enggai, literally means "My heart did not want to," idiomatically, "I did not want to."
Nama deh? ko ati aku dalam nyin, might literally be "'What's that?' said my heart within there," or idiomatically, "'What's that?' I thought to myself."

The first two examples resemble Western notions of "emotion" and "will" respectively, whereas the third is closer to thinking. Note that in all three instances, the bodily locus of such feelings, desires, or thoughts is the *ati*.

The third example employs the word *jako* (or its shortened form *ko*). *Jako* means to talk, though it is commonly used, as in the previous example, to refer to what is termed "thinking" in the English language. This points to a correspondence between the Western cultural concept of thinking and the Iban cultural concept of talking.

I do not wish to suggest that there is no Iban concept of "thinking." The word *runding*, for example, refers primarily to thinking. But it is important to note that *runding* can also be used to mean spoken interaction, where it might be translated as thinking through (say a problem or decision) with someone. Thinking through a decision, is an activity done with people as much as it is done by oneself.

With *jako* able to mean thought and *runding* able to mean speech, there is considerable overlap in Iban between the concepts of thinking and talking. In English the distinction is much sharper. It would be easy to overstate these differences between Iban and English. For it is true that in English there are many instances when thinking and talking blur into each other (such as inner voices or thinking aloud). And, as I have indicated, Iban people do make a distinction between silent inner thoughts and spoken words. One might summarize this comparison by stating that the distinction between thought and speech is not as culturally salient for Iban as it is for English speakers. And if there is an emphasis within Iban language and culture, it is one that privileges the idea of talking over that of thinking.

I examined other idioms that might approximate communication between individuals by thought alone, notably the concept of a separable soul that can be enticed out of the body by spirits during dreams or illness. The Iban soul, however, travels, experiences, and talks. It is not contemplative. Spirits and human souls interact verbally and through sexual attraction, not mental communion. Moreover, in contrast to the Christian God, spirits do not know what you are silently thinking unless you say it aloud; retribution only occurs in response to verbal behavior. The term for this – *puni jako* – refers to the ritual danger associated with *speaking* the wrong sentiments. There is no cultural model of other beings knowing your unspoken inner thoughts. There is a cultural model for disorders of the privacy of speech, not thought.

As a consequence, my attempts to ask questions concerned with the subjective experience of thought disorder were difficult for patients to grasp, as illustrated in the following two exchanges with Umang. She was a somber woman in her thirties, who had largely recovered from an episode of *sakit gila*, but who was still regarded by her kindly, elderly husband as vulnerable to a recurrence. The following translated transcripts of two tape-recorded segments of a diagnostic interview relate to "thought insertion" and "thought broadcast" questions respectively:

Thought insertion:

ME: Do you have thoughts in your head which are not your own?
UMANG: Thoughts in my head? [In a tone of surprise?]
ME: Yes.
UMANG: Not my own? [Again surprised?]
ME: Yes.
UMANG: How do you mean?

Thought disorder:

ME: Do people at large know your thoughts, even when you don't speak?
UMANG: They do. People know.
ME: Explain to me! Tell me! Your thoughts are known by a lot of people? Even though you don't talk?
UMANG: I don't talk much – I don't want to talk much when I am really ill.
ME: Oh. But do others know your thoughts?
UMANG: Other people?
ME: Yes.
UMANG: Yes, they know the thoughts that I have broadcast (put about).
ME: Ah. How do they know if you don't talk?
UMANG: That's because I have told them previously.
ME: Oh. You have told them previously.

In collaboration with Aru, I first sought to recast these questions within the "heart/liver" metaphor. Here, thought insertion became an idea of one's heart being influenced by people even when they had not talked to you. This made no better sense than thoughts being put into your head. Second, we recast these questions in terms of talking rather than thinking. Thought insertion now became an idea of inner speech within the heart being influenced externally. In Iban, however, it sounded as if we were asking whether other people were simply pressuring the person into doing something. In changing these questions into metaphors that resonated with Iban culture, they lost their core meanings as FRS.

The closest possible approximations to the FRS employed the idiom of magic. Iban magic involves the exertion of power from a distance by the use of dangerous ritual techniques and substances. It is exercised by malign humans or spirits and may make a person ill or alter his or her behavior. Spirits also have the capacity to exert an attraction over people, often sexual in nature. A clinical example concerned a young man who found himself being drawn away from the longhouse against his will into the jungle by a spirit who appeared to him in the form of a naked female. In the most general terms, these phenomena seem to be equivalent to the FRS of "made impulses" and "made volitional acts," for both are a form of external influence over an individual's behavior and will. Neither is concerned with an individual's thoughts.

In sum, though we explored and tested a range of Iban cultural idioms, we were unable to arrive at a satisfactory translation of the questions relating to the FRS of subjective thought disorder. These questions presuppose a Western cultural concept of personhood, which gives a privileged place to internal mental life as a defining feature of the person. It is a mental life that is recognized as located in the brain, and that is experienced as disembodied. And it is a mental life that is experienced as being quite separate from that of others. FRS of thought insertion, withdrawal and broadcast, and their associated questions in the PSE make sense in a culture where there are well-recognized paranormal and religious exceptions to the norm of mental privacy. Though they are strange questions, they are not inconceivable in such a Western context.

To the longhouse Iban, however, they are both strange and difficult to conceive, for this is a setting in which the body is experienced as the field of mental life. In Iban culture, personhood is defined less in terms of the uniqueness of an individual's mental life and more in terms of the interactions with those that surround him or her, with particular emphasis placed on the verbal aspect of these interactions. It is a world in which there are no cultural models, religious or otherwise, for thoughts being read or broadcast. It is a world where dangerous objects may be inserted from a distance into your body causing illness, or removed by the shaman to heal this illness, but where thoughts are neither inserted into your mind nor withdrawn from it.

This contrasts with the cultural phenomenology of hearing, which was remarkably similar across the two contexts.

Empirical Comparisons

Auditory Hallucinations: Qualitative and Quantitative Findings

The ease of translation of auditory hallucination questions was matched by the similarity between Iban and Australian respondents when

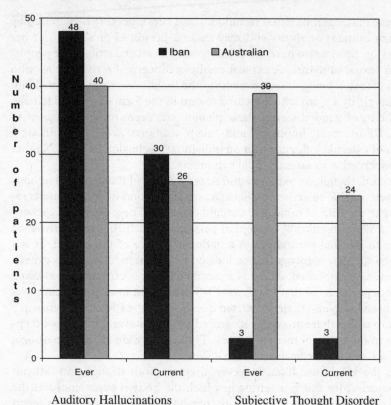

Figure 3.1.   Auditory Hallucinations and Subjective Thought Disorder in Iban and Australian Patients

reporting these hallucinatory experiences. Thirty of the fifty Iban patients and twenty-six of the fifty Australian patients reported having experienced auditory hallucinations in the month prior to the assessment (see Figure 3.1). This difference was not statistically significant. Since case finding among a people who live in remote riverine communities dispersed across difficult terrain is necessarily haphazard, these comparisons must be interpreted with caution. Nevertheless, somewhat more Iban patients (forty-eight) than Australian patients (forty) reported having experienced auditory hallucinations at some stage during the course of their illness and this difference was statistically significant ($\chi^2 = 6.06$, $df = 1$, $p < 0.05$).

At a qualitative level, the similarities were striking. Dom anak Igat, a twenty-nine-year-old man, had been hearing voices for more than ten years. They sounded like the voices of living people and seemed to come from somewhere near his ear:

I hear them for a little while, then no more, and then they come back again. They talk to themselves about me. They talk about what I say. They talk about what I do. They insinuate things about me.

Bidah anak Mangat, a forty-four-year-old woman living with her mother, described two different voices:

There is one person who helps me. She is my helper. But I don't know who she is. I am troubled by them. I don't agree with what they say. But the good one helps me. There is one who helps and the other disturbs me. I don't talk with them, I just laugh.

It was notable that Iban patients could describe the voices they heard in considerable detail – where they came from, who was talking, what they said. And the way they described them resembled the way Australian patients talked about auditory hallucinations – the qualitative experience of listening to them was very similar. Had Schneider come to Borneo, he might have recognized some characteristic features of these auditory experiences: commenting, disagreeing, derogatory, commanding. There were other similarities between the way Iban and Australian patients reported auditory hallucinations: the strange quality of the experience, the contradictory content of the words, the sometimes faint intensity of the sound, its indeterminate spatial origin. Qualitative impressions such as these are not often reported in the psychiatric literature because they are difficult to measure or verify but they are no less important for that.

Subjective Thought Disorder: Qualitative and Quantitative Findings

Given the difficulties in asking Iban respondents about the subjective experience of thought disorder, it comes as no surprise that these symptoms were much less commonly reported by Iban patients. Three of the Iban sample and twenty-four of the Australian sample reported the symptoms in the month prior to assessment. The same three Iban patients and thirty-nine Australian patients reported having experienced them during the course of their illness. That is to say, Iban patients reported significantly less subjective thought disorder than Australian patients, either within the previous month ($\chi^2 = 22.37$, $df = 1$, $p < 0.001$), or at any time in their illness ($\chi^2 = 53.20$, $df = 1$, $p < 0.001$).

In a further twelve Iban cases, there was equivocal evidence of thought disorder. These twelve at first responded affirmatively to the questions, but were unable to elaborate on their answer or provide any examples of their experiences. For some, the questions may have resonated with their experience, but only vaguely, and in a way that could not be put into words. For most, however, the initial affirmation is more likely to have reflected a sense of politeness that manifested as a wish to fit in with the researcher and his questions. Saying "Yes" can be the most expedient way of dealing with the puzzlement or irritation caused by a question that does not make sense. For this reason, there is a risk of overestimating the presence of such symptoms in psychiatric research, which is why it is prudent to record a symptom as present only if a patient is able to describe what he or she has experienced to the researcher. It was in applying these rigorous criteria that I determined that just three patients could clearly be regarded as having experienced thought disorder. The contrast with auditory hallucinations was noticeable, for as previously indicated, those patients who affirmed that they heard people's voices were able to talk about the experience in considerable detail.

Given how alien the questions were to Iban ethnopsychology, what is most surprising is that three patients did manage to grasp the questions and confirm that they had had these symptoms by describing the experience. All three were women; their mean age (thirty-one) was similar to that of the Iban sample, but their length of illness – eight years – was less than the mean of the sample. The first, Empiang anak Dagang, age twenty-three, lived with her mother and father in a single-family house situated on a main road at some distance from their longhouse. When at high school, Empiang had failed third-form exams (Malaysian high schools have five, sometimes six grades or "forms") and left the district to work in the capital city where she cared for her sister's children while her sister worked. There, Empiang had become intensely involved with an evangelical Christian group, and it was while traveling to another Malaysian state with a group of young churchgoers to carry out Christian work that she first became ill. She said she heard the voice of Satan pretending to be Jesus telling her, in biblical phrases, that if her eye made her sin she should throw it away. As a result, she tried to damage her eye with a needle. Empiang vividly described the FRS of thought insertion in terms of that thing (an indirect reference to Satan) putting thoughts into her head.

The second, Margaret Sandu anak Jenggie, was a twenty-six-year-old woman. At eighteen years of age she had graduated from fifth form at high school and then moved to the capital city, where she found a job working as a clerk in a timber company. It was then that she first became acutely ill. "At the time," she remarked, "I still held to the Christian religion." Not only did she hear people's voices coming from strange places such as the roots of her hair or from the toilet, but she also became convinced that people could hear what she was thinking, and that they could snatch (*ngerampas*) thoughts from her head. Margaret perceived her illness in terms of a vulnerability, in spite of her Christian faith, to the influence of traditional Iban charms that someone had placed on her.

The third was Bidah anak Mangat, whose auditory hallucinations were described previously and whose case has been published elsewhere in more detail (Barrett 1998a, 1998b). Both she and her mother, on whom she depended greatly, were devout Christians. Bidah had been educated to the fourth grade of primary school when, at the age of ten, her mother withdrew her from school to help in the house. In spite of her lack of formal education, Bidah could read and write. When describing her symptoms to me, she was quite clear that people around the longhouse knew what she was thinking because her thoughts were coming out of her brain. She said that if she read, others knew what she was reading. Bidah understood her illness, its cause and it symptoms, in terms of the influence of Satan and God.

It is notable that all three were deeply influenced by Christianity. The first two had advanced to high school and then begun to make a transition from the longhouse into an urban setting. Bidah had done neither, though she was literate. These three were not the only ones among the fifty patients who had received an education or were literate, nor were they the only ones who had converted to Christianity. It is not possible, nor is it the aim of this analysis, to demonstrate an association, let alone a causal relationship, between these factors and the presence of FRS of thought disorder. The more modest suggestion advanced here is that exposure to education, to reading, and to Christian concepts of thinking and communication with a personal God, provides a cultural context within which a disturbance in cognition associated with schizophrenia might be experienced in terms of FRS – a cultural context within which it is conceivable to imagine thoughts being taken from one's head, put into one's head, or broadcast about.

To summarize, it was relatively simple to translate questions concerning auditory hallucinations from English into Iban, and I found that auditory hallucinations were qualitatively and quantitatively similar in these two groups, occurring even more frequently among the Iban if one took into account the entire course of the illness. By contrast, with respect to the subjective experience of thought disorder, difficulties were encountered in translating FRS questions from English into Iban because of differences in the way in which thinking itself was culturally signified and understood. Subjective thought disorder was reported significantly less frequently in the Iban sample.

Accounting for Difference

Do these differences represent a minor artifact that stems from the methodology of translation? In other words, is it that Iban people subjectively experience disturbances in thinking but, being difficult to convey in the Iban language, these disturbances are less commonly reported? That there were another twelve Iban patients with equivocal evidence of subjectively experienced thought disorder might be taken as support for this argument, although as I have pointed out already, their responses were more likely to be expressions of polite agreement rather than a vague expression of thought disorder. Ultimately, it is not possible to answer this question with any certainty when words are virtually the sole means of access to others' thoughts. How can we know unless they tell us?

Observations provided by those close to the patients may cast light on the differences I have reported. Iban and Australian patients in this series both exhibited disturbances in speech when psychotic. Their speech was observed by family members and by mental health professionals to be incoherent, illogical, vague, or drifting from one topic to the next. In the Iban context, it was described as "going off track," "not straight," or becoming "tangled." In the Australian context, terms such as "talking nonsense" or "looseness of associations" were used. Iban and Australian patients manifested similar levels of disturbed speech production. It could be argued, therefore, that this disturbance is common to both groups, but that Australian people subjectively experience it as thought disorder, whereas Iban, given their "speech-rather-than-thought"-oriented ethnopsychology, preferentially interpret and express these experiences within an auditory idiom.

What are the implications of these data for the cross-cultural comparison of schizophrenia? Is it that auditory hallucinations hold true cross-culturally, and that subjective thought disorder is a more culturally contingent aspect of the syndrome? To this question, the data can reply more confidently: If there is one clinical dimension in which the resemblance, qualitative and quantitative, between the two samples is striking, it is that of persisting auditory hallucinosis (PAH). Both series of fifty patients contain a majority of cases of PAH that is cross-culturally recognizable and robust. Other clinical features associated with schizophrenia are less recognizable between these two cultures, and reported with greater variability, none more so than FRS. In the three exceptions from the Iban group, there were important cultural, religious, and cultural conditions that may have made possible the experience and expression of FRS of subjective thought disorder. Given how variable and culturally contingent they are, it is time to reassess the weight that is currently placed on FRS of thought disorder as diagnostic criteria for schizophrenia.

Psychiatric research, cultural and biological, might fruitfully focus its attention on patients who suffer from PAH rather than schizophrenia. The former is a clinical category that is generated more directly from culturally grounded phenomenology; the latter is a higher order construct, which is imbued to a larger extent with the cultural history of nineteenth-century European psychiatric science and its contemporary equivalents (Barrett 1997). A strand of biological research in schizophrenia has already begun to adopt this symptom-based strategy in seeking to identify brain function correlates of auditory hallucinations using functional MRI (McGuire, Silbersweig, Wright, Murray, Frackowiak, and Frith 1996) and other neuroimaging methods (David 1999).

It is important to avoid the trap of assuming that pathogenic is to pathoplastic as cross-culturally robust clinical features are to culturally contingent clinical features. A symptom that holds true cross-culturally is not necessarily a window onto the underlying biological processes of illness. It is equally plausible that such a symptom may represent a similar response in different cultural contexts to the predicament of psychosis, a final common pathway that is shared by more than one culture. PAH may in fact represent a transculturally similar mode of response to the social alienation that stems from psychotic illness. Thus, the search for biological correlates of such cross-cultural symptoms is best advanced hand in hand with social enquiry.

Conclusion

Cross-cultural psychiatric research involves the translation of diagnostic instruments, most of which have been composed in English. It involves the translation of diagnostic concepts, the provenance of which can usually be traced back to a European tradition of clinical science. Although there is some recognition within the field that diagnostic instruments carry meanings derived from their culture of origin, the English original frequently serves as a de facto etic version of the instrument, emic relevance being associated more closely with the translated version – an ideal toward which all translators are encouraged to aspire. This cross-cultural skewing will always remain the case as long as back translation into the original language remains the gold standard for the testing of translations. European diagnostic concepts similarly tend to be regarded, by default, as universals, with variations in different contexts being accounted for in terms of linguistic and cultural specificities.

It is not possible, nor is it useful, to escape entirely from such a project. The research that I have described is located within its broad framework insofar as it seeks to understand Iban linguistic and cultural conceptions of *sakit gila*, but takes as its starting point an English PSE-10 and a concept of schizophrenia that includes symptoms first described in the German literature. However, the approach advanced in this chapter is one that entails a more thoroughgoing reflexive analysis of the psychiatric instruments used in research by treating the process of translation as worthy of critical attention. Difficulties in translation of course require resolution, but at the same time they provide an opportunity to investigate cultural and language differences that may teach us about important variations in the subjective experience of psychiatric disorder.

The strategy I have outlined here was to treat the psychiatric diagnostic instrument as an ensemble of speech acts, thereby directing attention to the implied interactions between the person asking the questions and the person answering them. When working from English to Iban, it was thereby possible to discern, embedded within the English language of the PSE-10, a set of tacit markers of profession and class. They translated comfortably into a repertoire that was relevant to Iban individuals who had received higher education and had moved away from the longhouse to work in professions and white-collar occupations. In reorienting to a "longhouse" repertoire, however, profession and class were left behind. Instead, it became necessary to come to terms with the issues of verbal clarity and respect. The relationship between power and words was common to both settings, though secular forms of power were signified in one, ritual power in the other. In the Iban setting, the choice of translations was important in establishing appropriate forms of interaction between researcher and patient. Given the ritual power associated with particular words, it was even more critical in establishing appropriate forms of interaction between these two humans, on the one hand, and on the other, the spirits who were regarded as the sources of voices. Without the recognition that powerful words are the primary form of communication between Iban and spirits, and that the only avenue to an understanding of these communications is by means of appropriate words, a comparative culturally grounded phenomenology of psychiatric disorder is not possible.

Second, I have sought to employ a mutually reflective comparative strategy in which the analysis of data gathered in each cultural context was used to illuminate the analysis of data derived from the other. The modern history of cross-cultural studies in this field has been a narrative in which Western psychiatry's concept of schizophrenia has been transported to different places for testing under different cultural conditions. Very often these conditions are not as radically different as might be imagined. The enterprise has very often been managed by psychiatrists trained in European or North American postgraduate institutions. These psychiatrists rely, for their research infrastructure, on mental health facilities resembling old European psychiatric hospitals first established in colonial times.

This chapter differs insofar as it is a narrative of cultural critique. It has reported an attempt, first, to understand the cultural underpinnings of the schizophrenia concept and certain of its FRS diagnostic criteria; second to understand the cultural underpinnings of the Iban lived experience of *sakit gila*; and third to bring these two traditions into confrontation in order to examine some of the fine phenomenological detail at point of contact – a uniquely Western postmodern exercise, no doubt, but at least one that accords equal status to each party and seeks to avoid a stance of postcolonial Western mental health hegemony. By such means, comparative research can cast light on those components of the clinical definition of schizophrenia that may be tied more than other components to the cultural and intellectual history of Western psychiatry. It can thereby suggest how the illness category might be refined rather than simply reproduced.

Throughout, I have sought to make the case that comparative cultural phenomenology requires ethnographic underpinning. All too frequently, broad brush statements appear in the literature that use explanatory frameworks of spirit experiences, magic or witchcraft, to account for psychiatric symptoms, and vice versa. Before hastening to such conclusions it is fruitful to prepare the ground by learning in some detail what spirit voices normally sound like, how it feels when magic affects your body, or what it is like when your soul sees people, talks to them, is drawn away, or is frightened – a cultural phenomenology of unusual experiences, normative and pathological. It is equally important to examine the tacit cultural assumptions that define what it is to be a person, a body, a soul, a mind. Before comparing symptoms of schizophrenia, it is necessary to question rather than assume what it is for a person to think, feel, and interact with humans, spirits, Gods, or other beings.

The study of FRS is illuminating because it enables a reexamination of these taken-for-granted categories of person, thought, and speech in pursuit of a more sensitive understanding of strange psychotic phenomena. As a focus of comparative enquiry, FRS are pivotal because they lie at the interface between subjective experience, the definition of psychotic illness, and the cultural mediation of psychiatric disorder.

NOTE

This research was funded by the Australian National Health and Medical Research Council. I am grateful for the support of the Malaysian Medical Research Institute, Universiti Malaysia Sarawak, the Sarawak State Planning Unit, and the Sarawak Department of Health.

REFERENCES

American Psychiatric Association. 1994. *Diagnostic and Statistical Manual of Mental Disorders (DSM-IV)*. Washington, DC: American Psychiatric Association.

Andreasen, Nancy C. and William T. Carpenter. 1993. "Diagnosis and Classification of Schizophrenia." *Schizophrenia Bulletin* 19(2): 199–214.

Barrett, Robert J. 1993. "Performance, Effectiveness and the Iban Manang." In R. Winzeler, ed., pp. 235–80. *The Seen and the Unseen: Shamanism, Mediumship and Possession in Borneo*. Borneo Research Council Monograph Series Number 2. Williamsburg, VA: Borneo Research Council.

———. 1997. "Sakit Gila in an Iban Longhouse: Chronic Schizophrenia." *Culture, Medicine and Psychiatry* 21(3): 365–79.

———. 1998a. "Conceptual Foundations of Schizophrenia, I: Degeneration." *Australian and New Zealand Journal of Psychiatry* 32: 617–26.

———. 1998b. "Conceptual Foundations of Schizophrenia, II: Disintegration and Division." *Australian and New Zealand Journal of Psychiatry* 32: 627–734.

Barrett, Robert J. and R. H. Lucas. 1994. "Hot and Cold in Transformation: Is Iban Medicine Humoral?" *Social Science and Medicine* 38(2): 383–93.

Bernstein, Basil. 1973. *Class, Codes and Control*. St. Albans, UK: Granada.

Carpenter, William T. and John S. Strauss. 1974. "Cross-cultural Evaluation of Schneider's First-rank Symptoms of Schizophrenia: a Report from the International Pilot Study of Schizophrenia." *American Journal of Psychiatry* 131(6): 682–7.

Chandrasena, R. and A. Rodrigo. 1979. "Schneider's First-rank Symptoms: Their Prevalence and Diagnostic Implications in an Asian Population." *British Journal of Psychiatry* 135: 348–51.

Coffey, G. J., A. Mackinnon, and I. H. Minas. 1983. "Interethnic Variations in the Presence of Schneiderian First-rank Symptoms." *Australian and New Zealand Journal of Psychiatry* 27: 219–27.

David, A. S. 1999. "Auditory Hallucinations: Phenomenology, Neuropsychology and Neuroimaging Update." *Acta Psychiatrica Scandinavica* 99: 95–104.

Fabrega, Horatio. 1982. "Culture and Psychiatric Illness: Biomedical and Ethnomedical Aspects." In A. J. Marsella and G. M. White, eds., pp. 9–68. *Cultural Conceptions of Mental Health and Therapy*. Dordrecht, Netherlands: Reidel.

Fox, John W. 1990. "Social Class, Mental Illness, and Social Mobility: The Social Selection–Drift Hypothesis for Serious Mental Illness." *Journal of Health and Social Behaviour* 31: 344–53.

Freeman, Derek. 1970. *Report on the Iban*. London: Athlone Press.

Gharagozlou, H. and M. T. Behin. 1998. "Diagnostic Evaluation of Schneider First-rank Symptoms of Schizophrenia among Three Groups of Iranians." *Comprehensive Psychiatry* 20(3): 242–5.

Graham, Penelope. 1987. *Iban Shamanism: An Analysis of the Ethnographic Literature*. An Occasional Paper of the Department of Anthropology, Research School of Pacific Studies. Canberra: Australian National University.

Hoenig, J. 1984. "Schneider's First-rank Symptoms and the Tabulators." *Comprehensive Psychiatry* 25(1): 77–87.

Hymes, Dell. 1972. "Models of the Interaction of Language and Social Life." In J. Gumperz and D. Hymes, eds., pp. 35–71. *Directions in Sociolinguistics: The Ethnography of Communication*. New York: Holt, Rinehart and Winston.

Jensen, Erik. 1974. *The Iban and Their Religion*. Oxford: Clarendon Press.

Koehler, K. 1979. "First-rank Symptoms of Schizophrenia: Questions Concerning Clinical Boundaries." *British Journal of Psychiatry* 134: 236–48.

Lucas, R. M. and Robert J. Barrett. 1995. "Interpreting Culture and Psychopathology: Primitivist Themes in Cross-cultural Debate." *Culture, Medicine and Psychiatry* 19(3): 287–326.

Malik, S. B., M. Ahmed, A. Bashir, and T. M. Choudhury. 1990. "Schneider's First-rank Symptoms of Schizophrenia: Prevalence and Diagnostic Use. A Study from Pakistan." *British Journal of Psychiatry* 156: 109–11.

McGuire, P. K., D. A. Silbersweig, I. Wright, R. M. Murray, R. S. Frackowiak, and C. D. Frith. 1996. "The Neural Correlates of Inner Speech and Auditory Verbal Imagery in Schizophrenia: Relationship to Auditory Verbal Hallucinations." *British Journal of Psychiatry* 169: 148–59.

Mellor, Clive S. 1970. "First-rank Symptoms of Schizophrenia: I. The Frequency in Schizophrenics on Admission to Hospital; II. Differences Between Individual First-rank Symptoms." *British Journal of Psychiatry* 117: 15–23.

Ndetei, D. M. and. A. Vadher. 1984. "A Cross-cultural Study of the Frequencies of Schneider's First-rank Symptoms of Schizophrenia." *Acta Psychiatrica Scandinavica* 70: 540–4.

Padoch, Christine. 1982. *Migration and its Alternatives among the Iban of Sarawak*. The Hague: Martinus Nijhoff.

Schneider, Kurt. 1959. *Clinical Psychopathology*. M. Hamilton, trans. New York: Grune & Stratton.

Tandon, R. and J. Greden. 1987. "Schneiderian First-rank Symptoms: Reconfirmation of High Specificity for Schizophrenia." *Acta Psychiatrica Scandinavica* 75: 392–6.

Wing, John K., John E. Cooper, and Norman Sartorius. 1974. *Measurement and Classification of Psychiatric Symptoms: An Instruction Manual for the PSE and Catego Program*. Cambridge: Cambridge University Press.

World Health Organization. 1990. *Schedules for Clinical Assessment in Neuropsychiatry: PSE-10*. London: Institute of Psychiatry.

———. 1994. *Pocket Guide to the ICD-10 Classification of Mental and Behavioral Disorders*. Washington, DC: American Psychiatric Press.

Zarrouk, E. A. 1978. "The Usefulness of First-rank Symptoms in the Diagnosis of Schizophrenia in a Saudi Arabian Population." *British Journal of Psychiatry* 132: 572–3.

4 Living Through a Staggering World: The Play of Signifiers in Early Psychosis in South India*

Ellen Corin, Rangaswami Thara, and
Ramachandran Padmavati

I was frightened without my knowledge ... confusion only increased and I couldn't control it ... the fear, only this fear, not anxiety, only some kind of fear ...

The experience of psychosis is permeated by fear and confusion, radiating through the perceived world of suffering persons, infiltrating relationships with themselves and others. These feelings give to ordinary things an aura of strangeness and, to use Tellenbach's (1983) words, transform the "atmospheric quality" of the world. In the narratives of psychotic people, expressions of distress entwine and interlace to form the texture of a shifting world of agony. These aspects of the psychotic person's world cannot be neglected when considering the role of culture in psychosis; from such a frame emerge the questions and responses posed in this chapter.

An investigation of psychotic experience forces us to confront difficult ethical questions: How do we speak about others' suffering without redoubling the lived violence by an interpretive violence anchored in the position of the "well-informed" researcher? How do we find a language that may constitute or preserve the frightening dimension of that experience without succumbing to its fascination or objectifying it? Can we ever be justified in soliciting narratives and asking questions of people who are so deeply immersed in a world of suffering? The first two questions raise epistemological and methodological issues that will be explored in this chapter. The third requires that we weigh our own personal or intellectual questioning against what it might signify for those from whom we seek answers.

This chapter is about subjective experience and how it is framed and articulated among people with schizophrenia in the cultural context of South India. It is a first attempt to analyze data gathered in a pilot research project conducted under the auspices of the Schizophrenia Research Foundation (SCARF) in Chennai (previously Madras). The data comprise narratives provided by patients recently diagnosed with schizophrenia, as well as by one member of each patient's family. Our aim is to understand how culture mediates psychotic experience. We seek to generate hypotheses that explain how culture may shape the evolution of psychotic illness. Testing these hypotheses is beyond the scope of the present work. For this, we await the results of prospective longitudinal research.

Rethinking the Course and Evolution of Schizophrenia

In Western psychiatry, the old idea that patients with schizophrenia were condemned to deterioration has given way to the realization that the course of schizophrenia is heterogeneous (McGlashan and Carpenter 1988). Among the many potential factors that contribute to this heterogeneity, it is critical to take into account how patients' reactions to their illness influence the course of the disorder (Ciompi 1980; Strauss 1986). Strauss and Estroff (1989) call schizophrenia an "I" disorder in order to underscore how it affects the core of the person and to convey the extent to which persons remain active in dealing with it. Heterogeneity of course is the rule at a cross-cultural level. Since the work of Henry B. M. Murphy (Murphy and Raman 1971; Murphy 1982), cross-cultural researchers have consistently validated clinicians' impressions that schizophrenia differs according to culture, with a better course observed in non-Western societies (see Hopper this volume). Yet the mechanisms responsible for these differences remain poorly understood (Sartorius, Jablensky, and Shapiro 1978; Sartorius, Jablensky, Korten, Ernberg, Anker, Cooper, and Day 1986; Leff, Sartorius, Jablensky, Korten, and Ernberg 1992). Unfortunately, much research in this area tends to project onto other societies what is known in the West about course and outcome. It is quite limiting to test only those variables shown to be associated with course in Western countries. More importantly, the very meaning of such variables is very often left unexamined, as Jenkins ably demonstrated in the case of expressed emotions (Jenkins 1991; Jenkins and Karno 1992). When broader notions such as "tolerance" or "social support" are invoked (Cooper and Sartorius 1977), there is little attempt to question their meaning or explore the conditions that might reinforce or diminish their presence in different societies.

Progress in understanding cross-cultural variations in the course of schizophrenia requires that research methodology be anchored in a deeper set of reflections about the processes whereby culture might shape the evolution of schizophrenia. Our basic assumption, in this regard, is that experience is the key mediating variable; we propose here that it is critical to understand the pathways through which certain aspects of the social and cultural frame affect that experience. To do so requires the development of a richly textured approach to the complexities of both "culture" and "experience." It demands that we understand the manner in which culture and experience interrelate in contexts marked by psychosis. And it demands of us that we find ways to articulate the relationships between them.

Walking a Thin Line

We hold to a view of culture as paradoxical, multilayered, and contradictory, drawing on advances in two distinct fields of inquiry – psychological anthropology and French psychoanalysis. Though rooted in different intellectual traditions and concerned with different substantive problems, both have criticized a naive psychologistic notion of the person as being ironically disconnected from that very person. And both have argued, instead, for the reintroduction of personal experience and the human speaking subject within a broader symbolic and cultural frame.[1] When people experience psychosis, it is likely that their manner of resorting to the associative chains that constitute their culture[2] is influenced by the peculiarity of their experience (see Lucas this volume). They may privilege the articulatory power of peripheral representations available in their culture. They may also reinterpret mainstream cultural idioms and images to give more weight to certain connotations that resonate with what they experience. One could expect that patients and family members mobilize different representations and associative chains according to their respective position toward psychosis.

Experience is not transparent for the experiencing person, perhaps even less so for those who try to decipher that person's experience. Experience is a flow: It unfolds through time and always remains behind what one can tell of it (Bruner 1986); hence, the unavoidable discrepancy between what people experience and what they can say about that experience. Access to another person's experience is, perforce, partial and elusive, not only because people conceal, but also because "everyone censors or represses, or may not be fully aware of or able to articulate, certain aspects of what has been experienced" (Bruner 1986:5).[3] It therefore appears somewhat naïve or even violent to pretend to understand directly (without mediation) the words and behaviors of another person. In psychosis, interpretive difficulties are aggravated by a double context of reference; by which we refer to the context of the culture and of the interpersonal world of the patient, and those of his or her inner reality. For people suffering from psychosis, these difficulties are amplified because much of that experience lies in the realm of the unspeakable, the inexpressible. It is narrated through blanks and suspension points – conveyed through a particular rhythm of discourse characterized by hesitations and contradictions.

According to the European tradition of phenomenological psychiatry, major psychotic disorders alter the deep structure of a person's experience. For this school, inspired by the later writings of Hüsserl,[4] experience is not equivalent to an empirical reality that could be directly accessed and described. It refers to the basic spatial and temporal coordinates of a person's existence; to the dimensions that underlie his or her mode of being within the world; to the correlative qualities of his or her perceived, intentional world. This nonempirical reality is only accessible through phenomenological reduction, that is, through bracketing both common-sense and scientific knowledge. At the same time, experience is manifested through the empirical details of existence. Understanding therefore unfolds in the give and take between attention to the most mundane details of existence and sensitivity to the underlying basic coordinates of experience.

For phenomenological psychiatrists such as Binswanger (1970), Tellenbach (1979), and Blankenburg (1991), concrete behaviors, feelings, and narratives of psychiatric patients are understood as expressions of a basic alteration in their lived worlds. Phenomenological psychiatry encourages a particular way of listening to words and narratives that seeks to comprehend or grasp these altered feelings and disturbed perceptions. But it has two limitations: First, there has been scant interest in the dynamics of these basic alterations in experience; second, there has been little recognition of the embeddedness of personal experience in larger social and cultural frames. One must find ways to articulate these two facets of experience: its singular, most private aspect and its interpersonal, collective dimension.[5]

In postulating that experience contstitutes a mediating link between culture and the evolution of psychiatric disorders, we argue that transcultural psychiatry must consider schizophrenia "from the inside," that is to say, in relation to how it affects a person's self-experience and position toward the world. Experience, we believe, is constituted of affects, cognitive elements, and meaning. The turmoil and voids created at their junction provide a kind of energy that mobilizes particular associative cultural chains within patients, family members, and members of their immediate social environment.

Obeyesekere (1990) has explored the personal side of the transformation accomplished by culture. He hypothesizes a "work of culture" through which "unconscious motives are transformed into cultural symbols" (1990:56). Inspired by Ricoeur (1976) and Turner (1967),

Obeyesekere (1990:280) views symbols as rooted in diverse areas of life that produce "paradoxical, ambiguous, overdetermined and often contradictory meanings." "Personal symbols" are preconstructed forms that are isomorphic with personal experience. They are simultaneously personal and cultural, private and public; they provide a basis for self-reflection at the personal level and for communication with others at the cultural level. In this respect, they are amenable to a double hermeneutic that provides the person with options, choices, and leeway for manipulation. Obeyesekere argues that such personal symbols can be integrated into dynamics that are dominated either by a regressive orientation (when the individual remains trapped within personal conflicts and problems), or a progressive orientation open to reflexivity and elaboration.

When examining the role of culture in articulating personal experience of psychosis, we situate ourselves within a double perspective: On the cultural side, we examine how symbols referred to by individual persons articulate a larger framework of meanings; and on a personal side, we try to understand how the use of these self-same symbols operates at a personal level. In order to formulate hypotheses regarding the personal significance of recurrent signifiers or processes in patients' narratives, we were guided by their resonance with ideas developed by psychoanalysts familiar with the world of psychosis.[6]

Questions of Method

A comprehensive understanding of the work of culture in schizophrenia requires longitudinal studies of the processes whereby social and cultural contexts frame the experience of psychosis in particular settings and at particular times. This pilot project is limited to the generation of hypotheses that relate to aspects of such a larger frame. It builds on the idea that the early development of psychotic experience is a critical period for understanding how cultural referents and interpersonal dynamics may shape experience, and thereby, shape the course of schizophrenia. In those early moments of illness, what dominates is still a sense of movement, alteration, and flux; a feeling of strangeness and alienation; a quest for meaning or action triggered by these various transformations. Experience is not yet frozen into the familiar blocks of well-established roles. This study is thus well placed to explore how cultural signifiers are appropriated and eventually transformed by the people – patients and those around them – who are intimately involved in the experience of psychosis; by the same token it can explore the contribution of cultural dynamics in framing and modifying the interactions between patients and family members.

A pilot research project was conducted in Chennai, South India. Eleven patients in their twenties, recently diagnosed with schizophrenia,[7] were interviewed by a trained clinician. One family member of each patient was also interviewed by a different clinician.[8] All patients had been treated with neuroleptic medication but most of them responded poorly, despite the short duration of their problems. Most of the patients were attending the day care facility at the Schizophrenia Research Foundation (SCARF) in Chennai, and all interviews were conducted in this setting. Patients and relatives were interviewed in the language of their choice (English, Tamil, or Hindi). Interviews were recorded, transcribed, and then translated into English by translators. The quality of the translation was verified by one of us. Analogous sets of pilot narratives were also collected in Montreal and Toronto. We have focused our analysis in this paper on seven of the eleven pairs of narratives, chosen because they were all young men, thereby enhancing the homogeneity of our sample. Five of the patients were Hindu, one was Muslim (S1), and one was a Christian (S2). Narratives suggest the pervasive power of Hindu thought and Hindu signifiers in all patients' and relatives' narratives, including Muslim and Christian; they also indicate the fluidity of boundaries between these religious frames. In our interpretation, we therefore chose to focus on Hindu references.

Narratives were collected using an open-ended interview grid developed in Montreal by Corin, Lesage, and King. Called the "Turning Point/Period Interview" (TPI), following an expression borrowed from Strauss and colleagues (1985), it aims to reconstruct the main moments of transformation of experience that are associated with the early phase of psychosis, as perceived by key actors. The TPI focuses on the perceived evolution of signs, meanings, and practices before the first hospitalization or the first psychiatric diagnosis. The grid specifies areas to be explored but leaves open the formulation of questions. It is a crucial aspect of the methodology that these questions are worded and couched in a way that is determined by the unfolding narrative. That is, the questions are not preordained. For each period in the evolution of the illness, we reconstruct perceived signs, behaviors and feelings, meanings and reactions, coping strategies and help-seeking, as well as modifications of interpersonal relationships and social activities. Patients and family members were interviewed separately and encouraged to express their evolving experience in their own terms. Narratives were submitted to two parallel types of analysis. The first aimed to compare the interview dialogue with the published psychiatric and psychosocial literature, particularly with respect to symptoms and coping. We coded seven categories of variables: signs and symptoms, coping, explanatory models, reactions, help-seeking, the social network, and context. Subcategories were defined by moving back-and-forth between the literature and a content analysis of narratives collected in Montreal, Toronto, and Chennai. NUD*IST software allowed us to extract and compare the content of excerpts that related to variables across patients' and family members' narratives, or across cultures.[9] The second level of analysis was more qualitative. It involved the ordering of significant excerpts in three main columns: 1) subjective experience of the patient, comments about him, coping; 2) others' reactions, descriptions and comments about family, friends, or neighbours, help-seeking and comments about various sources of help; 3) all comments and hypotheses regarding etiology and meaning. The excerpts were organized to retain the sequence in which they arose within the narrative, while at the same time allowing us to identify temporal and conceptual associations. Colors were used to identify significant topics crossing various categories of variables, like reference to religion or spirituality, or withdrawal. This organization of the material enabled us to identify semantic organizing nodes, recurring themes within or between narratives and their contexts of occurrence. Their place within culture was explored through the literature, discussion with colleagues, and complementary ethnographic research.

Anthropologists are more aware now than ever before of their own participation in the creation of the data they are collecting (Crapanzano 1994). That the interviews were collected by clinicians within a clinical setting familiar to the patient is likely to have oriented the narratives, perhaps distorting a polysemic, fluid reality in the direction of a more unidimensional psychiatric account. On the other hand, this familiar setting provided the patients with a sense of reassurance, which supported them in disclosing and commenting on very private aspects of their experience. The richness, diversity, and personal character of their accounts suggest that the setting did not greatly inhibit the work of memory and reconstruction.

We have chosen here not to conduct in-depth analysis of individual narratives or to explore the idiosyncratic aspect of people's experience of psychosis. There were three reasons for this. The first one is conceptual. Access to the experience is always mediated through language and culture. In order to minimize the risk of projecting our explicit and implicit categories on other people's experience, it is necessary to identify the characteristics of the cultural idioms available to the actors: recurrences, contrasts, and associations that have to be examined across narratives. From that perspective, cultural hermeneutics is a prerequisite to single-case analysis. The second reason is ethical and relates to our reticence in appropriating singular narratives in our own work and publishing them in all their intricacies. The third reason is more pragmatic. It stems from the limits of our material but also, maybe, from anthropological approaches for accessing the subjective face of the experience – particularly in the case of psychosis. The risk of injecting our own words and sense of coherence within the narrative is particularly great.

However, our choice of analytic method also entails a violence toward individual narratives that are considered for what they reveal of a cultural idiom rather than for what they attempt to express of an always singular experience. The first step of our analysis entailed identifying words, sentences, and expressions through which individuals gave voice to the subjective experiences of their disorder. We were alert to descriptions of the strategies they developed in order to deal with suffering and fear. Pivotal experiences that appeared, to us, to be central to each patient's story, were singled out for analytic attention. The second step was to compare narratives to identify the main configurations common to all patients that organized their individual narratives. This comparison also revealed broader cultural themes invoked by the participants in this research project.

A complementary analysis conducted on narratives provided by family members focused on their attempts to deal with their relative and his psychotic illness. We were particularly interested in the attitude of "tolerance" of psychosis that has been ascribed to South Asian families in the cross-cultural literature (Waxler 1979).

While focusing essentially on patients' narratives, our (researchers') narrative was constructed with the aim of drawing attention to convergences and discrepancies between patients' and families' perspectives. Thus, it begins with the disruption introduced by psychosis: While patients are immersed within what is occurring, family members attempt to deal with their own anxiety and feelings of strangeness. In the course of this analysis, we identified three themes that appeared to us to be central to patients' narratives: a quest for significance, an appeal to religious referents, and the construction of a withdrawn space. We examined how these themes were addressed in family members' narratives. Family members' narratives will be the subject of another study. Here, we are limited to evoking a few themes illustrative of contrasts with patients' narratives. We then focused on the "cultural" elements mentioned by patients and family members and explored the associative chains in which these elements seem to participate. This examination led us to draw a tentative picture of the supranarrative frame in which individual narratives are embedded. This supranarrative frame is the focus of the last section of the chapter. We also formulated tentative hypotheses regarding the subjective significance of recurring themes in patients' narratives.

The Alteration of Experience in Early Schizophrenia

Narratives clustered around key experiences often generated a cascade of other problems or symptoms. Though weighted in singular ways, these experiences recurred in most stories. The most common was a feeling of fear – even terror – that threatened the core of the person. It derived from a deep alteration of patients' sense of self and of the world. Associative chains extended out in tangled, intersecting paths from that key experience. They pointed in three directions: a sense of the hostility of the outside world; a feeling that personal limits and boundaries had become porous; and a confusion that attacked the core of the person and undermined the possibility of that person forming an image of him or herself. Fear and distress were also manifest through alterations of bodily experience.

"Nothing. Only the Fear was There."

Fear often colored the entire story and sometimes threatened to engulf the person. In some narratives, fear appeared as a vague, insistent feeling. It escaped rational explanation. It had no clear focus:[10]

...I was frightened without my knowledge.... (S1)
...a kind of fear within myself, a kind of fear which could not be disclosed to others...a kind of fear without knowing... (S8)
...I had some kind of fear even without my knowing what it was. Without being able to do any work, I was preoccupied by that only.... (S11)

In other narratives, fear was more explicitly related to particular motives: a fear that others could cause harm; an impression that the social environment was hostile and threatening. Fear was also linked to the impression that personal frontiers had become blurred and invaded. People were frightened of becoming absorbed in a numbness of mind – lost in a world where meaning had become indecipherable, elusive, and shifting, without stable referents. And there was the fear that arose from a perceived failure to respond to those normative expectations that define one's place within society. Such fears attacked the core of the person, announcing death and madness:

...A fear of death...afraid that I would become mad actually...my energy was driven out of me.... (S2)
...A kind of fear came, a fear came as if all males would die.... (S9)

An Altered Atmospheric Quality

A number of patients became trapped in a hostile, inquisitive world in which they felt continuously under observation, surrounded and invaded by the gaze of others – a world in which they were commented upon and deciphered by innumerable others:

> ...I thought everybody was looking at me. I was feeling ashamed and I was self-conscious...I used to go by bus. I used to think everybody is looking at me, observing my movements, thinking that I am doing something wrong, something is wrong with me.... (S8)
> ...I felt everybody was doing wrong to me. Everybody is bad and only does bad things.... (S1)
> ...I also felt that others were looking at me differently. If anyone said anything, I would feel as if it had a double meaning.... (S10)
> ...Then if they spat, I would have a kind of fear within myself.... (S11)

We were struck by the contrast between the feeling that others possessed a knowledge about them, and the feeling of uncertainty about the content of this knowledge, as if the person felt absorbed within somebody else's narrative concealing an essential and mysterious truth:

> ...All were looking differently – wrongly – at me. They would keep their hands here and there, like that, fear came.... (S9)

Loose Frontiers

Parallel to this was a feeling of transparency, a feeling that others had the power to penetrate one's inner thoughts and feelings. The individual's intimacy was penetrated and known by indefinite others:

> ...Whatever I was thinking, they would hear. I was receiving double meaning messages, both positive and negative...soon, they became negative...I was frightened that they would do some harm.... (S10)

This could be associated with a deliberate paralysis of thinking:

> ...Whatever I was thinking, they would hear....I try not to think the way I used to do before. This time, I do not think because I feel that everyone will know what I am thinking.... (S10)

And it could evolve into a feeling of "transitivity" whereby they felt penetrated and directed by alien messages and thoughts. Some saw their own thinking or their own story reflected in the others' words. One narrative illustrates how personal frontiers could become so porous that self and other seemed to mirror one another continuously. This person recounted that his problems began with an urge to speak – a failure to follow common rules that organize what may be told, to whom, and when. In fact he began talking to everybody, without discrimination:

> ...I realized that I'm going wrong somewhere, the way I talk and all that was wrong....I started talking to everyone...to people who walk in the roads and

the ones in the company, with the ones I liked and the ones I disliked.... I was
talking without my knowledge....   (S4)

He experienced this at a bodily level as a feeling of outburst, overflow:

...I felt as if my head was going to blow, I felt like tearing my shirt and all
that....   (S4)

At the same time, personal frontiers became blurred. He appeared to
interiorize the outside world in his mimicking of a famous actor's style:

...I was acting like MGR (a famous actor turned politician) and like Rajinikanth
(another famous actor). I used to act like them....   (S4)

Yet he also saw himself reflected in the outside world:

...I felt able to see the things I thought in other people eyes. Somehow, it would
be visible... that's why I am not able to do anything....   (S4)

His personal story was mounted as a spectacle to the world:

...Even in TV, they used to show a film like the way I was, exactly the way I used
to be... something like my life, my story....   (S4)

This attack on distinctiveness also concerned his bodily envelope. Bodily parts seemed to become disconnected as if he was dissolving into the
world:

...My neck shrunk and I felt as it didn't stick to my body. I felt my body has
become very sensitive. I had goose pimples all over my body. I felt as if my foot
was not firm on the ground. When I drank water, I felt as if I was carried away
floating. I felt as if I was dragged to the cemetery....   (S4)

At another level, the violence of the voices echoed the extremities of verbal
and symbolic violence that had been exerted against him in his childhood:

...A voice would be constantly talking. It would say: "Your life is over, your fate
is done." Things like that. He (the patient's father) used to always scold me. Even
from my childhood... He doesn't talk as if I am his son, as if I'm somebody else's
son... "You are the cause of everything. Why don't you die?" And all that, he
used to say....   (S4)

Confusion

Feelings of confusion emerged in parallel with diffuse perceptions of
change:

...I was very troubled... something had changed... I was at home. I did not
do anything – sleep, eat, watch TV – I would be thinking of my problems....
                                                                              (S10)

It was clearly linked to the perception of being trapped in a hostile, frightening world:

...I think that everybody's plotting against me. I feel frightened, confused. I am confused. I think my life is finished.... (S10)

Equally confusion could generate a sense of fear:

...Suddenly thought changes and you will get negative thoughts and slowly it becomes negative and negative and you get fear.... (S8)

Patients' comments about their confusion pointed to a drift of significance at the very least, at worst, a wrecking of meaning which engulfed the self. At a simplest level, they talked of a difficulty controlling their thoughts:

...I was not in control of my thoughts, some thoughts were coming, I was hearing voices.... (S8)
...The confusion only increased and I could not control it...only physically I was present but mentally, my thoughts were not constant.... (S1)

Reality would become ambiguous:

...I started feeling that everyone did that (spitting, laughing). It could be real or unreal...real, maybe 50 percent, some 50 percent false.... (S11)

Confusion could come to absorb a person's whole attention. It could permeate the whole field of language, its categories, and the exercise of discernment in relation to the world. Everything would become indeterminate. The self, itself, was thrown into question, as if basic identity landmarks had gone missing:

...I was feeling everything is wrong. Everything was in a different angle actually....It's running. The mental thoughts are running. Would it be positive or negative? That kind of fear I had actually...I don't have any direction. So, it is a big problem.... (S2)

One narrative illustrates how a feeling of general confusion could develop from relatively minor discomfort:

...First, you are positive, you are confident. Then suddenly, doubts come in your mind, you can't do this, what is this – you will get confused, you are not sure about something and suddenly you feel you are not capable of doing things, then you feel afraid.... (S8)

His narrative indicates the pathways through which confusion progressively invades his life, his relationship to the world, and his sense of self. In his recollection, problems started with strange thoughts coming in to his mind, accompanied by a sense that other people were looking at him in a way that implied something was wrong in him:

> ... I used to think everybody is looking at me, observing my movements, thinking that I'm doing something wrong ... something is wrong with me.... (S8)

Initial small doubts grew – indeterminately, diffusely – to invade a larger reality:

> ... So, I thought lot of things were wrong and lot of things were right, but I never knew what was exactly wrong or right.... (S8)

And in order to resist this progressive indeterminacy of reality, he recalled having tried to generate a surrogate normative frame:

> ... I was making my own rules, thinking all sorts of things that were not sure. I was imagining that I shouldn't do this, I shouldn't do that.... I couldn't think which would say, "Oh, you can do this, you can do that."... (S8)

His image of himself vacillated:

> ... Some thoughts were making me ashamed of myself ... under inferiority complex ... some thoughts inducing superiority complex. Both sides thoughts were there.... (S8)

This tension ultimately became blurred as if everything was collapsing in indeterminacy:

> ... Now, I'm worried but I am not able to realize what my real talents are, my level of intelligence, what career would suit me. I'm not able to judge, that is my major problem. I'm not able to know whether I am normal, this is my normal self. I'm not able to identify my normal self.... Before, I had a picture of myself, I knew this is me; but now ... (S8)

In his words, what was lost was the presence of what he called a "Third," who could guarantee his existence and give him a sense of consistency:

> ... I'm not able to look out as a third person and say whether this is it, you are this, you have such capacity. I'm not able to understand myself like what a third person may be able to see from looking at me from outside. I'm not able to take over a subjective view of myself. (S8)

This person's narrative illustrates what Blankenburg (1991) refers to as a "loss of the natural evidence" (confer Sass this volume), an alienation from the world of commonsense that destroys the ability to think.

Afflictions of the Embodied Self

Narratives evoked the loss of mundane behavioral markers that frame the lives of common people and connect them to a shared cultural world:

... I wasn't taking food properly, or taking a bath, and I didn't go to the mosque for some days.   (S1)
... I never changed my clothes, took a bath. I didn't notice my body smelling....   (S2)

Analogous language expressed nostalgia for normalcy:

... I want to become active like before. I feel the difference. I just want to take a rest, eat, sleep, wake up, take bath in the morning and evening, read the newspaper. Just read the newspaper for one hour, take bath in morning and evening, then sleep for some time, waken and go for worship. Then, I can throw off everything... my old problem and become all right....   (S1)

Family members' narratives converged with patients' narratives in emphasizing the paramount importance associated in India with this kind of alteration:

... He was not as he used to be before. He was talking in a different way. He looked as if he hadn't taken food for many days. He didn't cut his hair, he had a beard....   (R2)
He would not take care of himself, not comb his hair; he would hurriedly eat his food while it was not very hot. He would drink water, coffee, very fast, drinking it all at once. He did not wear dress properly, he wouldn't shave...   (R11)
He was not relating well. He was alone, he didn't take food along with the family members....   (R1)

More generally, narratives revealed that patients' perspectives and family members' perspectives acknowledged the importance of fulfilling role expectations and in expressing intense grief about the patient's failure to do so.

Some of the excerpts we have cited illustrate how the alteration of self can be experienced through bodily sensations. Explaining that he felt everybody was against him, one person said: "If I went out, I felt as if my head was held tightly" (S11). S4's narrative, cited previously, indicated that a sense of dissolution of self ran parallel to a disintegration of his bodily schema. We formed the impression that the fragility of the self experienced by patients was inscribed directly on their body – corporeal metaphors were compensating for difficulty in articulating the experience at a symbolic level:

... My energy was drawn out of me. I felt much frightened, everything was a very hopeless situation.... I was emaciated very much. My knees were loosened – no blood in my body....   (S2)

In the same narrative, fear of death was associated with an sense irritation within the head. In another, a sense of the impending destruction of the world ("as if all males would die") was incorporated into bodily perceptions:

...At that time, I felt my head was burnt, things inside the head got burnt....I know because my head had become weak....   (S9)

Fighting Chaos, Tracing Borders

Narratives testified to the extent of damage associated with psychosis, in the face of which both patients and family members fought for meaning and significance, in an attempt to reconstruct personal and interpersonal spaces in which normal life would be possible. Their positions sometimes converged; at other times they would oppose each other. Here, we examine three main areas: the search for significance, the resort to religious referents, and the construction of a withdrawn position.

Causality and Significance

Even when problems developed incrementally or imperceptibly, the narratives we collected from patients who came for psychiatric consultation indicated that at some point, things came to a head, and all concerned – patients, family members – became overwhelmed by feelings of estrangement, alienation, and anxiety. At this point, the explanatory models of illness they described were fluid and shifting. We formed the impression that explanatory models, per se, were less important than a more fundamental quest for meaning characterized by the fluidity and fragility of meaning rather than by its content or product.

In fact, classical etiologies calling to local systems of beliefs occupied only a minor place in patients' narratives. Just two people briefly referred to "black magic" or "evil spirits" as possible causes for their problems. They mentioned these causes as personal guesses in the course of a process of self-questioning that attempted to clarify the feeling of alienation they were experiencing:

...I was okay and all that, I used to feel. Then only would I feel that someone would have planted some black magic....Would my relatives have done that? I used to think and feel worried....
...I think I have evil spirits in my body....   (S4)

In the second case, the patient later mentioned that a healer thought he was possessed by a female spirit. This resonated with past experiences involving the blurring of gender distinctions:

... My face had changed into a female face. The healer said that I was possessed by a woman.... Everyone was teasing me. Even in college, they were ragging me.... In college, one boy used to say that I was a girl.... (S10)

In the first of these two cases, that of a young man who felt harshly rejected by his father, recourse to a cultural etiology allowed him to formulate a personal hypothesis, though tentatively so:

... I had fits. My mother gets possessed sometimes. I don't know whether I was possessed or had fits.... (S4)

At another level, patients also mentioned scrutinizing their life history in search for the cause of what they were now experiencing. This reflection emerges either in particular childhood conditions (S4, as follows), or in something they should have done (S10, 9, and 11):

... I don't know whether my life has been spoilt because of him (a violent father).... (S4)
... I think that I have sinned. When I was young, I would stone and kill chameleons. I would hurt dogs and cats with a catapult. All these sins are now troubling me.... (S10)
... When I went home, there was a doll, a boy doll was there and I burnt it.... A kind of fear came, a fear came as if all males would die because I burnt it.... (S9)
... My neighbor saw me doing something and voiced the problem to the whole neighborhood.... (S11)

It is worth reiterating, however, that an etiological quest did not occupy a prominent position in the stories of the patients we interviewed. When causes were mentioned, they did not coalesce around a stable range of meanings; they unfolded along multiple pathways as if they had become subsumed within the general turmoil that characterized the patients' life. For others, such as S8, this form of questioning appears outside of reach:

... I never had an overall view of what was going on. Always, I was reacting to the incidents subjectively.... (S8)

More important were the larger questions about the significance (not just the cause) of what they were experiencing. Three narratives were especially illustrative in this respect. They suggest that significance is prospective rather than retrospective – indicative of a project rather than a cause. Meanings were highly personal, while at the same time building on collective signifiers available in the culture.

In a first example (S1), the person attempted to inscribe his experience within his vision of existence as built on Hindu philosophy. He recalled the fear he experienced from the very beginning of the illness and which persisted, for him, as a cardinal symptom:

> ... I thought, what is the problem I have got? Why am I like this? I can't understand anything. Why am I like this? ...   (S1)

He looked for a response in ideas of balance and compensation:

> ... Only recently I realized that I'm suffering now to live better in the future. It's to be well in life that I'm suffering now. I have suffered well in life – so, I want to live and show how well I can live. I have shown how bad a man can suffer – I have shown it to God. I've maintained a contact with God.... Furthermore, loss here and loss there, gain here and loss there, in the other world.... So I should live well and show to the world and again in the other world also I should live well....   (S1)

In a similar vein, another patient commented:

> ... I am a devotee of Lord Shiva. They say that if one is a devotee of Lord Shiva, then he will be 'mental.' So, I think I have Shiva Dosham....   (S10)

He saw the problems not so much as caused by Lord Shiva. Rather he saw them as a consequence of his own devotion, and in himself as manifesting the ambiguous character of Shiva. This allowed him both to acknowledge and to reshape positively the feeling of strangeness he experienced.

A third example illustrates a more idiosyncratic resort to cultural referents. Central to S2's quest for meaning was an enigmatic "vision" he had experienced at several points of his life. The vision conveyed a message or a "call" he was unable to decipher, but that was to leave a mark on the whole of his life. The first of these visions antedated the appearance of his initial problems. It was tinged with a sense of seduction and threat, as well as a blend of fear and confusion, which came to dominate the rest of his life:

> ... I was going to my church and I saw a man. He was very beautiful, very powerful. He looked like Moses. He was filled fully with an orange light... walking with a bird in his hand and he was saying, 'Yes, Yes,' something like that. That time, some strong force attacked me. A white light was inside my throat. He sent the powerful beam of light.... From then on, everything started decreasing. I started smoking excessively. So the problem is, I don't have that light....   (S2)

Later he described his reaction to the vision, thus:

> ... I thought I'm going to be some special person, some saint or something like that....   (S2)

The message nonetheless remained enigmatic and its seductive appeal he believed concealed a destructive power:

...He tried to communicate something through his silence. It was a very sweet experience but after that, slowly it started like a virus. Now, it has become very bad.... (S2)

The patient further explained how he resisted the enigmatic call with his whole body when the vision reappeared a few years later:

...Then the white light spread in my heart. Then again, an orange light came in my head but both were rejected. When the light comes, the body never accepts...Now, I feel I have lost everything. I have nothing. That kind of fear I have.... (S2)

The third time he had the vision, the figure of the man appeared to be contaminated by the degradation of his own experience:

...He was very old and all. He said, "Go! Go!" or something like that.... (S2)

This vision, he asserted, was responsible for the drift of his later existence:

...Yes, it totally changed my life. I was planning to become an engineer. I couldn't study. When I pick up the book, I would feel as if thorns are picking up my head.... (S2)

He continued to struggle with the significance of such an enigmatic message:

...I don't think he has harmed; he was full of love.... (S2)

Later he added:

...I never felt secure because I thought somebody is going to kill me, some religious person. (S2)

The centrality of a quest for significance in S2's life is further illustrated by his wide-ranging reading: religious, scientific, psychological, books about "creative thinking," even a study of "bodily language," which could help him to decipher others' character and intentions.

The data we report here represented a deep inquiry into the meaning of his existence rather than a search for the cause of his problems. The inquiry acknowledged the exceptional character of what was experienced. Perhaps it expressed resistance to a sense of confusion experienced by most of the patients. Discounting the value of this kind of quest from the start by calling it "delusional" is to miss the point. What is relevant is to explore how such a quest articulates the experience in a deeper sense and transforms it. It is now our task to examine which interpersonal, social, and cultural conditions could be influential in that regard. Etiologies calling to local representations and beliefs take a greater place in relatives' narratives. All but one family member mentions one or, more often, several possible causes of the problems. They pertain to two main areas. The most frequent explanations evoke black magic and evil spirits.

Somebody has done something to my son because of some business rivalry. We thought that: father death and all that ... because we are well off   (R9)
He used to say that a demon is coming in the backyard. ... He is not the person he used to be before ... looking as if he were possessed ... We thought, he was frightened by something ... we thought it was a kind of possession. ...   (R4)

Another strand of causality evoked by relatives pertains to astrology. It explains patients' problems by the position of inauspicious planets, therefore inscribing the drift of patients' life within an ordered world and a cosmic frame.

The astrologer said: 'his time is no good.' Saturn is within wrong side. He will be alright in a due course of things. ...   (R11)

Inscribing the Experience within a Religious Frame

Patients' narratives drew heavily on religious signifiers, as was also the case in a study conducted in Montreal (Corin and Lauzon 1992). At one level, religion provided a set of representations that helped to inscribe a personal, alienating experience into a larger drawing that transcended individual hazards. Religion equipped people with a range of symbols that they could appropriate to the context of their own quest for significance. A number of the excerpts from narratives quoted above exemplified how patients could borrow elements from a range of philosophical and religious conceptions that they could adapt to their personal world. This appeared, to us, to provide some stable reference points. For example, after an exegesis on the balance between well-being and suffering, between current and future life, S1 concluded:

... I have shown it to God. I have maintained a contact with God. ...   (S1)

In other cases, religious referents appear to be absorbed into the general flux of the patient's life. For example, in S2's narrative mentioned previously, there was a failure to resolve the enigmatic character of his call, and a failure to insert his experiences within a stable collective frame. These develop, in parallel, a progressive accentuation of the negative side of what was first ambiguous or indeterminate.

S9's narrative, on the other hand, illustrates how the protective function of a particular religious attitude reversed itself. He presented his story as one of total absorption within an image of God that he contemplated continually:

...I used to look at God's photo always, Pilhar's photo. They took me to a priest. He gave me a Goddess photo again, I started looking at that.... (S9)

This meditation appeared at first as an attempt to find a fixed reference point in a shifting world dominated by fear. Rather than resolving his difficulties, however, it accentuates the problems that then grew out of control:

...After that again I started to look at Meenakshi photo for many days....It increased, it increased....Sometimes I would be looking at the nose, suddenly looked at it at the eyes. Soon, my confusion started...as if I should look at it repeatedly again and again.... (S9)

It came to submerge any other interests:

...I didn't like anybody. Only God is enough. I started disliking family members.... (S9)

Ultimately, his absorption in a religious universe did not protect him against the emotions aroused by his father's death and, at that point, the protective system collapsed:

...After that, I started disliking gods. I said, "All Gods should die," and burnt all the photos.... Things inside the head got burnt. I was angry toward everybody – because father had died. (S9)

At a second level, religion provided an organizing frame that gave direction to people's lives, and ensured the ethical quality of human existence. Patients sought to interiorize or embody this frame through the repetition of gestures or rituals. One explained that his first reaction to the fear experienced at the beginning of his illness led him to the Muslim religion:

...I read the Quran, I was fasting, brushing my teeth with a mishma stick. People said that my memory would feel improved...I was going to the mosque almost every day.... (S1)

Feeling immersed within uncertainty and the drift of significance in his world, another recounted:

...I thought, What to do? That I join an ashram...I was interested only in joining an ashram because I never had a good idea of a good public life....I thought of going to an ashram and concentrate on something. Spiritually, I can do something good, I thought.... (S2)

In this case, his father mediated his son's relationship within a religious moral frame by introducing him to a religious person who played the role of confidant and advisor:

There was only one friend – whom my father told he is the only use for me. He was in the mosque conducting rituals. So I used to meet him and talk to him. . . . I used to disclose my problems to him regularly.   (S2)

In patients' narratives, family members were often mentioned as having been active in helping their sick relative to incorporate his experience within a religious frame. Family members privileged the collective, ritual dimension of religion and its reintegrative potential. They often mediated the celebration of rituals and recitation of prayers, creating a kind of protective web around the patient. For example, S8 presented himself as being engulfed within a general drift in which all certainties had become uncertain, so much so that he was unable even to form any stable image of himself. He reported that his mother took him daily to the temple and encouraged his devotion, thereby helping him to resist feelings of demoralization and the huge turmoil he was experiencing:

. . . Mother told me to read prayers. She was making me very devotional and taking me to temple daily . . . go to pray to the God there, just write and write prayers. It was useful. I felt moralization was there. I was getting moralized. I started believing in God . . . and I got back to my devotions. . . .   (S8)

In S4's narrative, the patient feared that his world would collapse, but his mother set up a kind of ritual safety net.

. . . A voice would be constantly saying, "Your life is over, your fate is gone." . . . I used to tell my mother and she used to do some pooja for that. Now, she takes me to temples. . . .   (S4)

He then appropriated his mother's practical religious intervention in his own way:

. . . My father and my sisters notice, "That he never used to talk to anyone before like this, but now he talks to everyone, goes to temples and sleeps. . . . He didn't like to go to temples but now, he sleeps there." . . . I used to go and sleep in a place where there is peace and silence. . . .

S9 also reported that his parents took him to priests and returned to their homeland to carry out rituals. He commented that "only when I went to temple did I become all right."

Family mediation was sometimes met with mixed feelings and reactions. Earlier, we mentioned S10's recollection of the failure of various ritual treatments attempted by his family, his father's friends, and neighbors:

...Before going to the doctor, they took me to a sanyasi....They did a lot of things. During the recital of the mantras, I used to shout at them, tried to beat them....   (S10)

The patient also recounted the parallel attempts by his mother and sister to create the kind of "security web" referred to previously:

...My sister would go to the temple to pray for me....My mother prays for me at the temple....   (S10)

He presented himself as quite distant from these attempts. If religion could offer him support, it was in providing him with a role he could enter in for survival:

...After that (his parents' death), I can beg at the temple....   (S10)

However, near the end of his narrative he indicated his desire to engage in a ritual treatment, but with the participation of his father who used to react very negatively to these problems:

...I feel frightened, confused. So I think that I should go to a faith healer. I will plan to go soon. My father has to take me....   (S10)

Family members' narratives confirm the importance they attach to religious rituals as a way to heal their ill relative. They also evoke the importance that faith in God and laying their fate in God's hands has for themselves. It helps them to detach from the situation, to confront heir own suffering and to keep on supporting the patient.

We have the belief that he will become all right. Anything is in God's will. Our only consolation is God and no else.   (R11)
I used to only pray. I had little confidence that it would become little better, that God would not let us down. We had done no harm to anybody. So he would be definitively all right.   (R10)

Taking a Distance: Withdrawal to Protect an Inner Space

All patients' narratives showed evidence of one form or another of withdrawal from the outside world. The more explicit form of withdrawal involved a change in behavior, activity, and social contacts. Sleeping and lying down came to occupy more and more of the patient's time. Sleep became a refuge – a place for forgetting. It embodied retreat:

...I will sleep as long as possible. I wouldn't think of anything....   (S2)
...Now, as I go home, I go to sleep. As soon as I go home....   (S4)

...I get up in the morning, immediately I want to go back to sleep. I am escaping from the situation.... (S8)
...Somewhere inside the house, I would sleep, cover myself and sleep....I would not like going out and all. I would sit with my head bent. I was not able to see anyone face to face.... (S11)

Withdrawal could derive from fear of the outside world or, perhaps, a defensive reaction toward a hostile world, as a means of enclosing private space:

...I don't have any friends, feeling detached from father, mother, sister, because from the time I burnt the doll, from that time onwards, I was having a kind of fear.... (S9)
...I was always thinking of who would shout at me at college....Voices would tease me, scold me, that I could not bear. But I was afraid of shouting back. So I imagined that I was shouting back at times in my mind.... (S10)

Retreat could be an intentional stance adopted by the person, or a larger attitude of inner detachment which may evoke the parents' attitude mentioned previously:

...I wanted to be left alone.... (S1)

After referring to his lack of basic knowledge, S8 said,

...I sit patiently, quietly, and wait. Since I don't have that much general knowledge, thoughts, I'm able to feel patient, be patient and sit quietly; I would go home, think about that only, feel about that.... (S11)

Family members would encourage this movement largely because of their own fear of neighbors' reactions:

...Mother said, 'We can stay here. We can live our life here itself and we don't need to go out and live alone to reach the other world.'...My mother asked me not to leave the home. (R1)
Always, they watch me and observe me: 'Don't get out often.'... (R11)

This gives the impression of a collusion between two attitudes arising from different motivations. However, patients tended to react negatively to this kind of pressure and would refuse to comply with such an injunction coming from outside themselves.

Several patients construct their withdrawal within a religious frame which legitimated their retreat. Thus, S4 found peace and silence by sleeping in temples, and S9 took refuge in the pooja room when he felt overwhelmed by a fear that others want him to die. Religion sometimes offered a moral space and a physical space of withdrawal, which could be used to justify extreme forms of retreat:

... I felt that living in this world is a waste. So, I thought I should live a simple life, give the share money I have to some poor people. I wanted to buy books related to religion and give to people who are not aware of it.... I wanted to stay in a hut and earn one day and spend for seven days with that: eat and rest, at time do worship, fasting, read Quran....   (S1)

On another level, patients' references to a "secret" could be seen in terms of an inner psychic space, sheltered from others' intrusion, malevolence, or curiosity. Protecting this space was, in part, a reaction to a more global feeling of shame. However, keeping things secret also served to protect a private space necessary for taming and elaborating what is occurring. In this case, inner detachment took the guise of reserve:

... I didn't tell it to anyone. I was hiding it from them.... Friends didn't ask. I was experiencing within myself....   (S1)
... I was not doing that well in studies ... but I never told them.... I started feeling shy, thought people were looking at me. I was more sensitive, started to become more and more reserved....   (S8)

Secrecy served as a protection against the porous personal boundaries described previously. However, it could expand and evolve toward a progressive isolation from the outside world:

... A kind of fear which couldn't be disclosed to others ... I wouldn't say anything. I wouldn't talk anything at all. So, I lost contacts and nobody has told me that something like this happened.... I wouldn't talk to anyone. I would hear something saying within myself, 'Don't talk.'... I didn't talk to anyone outside....   (S11)

Family members' narratives indicate that the patient's progressive isolation is not well tolerated and becomes a source of worry and concern. It often triggers their recognition that something is going wrong and some react vigorously to the patient's tendency to isolate himself.

He would go to the pooja room, keep the photo with him and stand there for a long time. He used to write in the book. When it became too much, we realized ... just staying in the pooja room, staying alone, going inside the room and staying alone.   (R9)
He had a separate room. Now, we have made it into one. We sleep in the same room.   (R1)

The Double Articulation of Psychosis in South India

The Hazards of Context Sensitivity

Fabrega (1989) has underlined the disturbance of self that is implicit in traditional formulations of schizophrenia. Diagnostic symptoms, which have been used in cross-cultural research, reflect Western views about "self-reflection" and "self-other relations." Fabrega invites scholars engaged in transcultural research into schizophrenia to attend to cultural ideas germane to the social formation, architecture, and temporal extension of the self.

A number of Indian and non-Indian scholars concur in identifying a particular type of context sensitivity characteristic of the Indian self and the Indian style of thinking. While actors' behaviors do respond to more ambiguous rules (as everywhere), context sensitivity is nevertheless a "preferred kind of rule" in India. Ramanujan (1989) traces its manifestations in linguistics, philosophy, and poetry, showing how this way of locating oneself in the world cannot be simply subsumed within Western distinctions and hierarchies: "The microcosm is both *within* and like the macrocosm, and paradoxically also contains it" (1989:51). Human and nonhuman agents are perceived as contiguous, constituting an ecosystem of which man's activities and feelings are also part: "To describe the exterior landscape is also to inscribe the interior landscape" and "culture is enclosed in nature, nature is reworked in culture, so that we cannot tell the difference" (1989:50).

The notion of appropriateness, central to Hindu thinking, expresses a similar idea regarding the continuity between different orders of phenomena. At the individual level, it may be broadly defined as the necessity for a person to behave and act according to his or her status and gender and according to the characteristics and the spatial and temporal coordinates of the situation. The Hindu notion of *jâti* (logic of class, gender, species) is seen as a paramount expression of context sensitivity: "Each *jâti* or class defines," according to Ramanujan (1989:53), "a context, a structure of relevance, a rule of permissible combinations, a frame of reference, a meta-communication of what is and can be done."

Interdependence between the person and the world is also expressed in McKim Marriott (1989) via the notion of the Indian "dividual" self rather than "individual" self. Similarly, in his paper, Ramanujan draws a parallel between the context sensitivity that he sees as characteristic of "an Indian way of thinking" and Alan Roland's description of the Indian self. He (Roland) posits a familial self, a "self-we regard," that sees no phase of separation/individuation from the parental family as in modern America (...). Roland remarks that "Indians develop a "radar" conscience that orients them to others, makes them say things that are appropriate to person and context" (Ramanujan 1989:53). The idea of a contiguity between the person and the world is pushed to its extreme in the notion of *moksha* as the ultimate goal of existence a state in which all distinctions between subject and object have been transcended, a unity of self and the world. Kakar (1981) describes it as the Hindu way of liberation, which would seek to undo the process of ego development achieved through education. The empirical self is constantly being eroded by the cosmic, metaphysical *âtman*, which Biardeau (1972:25) describes as "the immortal principle which, in man, is destined to deliver from the body, from every body to finally reach a perfect identity with Brahman." In the Ashtavakra Gita, the Master says:

I am the infinite deep
In whom all the worlds
Appear to rise
Beyond all form,
Forever still
Even so I am (Byrom 2001:20)

and:

As a wave seething and foaming
Is only water
So all creation,
Streaming out of the Self,
Is only the Self (Byrom 2001:6)

At a prima facie level, patients' narratives could be read as expressing a kind of "metonymic contiguity" between the person and his world, which resonates with Ramanujan's descriptions. They evoke an awareness of patients' location within his or her surrounding world. We have mentioned narratives that describe a transformation of the atmospheric quality of the lived world – one that is infused with hostility, suspicion, and invigilation. We have also mentioned a blurring of boundaries between self and the others and a sense of being invaded or controlled from within by outside forces. In all cases, these alterations are perceived as threatening the core of the person, and they are associated with fear and confusion.

However, two notes of caution are necessary to avoid superficial parallelism. First, the alterations described by the patients are not so different from those found in interviews done in Montreal and Toronto (Corin 1997); they could reflect basic aspects of the transformation of the experience associated with psychosis which underlie particular cultural elaborations. Second, divergences between patients' experience and cultural ideas are probably more salient than similarities between them. In fact, in patients' narratives, context sensitivity is characterized by a feeling of porosity rather than fluidity, by a sense of invasion by a flux that is beyond one's control as opposed to an experience achieved by an intense personal and spiritual work allowing one to transcend the boundaries of the self.

The emotional tone of our data suggest that the availability of a more flexible, context-sensitive notion of self does not mitigate the suffering that accompanies psychotic alteration of this self. However, we cannot rule out the possibility that fluid ego boundaries could help, in the long run, to mitigate the alienating force of psychotic experience and to integrate such experience, at least minimally, into the self.

The notion of appropriateness could be seen as expressing the normative dimension of context sensitivity and transforming it into an ethical stance. It could, therefore, also reinforce feelings of marginality and despair experienced by patients and families. Meeting one's family obligations is of paramount importance for patients and families. It is located within a larger framework of transgenerational exchanges and duties wherein investments (such as education) in one's child constitute a recognized pathway for improving family status in a changing society. People carry on their shoulders both their own and their family's future. The corollary of these norms emerge in the narrative material as a keen sense of failure on behalf of patients and prolonged grieving on behalf of parents. But several mechanisms mitigate the subjective impact of the illness and maintain the patient's probity as a person. Mentioning how the patient acted in the past keeps him defined in terms of appropriateness, as does projecting into an indefinite future the possibility that he will ultimately fulfil his family obligations. A fluid notion of appropriateness, we believe, serves as a symbolic device that integrates the patient into a shared imagined world. The concept of *dharma* defines moral duty and encompasses good thought, knowledge, conduct, and behavior, all of which lead to the acquisition of spiritual merit. Accomplishing culturally appropriate behaviors is a condition for personal progress. However, once again, Hinduism allows a certain flexibility; even if accomplishing one's dharma is a central imperative, this rule can be suspended in moments of great trouble (Mathur 1994).

Finally, narratives also reveal how links of interdependence, in Ramanujan's sense of the term, flow in the other direction. Interdependence is evident in the presence of family members, their attempts to adjust to the situation and the degree of tolerance they manifest toward the patient. It is clear that the availability of an extensive support system does not account for family's attitude: Its mobilization is severely constrained by the general stigmatization of mental illness for the patient and the entire family.

Furthermore, an elementary notion of "tolerance" is not very illuminating and cannot be explained as a simple reflection of larger societal values. It does not capture the intense and complex processes that operate at the cognitive, emotional, and pragmatic levels. Commenting on the unusual patterning of expressed emotion in India, Leff and his colleagues (1992) suggested that decreases in negative emotional attitudes toward the patient could be associated with the ability to understand disturbed behaviors in terms of disease. However, this does not account for the general low level of emotional overinvolvement the authors found in their study. The narratives we collected suggest that family members' attitudes and reactions are the product of an intense inner work that involves the spiritual dimension of life and one's relationships to the world.

Significance and Meanings

In our study, traditional cultural etiologies did not play a central role in shaping the experience of patients and their families. Perhaps those attending SCARF were a biased sample because they were consulting a psychiatric service. As found in our Montreal study, psychosis stimulates an intense quest for meaning that neurobiological explanations do not exhaust. When they do appear in narratives, cultural etiologies usually emerge as personal or family formulations, which enable people to name feelings of strangeness and alienation they experience, either from within, in the case of the patient, or in their interactions with the patient, in the case of family members. The evanescent, ever-shifting nature of these explanations may reflect the pluralism of Indian cosmology, but it may also reflect the fact that persistent psychotic phenomena resist inclusion in a single-meaning frame, no matter how protean that frame. Indeed it could be argued that psychotic experience, by its very definition, signals the limits of available cultural explanatory frameworks.

We have shown how patients moved beyond questions of the causes of their illness to grapple with their own position within the world. They sought to introduce coherence and purpose to their existence and to imbue suffering with a transpersonal, spiritual significance.

Comparing family members' narratives with those of patients, family members were oriented more to etiologies, while patients sought, above all, to communicate their unusual experience by locating it within a signifying frame. Both, however, made reference to the potential influence of malevolent humans or malevolent spirits (frequently ghosts of people who have met an untimely death). But it was family members who tended to rely more on the action of the planets, as diagnosed by specialists in astrology. Moreover, family members' narratives frequently referred to *karma*, thereby situating the illness within a larger order of things. Traditional cultural etiologies and astrological categories served family members' needs to normalize mental illness and assign it a place within the order of things. In regard to astrology, Fuller (1992) suggests that the movement of planets also evokes the cyclical oscillation of auspiciousness and inauspiciousness, which is a quality of time itself. If the influence of the planets is autonomous and irrevocable, and inscribes misfortune within the natural order of things, their position will continue to evolve so that more auspicious times can be anticipated for the future. On their side, patients remain more concerned with exploring the meaning of their experience from within, trying to read inner signs and experiences.

Elaborating an Inner Space

Research conducted in Montreal with people who have a diagnosis of schizophrenia (Corin 1990, 1998) led to the hypothesis that adopting a position outside, or at the margins, of the social field had a protective value for persons not rehospitalized during the past four years. Patients commented that withdrawal allowed them to construct an intimate, private space and to reconnect with themselves. This position was compensated by an opposite "relational" movement at the symbolic, imaginary, and pragmatic levels. The term, *positive withdrawal*, expressed this double orientation. Religious references played a significant role in articulating an inner space and renegotiating one's position within society. Religious referents were either borrowed from "marginal" religious groups or expressed as a personal spiritual attitude. A study of the factors associated with course and outcome of schizophrenia in India, and which included data gathered in Chennai, concluded that this protective function, among other factors, was associated with an increase in religious activities on the part of patients (Verghese, Rajkumar, Richard, Sethi, and Trivedi 1989).

Both patients' and family members' commented on patients' withdrawal. As has been shown in Western contexts, it was construed positively by patients and negatively by family members. In India withdrawal could also, perhaps, be a reaction to the intense care and support patients receive from family members. Their intimate presence may be an additional source of stress, which reinforces patients' retreat from social interaction.

Withdrawal must also be understood against the background of fear, disorganization, and confusion experienced by patients, and their sense of a blurring of personal frontiers. Withdrawal is a means by which patients create an inner space – an inner lived world – protected from intrusion. The importance that patients attach to not revealing what they experience suggests that this inner world is protected by an exclusion zone of secret. We hypothesized that building such a zone could be a way to restore boundaries separating the inner and outer worlds and support the possibility to form clearer ideas and representations about what is happening. This echoes the suggestions by Aulagnier (1991), a psychoanalyst who has written extensively on psychosis. She makes the point that capacity to keep things secret is an important precondition for the very act of thinking, a necessary prerequisite for forming personal thoughts that are more than an echo of other people's thinking.

Our narrative data also indicate that psychosis is experienced as engulfing the very movement of meaning itself, so that the world is perceived as both over- and undersignified. We suggest that withdrawal introduces the equivalent of an "empty space" – a "blank box" – necessary for thinking. Linguists have described the central role of negation and difference in the functioning of symbolic systems: Phonemes exist insofar as they can extricate themselves from the continuum of noise and distinguish themselves through a series of oppositions; symbols and metaphors build their power on the distance between signifiers and the objects they signify. In contrast to this productive cognitive function of negation, psychosis reveals the destructive work of the negative where links are attacked and representations dissolve (Green 1993). From that angle, withdrawal could be a way to create "embodied blanks" in an oversignifying reality as an attempt to stop the drift of significance.

In India, withdrawal builds on religious referents. Patients take advantage of locations of retreat associated with pilgrimage, temples, or mosques. Withdrawal evokes, explicitly or implicitly, a stance of renunciation central to the Hindu tradition. Madan (1987) describes the image of the *sannyasi* as a theatrical figure who gives away all of his belongings and conducts his own funerary rituals, thus rupturing all links with the world in order to live out an austere discipline. Though there was no explicit reference to *sannyasi* in the narratives we collected, we suspected that this religious archetype provided a model that allowed psychotic people to embrace withdrawal. Madan claims that while in principle renunciation is seen as the apogee of Hindu life, the real ideal of life in India is the figure of the householder who lives in the world under the light of the renunciant's philosophy. In the householder's language, renunciation becomes detachment in the context of worldly engagements: Engagements are not inherently bad but one has to be careful not to become enslaved to the world. Renunciation can be contemplated at a later stage of one's life, but would be strongly discouraged before the accomplishment of one's mundane duties. Madan also comments on the way renunciation is held to be inauthentic when it stems from a feeling of failure rather than accomplishment. He points toward the tension between these two ideals and the hostility expressed toward renunciants, who threaten the householder ideal, even if renunciation continues to hold supreme value in Brahmans' lives. Other authors have also described the tension existing between the ritualist and the ascetic trends in Hinduism.

This tension is echoed in the narratives we collected. Whereas patients resorted to religious signifiers in a way that resonated with a model of renunciation, family members were suspicious of this withdrawal. We have mentioned the strategies they used in trying to reintegrate the person within the social fabric, relying heavily on ritual dimension of religious practice. For themselves, however, family members sought to achieve a state of detachment. They turned to prayer and faith in an effort to achieve an inner attitude that would nourish and foster their further involvement with the patient and their larger attitude of tolerance.

Patients and family members thus draw on the tensions within the religious frame to deal with the challenges they confront. Further studies will have to examine the implications of such a tension in greater depth and locate it within the broader cultural frame and its transformation in contemporary India.

The Pragmatics of Culture

This research has revealed the extent to which the experienced self and lived world are altered in psychosis: how the world becomes overloaded with meaning and yet is totally enigmatic; how confusion invades feelings and thoughts, rendering reality itself ambiguous and unstable; and, how confusion attacks the capacity to think and undermines the sense of self. All of these trigger a quest for meaning, a search for fixed points of reference that might reestablish the possibility of stabilized meaning.

We have argued in this chapter that to understand the influence of culture on the evolution of schizophrenia, one must begin with the ways in which patients and family members situate themselves in a world that is deeply affected by psychosis. It is crucial to understand how cultural referents shape and articulate the personal and interpersonal experience of psychosis. It is critical to find a balance between an over- or under-culturalized interpretation. Traditional etiological models do not appear clearly in the narratives; they only surface in traces and fragments. One has to be careful not to confuse superficial similarities with deeper "family resemblances" between elements of narratives, behaviors, and key aspects of the culture. Yet while cultural elements may be transformed or distorted in psychotic experience, this does not mean that they do not play an important function. It probably remains true that, as suggested by Obeyesekere (1985), some cultures offer greater potential than others for a personal and interpersonal elaboration of psychosis.

Patients' and relatives' suffering form a fabric woven from narrative threads that knit together and then pull away from each other again, infusing the staggering world of psychosis with a sense of momentum. Culture does not impose its work on passive subjects. Actors circulate within culture; they choose, transform, and displace its signifiers. The researchers' task in transcultural psychiatry is to identify the range of possible signifiers available in particular cultures, to determine their relative weight within the culture and within actors' discourses, and to bring out the interplays of cultural signifiers, by observing their use in concrete cases.

Patients and family members relate to culture in different ways, echoing their particular position toward psychosis and the specific challenges it poses for them. The relative centrality or marginality of the signifiers they use reflects their own stance in relation to the social and cultural scene. Patients seem to favor a particular strand of religious signifiers that emphasize withdrawal and asceticism. While being an ideal horizon of human life, it is generally not supposed to be directly enacted, particularly before the fourth age of life (old age). Madan (1987) argues that detachment constitutes a culturally appropriate way to withdraw within the confines of worldly life and we have evoked its significance for family members. Some patients, however, seem to take renunciation literally and engage in extreme withdrawn behaviour. On the other hand, families do not encourage their children to follow this path and rather attempt to involve them in the ritual dimension of Hinduism.

For patients, cultural referents do not always articulate personal experience in a positive way. They may be absorbed by psychosis and remain embedded within a disorganized inner world. In other cases, it is as if there is a struggle to progressively tame, displace, or transform psychotic experience. This process unfolds through time. But it will require the development of prospective longitudinal studies to identify the specific elements of context that contribute to the progressive or regressive work of culture in a particular society and to grasp the unique pathways of its influence.

NOTES

* I thank Janis Jenkins, Jean Berggren, and Rob Barrett for their editorial work on this chapter.

1 In anthropology, one should mention the work of Crapanzano (1977, 1992, 1994), Obeyesekere (1981, 1985, 1990), and Csordas (1990, 1994). In psychoanalysis, Lacan (1966, 1981) is credited with having drawn attention to the central structuring role of the symbolic frame, transcending concrete interaction or exchange, in regard to the human subject. Aulagnier (1975, 1979, 2001) also anchors the development of the "I" within identificatory projects relayed by the parents; these projects imposed on the child are organized around a few *points de certitude* guaranteed by the culture, and which define the basics of generational and gender lines of differentiation as well as the rules of alliance and prohibitions prevailing in a particular society.

2 The idea that cultural representations and symbols condense several intersecting chains of meaning that connect to broader areas of the cultural life has been proposed by an interdisciplinary team of clinicians and researchers working in Senegal in the 1960s (Ortigues and Zempleni 1968). These associative chains may be mobilized in a variety of ways, depending on the actors' social position and social circumstances. Based on Levi Strauss' French structuralism and Lacan's psychoanalysis, this approach focuses on the singularity of individual and social actors and enlightens the heterogeneous pragmatics of culture.

3 In a paper on Antonin Artaud, Derrida (1967) reminds us of the essential shortcomings of words and narratives for conveying inner experience. He evokes the grieving process entailed by the necessity to resort to language or to borrow words that have always been used by other people, loaded by sets of meanings and associations that never coincide with singular semantic frames. This process does not mean that experience is outside culture, but that culture is only a partial reflection of the experience.

4 I refer here to Hüsserl's writings after the publications by his disciple Heidegger about phenomenology.

5 Modes of resorting to, transforming, and subverting cultural associative chains by people with schizophrenia and their families contribute to the recreation of the experience, as described by Crapanzano (1977:10) in his studies on the therapeutic potential of spirit possession rituals: "By articulation, I mean the act of construing, or better still constructing, an event to render it meaningful. The act of articulation is more than a passive representation of the event; it is in essence the creation of the event." The articles published in Crapazano and Garrison's edited collection (1977) illustrate how different persons use ritual idioms in different and opposite ways according to their own personal and interpersonal positions.

6 In a paper on the relationship between psychoanalysis and anthropology, I argued that each discipline enriches the other, not by transfer or application of concepts, but by resonance, their dialogue allowing each one to explore further what is developing at its own margins (Corin 1998).

7 All had been diagnosed between two and three years prior to the interview, except S8, who was diagnosed eight years previously.

8 Of these eleven patient-relative pairs, there was one (S6) in which we were able to interview the relative but not the patient. In reporting the interview material in this chapter we have preserved our original numerical identification running from S1 to S11.

9 The validation was done in collaboration with Alain Lesage, with the assistance of Amanda Hunt and Tonya Dominique. Ian Van Haaster and Marina Bandeira were also involved.

10 Patients are identified by subject number within brackets, (S1) and relatives as such: (R1).

REFERENCES

Aulagnier, Piera. 1975. *La Violence de l'Interprétation: Du Pictogramme à l'Enoncé.* Paris: Presses Universitaires de France.

———. 1979. *Les Destins du Plaisir.* Paris: Presses Universitaires de France.

———. 1991. "Le Droit au Secret: Condition Pour Pouvoir Penser." In P. Aulagnier, ed., pp. 219–38. *Un Interprète en Quête de Sens.* Paris: Payot.

———. 2001. *The Violence of Interpretation: From Pictogram to Statement.* Alan Sheridan, trans. Hove, East Sussex: Brunner-Routledge.

Biardeau, Madeleine. 1972. *Clefs Pour la Pensée Hindoue.* Vichy: Ed. Seghers.

Binswanger, Ludwig. 1970. *Analyse Existentielle et Psychanalyse Freudienne.* (Première édition, Allemagne: 1947, 1955, 1957 ed.) Paris: Gallimard.

Blankenburg, Wolfgang. 1991. *La Perte de l'Evidence Naturelle.* (First edition, German: 1971 ed.) Paris: Presses Universitaires de France.

Bruner, Edward M. 1986. "Introduction." In V. W. Turner and E. M. Bruner, eds., pp. 3–30, *The Anthropology of Experience.* Urbana and Chicago: University of Illinois Press.

Byrom, Thomas. 2001. *The Heart of Awareness: A Translation of the Ashtavakra Gita.* Boston: Shamala Publications, Inc.

Ciompi, Luc. 1980. "The Natural History of Schizophrenia in the Long Term." *British Journal of Psychiatry* 136: 413–20.

Cooper, John and Norman Sartorius. 1977. "Cultural and Temporal Variations in Schizophrenia: A Speculation on the Importance of Industrialization." *British Journal of Psychiatry* 130: 50–5.

Corin, Ellen. 1997. *At the Margins of Culture in Psychosis.* Paper presented at the American Anthropological Association Conference, Washington, DC.

———. 1998. "The Thickness of Being: Intentional Worlds, Strategies of Identity, and Experience Among Schizophrenics." *Psychiatry* 61: 133–46.

———. 1998. "Le rapport à L, AUTRE, Psychanalyse et anthropologie." In S. Havel, ed., pp. 21–42. *Résonances: Dialogues and avec la psychanalyse.* Montréal: Éditions Liber.

Corin, Ellen and Gerard Lauzon. 1992. "Positive Withdrawal and the Quest for Meaning: The Reconstruction of Experience among Schizophrenics." *Psychiatry* 55(3): 266–78.

Crapanzano, Vincent. 1977. "Introduction." In V. Crapanzano & V. Garrisson, eds., pp. 1–40. *Case Studies in Spirit Possession.* New York: John Wiley & Sons.

———. 1992. *Hermes' Dilemma & Hamlet's Desire: On the Epistemology of Interpretation.* Cambridge, MA.: Harvard University Press.

———. 1994. "Rethinking Psychological Anthropology: A Critical View." In M. M. Suarez-Orozco and G. L. Spindler, eds., pp. 223–43. *The Making of Psychological Anthropology.* Forth Worth, TX: Harcourt Brace College.

Crapanzano, Vincent and Vivian Garrison. 1977. *Case Studies in Spirit Possession.* New York: John Wiley & Sons.

Csordas, Thomas J. 1990. "Embodiment as a Paradigm for Anthropology." *Ethos* 18: 5–47.

_____. 1994. *The Sacred Self. A Cultural Phenomenology of Charismatic Healing.* Berkeley: University of California Press.

Derrida, Jacques. 1967. "La parole soufflée." In J. Derrida, ed., pp. 253–92. *L'Ecriture et la Difference.* Paris: Édition du Seuil.

Fabrega, Horacio J. 1989. "On the Significance of an Anthropological Approach to Schizophrenia." *Psychiatry* 52(1): 45–65.

Fuller, Christopher J. 1992. *The Camphor Flame. Popular Hinduism and Society in India.* Princeton, NJ: Princeton University Press.

Green, André 1993. *Le Travail du Négatif.* Paris: Éditions de Minuit.

Jenkins, Janis Hunter. 1991. "Anthropology, Expressed Emotion, and Schizophrenia." *Ethos* 19: 387–431.

Jenkins, Janis Hunter and Marvin Karno. 1992. "The Meaning of Expressed Emotion: Theoretical Issues Raised by Cross-cultural Research." *American Journal of Psychiatry* 149: 9–21.

Kakar, Sudir. 1981. *The Inner World: A Psycho-analytic Study of Childhood and Society in India.* Delhi: Oxford University Press.

Lacan, Jacques. 1966. "Fonctions et Champ de la Parole et du Langage en Psychanalyse." *Écrits* 237–322.

_____. 1981. *Le Séminaire, Livre III Les Psychoses.* Paris: Le Seuil.

Leff, Julian, Norman Sartorius, Assen Jablensky, Ailsa Korten, and G. Ernberg. 1992. "The International Pilot Study of Schizophrenia: Five-year Follow-up Findings." *Psychological Medicine* 22: 131–45.

Madan, Triloki N. 1987. *Non-Renunciation: Themes and Interpretation of Hindu Culture.* Delhi: Oxford University Press.

Marriott, McKim. 1989. "Constructing an Indian Ethnosociology." *Contributions to Indian Sociology* 23(1): 1–39.

Mathur, Kripa S. 1994. "Hindu Values of Life: Karma and Dharma." In T. N. Madan, ed., pp. 63–77. *Religion in India.* Delhi: Oxford University Press.

McGlashan, Thomas H. and William T. Carpenter. 1988. "Long-Term Follow-Up Studies of Schizophrenia: Editors' introduction." *Schizophrenia Bulletin* 14(4): 497–500.

Murphy, Henry B. M. 1982. *Comparative Psychiatry. The International and Intercultural Distribution of Mental Illness.* Berlin: Springer-Verlag.

Murphy, Henry B. M. and A. C. Raman. 1971. "The Chronicity of Schizophrenia in Indigenous Tropical People: Results of a Twelve Year Follow-up Survey in Mauritius." *British Journal of Psychiatry* 118: 489–97.

Obeyesekere, Gananath. 1981. *Medusa's Hair: An Essay on Personal Symbols and Religious Experience.* Chicago: The University of Chicago Press.

_____. 1985. "Depression, Buddhism and the work of culture in Sri Lanka." In A. Kleinman and B. Good, eds., pp. 134–52. *Culture and Depression.* Berkeley: University of California Press.

_____. 1990. *The Work of Culture: Symbolic Transformation in Psychoanalysis and Anthropology.* Chicago: The University of Chicago Press.

Ortigues, Edmond, Marie-Cécile, Zempleni, Andras, Jacqueline. 1968. "Psychologie clinique et ethnologie." *Bulletin de Psychologie* 21 (15–19): 950–8.

Ramanujan, Attipat K. 1989. "Is There an Indian Way of Thinking? An Informal Essay." *Contributions to Indian Sociology* 23(1): 41–58.

Ricoeur, Paul. 1976. *Interpretation Theory: Discourse and Surplus of Meaning.* Fort Worth, TX: Texas Christian University Press.

Sartorius, Norman, Assen Jablensky, Ailsa Korten, G. Ernberg, M. Anker, J. E. Cooper, and Robert Day. 1986. "Early Manifestations and First-contact Incidence of Schizophrenia in Different Cultures." *Psychological Medicine* 16(4): 909–28.

Sartorius, Norman, Assen Jablensky, and Ron Shapiro. 1978. "Cross-cultural Differences in the Short-term Prognosis of Schizophrenic Psychoses." *Schizophrenia Bulletin* 4(1): 102–13.

Strauss, John S. 1986. "The Life Course of Schizophrenia." *Psychiatric Annals* 16(10): 609–12.

Strauss, John S. and Sue E. Estroff. 1989. "Subjective Experience of Schizophrenia and Related Disorders: Implications for Understanding and Treatment. Foreword." *Schizophrenia Bulletin* 15(2): 177–8.

Strauss, John S., Hisham Hafez, Paul Lieberman, and Courtenay M. Harding. 1985. "The Course of Psychiatric Disorder, III: Longitudinal Principles." *The American Journal of Psychiatry* 142(3): 289–96.

Tellenbach, Hubertus. 1979. *La Mélancolie.* (First edition, German: 1961 ed.) Paris: Presses Universitaires de France.

———. 1983. *Goût et Atmosphère.* Jean Amsler, trans. (First publication, 1968.) Paris: Presses Universitaires de France.

Turner, Victor. 1967. *The Forest of Symbols.* Ithaca, NY: Cornell University Press.

Verghese, A., J. K. John, S. Rajkumar, J. Richard, B. B. Sethi, and J. K. Trivedi. 1989. "Factors Associated with the Course and Outcome of Schizophrenia in India: Results of a Two-Year Multicentre Follow-Up Study." *British Journal of Psychiatry* 154: 499–503.

Waxler, Nancy E. 1979. "Is Outcome for Schizophrenia Better in Nonindustrial Societies? The Case of Sri Lanka." *The Journal of Nervous and Mental Disease* 167(3): 144–58.

5   In and Out of Culture: Ethnographic Means to Interpreting Schizophrenia*

Rod Lucas

Introduction

Schizophrenia is often represented as an ineffable phenomenon, the meaning of which is almost impossible to grasp. Historically, it has epitomized an inaccessible subjectivity and a point of failed intersubjectivity (see Barham 1993). For some commentators it is the "essence of incomprehensibility itself" (Sass 1992:19). People diagnosed with it have been deemed to be "unununderstandable" (Jaspers 1963:577ff), to be "outside the human community" (Rümke 1990:336), to have repudiated the social world, or to have negated the "human role" (Shulman 1968:190). Such characterizations are encoded in clinical formulations of schizophrenia and are implicit in all of those institutional processes by which a person is identified as (and comes to know themselves as) a "schizophrenic." Such fraught understanding was also a feature of peoples' accounts of their experiences of schizophrenia elicited as part of an ethnographic research project. Both clinically and experientially, schizophrenia can be apprehended as lying outside of culture.

This chapter explores such resonances in the relationship between culture and schizophrenia. Classic clinical accounts suggest that assumptions about culture and its transgression are encoded in the very concept of schizophrenia. These assumptions are made available to patients through their own diagnosis. Patients' and clinicians' understandings of what constitutes "culture," and what it means to be outside of it, are shown to be remarkably similar.

But there is also a significant disjuncture between these formulations and the "culture" that ethnography identifies as the vehicle and expression of peoples' everyday lives. The ideas about "culture" that people hold, and the "culture" identified by anthropology, are not necessarily the same thing, just as the "culture" assumed by psychiatry is not the same as the "culture" that is lived in and through the extraordinary experiences of schizophrenia. By subjecting the notion of "culture" itself to ethnographic analysis, I seek to clarify the dissonance that often pertains between the

146

disciplines of psychiatry, anthropology, and the people who are the focus of each.

Background

This chapter draws on ethnographic research exploring the implications of a diagnosis of schizophrenia for peoples' day-to-day lives. Conducted in an Australian capital city, it was aimed at eliciting peoples' understandings of schizophrenia and the coping strategies that allowed them to live independently in an era of deinstitutionalization. Fieldwork was conducted with fifty participants, in their own homes or in other settings of their choosing. Material on each participant's biography, genealogy, social background, network, living skills, domestic arrangements, and interests was gathered by way of interviews and participant observation. This material was grounded in an immediate social context: the relationships established with individual participants and the meticulously recorded dialogues – developed over weeks, months, or years – at the heart of those relationships.

Beyond interviews and their resulting texts, the research process involved joining with participants in a variety of everyday activities. Whilst they provided important contextual data on participants' lives, such activities were more valuable for introducing me to the demands and possibilities of various situations in which participants commonly found themselves, and where some of their extraordinary experiences took place. They were privileged opportunities to be in certain settings – a crowded bus, the shopping mall, an outpatient waiting area – to witness participants' responses to those settings, experience them for myself, have problems or difficulties pointed out while they were occurring, and engage actively in the interpretation of phenomena to hand. Like the ethnographic technique of participant observation, these activities provided access to "the most fleeting and elusive, and very often the most decisive, aspects of social existence, such as the furtive strategies that are engaged in the most banal and therefore least observed moments of ordinary life" (Bourdieu 1983:112).

Such activities provided an education of the senses, as new significances were attached to previously unnoticed sounds, certain visual effects in art and advertising, the aural properties of radio and telephone, or the effects of closed and heavily curtained rooms. These activities were also an exercise in educating attention, as neglected or previously undisclosed relationships were established between people and everyday objects, unveiling alternative readings of speech or television imagery, of posters, and newspaper headlines. This heightened attention was often generated for both researcher and participants, as the very expression of interest caused some participants to reflect on and therefore to objectify such phenomena in order to bring them to attention (confer Rabinow 1977:118–19).

Many participants played an active and enthusiastic part in these processes – instructing the researchers, taking us to sites of anomaly, finding illustrative objects and settings, and explicating these. Shaun eagerly scoured the shopping mall for examples of the objects and activities that would demonstrate his concerns; Tony arranged for us to film the spirit "voices" that emanated from him in certain settings; while waiting at the interchange, Brian solicited and debated our responses to the bus ride we had just shared, thus setting up the intense reflexivity of our subsequent journeys that day.

Working together in these ways to bring certain perplexing phenomena into view required discovering (or creating) intersections between biographies, knowledges, and assumptions. This task was predicated on a view of culture as open and emergent, to be discovered in the resources – language, media, dispositions, stocks of taken-for-granted knowledge – that were available to both participants and researchers as elements of their everyday lives in local worlds of meaning (see Kirmayer and Corin 1998).

On the Edge of (Clinical) Experience

Historically, schizophrenia has focused attention on the bounds of community and the existential limits of what it is to be human. As a paradoxical and "multi-dimensional" concept encapsulating contradiction (Rümke 1960), schizophrenia's enduring characteristics are described as puzzling, enigmatic, mysterious, and unnerving (Sass 1992:13–14).

Classic clinical formulations presume the strangeness of schizophrenia; psychosis defies the shared communicative potential of thoughts and feelings. In delineating dementia praecox, Kraepelin had emphasized its essentially peculiar, unclassifiable, and undefinable qualities, warning clinicians against empathy as a source of understanding this perplexing condition (Kraepelin 1974b:10). Jung similarly emphasized the incomprehensibility of schizophrenic phenomenology and the "plain madness" of attempting to understand such madness:

There is an apparent chaos of incoherent visions, voices, and characters, all of an overwhelmingly strange and incomprehensible nature. If there is a drama at all, it is certainly beyond the patient's understanding. In most cases it transcends even the physician's comprehension, so much so that he is inclined to suspect the mental sanity of anybody who sees more then plain madness in the ravings of a lunatic. (Jung 1960: 236)

Rümke provides one of the clearest expressions of schizophrenia's ineffability with his notion of the "praecoxfeeling": an "undefinable attribute" that pervades all observed symptoms of schizophrenia and that is registered as "something that cannot be classified in the usual way" (Rümke 1990: 336). This "something" can only be intuitively felt.[1] It was the confounding of the basic urge to make contact with others – the weakening of what he called the "rapprochement-instinct" – that Rümke declared to be the fundamental phenomenon in schizophrenia (Rümke 1990). The investigator "cannot find the patient," who is absent even though present before him.

It is through such genealogies that the person with schizophrenia has come to be known as "psychiatry's quintessential other – the patient whose essence is incomprehensibility itself" (Sass 1992). It is not surprising, therefore, given the power to define persons that is encoded in these formulations, that those diagnosed with schizophrenia are able to articulate a similar positioning for themselves. Most participants were adept at reproducing clinical accounts of schizophrenia: Some had photocopies of the relevant portion of the DSM-III; all had extensive experience with psychiatrists, outpatient clinics, and mobile-treatment teams. All could articulate the terms in which their diagnosis had been reiterated in the various languages of treatment and support. They all rejected popular representations – violent, threatening, "split personality" – encountered in the media, or expressed by acquaintances, or even by members of their own families.

Apprehended in and by the Body

The difficulty of detecting a physical location for schizophrenia has been a principal expression of its indeterminacy. If, at a perceptual and interactive level, the essential phenomena of schizophrenia have remained ineffable, their cause has also been relegated to an as yet unknown and inaccessible location within the body itself (Sass 1992:19). The obscurity of this physical locus has recurred throughout a century of clinical formulations, from Kraepelin's "morbid insult" to the "human machine" (1992:518), to contemporary neurophysiological and genetic discourses.

The image of a yet-to-be-revealed bodily repository has contributed to schizophrenia's exclusion from "culture" – especially insofar as the latter concept is used to designate a distinctively human realm of language and meaning in counterpoint to material "nature" (see Littlewood 1996:247–51).[2] To construe schizophrenia in this way is to suggest that it be known by way of a sensate or embodied apprehension, rather than by hermeneutic means (and thereby further removing it from what culture is presumed to be). Rümke's concept of *Praecoxgefühl* was introduced to emphasize the circumvention of linguistic or discursive ways of knowing schizophrenia:

What is known as '*Praecoxgefühl*' – what we call the 'odour of schizophrenia' (in the jargon of the clinic, 'It smells to me like a schizophrenic,' or 'I have the presentiment that we are dealing with a schizophrenic') – is based, in part, on our impression of the patient's gestures, attitudes, and behavior. (Lopez-Ibor 1974:17)

Barrett (1996:58) has demonstrated how such tangible and sensate metaphors of knowing still direct work in a contemporary hospital setting, with clinical teams waiting for nurses to "get a feel for the patient" before instigating treatment regimens. There was also an abiding belief in older nurses that they have been able to "smell schizophrenia" (Barrett 1996).[3]

These images reinforce the indeterminate nature of schizophrenia itself, which can only be apprehended by clinical acumen, intuition, or a uniquely tuned sense. Participants were similarly struck and perplexed by the indeterminate yet sensate qualities of their own experiences: participants' accounts were full of unaccountable bodily sensations – "my brain's on fire," "my heart bleeding" – of bodies being distorted, twisted, manipulated, or transformed, and the physicality of "voices" as living presences "breathing within you." They saw the label "schizophrenia" as pointing to what could not be otherwise grasped or understood, and they said that this lack of communicable understanding was at the heart of what it meant to have schizophrenia. One research participant, for example, asserted the failure to find his experiences and concerns reflected in the world around him in the following terms:

There are few books about your everyday experience, there is no television, and the radio is rather flat. You are without a culture for your condition.

Another participant bemoaned the absence of a language that would signal and "translate" her experiences, such as the signing that she taught to the deaf on a voluntary basis.

Some participants had spent considerable periods of time investigating (and attempting to verify) the location and effects of schizophrenia within their own bodies. One described it as an "alien intelligence" that inhabited his "receptive" body; another cataloged "in-dwelling spirits"; others sought to measure bodily "vibrations," monitor "hormones," or manipulate sensory and physical inputs. What they emphasized was a phenomenology that was difficult for them to specify and one that was equally inaccessible to others. Some participants had even undergone a series of medical examinations, sometimes over many years, without any determination of a physical cause for their "symptoms." This further highlighted the distinctiveness of their experience, locking it into their own discrete bodies, unavailable to others. Most of these phenomena were unobservable, although one participant encouraged us to film what he saw as the physical manifestations of "interference" from the various electromagnetic fields that he had identified as emanating from the stove, the electric light, and the computer in his house. A number of people lamented the absence of physical stigmata by which their experiences could be made manifest to others – this had been the impetus behind one participant's attempt to drive nails through his hands in imitation, he said, of Christ's suffering. The presumed location of these phenomena in the inaccessible interior of bodies or minds further emphasized schizophrenia's intractability to cultural commonality.

Culture and Schizophrenia

Concepts of "culture" are as multiple and amorphous as the "daunting heterogeneity" that pervades understandings of schizophrenia (confer Sass 1992:25). Mapping the relationship between psychopathology and culture requires an examination of how each of these posit the other: that is, of how culture provides models of ineffability, strangeness, and extremity, and how psychiatry works with certain delineated forms of "culture" as a measure of what has gone wrong in schizophrenia.

Elsewhere (Lucas and Barrett 1995) I have traced some of the recurrent conceptual properties that have allowed images of society, person, and mental illness to signify each other, and for interpretations of both culture and illness to share a common framework. Here, I outline some of the ways in which notions of "culture" function in this domain by way of three formal analogies. The examples highlight the fact that participants worked with these notions in the same way as clinicians and other commentators. Participants could articulate representations in each of the three modes, thus emphasizing how pervasive and readily available these were as images of both culture and schizophrenia.

Analogy 1 – Primitivism

A persistent image, especially in the cross-cultural literature, sees in schizophrenia a replication of the supposed disordered state of primitive society. In this, the image of a volatile, unstructured cultural condition is held to illuminate the supposed fluid and undifferentiated state of psychosis. Transposing a representation of culture from a collective to an individual site posits a failed evolutionary progression being manifested within individual psychologies, or the "swamping" of a weakened psyche with archaic symbolism (Jung 1960:239–40).

While this theme is most readily associated with psychoanalytic interpretations, it is also present in the genealogy of biological psychiatry, Kraepelin believing that women, children, and primitive peoples exhibit more clearly what is universal in mental disease. The former are closer to nature and therefore more representative of the biological organism, expressing mental illness in a clearer form; primitive people have a lesser grasp on life and live in delusional or dreamlike states because their thoughts are governed more by sensory images than speech. All are less intellectually developed and therefore capable of metaphorically epitomizing psychosis, which also resembles an undeveloped intellectual life (Kraepelin 1992:519–20). In some constitutions the "lower" forms of psychological life – greed, impulsive acts of violence, repetitive behaviors, "vestiges of earlier stages of evolution" – attain "a disastrous autonomy by destroying the higher faculties" (Kraepelin 1992:522), splitting the "primitive" instincts from higher functional control.

The "primitivist" representation of a relationship between culture and schizophrenia was articulated by one participant who observed that he was trapped in "a Darwinian situation, failing the survival of the fittest." He added: "Many patients are trapped in the Stone Age, they are left behind by modern developments." Others reported a fear of "losing control," of going "berserk" or "running amok" – all primitivist analogies (see Lucas and Barrett 1995). One man feared that his "murderous" or "belligerent" thoughts were evidence of a potential violence lying deep within himself, which could erupt at any time, even though there had been no history of him ever responding in this way. His own fear of "lashing out" (as he put it) was so great, nonetheless, that he avoided meeting people and led a highly circumscribed existence within his own house.

Analogy 2 – Society as Mental Illness

Both psychiatrists and social scientists have articulated a structural analogy between culture and psychopathology. Kraepelin (1974a:6), for example, saw mental illness as equivalent to religion, customs, art, politics, and history in its capacity to give expression to racial and national characteristics.[4] Conversely, Adorno identified "paranoia" as an appropriate expression of the "irrational authoritarianism" of many contemporary societies, especially those dominated by bureaucratic organization and centralized control:

The similarity between the social and the paranoid system consists not only of the closedness and centralized structure as such but also of the fact that the "system" under which most people feel they work has to them an irrational aspect itself. That is to say, they feel that everything is linked up with everything else and that they have no way out, but at the same time the whole mechanism is so complicated that they fail to understand its raison d'être and even more, they suspect that this closed and systematic organization of society does not really serve their wants and needs, but has a fetishistic, self-perpetuating "irrational" quality, strangely alienated from the life that is thus being structured. (Adorno 1994:115)

This is a variant of the widespread analogy between schizophrenia and social development, in which modern culture – epitomized by an increasingly impersonal, competitive, and administered social environment – is seen to induce schizophrenia as an inherent result of accelerated change and complexity: schizophrenia as an extreme manifestation of a modern malaise (Sass 1992:10).[5] Such images belong to a long tradition, going back at least to nineteenth-century critiques of the asylum (see Scull 1979:200). Such analogies focus on the presumed degeneration of civilization, with the city represented as both a manufactory and a repository of mental illness.

The participant I shall call Zöe was an artist and writer whose pamphlet advocating "consumer" perspectives on schizophrenia had been published by the local mental health authority. In the mid-1990s she exhibited a body of artwork critiquing what she saw as society's failure to validate psychotic experience. She also articulated Adorno's structural analogy between culture and schizophrenia by way of a striking inversion in which she took into herself what she saw as the ills, paranoia, and fear of a corrupt society:

What schizophrenics are infringing upon when they get to that . . . liberated mind level is the destruction of the corrupted society that we live in. Of course, we cannot go against the will of society, which is narrow-minded, corrupted, evil, demonic – everything they say we are, that's exactly what they are. If you have insight then you are not going to have it for long. And if you have brains then you're not going to have them for long either.

According to Zöe, the image of schizophrenia was, in reality, the true picture of society itself, which is accordingly evil, corrupt, and demonic. She saw her imagination and spirituality as threatening to unmask the hegemony of rational thought and expose the corruption of a social order that allows men to dominate women. Because she had dared to dream, to explore her imagination and her intelligence – the various sources of what she called her "power" – Zöe believed that she had been punished and made to submit to society's norms. Her status as a published writer and exhibited artist contradicted her diagnosis as a "psycho." She got much amusement and some solace from embodying and exposing such contradictions.

Schizophrenia appears to be unique in evoking this reflexive mirroring of the personal in the social. Other illnesses (such as cancer or MS) are not accorded these attributes, or do not become a means of comparison. Even other diseases of the mind do not become a vehicle for representing a social condition or the state of culture – we do not talk about an "Alzheimic society," for example, but it is possible to talk about a culture of paranoia and a "schizophrenic society."[6]

Analogy 3 – Art and Madness as Equally Strange Artifacts

Sass' analysis (1992) is an exhaustive attempt to demonstrate a formal association between psychopathology and culture. His interpretive strategy is to view the poorly understood schizophrenic-type illnesses in light of the sensibility and structures of consciousness found in the avant-garde literary and artistic products of modernism. Difficult to understand and feel one's way into, schizophrenia and modernism are equally "off-putting" (Sass 1992:8).[7]

With his art school training as a sculptor, the participant I call Shaun had decorated every surface of his apartment with images and found objects in order, he said, to reflect the fragmented meaningfulness of his everyday world. At one point his self-proclaimed "media addiction" required the monitoring of two television sets simultaneously. He asked rhetorically: "We all receive messages from the television, isn't that its whole point?" Shaun saw himself as both artist and philosopher. He also made the analogy between art and schizophrenia explicit. He said, "the definition of an artist is that they're agents of rupture," rupture being the dominant motif of his accounts of schizophrenia. This rupture had both internal and external modalities that reflected each other, mapping a personal experience of biographical disjunction onto a representation of societal change and innovation. In Shaun's view, the effect of psychosis was to "destroy the architecture of everyday experience"; this was also the effect that the schizophrenic/artist/philosopher can have on society by challenging taken-for-granted assumptions, which is its potentially positive effect. Schizophrenia was, in his account, the "powerhouse of culture," ushering in the new by way of startling confrontation. Shaun's was a popular, "commonsense" expression of the equation between art and schizophrenia, madness and genius, which Sass has explored by way of an elaborate formal analogy.

It is as a reader of texts and paintings that Sass creates this analogy, implicitly suggesting that those who have the experiences associated with schizophrenia "read" them in the same way that one might read *Nausea*, view Picasso's *Violin and Fruit*, or watch *Waiting for Godot*. In this, Sass emulates the views of the writer Nerval and thus invokes a long history that concerns itself with the relationship between madness and reading:

Every reading, says Nerval, is a kind of madness since it is based on illusion and induces us to identify with imaginary heroes. Madness is nothing other than an intoxicating reading: a madman is one who is drawn into the dizzying whirl of his own reading. Dementia is, above all, the madness of books; delirium, an adventure of the text. (Felman 1985:64)

At a superficial level, many participants did appear to have an affinity with works of fantasy, mythology, and heroism (although few had knowledge of, let alone interest in, surrealism, cubism, or Artaud's Theatre of Cruelty, for example) and they did use texts as a way of explicating the experience of schizophrenia. Adam, for example, provided the following injunction:

Read fiction and get an idea of what is real in fantasy. Look into the projections of the future. Read about telepathy and other spiritual fantasies. Get a grip on the stuff which will take you into forever.

Genres such as Arthurian legend and books such as *Lord of the Rings* were the most frequently mentioned texts in this context.

Each of these analogies employs a reification of culture: "the production of culture as an object in itself" (Kapferer 1988:97) in which meanings, patterns, and traits are "systematically removed from their embeddedness in the flow of daily life, fashioned into symbolic things, and placed in a stable, dominant, and determinate relation to action" (Kapferer 1988:210). An organic metaphor has been one of the most pervasive means of this objectification:

A powerful structure of feeling continues to see culture, wherever it is found, as a coherent *body* that lives and dies. Culture is enduring, traditional, structural (rather than contingent, syncretic, historical). Culture is a process of ordering, not disruption. It changes and develops like a living organism. It does not normally "survive" abrupt alterations. (Clifford 1988:235; emphasis in original)

Here indeed is a counterimage of schizophrenia. Participants represented their distance from culture as precisely the result of a profound disruption.

Their experiences were quintessentially disordering; the meanings they attached to those experiences were rarely derived from dominant, stable patterns of symbolization, and broke with normative schemes of both subjectivity and social classification. Participants were surviving the most abrupt and severe alterations to their expectations and imaginings – both their own for themselves prior to the onset of schizophrenia, and those of their families and others with whom they had relationships. Culture was an unreliable structural support that provided some analogies for understanding yet failed to order their experiences.

Berger and Luckmann (1967:89–90) remind us that reification – the apprehension of a human phenomenon, such as culture, as if it were a thing – is intrinsic to the social construction of reality itself. As a "modality of consciousness" this is also an active production as humans continuously objectify the human world (Berger and Luckmann 1967). Here I have shown how the facility to reify culture is produced and reproduced, both in psychiatric discourses and in everyday representations by those whose lives are significantly defined by psychiatry. Clinicians and people diagnosed with schizophrenia were equally capable of objectifying culture (and positioning schizophrenia outside of it). In the following section, I explore the dialectically entailed capacity for "dereification" (Berger and Luckmann 1967:91) that reveals another kind of "culture": a culture that emerges contingently and syncretically from within the flow of people's everyday worlds and is made available to analysis through ethnographic engagement.

Participants' Culture

Participants evinced culture as a practical accomplishment, revealed through those actions and understandings that prevailed in their daily lives. Ethnography highlights what people actually *do*, as opposed to the reified concepts such as "culture" by which their actions and beliefs are accounted for by others. Here I present a view of culture as actively and strategically used to some purpose (confer Swidler 1986), that purpose being to induce understandings of schizophrenia as a human experience.

Participants were not simply an expression of the capacity of "psychiatry's culture" (Littlewood 1996) to designate their person as "schizophrenic" and their experiences as pathological. Participants' culture was focused on understanding their perplexing experiences and themselves as certain types of persons who attracted psychiatric attention because they had extraordinary experiences. This was a "deeply context-bound process," in which identities were construed in terms of immediate conditions and everyday existences (confer Friedman 1992:841).

Models of schizophrenia in which culture is objectified – such as Sass's reading of art and literary texts – do not account for how participants in my study interrogated the meaning of the various texts that they read, not as sources of madness, but as a verification of the reality of their own experiences: For "what is real in fantasy" as Adam put it. They did not perceive texts as "mad," and did not gravitate toward certain types of writing for that reason. Such a model for "reading" schizophrenia does not describe the way in which several participants actually used the Bible – not as a source of analogies for schizophrenia, but as a way of verifying and validating their own "mystical" and "esoteric" experiences. It was the Bible that offered Brian a model of reading thoughts – "God knows what I am thinking, so it is possible" – of hearing voices, having "visions," or experiencing "in-dwelling spirits." Several participants cited the Bible as validating their own understandings – "the Bible is an operator's manual for hearing voices" insisted Adam – but also as a document known to all that confirmed the perpetual puzzlement, mystery, affliction, and suffering of human beings, such conditions confronting them personally and dramatically in their own experience.

Most participants had never heard of, let alone read, the many obscure modernist texts from which Sass derived his "parallels" with "schizophrenic thinking." None had seemingly read Rimbaud's *A Season in Hell* or *Illuminations*, but many used precisely these images to convey aspects of their experience. Marco – a participant who spent much of his time making abstract expressionist artworks, the representation, he said, of his "disintegrating" perception – may not have read Robert Musil's *The Man Without Qualities*, but his knowledge of popular physics and the effects of hallucinatory drugs was sufficient for him to create analogies with a world of perceptual forms dissolving into an immaterial whirling of atoms and subatomic forces.[8] Marco had read Huxley's *The Doors of Perception*; no one else seemed to be aware of this work, nor of William Blake (from whom the title was derived),[9] but several participants talked about the 1960s rock band "The Doors" (who had derived their name in the same way) and, by means of this reference, used the image of "opening the doors of perception" as a description of their experiences. Such images formed the basis of new metaphoric and tropic combinations that highlighted the confluence of ideas about psychic openness, unusual perceptual capacities, and religious propositions as when Karen said: "I don't know if I believe in hell, but the voices keep talking about the gates of heaven and hell."

Without direct or conscious access to the various portrayals of "psychotic" states in literature and art, participants were able to utilize a practical knowledge of their culture to create such analogies for themselves, using the more prosaic materials that were readily at hand. Their experiences suggested a set of correspondences that were neither indexical nor intentional, but that generated logical schemes of interpretation and production that fit together as intelligible and predictable, and therefore, as taken for granted. People perceived in the phenomena of language, film, and music an already existing identity with their own experiences. This material was not merely illustrative, but formed by the same concerns and dispositions that pertained in their own lives. This was a cultural facility used by people with schizophrenia, as much as anyone else. The references that most people used in this way did not require specialist knowledge; rather, they required a familiarity with a wide range of popular cultural forms that frequently pointed up the researchers' own limits and elitism. Analogies for the experience of schizophrenia were never presented in a merely illustrative way – "this image is like that experience." Rather, they were the very vehicle by which schizophrenic experiences were apprehended by participants and then conveyed in communications that drew on common, orchestrated understandings that were shared between participant and researchers because we each had a practical, working knowledge of our culture in some of its aspects. In this, they were like the Fang sermons described by Fernandez (1986:179), which "knit the world together" by means of subtle reference, neither didactic nor expository, but spontaneous and free associative.

Participants' explanations of schizophrenia drew on everyday media and situations in order to gain an understanding of those phenomena that were less well understood or perplexingly inchoate (confer Fernandez 1986:28ff). Television was itself a "delusion of real life," using technology to bring "visions" and "disembodied voices" into every lounge room: "Why are they more real than my voices?" queried Shaun. Such tropes were employed by participants to understand what had happened to them, and they subsequently used some of them to induce a measure of understanding in me. They were invoked inferentially from within a person's life, from the sources that had been happened upon as a result of biographical and social contingencies and were matched (or negotiated) from within the practical knowledge that I had similarly gleaned through my own history and experiences.

For most participants, the sources of knowledge about their culture and the wider world were current films (especially those available cheaply on video), contemporary popular literature, television programs, and radio commentary. Adam did not search twentieth-century literature to come up with poetical accounts that illustrated his experiences. His own understandings were informed, not by reference to texts, but by a logic of practice that aligned his experience to mysticism, religion, physics, excess, and transgression. It was this cultural utility that allowed innovative metaphors to make sense if they drew upon, for example, images of heaven and hell, drugs, altered perceptions, and a 1960s rock band, whether or not the speaker had ever heard of William Blake, Aldous Huxley, or Jim Morrison. It was this logic of practice, embedded in biography and drawing upon meanings that were readily at hand, that brought individual experience into alignment with social conditions and permitted its interpretation in terms of specific cultural referents.

Culture and Method

The culture evinced by participants in the research project was inseparable from the methods that we used to work with them. Accounts of schizophrenia were grounded in the relationships that we entered into with people for the expressed purpose of bringing this phenomenon into clearer view. Such accounts emerged from a dialogic engagement that sought to disclose (or build) the points of biographical familiarity, recognition, and empathy that meant some form of meaning could flow between us and enlighten what each of us could know about having schizophrenia. It required the reclamation of those common experiences that come from sharing a language, growing up in similar places at similar times, seeing the same films, watching the same television programs, reading the same books, or having ideas emerge from a stock of taken-for-granted knowledge. In this, the culture that was brought into view had a concrete material base in the objects, practices, and media that were readily at hand in the everyday world. This culture was revealed when (to take one example) the extraordinary experiences of psychotic hallucination, Biblical accounts of visions, and the contents of a record collection coalesced to produce a set of beliefs that fundamentally oriented an individual's identity and provided a framework for their activities on an ordinary day.

The necessity for exploring the mundane, material basis of belief was emphasized by Shaun when he complained about the absence of "artifacts" in his psychiatrist's office. He said: "When I am having a breakdown I can walk through [the shopping mall] and see fifteen or twenty messages on T-shirts that are all directed at me." He was frustrated that he could never convey the reality of this "referencing process" in a treatment setting that lacked these "cultural artifacts." In his own home he got out all his referencing artifacts and spread them on a table. They included record covers, magazines, collected images, and found objects. It was soon evident, however, that not even this display was sufficient as, in Shaun's case at least, the referencing was site specific and required moving around the city for it to be appreciated. He challenged us to go and see a poster in a city shop that he said would support his claims, especially those most secret things that alluded to his "true" identity. The excursion resulted in a long discussion of the researcher's own responses to the poster and of Shaun's criteria for validating his experiences. What this example suggests is that it is only by attending to the very specificity of everyday objects and actions in their time and place, within the framework of a particular biography, that the meaning of experiences associated with schizophrenia can be apprehended as both deeply personal and eminently cultural.

Conclusion

Notions of culture are produced and reproduced by both psychiatry and those who are its object. Psychiatric characterizations of schizophrenia historically locate its source outside of culture: in nature, primitivity, and the body as a material organism. At the same time, a limited repertoire of analogies allows culture to stand in for schizophrenia and give it substance. Schizophrenia is, accordingly, apprehended as both in and outside of culture.

I argue, following Fernandez (1986), that to employ the trope of culture across an inchoate ground – here comprising a range of puzzling and ineffable phenomena given an indeterminate physical location – is itself a preeminently cultural act, bringing meaning to otherwise ungraspable experience. Thus, while psychiatrists, anthropologists, and people diagnosed with schizophrenia can all share in a characterization of schizophrenia as being "beyond culture," culture is in fact central to this very proposition. Moreover, I have shown that people diagnosed with schizophrenia are equally capable of employing everyday cultural practices to accommodate schizophrenia in their lives, to generate meanings around it, to engage others in its interpretation, and that all of these processes are amenable to ethnographic interpretation.

I do not propose that by this means the experiences of schizophrenia become understandable in any absolute sense. That was not the case, as some aspects of participants' experiences remained intractable to empathy or intersubjective communication (at least for me). What was highlighted by close attention to the minutiae of everyday belief and practice – to culture in the specific sense – was the multiple levels at which both understanding and "ununderstanding" might operate, or rather, the multiple domains from which understanding could equally emerge, or recede again into "ununderstanding." It was everyday tools – language, objects, shared biographical experience, popular texts, and media – that seemed to effect this movement best. It was ethnographic engagement that served the task of building intersubjectivity and having patients' difficult experiences mean something to me as well as to them.

NOTES

* The ethnographic project on which this chapter is based was supported by the Australian Department of Health, Housing, and Community Services (later Health and Family Services) Research and Development Grant. Robert J. Barrett and Megan Warin were my inspired coresearchers on that project. The chapter's core argument emerged in discussion with Agapi Amanatidis, for whose insights I am indebted.

1 Confer Shulman (1968:x), who repeats the clinical advice handed down by generations of clinicians: "I can recognize the schizophrenic by the funny way he makes me feel when I try to interview him."

2 The contrast reflecting Birnbaum's distinction between an essential pathogenic determinant of mental disorder – those biological processes that are held to be necessary and sufficient to cause it – and its pathoplastic expression through personal and cultural variations. Littlewood (1996:248–9) demonstrates how the resulting form/content distinction is mapped onto a nature/culture distinction.

3 The popular press has recently revived this historical claim with reports on having smell accepted as a diagnostic tool for schizophrenia (see Aldersey-Williams 1998). The assertion emerges from the Highland Psychiatric Research Group (HPRG) at Craig Dunain Hospital, Scotland, where they are reportedly using breath samples, gas chromatography, and a mass spectrometer to reinstate (via technology) the "lost skill" of detecting schizophrenia's "anomalous" odor. One of the group's researchers is also quoted as having observed the routine training of Romanian clinicians to recognize the "smell of schizophrenia."

4 Not coincidentally, perhaps, this reflected turn-of-the-century German anthropology and its interest in the Volkgeist or "folk spirit" of cultures: "This spirit was believed to be anchored in passion and emotion, not in reason, and manifest in art, folklore, and language" (Woolf 1994:5).

5 Kraepelin (1992:518) had similarly seen mental illness as a waste product of development.

6 Such analogies are popularly applied to Australian society: "Australia has always suffered from schizophrenia – an identity torn between the heavily populated and ethnically diverse eastern cities and the vast empty interior where pioneering resourcefulness inspires romanticism" (Legge 1995:3). The work of prominent Australian artist Brett Whiteley has been seen to convey the "duality between pleasure and pain, calm and turbulence, beauty and evil and a condition of schizophrenic fragmentation" (Pearce 1995:46), itself a reflection of the "schizophrenic" nature of Australian society (McGrath 1979:71), citing Robert Hughes on an "historical obsession" with images of Australia as both paradise and hell.

7 Sass does not propose an explanation of schizophrenia with this analogy and makes no claim of aetiological connection between madness and

modernism; he is concerned with affinities rather than influences and an "understanding which consists in seeing connections" (1992:9).

8 Sass (1992:16) sees Musil's *The Man Without Qualities* as epitomizing the dissolution of an anthropocentric way of relating, thereby illustrating a parallel or affinity that will help elucidate the baffling inner lives of people with schizophrenia.

9 Huxley's (1954) *The Doors of Perception* is introduced by an epigraph from Blake: "If the doors of perception were cleansed everything would appear to man as it is, infinite."

REFERENCES

Adorno, Theodor W. 1994. *The Stars Down to Earth and Other Essays on the Irrational in Culture*. London: Routledge.

Aldersey-Williams H. 1998. "Smelling Faults." *The Australian Magazine* October 17–18: 80–1.

Barham, Peter. 1993. *Schizophrenia and Human Value: Chronic Schizophrenia, Science and Society*. London: Free Association Books.

Barrett, Robert J. 1996. *The Psychiatric Team and the Social Definition of Schizophrenia: An Anthropological Study of Person and Illness*. Cambridge: Cambridge University Press.

Berger, Peter L. and Thomas Luckmann. 1967. *The Social Construction of Reality: A Treatise in the Sociology of Knowledge*. Garden City, NY: Anchor Books.

Bourdieu, Pierre. 1983. "Erving Goffman, Discoverer of the Infinitely Small." *Theory, Culture, and Society* 2(1): 112–13.

Clifford, James. 1988. *The Predicament of Culture: Twentieth-Century Ethnography, Literature, and Art*. Cambridge, MA: Harvard University Press.

Felman, Shoshana. 1985. *Writing and Madness (Literature/Philosophy/Psychoanalysis)*. M. N. Evans and S. Felman, trans. Ithaca, NY: Cornell University Press.

Fernandez, James W. 1986. *Persuasions and Performances: The Play of Tropes in Culture*. Bloomington: Indiana University Press.

Friedman, Jonathan. 1992. "The Past in the Future: History and the Politics of Identity." *American Anthropologist* 94(4): 837–59.

Huxley, Aldous. 1954. *The Doors of Perception*. New York: Harper.

Jaspers, Karl. 1963. *General Psychopathology*. J. Hoenig and M. W. Hamilton, trans. Manchester: Manchester University Press.

Jung, Carl G. 1960 [1939]. "On the Psychogenesis of Schizophrenia." In R. F. C. Hull, trans., pp. 233–49. *The Psychogenesis of Mental Disease*, Bollingen Series, 20. Princeton, NJ: Princeton University Press.

Kapferer, Bruce. 1988. *Legends of People, Myths of State: Violence, Intolerance and Political Culture in Sri Lanka and Australia*. Washington, DC: Smithsonian Institution Press.

Kirmayer, Laurence J. and Ellen Corin. 1998. "Inside Knowledge: Cultural Constructions of Insight in Psychosis." In X. F. Amador and A. S. David, eds., pp. 193–220. *Insight and Psychosis*. New York: Oxford University Press.

Kraepelin, Emil. 1974a [1904]. "Comparative Psychiatry." In S. R. Hirsch and M. Shepherd, eds., pp. 3–6. *Themes and Variations in European Psychiatry: An Anthology.* H. Marshall, trans. Bristol: John Wright and Sons.

———. 1974b [1920]. "Patterns of mental disorder." In S. R. Hirsch and M. Shepherd, eds., pp. 7–30. *Themes and Variations in European Psychiatry: an Anthology.* H. Marshall, trans. Bristol: John Wright & Sons.

———. 1992 [1920]. "Die Erscheinungsformen des Irreseins (The Manifestations of Insanity)." D. Beer, trans. *History of Psychiatry* 3, 4 (12): 509–29.

Legge, Kate. 1995. "Unplugged." *Weekend Australian Review* June: 2–4.

Littlewood, Roland. 1996. "Psychiatry's Culture." *International Journal of Social Psychiatry* 42(4): 245–68.

Lopez-Ibor, Juan J. 1974. "The Delusional Schizophrenic Mutation." In A. Burton, J. J. Lopez-Ibor, and W. M. Mendel, eds., pp. 1–35. *Schizophrenia as a Life Style.* New York: Springer.

Lucas, Rodney H. and Robert J. Barrett. 1995. "Interpreting Culture and Psychopathology: Primitivist Themes in Cross-cultural Debate." *Culture, Medicine and Psychiatry* 19(3): 287–326.

McGrath, Sandra. 1979. *Brett Whiteley.* Sydney: Bay Books.

Musil, Robert. 1953. *The Man Without Qualities.* E. Wilkins and E. Kaiser, trans. New York: Coward-McCann.

Pearce, Barry. 1995. "A Soul Set Free: Brett Whiteley Retrospective." *State of the Art* (14) 46.

Rabinow, Paul. 1977. *Reflections on Fieldwork in Morocco.* Berkeley: University of California Press.

Rümke, Henricus Cornelius. 1960. "Contradictions in the Concepts of Schizophrenia." *Comprehensive Psychiatry* 1(6): 331–7.

———. 1990 [1941]. "*Het Kernsymptoom der Schizophrenie en het Praecoxgevoel* (The Nuclear Symptom of Schizophrenia and the Praecox feeling)." J. Neeleman, trans. *History of Psychiatry* 1, 3(3): 334–41.

Sass, Louis A. 1992. *Madness and Modernism: Insanity in the Light of Modern Art, Literature and Thought.* New York: Basic Books.

Scull, Andrew. 1979. *Museums of Madness: The Social Organization of Insanity in Nineteenth-Century England.* London: Allen Lane.

Shulman, Bernard H. 1968. *Essays in Schizophrenia.* Baltimore, MD: Williams & Wilkins Co.

Swidler, Ann. 1986. "Culture in Action: Symbols and Strategies." *American Sociological Review* 51: 273–86.

Wolf, Eric. 1994. "Perilous Ideas: Race, Culture, People." *Current Anthropology* 35(1): 1–7.

Part 2

Four Approaches for Investigating the Experience of Schizophrenia

6   Experiences of Psychosis in Javanese Culture: Reflections on a Case of Acute, Recurrent Psychosis in Contemporary Yogyakarta, Indonesia

Byron J. Good and *M. A. Subandi*

It was nearly noon on a hot, sunny day in August, 1997, when Subandi and I went to visit Yani, a thirty-six-year-old Javanese woman who was participating in our study of mental illness in the old city of Yogyakarta in central Java.[1] We had first met her for an interview two months earlier, but now, because another young woman participating in the study had recently phoned to express her concern about how much she had told us in a similar interview, we approached Yani's house with a bit of anxiety. We walked down a narrow alleyway that wanders through one of Yogya's poor *kampungs*, a crowded neighborhood that spills downward to one of the rivers running through the town, passing women, children, and young people sitting in open doorways and little shops, chatting in the heat of the day. We found Yani and her mother in their small house, which has one doorway opening onto a small sitting room and another doorway onto a room serving as a kiosk from which they sell a handful of everyday food items in an attempt to supplement a small pension the older woman receives. The sitting room was opened for us, and we were relieved to be greeted warmly, to find Yani in apparent good health, and both she and her mother happy to see us. We chatted with the two of them, took out our tape recorder and picked up our interview. It was some time into our conversation before we learned that Yani had had another acute psychotic episode in the brief interval since we had last seen her. Her mother said that she had just begun to recognize the signs that Yani was getting sick when we were last there, signs she knew well from previous episodes. Together, Yani and her mother told us how she had become sick again, decided not to return to the private psychiatric hospital where she had been taken for treatment on several previous occasions, but elected to rely on the prayers given Yani by Pak Han, a *kiyai*, or Islamic teacher, whose group she had been attending for some time. Both Yani and her mother were delighted to tell us how they recited the prayers and how quickly and completely she had recovered this time.

Subandi and I were startled to hear of Yani's illness because she showed no apparent residual symptoms of the rather severe episode she described as having begun only two months earlier. Hearing her story, however, reminded us of several other patients we recently interviewed and crystallized our sense of a common pattern. These were persons with relatively brief, acute psychoses, some of whom suffered only one episode, some of whom suffered regular recurrences. The symptoms often began quite suddenly – sometimes in a few days or even a few hours. They experienced classic auditory hallucinations and confusion, and in several cases, also told stories of having gone off on a kind of trek – around the city, to a nearby town, along the river, and into the countryside – remaining lost for some time before being returned home. The episodes tended to be rather short, not lasting long enough to meet DSM-IV's six-month duration criterion for schizophrenia, and we met these patients when they were clearly intact – interestingly diverse people, both men and women, often young, who had no apparent residual symptoms of hallucinations or thought disorder. Some had enough depressive symptoms to further confuse the diagnostic picture. As we heard the stories of the illnesses from these individuals and their families, classic themes from Javanese cultural psychology emerged, reflecting a broadly shared lifeworld in this highly diverse but predominantly Javanese and Islamic old city. It is this general pattern of psychotic illness and psychotic experience that we reflect on in this chapter, focusing primarily on a number of interviews we conducted with Yani and her mother from 1997 through 2000.

These reflections represent an effort to make sense of early observations and still-vivid experiences, rather than a fully elaborated cultural or theoretical analysis. I (BG) was a newcomer to Indonesian studies, having spent only sixteen months doing initial field research in Yogyakarta in 1999 when this case report was first formulated. With the support of a Fulbright senior lectureship and an NSF grant, and with the collaboration and assistance of Dr. Subandi, a member of the Faculty of Psychology in Gadjah Mada University, I developed a set of case studies of persons suffering a mental illness or drug addiction, interviewing and observing the work of healers in various Javanese and Islamic traditions, interviewing psychiatrists and psychologists, and visiting mental health services. This research was aimed at exploring Javanese "cultural psychology" by examining the experience of and response to major mental illness, while investigating the basic structures of formal and informal mental health services in Indonesia. With time, the research has increasingly focused on psychotic illness and has come to focus increasingly on cases with very rapid onset.

Our research in Java entailed working in three languages, demanding that close attention be paid to issues of translation. Interviews were conducted conjointly with Dr. Subandi in Bahasa Indonesia. If the person being interviewed preferred, however, it was conducted in Javanese, in which case Subandi translated orally into Bahasa Indonesia during the interview, or sometimes directly into English. He is fluent in all three languages. Most interviews were tape-recorded and transcribed, and here again, where transcriptions are in the Javanese language, Subandi was responsible for translation. Careful collaboration on the interpretation of interview data became a critical component of our research method.

Our research was carried out in Yogyakarta, a center of classic Javanese culture and site of a still functioning Javanese court. The city and the court have a special place in Javanese cosmology, mediating between the spiritually powerful Mount Merapi, an active volcano to the north of the city, and the Queen of the South Sea, who inhabits the coastal waters to the south. The city, its sultan, and its population also have an important place in Indonesian nationalist history, having been active in the independence struggle against the Dutch. The city was the site of Sukarno's first national assembly, and more recently, was the setting for massive demonstrations, led by the Sultan himself, as part of the movement that gathered under the banner of *reformasi*, which ultimately led to the ouster of Soeharto. Yogya is known as a city of universities and students, politically and intellectually progressive, an active center of modernist Islamic thought and political organization, and a center of traditional arts and culture. It is religiously diverse, with a sizeable Christian minority and numerous Islamic traditions and organizations. And it is a city with a postmodern flavor, dotted with *warnet*, tiny *warungs* or shops with computers linked into the worldwide web, banners announcing lectures and seminars on diverse aspects of *globalizasi* or globalization, and malls that were filled with international commodities before the disastrous *krismon* or monetary crisis that began late in 1997, while at the same time maintaining a commitment to organized forms of Javanese spirituality, cultural performances, and aesthetic life.

This complex center of Javanese and Indonesian urban culture, along with its network of rural and periurban villages, serves as the context and focus for our investigations. The research is classically anthropological, attempting to explore dimensions of Indonesian and Javanese culture and society by examining the language and experience of major mental illness, while at the same time investigating the influence of Javanese culture and aspects of Indonesian modernity on the phenomenology and course of psychotic illness. It provides the context for questions we raised here about the nature of the experience of psychosis.

Reading through the literature on schizophrenia and other psychotic illnesses, it is remarkable how often "the experience of schizophrenia" – the focus of the chapters in this collection – is equated with psychotic experience. It is now well known that the course of schizophrenia varies greatly from case to case, as well as across social and cultural settings (for example, Lin and Kleinman 1988; McGlashan 1988; Hopper 1991; Good 1997), and that many persons suffering psychotic illness are symptom-free for large parts of their life – experiencing an illness course the DSM-IV labels "Episodic With No Interepisode Residual Symptoms" (APA 1994:279). Nonetheless, to the extent that illness experience enters the medical literature, the focus is almost exclusively on the classic psychotic symptoms and resulting disability. Researchers writing in the European phenomenological tradition often describe schizophrenia as a distinctive mode of being-in-the-world (see Corin and Lauzon 1994 for a review). Even anthropologists writing about the experience of schizophrenia tend to focus primarily on culturally distinctive aspects of psychotic experience, rather than on the diverse forms of social and psychological adaptation of persons who sometimes experience psychotic episodes. While our research in Indonesia includes individuals who are chronically psychotic, many of those we interviewed have suffered episodes of psychosis followed by complete remission or relatively long periods without psychotic symptoms. This suggests the importance of studying psychotic illness in broader, nonessentializing terms – that is, not focusing solely on particular characteristics of psychotic experience as the distinguishing features of the experiential world of persons suffering schizophrenic illness.

In what follows, we first present data from our interviews with the woman we call Yani, interviews conducted largely with both Yani and her mother participating. Second, we discuss the implications for research, as well as for diagnosis, of working with samples that include persons who suffer a single psychotic episode or relatively brief, recurrent episodes – forms of illness that epidemiological research (for example, Susser, Finnerty, and Sohler 1996) suggests are quite common in so-called developing or low-income societies. Third, we draw on our discussions with Yani and her mother to outline some dimensions of a cultural phenomenology of the experience of psychosis among Javanese. Finally, we conclude by raising questions about potential influences of Javanese culture and society on the course of psychotic illness. Throughout, we focus on how one might approach the study of culture and the experience of schizophrenia in cases where psychosis is episodic.

The Case of Yani

We first met Yani and her mother for an interview in June 1997. We learned of her through a private psychiatric hospital in Yogyakarta where she had been a patient in 1996. We introduced ourselves, talked a bit about our research, and asked permission to interview her about her illness experience. Both Yani and her mother agreed, and both participated in our conversation.

We first talked briefly about her life history. Yani was born in 1961, the last of four siblings. Her father was a tailor in the university hospital, working personally for the prominent physician who was the hospital's first director. When Yani was six years old, her father died, leaving her to be raised by her mother and her mother's mother, who relied on a small pension left from her father's death. The family was poor and Yani is the only one of her siblings to have gone to the university. She entered the university in 1980 and graduated with a degree in agriculture in 1987. When we said to her mother that she must have been happy with what her daughter had achieved, she replied, "yes, very happy. But after she got sick, my feeling, I don't know . . . I don't know, it was like when you plant a tree and expect it to bear fruit, but in the end it does not bear fruit, like that . . ." And thus we began to talk about Yani's illness, with her mother's open, poignant acknowledgement about what a disappointment Yani had been.

Yani and her mother sat side by side, speaking in a kind of joint and over-lapping voice, at times enacting an apparent long-standing conflict in a way that seemed unusually explicit for Javanese speaking with strangers, a conversation that was sometimes uncomfortable for us as well as for them. They described how Yani had become ill as a student, had been treated, and recovered so that she could complete her exams and graduate, but then had fallen ill and recovered over and over again, being hospitalized a number of times. They complained of the effects of the medications on her body – that they made her weak, that she would sleep all the time, that she became fat. And they told, with some anger, of one incident when the medicine prescribed was "too strong," when one of the physicians apparently failed to provide anti-Parkinsonian medications and her body had become so stiff that she could hardly move or turn her head until they returned to the hospital physician for the correct medications.

And how did she feel when she was sick? She would become irritated, *mangkel*, they said, using the Javanese term, *kecewa*, meaning frustrated or disappointed. And at whom was she irritated? It isn't necessary to say, since that was in the past. But yes, in the beginning she was irritated with one person, an acquaintance in the university, but as time went on and the situation at home was difficult, it all piled up. And so she would get sick, then get better, then get sick again. "And when you were sick the first time, what did you feel?" Bandi asked Yani:

YANI: The first time, it was because of being *jengkel*, but the cause of the following times, sometimes it was because the attitude of my mother was not *cocok*, not compatible with me.

BANDI: So what were you feeling and experiencing at that time?

YANI: Yes, at that time, the feeling of my heart was not at peace. I didn't have (enough) religious knowledge (*ilmu agama*). Then I learned how to read the Qur'an, then I studied religious knowledge, so that I was not so easily *jengkel*, irritated, by other people. But when I studied religious knowledge, what happened to me was that I sometimes couldn't understand clearly, so that [I questioned why what I saw another person doing didn't fit with the religious knowledge that I was learning].

BANDI: So what did you do?

YANI: What I wanted, I wanted to have religious teaching. I wanted to have an Islam that is pure, *murni*, original. Therefore, I wanted to go out of the house.

BANDI: Oh, to go? To go where?

YANI: I wanted to have a pure Islam, for example like that in Saudi Arabia.

YANI'S MOTHER: At that time she left the house. She has already (run away from) the house two times. At that time when she was in Yogya she went and then returned home again, she turned herself in to the police, and asked the police to tell her mother, and then we picked her up in the police office. The second time, in Jakarta, at the place of her older sister, she also ran away. She was sick again at that time, she said that she was going to go to Saudi Arabia. But in reality, because she was sick, she was walking along the toll road. [When she was asked by the police where she was going, she said,] "I want to go home but I don't remember the way."

Her mother completed the story of the Jakarta episode by telling how the police sent her home by a motorcycle taxi, in the care of a driver who took her home even though she had no money. Meanwhile, she – the mother – had spent the night worrying, saying in her heart, "Where has this child gone that she hasn't come home? What will happen to her in Jakarta? My thoughts were upset. That night it was raining, and she got drenched and was cold, all wet." And then the door opened, and she walked in and said she had been off to Kampung Rambutan, a distant part of the city.

And thus, with these brief vignettes, the initial outlines of Yani's story emerged. She hinted at a relationship with someone she had known as a student that had gone awry, leaving her disappointed, frustrated, and angry, but she refused to speak about it. Her mother later confirmed that he was a boyfriend, someone she had been close with. After graduating, she had gone to live and work in Jakarta. She found it hard to make friends, got sick, and after seven months returned home. She has continued to live at home since that time, remaining in the small home in which she grew up, locked into an intense relationship with her mother, who is primarily responsible for her whenever she is sick. She has been sick many times, and during one of her episodes, she left home, went off wandering along a river, and did not return for many days. It was this brief outline of a story that we attempted to make sense of, to explore during this visit.

From the beginning, while acknowledging that she is someone who becomes sick, Yani framed the story as an attempt to find a pure Islam, to escape from conflict with her mother and find a place that is pure. Her mother, by contrast, described her as sick (*sakit*) and described the episodes in which she went off as times in which she became sick and "ran away," returning home in a state of confusion. These competing narratives continued throughout this interview, as we attempted to understand what we were being told.

We tried to ask a few simple questions about symptoms. Did she feel sad (*sedih*)? No, *jengkel* (annoyed, irritated). Feelings of guilt (*rasa salah*)? No, irritation. But she returned to her concern about practicing a true, deep, correct Islam, and the conflict with her mother that led to her feelings of irritation or anger:

YANI: ...as a Muslim I want to pray *khusuk*, with full involvement (deep absorption), I want to get the knowledge and study religious knowledge, but until now, I can't read the Qur'an, or if I read, not fluently...I don't care how my mother practices,... what I want is to practice my religious obligations (*ibadah*) correctly....

SUBANDI: But in the past, did you try to force others to follow your opinion?...Do you have this kind of tendency?

YANI: Yes, I have this desire, for example, but my mother forces me to do something different.... so I want to live my life one way, my mother, my grandmother another...therefore *jengkel*. So now about what my mother and grandmother want me to think, to be different, to burden me, I let it go, say I don't care, it's up to you, each one . . .

BANDI: So in the past you felt sick . . .

YANI: Actually, the feeling was *jengkel*, but my body was sick because of the drugs.

MOTHER: Because of *jengkel*, you feel stress, and then you get sick. . . .

Her mother made it clear that this was not simply "irritation," but much more serious episodes:

MOTHER: Yes, sometimes in the past she felt *mangkel*, then would become *muni-muni* (irritated and say whatever she felt like). She didn't get along with me (*tidak rukun* – not harmonious). So then I know [that she is sick] and I put her in the hospital. When she was there, she was treated with ECT, given medicine, and after three days I visited her again and she had gotten better.

BANDI: So at that time of stress, what was felt by Yani?

YANI: I just wanted to be by myself, not to get into fights (*tidak mengamuk* – not to run amok), to lock myself in my room, just to be by myself.

MOTHER: Yes, for four days and four nights, she didn't want to eat. So when you get sick, you usually lock the door.

As we read back through the interview, we see much of it was in this vein, with Yani talking about her desire for a proper Islam, suggesting that her mother and grandmother had different ideas about Islam, and that this made her *jengkel*, not sick. It was the medications that made her sick. Her mother, on the other hand, described the difficulties of caring for a daughter who periodically becomes sick, becomes contentious, locks herself in her room, and at times runs away in a state of confusion:

BANDI: So according to Yani, is this really a sickness, or only *jengkel* ?

YANI: According to me, I just wanted to be alone, but my mother could not accept this condition. Then I was brought to the hospital. It was my mother's business, not mine.

MOTHER: Yes, if you lock yourself in the room for four days and don't eat and don't drink. Once she felt that wearing clothes is *haram* (religiously impure), so she didn't wear anything in her room. *Itu namanya sakit!* 'The name for that is sick.' So when I approached her, she asked me to get away.

We asked about Yani's relationships. Yes, she has had another *pacar* (boyfriend) but, for religious reasons, she keeps a distance and this may make others think that she doesn't like him. Would she like to be married? Of course, as a human, she prays for that, but it would have to be someone willing to sacrifice themselves, given her physical condition. We asked about the possibility of black magic being involved. (Bandi: Did anyone do black magic to her? Yani: Actually, the cause is often from someone in the house, who has a different opinion, for example, one's mother. . . . Bandi: Do you feel there is jinn or *shetan*? Yani: No.) Did she go to alternative healers? My mother would know about that. Yes, she had taken her to a number of healers, but finally her family said she had spent enough money on that, and she hadn't gotten better, so why not take her to the hospital.

We asked about the time that she had gone off, wandering along the river. "Do you remember?" we asked. "Yes, I walked to the east, I know. . . ." "Do you remember? . . ." "Yes, I went along the bank of the river." "Weren't you afraid of snakes?" "No, because I wasn't really aware (*sadar*), so I wasn't afraid." "So you weren't really aware, you just wanted to walk?" "Yes, basically at that time I considered food as *haram* (impure, forbidden), clothes also *haram*, my desire was to find a spring that was pure, clean, like that." "Were you confused, *bingung*?" "Ya . . . it seemed, usually, because of the attitude of mother, so I felt that she was not really my mother." "Yes," her mother interjected, "when she was like that, she would ask me to go away. . . ."

We concluded with discussions of the *kiyai*, the Islamic leader whose services (*pengajian*) she has been attending, a suggestion that we might visit him, and a discussion of what she hopes will happen in the future.

We went to visit Yani again two months later. In the meantime, we had spent an afternoon with Pak Han, the *kiyai* whom Yani had been visiting as a form of religious treatment, discussing his religious services and healing activities. He knew Yani, but knew little of her story; he was clearly not involved in a psychotherapeutic relationship with her, in the usual sense of that word. In addition, Subandi had stopped by to bring Yani an Indonesian translation of the Qur'an, as a gift, and had been told by Yani's mother that she was sick and could not see him at that time. We were thus concerned that Yani might be sick and feel that our discussion had been too stressful for her. When we arrived, we were relieved to find Yani well and both Yani and her mother happy to see us. We chatted comfortably with them for some time before moving more formally into an interview, which, this time, took place almost exclusively in Javanese with Subandi translating for me occasionally. Yani seemed in good spirits, showing no appearance of illness, and she and her mother seemed more at ease than the last time we were together.

Subandi and I were thus surprised when Yani launched into the story of her most recent illness:

I've got the *doa* (an Islamic prayer), the *doa*, which should be recited when I get sick. So I have recovered (become aware, *sadar*) from the illness, because every time after practicing *sholat* (the formal ritual prayer, done five times per day), I recited this *doa*. When I was sick, my hand was involuntarily pinching myself, twisting the skin, and pulling my hair, twisting, pulling my ears. It could not be controlled. I continued this, pulling my hair, pulling my hair, and it hurt. My mother also knew. She held my hand, trying to stop me. Then every time after practicing *sholat*, I said this *doa*. Then, I told Pak Han, that the *doa*, which was taught by the Prophet was already proven. The *doa* was accepted.

Yani's mother elaborated the story, from her perspective. "So right after you left the house, she became sick. Then when you came here to give her the Qur'an, she could only sleep. I asked her to do some things. She didn't want to do anything, she didn't even want to eat." "When my feet were cold," Yani broke in, "my feet were rubbed with kerosene, and then my mother *ndremimil* (mumbled a prayer or mantra to me)." "Her feet were so cold, I was so worried. . . ." her mother responded. "Mother recited a mantra," Yani continued. "Why did you recite mantras? It isn't fitting (*cocok*) for me to be brought to a *dukun* (a traditional healer)." "It wasn't a mantra," her mother responded in good spirits. "It was a prayer from Islam. I recited whatever I could, like *astagfirullah alhazim . . . nggih lhailahhailaahaa . . .* whatever I could do. But Yani was angry." "Why do you do that? Why do you like using mantras?" asked Yani. "This isn't a mantra, this is a prayer from Islam," I said like that. "When she got sick, I became like her enemy, so I had to be really patient (*sabar*). She recovered after I recited Sholawat nariah every night forty-one times, for almost one hour."

The illness began, they agreed, after Yani's feelings had been hurt by being teased by Pak Han. She had gone to his *pengajian*, his religious service, was given the role of greeting the guests, and was asked to help set up the chairs. When she refused, saying she was too weak, Pak Han teased her, saying "so you don't want to help with the *pengajian*." "Actually Pak Han wanted me to have an activity," Yani said. But she had already become very sensitive, they agreed. "I already knew she was *kagol*, " her mother said, using a word used when a child longs for something, expects it, and is then disappointed. "I already knew. I recognized it. . . . Actually, I was already treating her carefully, gently."

Although apparently triggered by this event, Yani's recent illness seemed to have little logical relation to this story. Perhaps because we were so close to her recovery, Yani provided vivid descriptions of what she had just been through. Unlike our previous meeting, when she seemed to blame her mother for her difficulties, she seemed to have a relatively clear sense of her experience as illness.

"When I was sick, it seemed as though there was a whisper (*bisikan*) in my ear, my hand twisting my skin until I hurt. . . ." "It was involuntary. . . ." her mother interjected. "What was the whispering like?" Bandi asked. "The whispering was continuous. . . . 'You are still small (*cilik*, a word used commonly for a small child), but you have to be responsible' – many times, so my thought was pressed down, suppressed." She described how she avoided people, because her feelings would be hurt and she would get into quarrels. "That is why I stayed in my room. But when I didn't want to eat, my mother struggled to make me eat, so I have become small (*cilik*)," she said, suggesting an image of regression.

She returned several times to a description of the strange changes in her thinking:

It seemed that there was something pressing down, so my thoughts were not my own, the thoughts were pressing down, being pressed down continuously, the whispering overlapping, one coming before the other finished. . . . It was not me. Why was I controlled by something bad? Even inside, there was a being inside me. . . . Inside my body, there was a being that was not me myself, like that, like that. . . . Or again, the thought was suppressed (*pikiran itu ditekan*) from the inside of my thought, as if continuously, the ears were whispered (into), as if my life was not my own. So I was like a robot. Why was I like a robot? Thoughts were not my own thoughts. Whispering. Hands were controlled. . . . When I performed *sholat*, I had little consciousness. The rest, it was not my own consciousness (*kesadaran pribadi*).

"According to Yani, who took control?" Bandi asked. "According to me, there was an attack from the outside. So there were other people who hate, then attack, with *kejawen* (Javanese)," she said, using a term that implied Javanese magic. "So 'black magic' (said in English) – last time you asked me, and I said there was no one who attacked, that the problem was in the house," she said, drawing our previous interview into her story. "After I became aware of this, there was this attack from other people." "By whom? Who might it be?" Bandi asked. "Yes, there was someone who was suspected," Yani replied. "My mother already knew. . . . It was not his own hand," she said, suggesting that the perpetrator had hired a specialist to attack her.

Yani went on to tell a long story about the man she suspected of doing this. The man she suspected, it seems, was a friend of the man she had previously mentioned as her *pacar*, the boyfriend she had had since returning to Yogya. She told a rather vague story about knowing him since she was small, then rooming in the same house with his sister when she worked in Jakarta, and that he lived nearby. One night she woke to find him standing near her bed. Though apparently nothing happened, she suspected he might want to do something "inappropriate." Another time she went to his house, was given something to drink, and became quite ill.

Yani then returned to the present and told an elaborate story about finding a fishhook in her prayer gown, thinking her mother had done something to her, then remembering that this man often talked about fishing and that she had found *kejawen* books in his house. It is difficult to tell if this story represents paranoia, or simply has a "subjunctive" quality (Good 1994:ch. 6), a sense of the mysterious. Such stories are thoroughly reality based in the lifeworld of Yani and her mother, and it provided a reasonable interpretation of her strange experiences as resulting from a kind of possession – by thoughts not her own, by a power that was not herself.

Yani and her mother had noted at times that when Yani was sick, she would see her mother differently, as her "enemy." As we talked, she provided a vivid description of the perceptual changes that led her to suspect even those close to her. "It seemed that outside, there were different beings. It seemed if I met other people, I was not really a human being. "For example," she told us, "if I met my neighbor, her voice was changed, her face was changed, so how could I interact with others?" "So how did you see them?" Bandi asked. "For example, I met Ningsih, like that, she changed and became Bu Jum. Bu Jum is the nurse at [the hospital]. The voice of Bu Jum . . . the face changed to be like Bu Jum, but only a little. Then, for example, there is someone who lives behind my house whose name is Arif, his voice changed, became the voice of someone . . . it turned out like that. So it was as if someone frightened me or there were voices, like 'dug-dug-dug' . . . it seemed to frighten me. . . . People who usually help me became like my enemies when I was sick." And those who usually helped her, she said, were the same persons who took her to the hospital.

She went on to complain again about the hospital and about the doctor who had given her a mistaken prescription. Then she returned to her theme. ". . . people seemed like different beings, because of changes in faces, in voices. I even asked my mother, are you a spirit, or are you a human being?" "When she got sick, she thought I was a *shetan,*" her mother interjected, "so we were in conflict. She thought I was her enemy." "Yes, because there was the fishhook like that, that is why I got angry," Yani agreed. "She thought I was the one who put the fish hook there," her mother told us. "I said, 'Am I crazy to put a fish hook there like that? I am a Muslim. I swear in the name of the truth, I swear I didn't put the fish hook there.'"

Finally, Yani returned to the story that she and her mother had mentioned earlier in the interview about how she had left the house, run away, and gone off to the river again. She had been bothered by sounds, she told us, for example, the noise of the small children playing outside her window, and she wanted to go to someplace quiet. So she had gone out to the river again, with a rice field beside it. A farmer found her lying beside the river, offered her lunch, and urged her to come to his house, to be with his wife, so that she would not be bothered by young people. And then suddenly her legs had begun carrying her home, beyond her control, simply moving as though they had their own will.

Yani returned to the story. "I just wanted to find a quiet place. I told my mother, basically, I want to clean my body. . . . I just wanted to stay quietly in my room to clean my body. My body was a dirty thing. I told my mother I wanted to pray. Maybe it would take six months, but if I wasn't yet clean, I would not go out from the house. I ate, but I said if you disturb me, I will run away. So I cleaned myself by using prayers." "You cleaned yourself because? . . ." Bandi asked. "There was whispering, the feeling of pressing, automatically, because it was not my own self, it was hard. So when I got sick, I often fought with my mother. She offered me medicine, but I wanted prayers. The medicine made my *doa* weak. And then we argued until I cried." And thus she returned to tell us about how she had used prayers, rather than medicine, to achieve her recovery.

We concluded this second interview by asking Yani to tell us about the initial relationship she had with her fellow student, the relationship that had been broken off leading to her first illness episode. She told the story in detail, without particular affect. We returned to talk a bit about her participation in Pak Han's religious group, promised to see her when we returned to Indonesia in June, and left.

We returned a year later, in August 1998, to visit Yani again. This time her mother greeted us, saying, "Oh, Yani remembered that you were supposed to return in June, and she was looking for you." She then went to call Yani. Though it was midday, we heard her asking Yani to get up, and we realized she must be sick again. Yani joined us, looking rather disheveled. Her hair was wet, from rinsing her face, and she wore an open dress, not appropriate for meeting guests. She spoke with us quite coherently, but in very abstract terms. She refused to be tape-recorded, and her conversation was so abstract it is difficult to reproduce. My notes read as follows:

It is difficult to remember what Yani said – because, with rare exceptions, she spoke quite abstractly and rather obsessively, not in a narrative style, talking about what life means, about Islam, about her disappointment in her environment, her disappointment in Islamic values – and resisted talking about specifics or real events. Examples of her talk: With all of these conditions, who is responsible . . . for all of what happened to me. I feel that my life is not my own, not decided by myself. Someone always takes control of my life. So what is the meaning of this, of life. For example, she recalled asking her father for money, but her grandparent asked her to save money in a piggy bank. What does this mean, she asked Bandi. He laughed, and didn't answer clearly, because there is no clear answer. I asked Bandi to ask her about her father, about her memory of her father. She said that her father died – he died in 1967, and she was born in 1961, and that was a very long time ago. She refused to speak any further about her memories of her father. Instead, she kept talking about the meaning of life, which she related to conditions in Indonesia.

Yani left, and her mother returned to talk with us. Yani had become sick again in June, when the sister of the man she spends time with told Yani that she is opposed to their relationship and tried to stop them from seeing each other. This hurt her feelings, made her feel *kagol*, and she became sick again. Yani's mother was in despair. She had had a nurse coming by to give Yani injections, but the Indonesian economic crisis had left her without resources to buy any more medication. We have nothing left but prayer, she told us. After giving her a gift, which could be used to buy medicines, we left, promising to see her after a year. Subandi returned to visit Yani six months later, in February 1999, and found her to be quite well again. She had been hospitalized for eighteen days in October, treated with neuroleptics, and had finally recovered and returned home. She was continuing to take her medications, and had tried to make a small business selling fried food. She gave this up because the economic crisis continued to make any small business activities difficult. However, she was active and talked about finding work.

Our last visits with Yani to date were in July and November of 1999. She was still quite healthy at this time, although this time she had decided to continue taking antipsychotic medication, while complaining about how much weight she had gained. She was open and reflective and told us several additional stories related to her experiences. She described how when she was sick, she felt the bed she was using was former President Sukarno's bed. Since she understood that Sukarno had been killed by his own assistants, persons she said were members of the Indonesian Communist Party, she did not want to remain in her bed. She also told how when she felt sick that one her neighbors, a man who had once been jailed for being a member of the Communist Party, was able to divert to her the punishment that he should have received. This was the reason that she would shout out her neighbor's name, calling him a genius.

Yani also told us that when she was ill, she sometimes heard two groups of voices. One set of voices were bad voices, which she associated with the voice of one of her boyfriends. These voices sometimes urged her to kill herself. Another set of voices, good voices, she identified as voices of Pak Han and another religious leader. These would whisper prayers in her ears, and would tell her that she should not kill herself, that she should die as a good Muslim. She described how these voices helped her respond to the voices urging her to kill herself.

Finally, we learned from Yani's mother that her husband, Yani's father, had had an episode of paranoia not long before he had died from a heart attack.[2] The father had secretly borrowed money and set up a small sewing business with another man in the neighborhood, refusing to tell his wife about the business. They were poor managers and the business was failing. About this time the father began acting strangely, staying awake at night and holding a weapon to protect himself. He began to feel that the Communists were threatening him, or that he might be accused of being a Communist, though he was not. This was 1967, a time when many members of the Indonesian Communist Party were killed throughout Indonesia, including in Yogyakarta, so fears of this kind were potentially realistic. However, Yani's mother insisted that her husband had become sick and withdrawn, had dug a large hole in the ground in the neighborhood, which he said was for the Communists, had dropped out of work, and had finally been hospitalized. Unfortunately, while hospitalized for his psychiatric problems, he died quite suddenly of a heart attack.

Remitting Psychoses: Diagnosis, Course, Experience

Hospital records indicate minor disagreement about the diagnosis of Yani's illness. The private psychiatric hospital, where Yani has been seen as both outpatient and inpatient for a number of episodes, records her diagnosis as Schizophrenia, Undifferentiated Type. The state hospital where she was seen in 1998 recorded her diagnosis as Schizoaffective Disorder, Manic Type, probably reflecting the prominence of positive symptoms, in particular the anger and agitation she displayed during the hospitalization. (On one occasion, Yani was angered when she was not given permission to perform prayers in the *musholla*, the prayer room of the hospital. She became violent, broke a window, and was placed in seclusion for one day.)

In our opinion, Yani meets DSM-IV criteria for Schizophrenia, Undifferentiated Type, with a longitudinal course classified as Episodic With No Interepisode Residual Symptoms. Positive symptoms are prominent during the acute episodes of her illness, and her levels of social and occupational functioning have been adversely affected since the first episode of her illness. The primary diagnostic question relates to duration. Her psychotic episodes are usually of rapid onset, most episodes have been quite brief, often (though not always) remitting in response to neuroleptic medication and/or ECT, and there is some question whether signs of her illness have persisted for six months. (During the 1998 episode, when financial hardship delayed her entry into treatment, the illness apparently persisted long enough to meet that criterion – perhaps for the first time.) In our experience, she is without serious negative symptoms, and her positive symptoms do not persist, even in attenuated form. ("Beliefs" associated with her delusions that some might consider "odd beliefs" when they persist – for example, that a neighbor is doing black magic to her – are normative in her cultural setting and shared in her family and neighborhood.) We find no evidence that she has met criteria for schizoaffective disorder.

It is particularly important to highlight the remitting course of Yani's illness, given the cross-cultural literature on the effects of social and cultural factors on the course of psychotic illness. Yani's illness displays many of the features noted in the DSM-IV (APA 1994:283) as associated with positive outcomes: good premorbid adjustment, acute or relatively rapid onset, female patient, presence of precipitating events (this is open to question, though she cites events in her narratives of episodes), brief duration of active-phase illness, good interepisode functioning, and minimal residual symptoms. She certainly experiences enduring disability – she is not married, she has never maintained a job appropriate to an Indonesian with a university degree. However, her personality – and personhood – are intact, and during long periods between episodes of acute illness, she is able to interact socially and reflect on her illness experiences with insight.

The cross-cultural literature suggests that remitting psychoses are far more common in some social settings than others, particularly in "developing" countries in contrast with North America and Europe. The WHO studies on schizophrenia (including the IPSS and the Determinants of Outcomes Study – WHO 1973; Jablensky, Sartorius, Ernberg, Anker, Korten, Cooper, Day, and Bertelsen 1992; Jablensky 1995) have consistently shown differences in overall outcomes between samples from nations classified as "developing" versus "developed" or "highly industrialized."[3] Recent analyses suggest that part, though not all, of these differences are accounted for by the higher incidence of acute onset, remitting psychoses in the developing country samples. Susser and his colleagues have argued strongly that Non-affective, Acute, Remitting Psychoses (NARP) should be considered as distinct from schizophrenia, proposing criteria to replace DSM-IV criteria for Brief Psychotic Disorder and ICD-10 criteria for the Acute and Transient Psychoses (Susser, Finnerty, and Sohler 1996). NARP – psychoses (with psychosis broadly defined) that are nonaffective (not meeting criteria for a mood disorder), have acute onset (less than two weeks from symptom onset to full-blown psychosis), and brief duration (less than six months to full recovery) – show distinctive clinical and epidemiological characteristics, they argue. Based on review of a number of recent epidemiological studies,[4] Susser and his colleagues suggest that incidence of NARP is as much as tenfold higher in developing countries than developed countries and twofold higher among women than among men, that the clinical presentation is often atypical for either schizophrenia or affective disorders, that the illness seldom becomes chronic, and that duration is typically four to six months (Susser and Wanderling 1994; Susser et al. 1995a; Susser, Fennig, Jandorf, Amador, and Bromet 1995b; Susser, Finnerty, and Sohler 1996).

For purposes of the current discussion, it is enough to note that psychoses with rapid onset and remitting course may be quite common in some settings, including Indonesia,[5] that classic discussions of "atypical psychoses" may be relevant even for samples that meet current criteria for schizophrenia,[6] and that care should be taken to guard against assumptions of chronicity when writing about subjective and experiential dimensions of schizophrenia. Indeed, questions about how diverse courses of psychotic illness are reflected in experience, as well as about how psychocultural dimensions of experience may feed back to contribute to more positive or adverse illness course, should be at the heart of the study of culture and schizophrenia.

Toward a Phenomenology of the Experience of Psychosis in Javanese Culture

Background

Several assumptions frame our reflections on Yani's experiences of psychosis and the implications of these for understanding subjective dimensions of psychotic illness in Java. First, we follow Fabrega in assuming that in addition to studying schizophrenia as a disease by focusing on "behavioral, neuropsychological, and psychophysiological" symptoms and processes, "psychotic disturbances can also be conceptualized in terms of ideas pertaining to the self" (1989:53–4). Fabrega argues that "in this type of conceptualization, one must take into account factors involving the formation, architecture and temporal extension of the self in a social

system" (Fabrega 1989:54). Because "the unfolding of a psychotic illness in a particular setting involves a pattern of destruction of selves
and subjectivities in that setting – selves and subjectivities constituted by
distinctive cultural models and social-familial environments" (Fabrega
1989:57), investigations should explore social and cultural dimensions of
the self. Our research thus focuses on dimensions of selfhood in Javanese
cultural psychology.

Second, we assume that psychotic illness produces dramatic episodes
of strange, disorienting experiences, experiences that occur in the midst
of everyday worlds and often lead to distinctive forms of withdrawal.
Lucas (1999) reports that although he would often interact "in perfectly
ordinary ways in a range of everyday settings" with persons participating
in his study of schizophrenia in community settings in Australia, there
"were times and places when these people were compelled to talk about
the most remarkable, difficult and ineffable experiences as a way of disclosing what they insisted was 'really' real about themselves and their
situations" (1999:2). He follows phenomenological writers such as Van
den Berg (1982) in observing the interpenetration of the extraordinary
into everyday perceptual worlds, and pursues questions about how these
experiential modalities were integrated into personal identity as well as
social and institutional worlds. Corin and her colleagues have focused
particular attention on distinctive modes of "withdrawal" characteristics of subgroups of persons suffering psychotic illness in Montreal, and
more recently in India (Corin 1990, 1998; Corin and Lauzon 1992, 1994;
Corin, Thara, and Padmavati this volume). These forms of withdrawal
appear closely linked to core experiences of psychosis – a feeling of fear
or terror, which derives from a perceived deep alteration of oneself and of
the world and the need to protect an "inner space" (this volume p. 118).
They are then linked, Corin hypothesizes, to patterns of constituting and
ritually respond to withdrawal and alterity particular to a given society
and culture. Our research is aimed at exploring the influence of culture
and religion on the ineffable experiences of psychosis and their integration
into everyday life in contemporary Java.

Third, we assume that the experience of psychosis is always a *social*
experience – at once social, psychological, and interpersonal. Experiences
of psychosis are mediated by life history and psychological development,
by interpersonal relations, particularly with intimates, systems of power
and institutional structures, and patterns of cultural interpretation and affective responses to persons suffering psychotic episodes. In societies like
Indonesia, attention to families is particularly crucial. Jenkins' work (for
example, Jenkins 1991, 1997; Jenkins and Karno 1992) highlights the
extraordinary import of emotional climate and affective dimensions of

social relations for persons with psychotic illness, particularly relations with family members. Her work shows how cultural interpretations influence emotional responses within families, and how these, in turn, are integrated into self processes. In a similar vein, Corin and her colleagues show that accounts of subjective experience require careful methodological attention to perspectives of both the sufferer and members of families (Corin, Thara, and Padmavati this volume). Our research thus focuses on families as the context for social experiences of psychosis.

Yani and her Javanese Lifeworld

Yani's narrative points to several psychocultural domains relevant to our understanding of the experience of psychosis in Java. We briefly outline these, drawing on the analytic frames we have reviewed.

It is impossible to listen to Yani and her mother without sensing the significance of Javanese culture and Javanese Islam for efforts to understand Yani's experience. Although medications, ECT, hospitalization, psychiatrists, and nurses have all been crucial in the treatment of Yani, psychiatric interpretations of her illness are far from hegemonic. Indeed, psychiatric conceptualizations of schizophrenia are almost absent from our conversations – there is no talk of chemical imbalances in the brain here – and the word "schizophrenia" is of little relevance. Instead, classic Javanese and Islamic themes – sometimes in tension, sometimes seamlessly integrated – as well as echoes of Indonesian political memory permeate their accounts of Yani's extraordinary experiences.

The Javanese lifeworld is deeply vitalistic, a world of powers and forces, of persons who have the ability to cause harm by destroying one's vitality, a world of spiritual practices aimed at enhancing one's *tanaga dalam* (one's inner powers). Underlying much reasoning and action in diverse Javanese worlds – *prijaji* (mysticism), village or neighborhood syncretism, Islamic practices, particularly those associated with Sufism[7] – is what Benedict Anderson described as "the idea of power."

Power...is not a theoretical postulate but an existential reality. Power is that intangible, mysterious, and divine energy which animates the universe.... In Javanese traditional thinking, there is no sharp division between organic and inorganic matter, for everything is sustained by the same invisible power. This conception of the entire cosmos being suffused by a formless, constantly creative energy provides the basic link between the 'animism' of Javanese villages, and the high metaphysical pantheism of the urban centers. (Anderson 1972:7)

In this setting, the self is constituted in terms of potency and is cultivated through a variety of spiritual practices, forms of self-restraint, and "concomitant refinement in language, sentiment and behavior that Javanese culture prizes in both men and women," which are, in turn, linked to one's position in the social hierarchy (Keeler 1990:130).[8]

There are two immediate implications of this conceptualization of the self for the understanding and experience of psychosis in Javanese culture. First, the break with decorum associated with psychosis is interpreted as a loss of ability to maintain a refined (or *halus*) self. It is thus deeply embarrassing, both to the sufferer and to his or her family members, threatening the place of the self in the status hierarchy of everyday life. The word *mengamuk*, "to run amok," is most typically used, not for a dissociative killing spree, the "amok" of the classic literature on culture-bound syndromes, but for outbursts of anger and violence that indicate an inability to maintain a restrained, refined self in interpersonal relations.[9] Such outbursts are, of course, common during psychosis, and in the old urban neighborhoods of Yogya, the sounds of such an outburst intrude violently into the soundscape of the *kampung*, making psychosis a highly public affair. Second, experiences of black magic or spirits are by no means essentially pathological. The self is by nature permeable to the *batin* world, to "what is generally imperceptible, mysterious, and resistant to obvious explanation" (Keeler 1987:39). There is thus less of a disjuncture between the everyday world and the lifeworlds of those who are psychotic than in some societies. A sense of something being done to one, of harm sent one's way, belongs to both worlds, to that of Yani and her mother, though we do not know what others think of their hypothesis that a friend's black magic is causing her illness episode. Spirits, too, belong to both worlds. Yet, as persons with psychoses recover they may realize that the powerful feeling that there are spirits in the house, speaking with them, is part of their illness. On the other hand, a potent or powerful person is able to relate to the unseen world without being harmed, and madness may result from contact with spiritual forces by one without adequate preparation or potency.

Yani's experience is deeply influenced not only by Javanese *kampung* culture, but by Javanese Islam. Indeed, much of her talk about Islam is predicated on conflict between that which is Javanese, *kejawen*, and that which is Islamic, probably reflecting contacts she had as a student with "modernizing" forms of Islam (such as Mohamadiyah), which call specifically for purifying Islam by excluding syncretic practices. There is an obsessive quality to Yani's talk about religion. She wants to practice only what is true Islam, the practices that are correct. She talks about the rules on fasting, about replacing fasting days lost because of her menstrual period, or her illness. She complains that her mother's wish that she fast on certain calendar days is not true Islam. On the other hand, when asked if she has been praying regularly or routinely practicing *dzikir* (Sufi chanting) she says "no, she is too lazy (*malas*)," or that it is not necessary because she has been ill. When she becomes ill, she continues to talk about these themes, but now much more abstractly, in global terms, focusing on the lack of a true Islam in Indonesia.

Themes of Islamic purity and impurity, linked more generally to themes of purity in Javanese culture, are also important mediators of her experience. She begins to feel that the house is *haram* (defiled, forbidden) that the food, her clothing, and the neighborhood are all *haram*. Her body is a dirty thing. And so she goes on a quest for a place that is pure, holy, to find a spring. The category of purity is no cognitive abstraction, for Yani, but an embodied sense. In cases of depression in Java, feelings of the body being impure often play powerfully along with feelings of being sinful or guilty, of having disappointed God, of having lost his favor – in ways that are familiar to those who treat Christian and Jewish patients. Yani's discussion of the impure has a more obsessive, less depressive quality, and it provides a motive for her extraordinary periods of wandering.

Islam is also present in her discourse as a potent source of healing. The *doa* she recites, along with her mother, offers the possibility of recovery. It has power, potency that is threatened by pharmaceuticals, Yani feels. The ritual practices – *sholat* in response to the call to prayer five times per day, repetition of various *sura* from the Qur'an, recitation of *doa* – organize her behavior and mark both her illness and recovery as she loses and regains her ability to concentrate.

Stories of withdrawal, mediated by both Islamic and Javanese forms, are explicit in Yani's narratives. When she has an episode, she withdraws into her own room, locks herself in, and seeks solitude. Indeed, after one of her episodes, she urged her mother to reorganize the space in the house, build rooms that could be rented out to students, and create a room that she could use as her own private space.[10] She describes her desire to withdraw as growing out of a feeling that the house has become impure (*haram*). She also describes the need to withdraw from her mother, to withdraw from conflict, and be alone in a clean space. Her stories of running away also seem to be culturally distinctive narratives of withdrawal rather than simply stories of confusion and wandering. She flees her house and neighborhood and wanders explicitly into marginal spaces along the river. She seeks a source of purity like a pure spring. She confronts dangers and returns. There are echoes here of classic themes in Javanese literature of heroes who go off, wander in the forest, confront demons, and return empowered to everyday life, a theme that also structures Javanese ascetic or mystical practices.[11] It is unclear how these classical themes are related to Yani's wandering, but her stories are consonant with Javanese themes, which organize a "culturally constituted space of illness."[12]

Finally, any discussion of Yani's experience must include careful attention to her personal and family history and the dynamics of her relationship with her mother. Yani suffered the loss of her father at age six, and grew up in an intense relationship with her mother and grandmother. Clearly, her mother – a strong, intelligent woman – is deeply invested in Yani, but their relationship seems always to have been conflicted. They were not *cocok*, not compatible, Yani says, from the time she was small. It turns out that her mother grew up Christian, not Muslim, and she apparently remains committed to Javanese practices, though she is now Muslim. Thus, the problems between Yani and her mother have cultural and religious dimensions, even though Yani remembers their disagreements having gone on since her childhood. During our interview in 1998, though she was not well, Yani told us that her mother and mother's mother used to argue with each other, and still do, and that she has long had to try to mediate between them. She said explicitly that when she got sick, they stopped arguing, suggesting a possible meaning of her sickness.

Yani's relationship with her mother seems to become more difficult when she begins to become ill, and when she is sick, she sees her mother "as her enemy." Indeed, her illness symptoms and her recovery are discussed by both mother and daughter through the medium of their relationship. Yani attempts to withdraw, while her mother actively resists her withdrawal. Yani's mother sleeps with her when she is ill to make sure she doesn't run away, or Yani resists sleeping with her, or the mother tells us that now that she is better Yani sleeps with her again. Similarly, her eating problems not only index her illness but do so via indexing their relationship. When Yani became sick, her mother told us, she ate almost nothing, one banana a day. Later she ate a bit of rice, then rice and vegetables. "Later she became bored with this kind of food, and wanted to eat what I ate. But she didn't want to eat together with me. So I had to separate the food – her food from mine. Finally, she was able to eat together with me." Their eating together is thus described as iconic of Yani's return to the world of sociality.

Yani also seems quite sensitive to losses. She uses the word *kagol*, a word translated literally as "frustrated" but suggests the kind of feeling a child has when he or she does not receive something longed for and expected, to describe her feelings of loss when her relationship with the young man she hoped to marry was cut off. Her stories of her relationships with men since that time are colored by the fact that she has been ill, but they describe an ambivalence about how close to get to men, a longing for a relationship but the experience of relationships as dangerous. And ultimately a man she thought was a friend who appeared threateningly in her bedroom in Jakarta is now suspected of causing her most recent illnesses by doing black magic against her.

Although our data are limited, we are suggesting simply that the need to explore developmental issues and primary relationships is particularly important for individuals who suffer intermittent psychoses. It is necessary for understanding their strengths and vulnerabilities, the psychocultural themes that emerge in psychotic experience, as well as how psychotic experiences are later understood and integrated into experience. We cannot understand the "experience" of these individuals without exploring their subjective and intersubjective worlds, their psychological functioning and styles of interpersonal relating. Families are often at the center of their interpersonal worlds. We do not yet have enough data to map the range of family responses to a member with psychotic illness in Java, as Jenkins has developed for Mexican-American families, or the patterns of relating to their families by persons with psychotic illness, as Corin and her colleagues have developed for Montreal. But Yani's case makes clear that Jenkins' insistence that research should focus on families – on their interpretations of illness, the affective climates of families, and interventions by particular family members – is particularly important for this research.

Conclusions

We conclude by restating two sets of questions that inspired this chapter and seem to grow out of it. First, does the study of psychotic experience for persons suffering from acute, recurrent psychotic disorders require different questions and different approaches than the study of more chronic thought disorders? Do such disorders require more intensive psychological interpretations – a search for psychological dynamics to the onset of psychotic symptoms or to recovery? What is the experience of psychosis like for those who have intact personalities, who have been psychotic and worry they might be again, but are currently without thought disorders? Katharine Shaw and her colleagues (Shaw, McFarlane, and Bookless 1997) suggest that psychosis may be traumatizing, that PTSD may be an appropriate model for examining the effects of the trauma of psychosis and hospitalization. What are the continuities, as well as disjunctures, of experience across psychotic and nonpsychotic experience for such persons? Are some groups of intermittent psychotic disorders to be distinguished from schizophrenia? Do current diagnostic systems provide an adequate basis for making appropriate distinctions? Is it true that acute psychoses are more prevalent and unremitting psychoses less frequent in some cultural and social environments? If so, how do we understand this? How can close attention to the cultural phenomenology of the experience of such disorders help answer these questions?

Second, how can we better conceptualize the interactions between broad social and cultural processes and self-processes linked to psychosis? May it be that psychotic symptoms trigger a set of distinctive social and cultural responses, which influence self-processes of those who are ill, and these in turn interact with neurobiological processes to determine the course and prognosis of psychotic illness? Corin's suggestion that we focus on "withdrawal" provides one potential model for linking social and self-processes. Both Corin and Lucas found that many persons suffering schizophrenia in their samples (in Montreal and Adelaide) turned to marginalized religious groups or forms of parapsychology where they found some validation for their extraordinary experiences. In Java, by contrast, although psychotic experiences (of voices, spirits, and black magic) are also extraordinary and deeply troubling, they do not require resort to alternative psychologies. Indeed, those who seem most fascinated by parapsychology are Javanese academics, particularly psychologists, whose extraordinary experiences, highly valued among Javanese spiritual groups, can only be validated by parapsychology or psychologies alternative to Western academic psychologies. Corin's suggestion that we compare ritualized forms of withdrawal across cultures – for example, Hindu asceticism, African spirit possession, and North American retreat to marginalized religious groups – offers an important direction for continued research. Studies of families may provide a second model for linking social and self-processes. Examining the complex interactions among psychotic symptoms, responses by family members most deeply affected, interpretations of these responses by those who are ill, and course of illness may provide insights into how social and cultural processes influence course of psychotic illness.

Answers to the questions raised here will require detailed, longitudinal research that is cross-cultural and focused on diverse naturalistic settings, yet uses careful methodologies that make comparison possible. It is precisely such work that is required if cross-cultural studies of psychosis are to contribute to our understanding of schizophrenia as they should.

NOTES

1 When the first person is used in this chapter, reference is to the first author Byron Good. Good is responsible for the written text of this manuscript, while Subandi is a full collaborator, playing the primary role in conducting the interviews and participating in analysis of the data. This project was supported by a Senior Fulbright Lectureship in 1996 and an NSF Grant in 1997–98.

2 This story emerged in an interview carried out jointly with Dr. Rob Barrett, who was visiting Yogyakarta and accompanied us for a visit to Yani and her mother.

3 These findings, particularly the relevance of the distinction between "developing" and "developed" or "industrialized" societies, have been roundly debated (see particularly Cohen 1992, followed by responses and a debate in the same journal; cf. Kleinman 1988, Hopper 1991, Good 1997 for discussion).

4 Cross-cultural longitudinal studies of acute psychoses include the WHO Cross-Cultural Study of Acute Psychosis (Cooper, Jablensky, and Sartorius 1990), the Indian Council of Medical Research Collaborative Study of Acute Psychosis (1989), the WHO Determinants of Outcome Study (Jablensky et al. 1992), a series of studies in Chandigarh, India (for example, Susser, Varma, Malhotra, Conover, and Amador 1995; Varma, Wig, Phookun, Misra, Khare, Tripathi, Behere, Yoo, and Susser 1997; Malhotra, Varma, Misra, Das, Wig, and Santosh 1998), Egyptian research (Okasha, Dawla, Khalil, and Saad 1993), and recent Scandinavian research (Jorgensen, Bennedsen, Christensen, and Hyllested 1996, 1997).

5 We are currently carrying out an incidence study of psychotic illness in the Yogyakarta region, attempting to determine rates of rapid or acute onset illness.

6 These include classic writing on "reactive psychosis" (Jaspers 1913; confer Stromgren 1986; Munoz, Amado, and Hyatt 1987), "psychogenic psychosis" (Wimmer 1916), "schizophreniform psychosis" (Langfeldt 1939), "bouffee delirante" (see Pichot 1986 for a discussion), and "cycloid psychosis" (Leonhard 1961; Brockington, Perris, Kendell, Hillier, and Wainwright 1982; Brockington, Perris, and Meltzer 1982; Lindvall, Hagnell, and Ohman 1990; confer Perris 1990), as well as more general reviews of "atypical psychoses" (Manschreck and Petri 1978; Wig and Parhee 1987; Menuck, Legault, Schmidt, and Remington 1989).

7 This formulation reflects Geertz's (1960) classic categorization of forms of Javanese religion and culture as *prijaji, abangan,* and *santri.* These are reflected, respectively, in the elite, court-based practices of Javanese mysticism, village practices of ritual exchange (*slametan*), and relations with the spirit world and Islamic practices.

8 "In Java, the self is defined most crucially in two ways: as placed in the social hierarchy, and as in possession of a particular concentration of power" (Keeler 1987:19). Keeler elaborates this formulation in his remarkable exegesis of the Javanese shadow plays. See also J. Errington 1984; Stange 1984; and S. Errington 1989 for relevant discussions.

9 *Amok* is also used to describe mass behavior by unruly, violent crowds (confer Good 2001).

10 I was made aware of the significance of this by reading Lucas's discussion of the organization of space and the special significance of their own bedroom for persons with schizophrenia, living in their own apartments, or with their family in the community sample he studied in Australia (Lucas 1999:153–70).

11 I am grateful to John MacDougal for suggesting this interpretation.

12 Rob Barrett suggested this term during a discussion of this chapter at the Russell Sage Foundation.

REFERENCES

American Psychiatric Association. 1994. *Diagnostic and Statistical Manual of Mental Disorders, Fourth Edition* (DSM-IV). Washington, DC: American Psychiatric Association.

Anderson, Benedict R. O'G. 1972. "The Idea of Power in Javanese Culture." In C. Holt, ed., pp. 1–69. *Culture and Politics in Indonesia.* Ithaca, NY: Cornell University Press.

Barrett, Rob. 2002. "Kurt Schneider in Borneo: Do First-Rank Symptoms of Schizophrenia Apply to the Iban?" In R. Barrett and J. Jenkins, eds., pp. 87–109. *Schizophrenia, Culture, and Society: The Edge of Experience.* Cambridge: Cambridge University Press.

Brockington, Ian, Carlo Perris, R. E. Kendell, V. E. Hillier, and S. Wainwright. 1982. "The Course and Outcome of Cycloid Psychosis." *Psychological Medicine* 12: 97–105.

Brockington, Ian, Carlo Perris, and Herbert Meltzer. 1982. "Cycloid Psychoses: Diagnosis and Heuristic Value." *Journal of Nervous and Mental Disease* 170: 651–6.

Cohen, Alex. 1992. "Prognosis for Schizophrenia in the Third World: A Reevaluation of Cross-Cultural Research." *Culture, Medicine and Psychiatry* 16: 53–75.

Cooper, John E., Assen Jablensky, and Norman Sartorius. 1990. "WHO Collaborative Studies on Acute Psychoses Using the SCAAPS Schedule." In C. N. Stefanis, A. D. Rabavilas, and C. R. Soldatos, eds., pp. 185–92. *Psychiatry: A World Perspective.* Amsterdam: Elsevier Science Publishers.

Corin, Ellen. 1990. "Facts and Meaning in Psychiatry: An Anthropological Approach to the Lifeworld of Schizophrenics." *Culture, Medicine and Psychiatry* 14: 153–88.

———. 1998. "The Thickness of Being: Intentional Worlds, Strategies of Identity, and Experience Among Schizophrenics." *Psychiatry* 61: 133–46.

Corin, Ellen and Gilles Lauzon. 1992. "Positive Withdrawal and the Quest for Meaning: The Reconstruction of Experience among Schizophrenics." *Psychiatry* 55: 266–81.

———. 1994. "From Symptoms to Phenomena: The Articulation of Experience in Schizophrenia." *Journal of Phenomenological Psychology* 25: 3–50.

Corin, Ellen, Rangaswami Thara, and Ramachandran Padmavati. 2002. "Living through a Staggering World: The Play of Signifiers in Early Psychosis in South India." In R. Barrett and J. Jenkins, eds., pp. 110–145. *Schizophrenia, Culture, and Society: The Edge of Experience.* Cambridge: Cambridge University Press.

Errington, J. Joseph. 1984. "Self and Self-Conduct among the Javanese *Priyayi* Elite." *American Ethnologist* 11: 275–90.

Errington, Shelly. 1989. *Meaning and Power in a Southeast Asian Realm.* Princeton, NJ: Princeton University Press.

Fabrega, Horacio. 1989. "On the Significance of an Anthropological Approach to Schizophrenia." *Psychiatry* 52: 45–65.

Geertz, Clifford. 1960. *The Religion of Java.* New York: Free Press.

Good, Byron J. 1994. *Medicine, Rationality and Experience.* Cambridge and New York: Cambridge University Press.

———— 1997. "Studying Mental Illness in Context: Local, Global, or Universal?" *Ethos* 25: 230–48.

Good, Byron with M. A. Subandi and Mary-Jo DelVecchio Good. 2001. "Le Sujet de la Maladie Mentale: Psychose, Folie Furieuse et Subjectivité en Indonésie." In A. Ehrenberg and A. M. Lovell, eds., pp. 163–195. *La Maladie Mentale en Mutation: Psychiatrie et Société.* Paris: Éditions Odile Jacob.

Hopper, Kim. 1991. "Some Old Questions for the New Cross-Cultural Psychiatry." *Medical Anthropology Quarterly* 5: 299–330.

Indian Council of Medical Research. 1989. *Collaborative Study on the Phenomenology and Natural History of Acute Psychosis.* New Delhi: Indian Council of Medical Research.

Jablensky, Assen. 1995. "Schizophrenia: Recent Epidemiologic Issues." *Epidemiologic Reviews* 17: 10–20.

Jablensky, Assen, Norman Sartorius, G. Ernberg, M. Anker, Ailsa Korten, John E. Cooper, Robert Day, and A. Bertelsen. 1992. "Schizophrenia: Manifestations, Incidence and Course in Different Cultures. A World Health Organization Ten-Country Study." *Psychological Medicine Monograph Supplement* 20: 1–97.

Jaspers, Karl. 1963 (1913). *Allegemeine Psychopathologie (General Psychology).* J. Hoening and M. W. Hamilton, trans. Manchester: Manchester University Press.

Jenkins, Janis. 1988. "Ethnopsychiatric Interpretations of Schizophrenic Illness: The Problem of *Nervios* Within Mexican-American Families." *Culture, Medicine and Psychiatry* 12: 301–29.

———— 1991. "Anthropology, Expressed Emotion, and Schizophrenia." *Ethos* 19: 387–431.

———— 1997. "Subjective Experience of Persistent Schizophrenia and Depression among U.S. Latinos and Euro-Americans." *British Journal of Psychiatry* 171: 20–5.

Jenkins, Janis and Marvin Karno. 1992. "The Meaning of Expressed Emotion: Theoretical Issues Raised by Cross-Cultural Research." *American Journal of Psychiatry* 149: 9–21.

Jorgensen, Peter, B. Bennedsen, Jakob Christensen, and A. Hyllested. 1996. "Acute and Transient Psychotic Disorder: Comorbidity with Personality Disorder." *Acta Psychiatrica Scandinavica* 94: 460–4.

———— 1997. "Acute and Transient Psychotic Disorder: A 1-Year Follow-Up Study." *Acta Psychiatrica Scandinavica* 96: 150–4.

Keeler, Ward. 1987. *Javanese Shadow Plays, Javanese Selves.* Princeton, NJ: Princeton University Press.

———— 1990. "Speaking of Gender in Java." In J. Monnig Atkinson and S. Errington, eds., pp. 177–206. *Power & Difference: Gender in Island Southeast Asia.* Stanford, CA: Stanford University Press.

Kleinman, Arthur. 1988. *Rethinking Psychiatry: From Cultural Category to Personal Experience.* New York: Free Press.

Langfeldt, G. 1939. *The Schizophreniform States.* Copenhagen: Munksgaard.

Leonhard, K. 1961. "Cycloid Psychoses – Endogenous Psychoses which are Neither Schizophrenic nor Manic-Depressive." *Journal of Mental Science* 197: 632–48.

Lin, Keh Ming and Arthur Kleinman. 1988. "Psychopathology and Clinical Course of Schizophrenia: A Cross-Cultural Perspective." *Schizophrenia Bulletin* 14(4): 555–67.

Lindvall, Marika, Olle Hagnell, and Rolf Ohman. 1990. "Epidemiology of Cycloid Psychosis." *Psychopathology* 23: 228–32.

Lucas, Rod. 1999. *Uncommon Lives: An Ethnography of Schizophrenia as Extraordinary Experience.* Doctoral Dissertation, Departments of Anthropology and Psychiatry, University of Adelaide.

Malhotra, Samit, V. K. Varma, A. K. Misra, S. Das, N. N. Wig, and P. J. Santosh. 1998. "Onset of Acute Psychotic States in India: A Study of Sociodemographic, Seasonal and Biological Factors." *Acta Psychiatrica Scandinavica* 97: 125–31.

Manschreck, Theo C. and Michelle Petri. 1978. "The Atypical Psychoses." *Culture, Medicine and Psychiatry* 2: 233–68.

McGlashan, Thomas H. 1988. "A Selective Review of Recent North American Long-Term Followup Studies of Schizophrenia." *Schizophrenia Bulletin* 14: 515–42.

Menuck, Morton, Sandra Legault, Peter Schmidt, and Gary Remington. 1989. "The Nosologic Status of the Remitting Atypical Psychoses." *Comprehensive Psychiatry* 30: 53–73.

Munoz, Rodrigo, Henry Amado, and Sharon Hyatt. 1987. "Brief Reactive Psychosis." *Journal of Clinical Psychiatry* 48: 324–7.

Okasha, Ahmed, A. S. el Dawla, A. H. Khalil, and A. Saad. 1993. "Presentation of Acute Psychosis in an Egyptian Sample: A Transcultural Comparison." *Comprehensive Psychiatry* 34: 4–9.

Perris, Carlo. 1990. "The Importance of Karl Leonhard's Classification of Endogenous Psychoses." *Psychopathology* 23: 282–90.

Pichot, Pierre. 1986. "The Concept of 'Bouffee delirante' with Special Reference to the Scandinavian Concept of Reactive Psychosis." *Psychopathology* 19: 35–43.

Retterstol, Nils. 1986. "Classification of Functional Psychoses with Special Reference to Follow-Up Studies." *Psychopathology* 19: 5–15.

Shaw, Katharine, Alexander McFarlane, and Clara Bookless. 1997. "The Phenomenology of Traumatic Reactions to Psychotic Illness." *Journal of Nervous and Mental Disease* 185: 434–41.

Stange, Paul. 1984. "The Logic of *Rasa* in Java." *Indonesia* 38: 113–34.

Stromgren, Erik, 1986. "The Development of the Concept of Reactive Psychoses." *Psychopathology* 20: 62–7.

Susser, Ezra, Shmuel Fennig, Lina Jandorf, Xavier Amador, and Evelyn Bromet. 1995b. "Epidemiology, Diagnosis, and Course of Brief Psychoses." *American Journal of Psychiatry* 152: 1743–8.

Susser, Ezra, Molly T. Finnerty, and Nancy Sohler. 1996. "Acute Psychoses: A Proposed Diagnosis for ICD-11 and DSM-V." *Psychiatric Quarterly* 67: 165–76.

Susser, Ezra, Vijoy K. Varma, Savita Malhotra, Sarah Conover, and Xavier F. Amador. 1995a. "Delineation of Acute and Transient Psychotic Disorders in a Developing Country Setting." *British Journal of Psychiatry* 167: 216–19.

Susser, Ezra and Joseph Wanderling. 1994. "Epidemiology of Nonaffective Acute Remitting Psychosis vs Schizophrenia: Sex and Sociocultural Setting." *Archives of General Psychiatry* 51: 294–301.

Van den Berg, J. H. 1982. "The Schizophrenic Patient: Anthropological Considerations." In A. J. J. de Koning and F. A. Jenner, eds., pp. 155–64. *Phenomenology and Psychiatry*. London: Academic Press.

Varma, V. K., Narendra N. Wig, H. R. Phookun, A. K. Misra, C. B. Khare, B. M. Tripathi, P. B. Behere, E. S. Yoo, and Ezra S. Susser. 1997. "First-onset Schizophrenia in the Community: Relationship of Urbanization with Onset, Early Manifestations and Typology." *Acta Psychiatrica Scandinavica* 96: 431–38.

Wig, Narendra N., and R. Parhee. 1987. "Acute and Transient Psychoses: A View from the Developing Countries." In J. E. Merrich and M. von Granach, eds., pp. 115–21. *International Classification in Psychiatry*. Cambridge: UK University Press.

Wimmer, A. 1916. "Psykogene Sindssygdomsformer (Psychogenic Varieties of Mental Diseases)." In A. Wimmer, ed., pp. 85–216. *St. Hans Hospital 1816–1915*. Copenhagen: GEC Gads Forlag.

World Health Organization (WHO). 1973. *The International Pilot Study of Schizophrenia*. Geneva: World Health Organization.

7   To "Speak Beautifully" in Bangladesh: Subjectivity as *Pāgalāmi*

James M. Wilce, Jr.

Introduction

This chapter demonstrates that what Bangladeshis call *pāgalāmi*, madness, is shaped by metacommunicative pressures and cultural sensibilities touching gender and the aesthetics of behavior and experience.[1] My analysis, inspired by linguistic anthropology, uncovers one aspect of the relationship between Bengali culture, language, and interactive style. I analyze a transcript of videotaped conversation with a person with schizophrenia to focus on speech as contextually embedded interaction rather than simply a manifestation of individual psyche. I focus on conversational turn taking and breakdowns therein to uncover a Bangladeshi family's embodied sense of beauty in interaction. Videotape reveals uses of the body in gesture and postural orientation. Through their bodily and verbal acts, we can witness Bangladeshis struggling to achieve or maintain intersubjectivity, enacting local gender sensibilities, and responses to modernity.

Schizophrenia and *Pāgalāmi*: Dual Perspectives on Bangladeshi Cases

I focus my analysis on a woman I call Rani, about twenty years old at the time her encounter with madness began, whom I met in the course of doing anthropological fieldwork in Bangladesh. I describe her case in the context of families and villages, which is where the realities of Bangladeshi *pāgalāmi*, or madness, are still largely constructed, rather than in the framework of medicine, psychiatry, and mental institutions. In relation to Rani's case and a number of others, I had the advantage of collaborating with Dr. Chowdhury, a practicing Bangladeshi psychiatrist, who was trained in the United Kingdom and who diagnosed these cases as fulfilling the ICD criteria for schizophrenia. I will contextualize the story of Rani and draw attention to some of the features she has in common with others who are called *pāgal* (mad). The *pāgalāmi* model inflects the broad range of local forms of madness; consistencies across these cases warrant

196

attention to that model insofar as it is itself a factor in the behavior and experiences associated with madness in Bangladesh. Thus, I also draw upon my knowledge of other cases – and of ample interactions (some recorded) in normal families – that I am unable to present here (Wilce 1998, 2002).

Gendered Identity and Language in Bangladesh

Bangladesh is the product of river deltas. Its floods constantly renew the topsoil on which rice depends, though they can also wash away whole villages and, over the long term, threaten the whole city of Chandpur, capital of the district that includes the subdistrict Matlab where I undertook two periods of fieldwork (in 1991–92 and in the summer of 1996). Rani's first acute psychotic episode followed a particularly frightening flood. Her insistence some four years later that she was seeing snakes invisible to others might represent a memory of snakes floating in the muddy waters at that time.

Rani's family represents the rapidly shrinking Hindu minority in Bangladesh (Nasrin 1994), while the other cases I draw on are Muslims.[2] Hindus and Muslims share some of the ethos of *pardā*, a more or less strict gender segregation, most visibly represented by the "veils" or head-to-toe coverings that Muslim women wear. Gender relations have changed radically since the times of the original *ādibāsis*, the indigenous residents of Bangladesh, now largely swallowed up or driven off. The female spirits of the *ādibāsis* (the sometimes sexually charged *bhut* spirits), and the gendered *jinn* (male) and *pari* (female) of orthodox Muslims' spiritual world, are still feared by Muslims and Hindus alike. A wildness beyond control is associated with *ādibāsis*, as well as with the *bhut*, *jinn*, and *pari* spirits. The following proverb links two other categories within Bengali culture that exemplify behavior that is out of control:

chāgale ki nā khāy, pāgale ki nā kay.
What won't a goat eat – and what won't the mad say!

Wildness is thus associated with those who are mad as well as animals, spirits, and jungles.

Rice agriculture (symbolized by the plow) occupies a central place in the Bengali cultural order and represents the subjugation of the "wild" *ādibāsis* and the end of their way of life. Given the associations between the *ādibāsis* and female spirits, agriculture is also a highly gendered symbolic field. The plow is likened to the phallus and represents male dominance, while the field represents the auspicious form of female fertility: the form under male control. Muslim folklore in Bangladesh depicts

Allah appointing Adam to the task of growing rice; this male work thus takes on religious significance, and these discourses in turn reproduce gender ideologies and gender relations.

The Bangla language and attitudes toward it were deeply influenced by the agencies of colonialism (Kopf 1969), which associated the Bangla-speaking Other with the poets of the Bengal Renaissance and with femininity, in contrast to the masculine British self (Nandy 1983; Banerjee 1989). The Raj's symbolic feminization of its colony provoked resistance movements that engaged the feminine (images of Mother and Motherland invoked again by India's current ruling party) in a rhetoric of violent resistance (Kakar 1978:260–81). Gender distortions and rage may reach unique levels among the mad in Bangladesh, but they still need to be seen against the backdrop of that history of colonial insult. Violent assertions of national pride are neither limited to present-day India nor to rhetoric. A rickshaw puller once told me about his participation in the Bangladesh Liberation War, during which he and his companions had faced daunting odds with great courage. He boasted that Bangladeshis fear nothing. The level of violence in Bangladesh must surely have grown significantly since 1971, with many weapons "left sitting around." To the extent that a willingness to commit violence – sometimes described as "fearlessness" – is now a part of the construction of male Bangladeshi identity, it is a problem (for some men) against which the profound fears typifying paranoid ideation are further shaped in personal and culturally typifying forms of "meta-emotion" (Gottman, Fainsilber Katz, and Hooven 1996), feelings and values in relation to emotion.

In recent decades, new forms of language have emerged in Bangladesh, particularly those representing the language of the new state. Increasing emphasis is being placed on rational and efficient "clear" speech. Valued speech forms exhibit both semantic discipline in the service of this clarity of reference and a commitment to intersubjective engagement – to common understandings, politeness, and mutuality that link speaker and audience. As mass public education has spread, even to the rural areas of Bangladesh, the challenge of helping children succeed in school has led to a proliferation of a new form of wage labor – late adolescent boys and girls tutoring younger children. Rani's sister earned money this way, making an important contribution to their household income. Such tutoring, along with the encouragement of public speeches by schoolchildren (that is, most of Bangladesh's children) on national holidays, enable role models of loud, clear speech to reach and influence many if not most Bangladeshi children, even in rural areas.

In this and other ways, modernity touched all the cases of madness that I became acquainted with insofar as even rural Bangladesh has been incorporated into the cash/wage economy. Mass education is becoming a reality even for girls, and some expectation of salaried employment is held out for male and female graduates of high school and college. The clash between these inflated expectations on the one hand, and severe unemployment and underemployment on the other, has a negative impact on the illness careers of the mad. Gender roles and ideologies are changing, too, but when troubled people violate gender norms – particularly notions of modesty and appropriate gender segregation (*pardā*) – they suffer from the sense of being abnormal and sometimes from open ridicule or even violent reactions from their families. Thus, cultural as well as economic values and pressures affect the lives of those called *pāgal*; gendered dimensions of the self are particularly vulnerable to both sorts of pressure.

Pāgalāmi: Bangladeshi Models of Madness

The "madness" label deserves our attention. In Bangladesh, much like West Bengal where it has been described in one ethnography (Bhattacharryya 1986), human *pāgalāmi* is likened to the behavior of goats – out of control, oral, intrusive, and sometimes embarrassing if not harmful to the household to which it may be tethered. Madness is norm-defiant behavior. Even so, it can be a divine gift. This equation of madness and divinity reflects socioreligious movements outside of Brahmanical Hinduism in medieval Bengal, movements involving more charisma than routine, which overtly rejected such pervasive norms as ritual purity and caste.

None of the twenty rural Bangladeshis whom I asked to list all the illnesses they knew mentioned madness. Yet whenever *pāgalāmi* shows itself to be not divinely inspired ecstasy, but insanity, people tend to call it a *rog*, or "illness." Help is needed, first in divining or diagnosing its cause (Bhattacharryya 1986). Even if someone can determine the cause, they might well have no medication for it. For "spiritual causes," treatment is of a ritual nature and is oriented to restoring moral balance.

Thus, the complex Bengali model treats at least some of the mad as agents, responsible for at least exacerbating their symptoms if not causing them. In other cases – even where patients are held to be the ultimate cause of their own madness – through violation of a taboo – people attribute mad behavior to an external agency. Among the external causative factors is *ālgā*, "[the influence of something] loose [like a "wild" spirit]" (Wilce 1998). In some parts of Bangladesh this loose thing is a "wind," but wind can be a euphemism for a spirit. A study of Bangladeshi immigrants in London (Bose 1997) found that family members attribute mad behavior to another euphemism – *upari*, "[the influence of something from] above."

During my fieldwork in rural Bangladesh, *jinns* "grabbed" (*jinn-e dhar-ech-e*) or possessed two recently married women, causing them to speak in a shockingly brash manner. In such cases of spirit possession, medication is not prescribed. Traditional practitioners treat the problem by magical use of select passages from the Qur'an, or in some cases, combine this practice with a very firm talk to the spirit by an exorcist, a talk involving negotiation, but finally a firm command to leave. Rani's family tried at first to treat her madness as a case of possession and arrange multiple exorcisms. Her mother says these failed; Rani agrees. After that, they gradually, if sadly, accepted her *pāgalāmi* as a part of her rather than the effect of a spirit. Thus, it often takes time for people to come to an agreement about the nature of a particular case of deviance. In the case of Rani, the possession hypothesis led to an intervention that failed; the family and their practitioners then turned to other hypotheses. Such trial and error is part of the local process of diagnosis. In greater Bengal (which includes Bangladesh and West Bengal), people distinguish between endogenous madness and "divine madness" (McDaniel 1989). If deviance lasts and exorcism fails, the madness will eventually be considered endogenous, *māthākhārāp* (bad head). Hopes dim. Exorcism either works quickly or never does, and there is no quick cure – perhaps no cure at all – for *māthākhārāp*.

This discussion of possession and madness leads us to a broad assertion. No classificatory, diagnostic, or therapeutic term has meaning on its own but rather derives meaning from the network of terms used with it or as alternatives to it. Regardless of whether a particular case is blamed on spirits at a particular stage, the semantic network (Good 1977, 1994) in which Bangla *pāgalāmi* is embedded, includes wildness and spirits – one reason to avoid reducing it to psychosis as a secular disease.

An ethnopsychiatric system that is as deeply pluralistic as is that of greater Bengal resists being placed on either side of the divide between optimistic and pessimistic, or exogenous and endogenous understandings of the cause of madness (Barrett 1988). In fact, the Bengali model assigns a role to body, spirits, substances, and actions. The body is both the ground of potentially "mad" behavior and its affected object. Bangladeshis may describe madness in terms of a heating of the head. They ascribe that heating to foods, acts (including, or perhaps particularly, speaking), or envision "the madness" as an entity localized in the head, with wild eating as its symptom.[3] Willfulness or willful behavior can be flexibly ascribed to madness or blamed as its cause. Eating or speaking with too much enthusiasm can be a problem. Lamenting – loud melodic weeping – that is judged excessive may be simultaneously used as evidence that the performer "is" mad and blamed as at least an exacerbating factor in her madness – an act of passion that must certainly heat her head further (Wilce 1998). Likewise, Dr. Chowhdhury can, within the course of a minute, hear a patient speak in a "paranoid" fashion, turn to me, and tell me in English that he suffers from paranoid ideation, and then turn to him and tell him that his thoughts will make him worse and he should control them. Thus, whether one is a psychiatrist or a "layman," to speak of *pāgalāmi* is to speak of a model of the self and its moral universe.

"Madness" and the Rhetorics of Bangladeshi Self hood

One reason *pāgalāmi* requires moral-ritual intervention is that it can arise from perceived moral violations including talking too much, too subjectively, or just wildly. We must see this madness as transgression in relation to legitimized and delegitimated Bengali strategies for handling subjectivity and achieving intersubjectivity. As I will show, Bangladeshis often express these strategies metacommunicatively (Bateson 1972), particularly in communicative acts that judge or guide the speech of others. *Pāgalāmi* is constructed largely in terms of morally deviant attraction of attention to the self.

Strategies for balancing subjectivity and intersubjectivity are culturally relative. We see this in the Bangladeshi tendency to find signs of madness in the very marks of individualism praised in the West. An anecdote related to me by Dr. Chowdhury from her mostly urban experience illustrates how madness becomes a key sign in the semiotic network around Bengali selfhood. Dr. Chowdhury needed to renew her passport; the bureaucrat dealing with her discovered that she was a psychiatrist, whereupon he opined that both madness and visiting a psychiatrist were *bilāsitā* (luxurious self-indulgences). I heard rural people voice similar judgments of a man who sang prayers lamenting his fate. Self-assertion appears to be self-indulgence in a context where interpersonal autonomy is not idealized. In South Asia, the idealized self is radically embedded in the hierarchical structure of the extended kin group. The positive individual self-regard encouraged by so much self-help literature in America is, in South Asia, matched by a family-based "we-self-regard" (defining self in relation to family, staking one's self-regard in the whole family's reputation – Roland 1988; Kurtz 1992). Where cultural traditions sing the virtues of group loyalty rather than individual self-expression, what one rural Bangladeshi called "singing your excuse" – probing or expressing one's subjective experience – is a disapproved luxury.[4]

Societies that regard madness as an illness bearing some relation to emotions that need to be worked through, may validate such work. But the *pāgalāmi* model values other sorts of work. Those Bangladeshis whom I prompted to talk about *pāgalāmi* described it in moral terms – as a failure of moral discernment entailing neglect of one's duty, the responsibilities accompanying one's gendered social role. Most Muslims, especially women, should not desire the position of those who legitimately lead prayers at the mosque or play other public roles. It is regarded as *pāgal* to raise one's voice – in lament song or even in prayer – in a public sort of way when one's role is understood to be much more circumscribed (Wilce 2002).

As an ideal type, bureaucracy is a product of "rational" states and cultures of efficiency (bureaucratic realities notwithstanding!). Dr. Chowdhury's bureaucrat was efficient to the end, providing a single word – *bilāsitā* – that condenses many views of madness I gleaned from the neighbors and family members of the mad. For instance, Rani's economically marginal family expressed a concern that Rani accepts no limits on what she eats. The fact that they consider Rani's appetite a form of self-assertion resonates with my American commonsense. What is striking, however, is the fact that self-assertion itself is so "marked" that it is taken as a symptom of madness. In such an interpretive climate, open displays of subjectivity by the well or the mad are threatening rather than desirable. One does not speak of one's innermost experience, nor do criticisms of the "luxury" of madness focus on their subjectivity. Experience is not expected to be the theme of discourse, and in fact is not even the explicit theme of those criticizing madness as a "luxury." Characterizations of the mad thematize what they do and say more than what they see, hear, dream, or perceive. The proverb cited earlier, linking goats and the mad, epitomizes the characterization of madness as (out of control) behavior rather than experience.

Thus, Bangladeshi discourses find indexes of madness in a range of acts, from singing one's prayers to eating "too much." What makes those indexes cohere into a single model, the *pāgalāmi/bilāsitā* model, is the notion of a deviant attraction of attention to self.

Subjectivity, Intersubjectivity, and Empirical Research: Interpreting Naturalistic Interaction

Unless we reflect deeply upon it, we in the West take language as a tool for referring to things in the world, things presume to exist quite apart from our speaking of them. Among these things that we often include in our image of "objects" to speak about are feelings. We speak of subjectivity as if feelings were stored "inside" a person, awaiting verbal expression in a transparent medium (language) that we don't imagine will have much impact on the feeling itself. It takes a little more reflection to realize that much speech is at least a kind of impression management. Wittgenstein went so far as to describe all uses of language as so many language games, by which he meant to draw an analogy between conversational moves and moves in a game like chess.[5] I think we err when we describe interviews as if they uncover the interviewee's truth, as if all interaction did not also serve the central function of negotiating the terms of relationships, or creating some relational dimension afresh. And it is important to realize that Bangladeshis and many other peoples do not share our model of subjectivity, or our value on "direct" and "sincere" expressions of feeling.

Spoken interaction is like a dance; it reveals joint achievements or failures as much as individual psychological realities. We can use videotape to get at both. When I videotape my own interaction with a family like Rani's, I learn as much from their semiprivate talk amongst themselves as from my questioning. Naturalistic moments of familial interaction that I have recorded on videotape often reveal more than do answers by those same persons to my questions. As speech events structured by outsiders, interviews are problematic (Briggs 1986); social scientists are at times confronted with the paradox of wanting to observe how people are with each other when they are not being observed.

I got to know Rani and her family in unstructured interactions, participating with and observing them in their life at home on several occasions. On some of those occasions I made audio- or videotapes of the interaction. Rani's sister Shapla and a male field assistant (Faisal) helped me transcribe and interpret the audiotapes *in situ*, and I was also assisted in my work with the videotapes by a number of Bangladeshi people in the United States – all of whom had been away from home less than two years – upon my return. Providing accurate transcripts is basic to my task; their accuracy primarily reflects the help of Shapla and Faisal on site in 1992. I relied on Bangladeshi consultants in the United States, not so much to translate, as to transcribe portions of the many hours of tape that serve as context to what is described here, and to reflect with me on the visible behavior which my U.S. video lab enabled me to show them – an advantage I did not have on the field in 1992.[6]

The sort of participant observation in which I got to know Bangladeshi families is the most fundamental, but also ineffable, of the methods anthropologists use. By no means did I videotape all of my interactions with Bangladeshi families during my five years there. I have no videotapes of normal families rebuking children for not answering questions adults put to them – but it does happen. At least when someone – for example, an adult – asks a question, families treat failure to answer clearly as a real infraction. In this sense, people expect clarity (as opposed to irrelevance or mumbling) at least as much at home as in public encounters. The presence of a visitor like myself does not make any given home encounter that unusual, given the frequency of social visits by neighbors and friends. Family members care about but can more easily overlook failures in the dance of interaction when no visitors are present, but the stakes are higher during a visit.

In a recent trip to Bangladesh it was after I had turned off my two video cameras and left the home of Pomul – a fifty-year-old man who had suffered with schizophrenia for thirty-five years – that his brother, Baro, walking with me to a corner where I could get a cab, described what it had been like to live with Pomul. Baro told me that, before that night, no one had ever told them that hearing voices was a symptom of Pomul's illness. Baro said that they used to punish the fifteen-year-old Pomul, at the outset of his illness, when he would plug his ears with his fingers. I presume this was to shut out his voices. Baro also admitted that for years the large family had blamed Pomul for ruining their reputation, since they "had never had another problem."

Although I did not tape that conversation with Baro, or other events in which Bangladeshi families work hard to get deviant members back into the dance of interaction or may even punish deviance, they form the context of the case study that follows. We lack broad surveys of what constitutes "normative" familial interaction there. We do not know what might constitute "hypercritical" emotional engagement in families with or without schizophrenia. What is clear, though, is that Bangladeshi families invest great energy to achieve a "beauty" that, for them, is constituted in the give and take of interaction.

Fortunately, people tend to forget about recording equipment after a while, and thus my recordings capture some sense of the everyday. In relation to families like Rani's and Pomul's, my open-ended interactions and loosely structured interviews are most revealing when they are least like interviews and most chaotic, multiparty, and Bengali in their structure and norms – most like naturally occurring family interactions. My presence itself had an effect. Even so, in the analysis of Rani's case, the videotape enables us to focus on what family members do with each other. When I examine their interaction, I discover how families may expect to verbally and gesturally "dance with each other," and if they fail, how they try to shape each other's moves. The metacommunicative moves of mother and sister – the signs they give in word and gesture of how they think Rani ought to communicate – deserve special attention.

Thus, what I tape – while not quite "natural" – deserves the label "naturalistic interaction," and in it we see naturalistic evidence of subjectivity. Although Bangladeshis do not talk much about subjectivity, their subjectivity and attempts to achieve and maintain intersubjectivity are still amenable to our analysis. Emotion, after all, is often signaled without being named or talked about. The "preference" – at least among the economically and politically marginalized majority in Bangladesh – for indirect signaling of experience simply constrains the methods of inquiry. It is best in this instance to approach subjectivity through naturalistic interaction. Of particular import are the ways in which those categorized as *pāgal* may index their subject position (that is, their right to experience or assert some desire) if not their inner experience.[7]

Embodiment offers itself as a relevant paradigm for the empirical study of subjectivity (Csordas 1990).[8] Videotaped interactions provide opportunities for studying how people strive to make sense of each other's actions, creating intersubjective understanding with or without verbal reference to inner experience (for example, emotion labels). Interpreters – kin as well as anthropologists – use embodied and verbal signs to signal tentative "readings" of each others' moves in the game of interaction, and correct misreadings, thus achieving common understandings through interaction (Garfinkel 1967; Schutz 1970; Duranti 1997). This works much of the time, but it is always tentative and fragile. Rani's case, which follows, reveals how repeated failure to achieve intersubjectivity can cause suffering, exacerbated when high expectations for this achievement are upheld. For the mad, the expectation that mutual coordination of talk and action should be counted on as a given appears to be more an ideology than a possibility within their grasp (Desjarlais 1997). My case study also exemplifies the contribution that analysis of videotaped interaction can make to the study of madness in domestic and therapeutic contexts.

To uncover these phenomena in videotaped interactions requires a fine-grained transcription of that interaction (Duranti 1997). Because of the importance of interactional timing in the achievement of intersubjective attunement (Sacks, Schegloff, and Jefferson 1974; Schutz 1976b) and thus in the analysis of interaction with the mad (Scheflen 1973), I attend closely to pauses and overlaps. I also attend to grammar and the poetics of psychotic speech because of what those features reveal about the orientation of the speaker, often in contrast with interlocutors' orientation.

Rani: A Case Study

I met Rani in 1992. Like many of the Hindus left in Bangladesh, Rani's family is barely able to survive. They live in a house of thatch, with a tin roof, within a few meters of the banks of the Dhonagodha River in which they must bathe, and which flooded in 1988. Rani spent much of her time squatting on the hardpacked dirt floor inside, or keeping the courtyard outside swept clean of leaves and debris. The household had no permanently resident males. It subsisted largely on what Rani's sister Shapla earned tutoring neighborhood children.

Shapla would lead the children in a polyphonous chorus of reading, demanding that each child speak out in a loud, clear voice. This is a highly valued form of oral literacy that bears some resemblance to political oratory in its marked intonation contours. Loud speech that remains on a high pitch until reaching a sharp drop at the end of each sentence achieves what Shapla calls "beauty," and does so in one of two ways. For individual orators it is associated with an aesthetic of clarity that is appreciated by audiences, especially so if the pitch is well controlled. For choruses of students or worshippers, it achieves a sense of ensemble and intersubjective attunement.

Rani had first become ill at the age of twenty, some four years before I first met her. Talking about the onset of symptoms with her mother, Mashima – my term of address for her as my fictive maternal aunt – focused on how hard it was for Rani when her sister, Shapla, sold her old books rather than pass them on to Rani so that she might, too, attempt the matriculation examination. Rani was hurt that her brother and sister would not put her through school.

Gender symbolism pervaded Rani's symptoms. She refused to bathe in the river because she (and no one else) saw snakes – an image Hindus connect with sexuality, the Serpent goddess, and Tantric Hinduism (Sullivan 2000). She dressed in a way that failed to meet the requirements of feminine modesty – in a *shalwar-kemiz* (loose pants, long blouse) but without a *dopatta*, the long and broad scarf to "cover the breasts." She also ate voraciously, a trait that stands out in a culture where households are male-dominated and women are expected to eat last and least. Rani's food demands violated gender norms; the societywide constraints on self-assertion fall particularly on women. Just as the Bangla proverb links goats with the mad and eating with speaking, so Rani's family viewed both her orality – eating and speaking – as out of control.

As I spoke to Mashima, Rani would change from staring, to shouting, to standing silently with one hand raised for minutes on end, to eating rice so greedily that some spilled out of her mouth – highly unusual for Bangladeshis, who try not to waste even one grain of rice. At one point Rani chased a rooster and hen away, shouting angrily. Though Mashima and Shapla had previously claimed to understand everything Rani said, on that occasion they told me, "She's speaking her own language, and we do not understand." They desperately sought my help to cure Rani so that she could be married into the family of some man who would at least have more to feed her than Mashima.[9]

Transcription Conventions

It was impossible to interview Rani about her subjective state, but it was possible through video and audio recordings to observe her spoken interactions, her bodily postures and movements, and the style in which her family interacted with her. In the following transcript, the participants are designated as follows: R is Rani, W is Jim Wilce, M is Mashima, S is Shapla, and B is a boy from the neighborhood. Pauses, measured in seconds, are recorded in parentheses. Parentheses also enclose words that are uncertain or hard to make sense of. Indecipherable syllables are designated with an x. A bracket between lines marks an interruption or overlap and is located at the point at which the overlap begins. "Stage cues," descriptions of a speaker's vocal quality, her addressee, and so on, are enclosed in brackets. Latching – a near overlap with no perceptible pause between speakers – is designated by =. Degree signs around a word or segment (°x°) indicate markedly quieter speech. Exclamation points represent markedly louder speech.

```
01   W: How did you sleep?
02   R: (2) (?? in my mind??)
03   W: Did you sleep?
04   R: On the day my mind was burning.
05   W: (1.5) Hmm?
06   R: It burns.
07   W: (2) I didn't get that.
08   R: (2) (for Allah's sake??), OK?
09   S: Speak (like a recitation) – can't you speak like that?
10   R: [They] don't take [it].
11   S: Speak! (.5) Speak beautifully.
```

For several minutes I talk with Mashima about what sorts of treatment she had previously arranged for Rani. The transcript resumes.

```
12   W: Now what will you do?
13   M: (.6) Son, what am I supposed to do (laughing)?
14   M: Can you, would you make her well?
15   (3)
16   W: (to R) Now (.2) what do you want?
     (2)
```

17   w: Rani.
18   m: (.1) Say, "I want to be well."
19   r: (laughing xxx)
20   r: (xxxx xxxxx)
21   m: Rani! Hey!
22   m: Say, "I want to be well."
23   r: (Mother, why would you need to get well?)
24   m: [Say] "I want to be well."
25   r: (2) [in normal, end-falling intonational contours] In whatever
     direction [Bangla dik-e].
26   r: The earth underneath this homestead [goes].
27   r: [goes], that's the direction (of the homestead?)
28   r: Let [someone] give [Bangla di-k e] this.
29   r: Let someone give (giv-). Give this.
30   r: Let someone give (xxx).
31   w: Ra . . .
32   r: If someone says to give.
33   m: The value=.
34   b: =(What was the cost?)=
35   w: =How did you feel about the healers?
36   w: How did you feel about the healers' treatment?
37   r: [smiles] °It went like (x)°.
38   s: Speak.
39   m: Speak!
40   s: [softly] Rani.
41   m: [leaning forward] The healers' treatment . . .
42   m: How was it?
     [
43   r: [shaking head negatively] Healers don't succeed.
44   m: Say "do not succeed."
     [
     [starts echoing M's head shake]

I first wish to focus attention on the spoken interaction between Rani
and her family members rather than the features of Rani's speech that may
arise from her schizophrenia. Conversation is probably a universal speech
genre defined by the norm of one person speaking at a time, with turn
taking determined by a range of culturally and situationally specific rules
(Sacks et al. 1974). Although speech communities differ in what they
consider a normal pause length, Bangla conversation shares with a number of other languages, including American English and Thai (Moerman
1988), a tendency to minimize interturn pauses and overlaps. Hence,

long pauses mark a break in synchrony. Short pauses are an achievement that reflects intersubjective attunement between interlocutors that enables them to anticipate that one is coming to a point at which another might appropriately take a turn. The short pauses between lines 12 and 13 and between 17 and 18 reflect how it is possible for intersubjective attunement to the rhythms of interaction to be achieved even when one interlocutor is a foreigner. Mashima knew my turns were complete. By contrast, attempts to engage Rani lead to awkwardly long pauses, evident throughout lines 1–8. After line 15, my question to Rani would make her an appropriate next speaker, but there follows, instead, a two-second pause. Such difficulties lead to overlaps. After my question in line 1, there was also a pause of two seconds. I gave up waiting for an answer and began reiterating the question, only to discover Rani had begun speaking. In line 19, Rani overlapped her mother's attempt to elicit a proper response to another of my questions. The transcript brings to light the contrast between the effortless interactive coordination between most of those present, and the awkward, disjointed attempts at interaction with Rani.

Shapla and Mashima enact a Bangladeshi value system that ranks the achievement of intersubjectivity over the expression of subjectivity. This culturally specific aesthetic, captured in the term *sundar* (beautiful), merges moral and emotional domains into bodily and linguistic interaction (Desjarlais 1992). We see this aesthetic evaluation of interaction, and particularly of Rani's speaking, in lines 9 and 11. Shapla tries to rein in Rani's discursive wandering, first goading her with a rhetorical question (9) then a very direct imperative (11), *bal, sundar kare bal,* "Speak – speak doing beauty!" It is the juxtaposition of 9 and 11 that reveals some of what "beauty" meant for Shapla – that is, speaking out clearly as one would in a recitation (such as Shapla elicited from the children she tutored). Yet more importantly, this was Shapla's way of urging her sister to understand and join in the normative moves of their interaction games. "Speaking beautifully" would entail appropriate participation, including giving clear answers to my questions about how she had slept, and so on. "Beauty" in relation to speech, for Rani's family, meant polite interactive participation and verbal clarity. Such polite participation normatively involves ways of deploying the body as well as words.[10]

Some familial efforts to achieve intersubjectivity involve optimistic interpretations of Rani's words. In lines 33 and 34, Mashima and a little neighbor boy try to interpret her words as an attempt to engage her interlocutors. They respond to her talk of "giving" with interpretive guesses, filling in the blanks in Rani's discourse, addressing the value of whatever it is that needs to be "given." These responses are best seen as desperate attempts to channel flights of subjectivity into the common stream of intersubjectivity. Given that expressions of one's own subjectivity are usually seen as a *bilāsitā*, self-indulgent luxury, lines 33–34 reflect an attempt to rein in Rani's rampant, "self-indulgent" subjectivity as they guess what she at least should have "meant" to say.

We also see Mashima's concern for her daughter's "beauty" – her well-attuned deployment of words and embodied movement – especially in lines 43 and 44. Throughout the transcribed interaction, Rani was seated, facing toward me, though almost never looking at me. Mashima was standing behind her in the shaded doorway of their home, while Shapla stood with her gaze mostly on Rani, holding a microphone toward her. Rani had certainly not been attuned to our questions. She did not even orient herself in any obvious postural or gestural way to the physical presence of her interlocutors. Seeing this, her mother took matters into her own hands. Even from behind Rani, Mashima used her words and her body in a last ditch attempt to help Rani attune to the flow of their interaction. I had asked Rani about her experience of what I know to be sometimes violent folk treatment (lines 35 and 36). Shapla (38) and I had failed to get her to respond. Yet, when Mashima repeated my question (41–42), she succeeded – Rani shook her head from side to side, saying such treatment does not "turn out well." In lines 43 and 44, Mashima actively constructed her interaction with Rani as mutual by echoing Rani's moves and words. She repeated Rani's long overdue answer about how traditional healers failed and, as she did so, shook her head from side to side immediately after Rani had done so. This appears to have been a sort of compensation for Rani's failure up to that point to echo others' moves or engage them in any sustained interaction. If Mashima could help Rani engage any of us in the mutual give and take of interaction, she could lend a sense of "beauty" not only to the moment but also to her daughter. But she was able to do so only by going beyond helping Rani to actually making interactive moves on her behalf.

Mashima's behavior reflects and sustains her aesthetic of language as intersubjective achievement, as orderly and polite exchange. Such a strategy enables the family to carry on, glossing over Rani's problems, or propping up her efforts to produce the appearance that she was doing her share of the interactive work. Yet, Rani had her back turned to Mashima when Mashima echoed Rani's head shake; that misalignment suggests the greater suffering of Rani and her family together. It also suggests how inadequate purely cognitive models are to capture the embodied, moral, emotional collisions of people with life's resistance (Kleinman 1992). Rani's turning her back during her mother's attempts to build a facade of intersubjectivity becomes a trope for the breakdown of mutual attunement in the family. Such a breakdown is all the more painful in a cultural system that values the centripetal force of intersubjectivity above the centrifugal force of subjectivity.

Intersubjectivity is a tenuous achievement (Schutz 1976a). To take intersubjective attunement as an unproblematic given is misguided and potentially injurious. Far from engaging her interlocutors Rani was playing a solitary sort of language game (Wittgenstein 1958; Duranti 1997). Her language was turned in on itself, playing with and celebrating its own capacities. In giving herself over to play on Bangla homonyms (the punning connection between *dik-e*, "in the direction of," and *di-k e*, "let him give this") and then a whole paradigm of the verb *di*, "give," she neither invites nor seems to expect any participation. This game is her own. To Rani's private play her family responded by beckoning toward shared values, connection, and mutuality, but as fast as they repaired ruptures in attunement Rani created more. From the outside these attempts by members of her family appear doomed and perhaps akin to the sort of negative emotion expressed by families of people with schizophrenia who are associated with poor prognosis (Karno, Jenkins, de la Selva, Santana, Telles, Lopez, and Mintz 1987).

Rather than complying with our multiple proddings to talk about something, Rani plays with a verb paradigm, as some foreign student learning Bangla might do. In a few quick lines (28–32), she produced five different forms of the verb "to give": the third person imperative (let someone give), the naked verb root (which never occurs in normal speech), the conditional, the infinitive, and the demeaning (or very intimate) form of the imperative. Playing with a verb paradigm entails taking pleasure in structure for its own sake, quite different from a semantic use of language. Whatever Rani's goal might have been, the effect was not to achieve intersubjectivity. Clear reference focuses the self and puts it in the service of intersubjectivity. A clear pointing gesture, an utterance referring to something topical at a given moment of shared understanding – these illustrate both how interaction imposes a certain focus and how such reference makes mutual understanding possible. Rani's paradigm play is a kind of self-involvement radically different from intersubjectivity. Psychotic experience and actions lie beyond a "symbolic" or semantico-referential mode of linguistic expression.[11]

So, "beauty" in relation to speech, for Rani's family, meant interactional politeness and verbal clarity, not subjective fancy such as they perceived in Rani. Rani's preference for a kind of linguistic solitaire frustrated her family's efforts to include her in a shared game. Intersubjective attunement as a norm (for conversation analysts as for Rani's family) represents a partial "take" on reality, a value with its own context of power (altruistic though a family's power might be). It relates to the political economy; the ideological valorization of intersubjectivity is inflected by motivations related to political-economic interests (Desjarlais 1997). The insight applies as well to Rani's family, anxious as they are that she regain her footing on the normative paths to subsistence available to Bangladeshi women, particularly marriage or nowadays, tutoring neighborhood children.

Note that Rani's family does not mention their distress at her performance failures any more than Rani confesses the pleasure she takes in linguistic structure. Both signal these emotions in a manner revealed by careful analysis of this excerpt of their videotaped interaction. Bangladeshi bodies and voices embody metacommunicative value judgements. They critique and guide the communicative behavior of individuals, in this case, Rani. Conversely, bodies and voices are objects of this sort of regimentation of behavior (Schieffelin, Woolard, and Kroskrity 1998). Rani's unintelligible speech and awkward behavior served as a screen onto which her family projected norms of interaction. Videotaped events, I argue, provide a unique close-up view of breeches in intersubjectivity and attempts to repair them, played out in this Bangladeshi context within the arena of the cultural aesthetics of *sundar*. This analysis also reveals the clash of worlds and of two different subject positions: Rani's very tenuous position, like that of a child striving to magically create a world (one of nurture to which she can cry, "give!"), and that of her family, relatively stable "on the ground," controlling a space suitable for a fulcrum to leverage others' actions (de Certeau 1984; Desjarlais 1997). Their desperation to restore Rani's sanity reflects the weakness of women's position in two ways. First, Mashima and Shapla are called to constrain Rani's verbal playfulness – because a woman in rural Bangladesh who exceeds her limits is vulnerable to censure at the very least. Second, they have so few resources that they need her to be marriageable, if not restored to mental parity with her economically productive sister.

Postscript: My friend the psychiatrist, Dr. Chowdhury, traveled on my invitation to Rani's rural home in April 1992. She spoke with her in the presence of family members, and turned to comment to me in English on the irrelevance of Rani's "answers" to her questions. (This despite the fact that Rani was actually much more coherent at that moment – after initially running away from the psychiatrist and speaking incoherently in a far corner of her homestead – than she had been in the interaction transcribed previously). After spending almost an hour there, Dr. Chowdhury prescribed antipsychotic injections to be administered back at her office in Dhaka. The family complied and maintained a regime of monthly travel and injections for two years. I saw an almost immediate improvement.

Sadly, Rani's family could no longer make the trips after two years, and she had relapsed completely when I met them again in 1996.

Conclusion

Bangladeshi *pāgalāmi* encompasses forms of deviance from silliness to psychosis and bestows on them the kind of semantic unity engendered by lumping items together in thought and discourse. The category, the label, and its manifold associations all play a role in shaping the imagination and experience of madness. The widespread knowledge that being *pāgal* entails an expectation to eat and speak wildly, licenses wild appetites expressions. I have argued that the Bangladeshi understanding of sanity as intersubjective attunement and madness as subjective flight relativizes subjectivity and its relation to intersubjectivity. Rani and others (Wilce 1998, 2002) exemplify a tendency for the so-called *pāgal* to revel in their subjectivity. This tendency takes on a particular meaning in Bangladeshi cultural context. Reveling in subjectivity challenges Bangladeshi communicative norms and evokes criticism. It is just such criticisms that reveal local ideals of interaction. The criticisms take on an ideological flavor in these histories of interaction. Because the "mad" violate expectations, they become the objects of metacommunicative, ideological attempts to regiment their speech. The very affectivity, self-exploration, self-sensitivity, and the modes of expression associated with such states are taken as threats to the Bangladeshi value system. The very tendency of some of the "mad" to focus on their experience, per se, invites negative attention and objectification (Wilce 1998). Bangladeshi discourses about "madness as *bilāsitā*," the luxury of "self-indulgence," entail just that sort of critical objectification.

Thus, the centrality of speech-interaction among locally designated "signs of madness" – but also the central role of speech, metalanguage, and metacommunication (including gesture) in the formulation of local criticism and shared cultural ideas about madness – invite the sort of interpretation linguistic anthropology can provide. Linguistic anthropologists often work intensely with a few cases, painstakingly transcribing long stretches of talk and providing ethnographic contextualization. When they do analyze single utterances or turns at talk, they do so within the larger context. Increasingly, they turn to videotape to preserve much of this richness. These methods have provided us with a fine-grained view of the problems madness presents for Rani's family and their interaction. Analyzing the transcript uncovered local actors' attempts to use metacommunicative acts – from saying "Speak beautifully!" to echoing Rani's gesture as if to reestablish the link between them – to shape the communicative acts of the deviant. Madness presents these families with the particular problems it does partly because of their expectations, which reflect Bengali culture and its values vis-à-vis subjectivity and language. Shapla and Mashima enact a Bangladeshi value system that valorizes intersubjectivity and fosters its achievement rather than individual self-expression. The culturally specific aesthetic captured in the term *sundar* merges the moral and the emotional into embodied linguistic interaction. The methodology of linguistic anthropology has provided insights into such interactions. Such an approach may well be relevant to the study of expressed emotion in schizophrenia (Jenkins 1991; Jenkins and Karno 1992). Shapla's call to "speak beautifully . . . like a recitation" and Mashima's gestural-echo might escape being coded as overt criticism, or even open longing for "the old Rani." Perhaps it is not hypercritical – that remains unclear so long as baseline research into madness and its family context in Bangladesh is in its infancy. However, the videotape reveals what I think we must call Mashima's "surplus of desire" to see her daughter engaged in the normal exchange of gestures and verbal sequences.

My analysis reveals the centrality of gender in the transformations of the self that come to be called madness.[12] Economic, cultural, and metacommunicative pressures present challenges for the full recovery of Rani and others like her. But those called *pāgal* also present challenges of their own – to Bangladeshi gender stereotypes, for instance – as they play with gender and other signifiers. Exceptional gender role behavior was common to all the so-called *pāgal* I knew, regardless of their particular psychiatric diagnosis or lack thereof. This attests to the powerful influence of the *pāgalāmi* label and the model it distills.

The symptoms of madness receive particular marking in Bangladesh. One may be diagnosed according to international criteria, but one must still face local interpretations and pressures. The appetite of the mad becomes a particular object of scrutiny. If they resort to a traditional genre of emotional performance, the lament, or in some other way put marked energy into the expression of private thoughts and feelings as did Rani, that also comes in for critical attention. Thus, the symptoms of *pāgalāmi* engage context and expectations; in a limited sense, *pāgal* behavior is a performance. However, like all performance, it is highly interactive, and my calling attention to its performative qualities, paradoxically, challenges local views of madness as a kind of malingering (Wilce 2002). The construction of madness as label, and the performance of madness as behavior, are both crucially affected by, and entail a dialogue with, rural Bangladeshi norms of intersubjectivity and of gendered speech and behavior.

NOTES

1 I gratefully acknowledge the support of Provost Susanna Maxwell and the Organized Research Committee of Northern Arizona University in writing about the matters presented here and in revisiting Bangladesh in 1996. My 1991–92 fieldwork was supported by IIS/Fulbright, the National Science Foundation, the American Institute of Bangladesh Studies, and the International Centre for Diarrheal Disease Research, Bangladesh (ICDDR,B). I am also deeply grateful to Rob Barrett, Janis Jenkins, the Russell Sage Foundation, and all those who participated in the symposium for their support and insights.

2 This reflects ongoing emigration of Hindus to West Bengal, India, leaving well over 90 percent of Bangladesh's citizens identifying themselves as Muslims (VanGinneken 1996). VanGinneken's estimate is based on demographic research conducted by the International Centre for Diarrheal Disease Research, Bangladesh (ICDDR,B).

3 Compare Cohen (1998:243–4) for an account of the elderly whose "bad voices" – for example, demanding too much food – can be considered symptoms of madness.

4 Singing is used as a metaphor for odd, "selfish" speech in rural Bangladesh (Wilce in press).

5 For the particular way that linguistic anthropologists have used Wittgenstein's notion of language game, see Duranti (1997).

6 I exported the audio track of *some key portions* of my videotapes – those transcribed here – in 1992 to play for Faisal and Shapla, which was the best I could do at that time. One of these limits was the VHS/PAL conversion problem, but the primary constraint was that 1992-era cameras had no adequate built-in monitors. Thus, I could only play the much longer portions of video that form the context of the transcribed portions with technology available to me here.

7 I thank Arthur Kleinman and Byron Good for stressing the importance of "subject position" (and not only subjectivity traditionally construed) during the Russell Sage Foundation symposium, at which I presented a version of this chapter.

8 This despite the problematic gap between embodied and conscious affect found in Americans suffering from schizophrenia (Kring this volume).

9 This hope that Rani would one day fit back into a productive socioeconomic role led to no overt pressure of the sort I describe as follows; that relates, instead, to polite interaction. But the now-common observation that families, or staff members at a homeless shelter (Desjarlais 1997), or officials at asylums and mental hospitals (Foucault 1973) steer patients toward moral and economic conformity is also relevant in Bangladesh. Here I refer not only to the hopes of Rani's family, which they would voice in her presence, but to the direct attempt by Dr. Chowdhury to persuade another patient and neighbor of Rani's to conform. When the psychiatrist came to visit my rural site in April 1992 she met Hamid, a young man who had partially recovered from an acute episode of psychosis five years before we met him, but who was so paralyzed by fears that he felt unable to work. Dr. Chowdhury insisted he work a bit every day, whether in his brothers' rice fields or in a shop in his village. She urged him to give up his longheld fear that he had been poisoned. Her attacks on his fears

reflect a Bangladeshi moral discourse (against dangerous subjectivities) manifested also in Rani's family, and somewhat parallel to moralizing discourses heard elsewhere.

10 I have videotapes of families teaching their toddlers not only to respond to adults making "first moves" that expect a response, such as questions or greetings, but of moving the toddler's bodies to properly achieve the polite act, especially a handshake or a goodbye wave to accompany introductions or leave takings. Parents teach these lessons because such demonstrations of interactive engagement are normative.

11 Kristeva argues that psychotic speech is a kind of reemergence (from children's first echolalias) of an earlier semiotic modality. This reemergence produces nonsensical effects that can destroy syntax itself. This "poetry" of psychosis serves as the last prop of the speaking subject threatened with the complete collapse of the signifying function (Kristeva 1993:155, 156).

12 In Dr. Chowdhury's psychiatric interview with Hamid mentioned in an earlier note, she asked him whether he had married, using an active verbal construction as is the norm in talking about men marrying. The passive construction he used to answer her, saying he could not *be married* because of his illness (in effect, "to be married off"), is more typical of a women's Bangla idiom.

REFERENCES

Banerjee, Sumanta. 1989. "Marginalization of Women's Popular Culture in Nineteenth Century Bengal." In K. Sangari and S. Vaid, eds., pp. 127–79. *Recasting Women: Essays in Colonial History*. New Delhi: Kali for Women.

Barrett, Robert J. 1988. "Interpretations of Schizophrenia." *Culture, Medicine and Psychiatry* 12: 357–88.

Bateson, Gregory. 1972. *Steps to an Ecology of Mind*. Scranton, PA: Chandler.

Bhattcharyya, Deborah. 1986. *Pāgalāmi: Ethnopsychiatric Knowledge in Bengal*. Foreign and Comparative Studies/South Asian Series, No. 11. Syracuse, NY: Maxwell School of Citizenship and Public Affairs.

Bose, Ruma. 1997. "Psychiatry and the Popular Conception of Possession among the Bangladeshis in London." *International Journal of Social Psychiatry* 43(1): 1–15.

Briggs, Charles. 1986. *Learning How to Ask: A Sociolinguistic Appraisal of the Role of the Interview in Social Science Research*. Cambridge: Cambridge University Press.

Certeau, Michel de. 1984. *The Practice of Everyday Life*. S. Rendall, trans. Berkeley: University of California Press.

Cohen, Lawrence. 1998. *No Aging in India: Alzheimer's, the Bad Family, and Other Modern Things*. Berkeley: University of California Press.

Csordas, Thomas. 1990. "Embodiment as a Paradigm for Anthropology." (The 1988 Stirling Award Essay). *Ethos* 18: 5–17.

Desjarlais, Robert R. 1992. *Body and Emotion: The Aesthetics of Illness and Healing in the Nepal Himalayas*. Philadelphia: University of Pennsylvania Press.

———. 1997. *Shelter Blues: Homelessness and Sanity in a Boston Shelter*. Philadelphia: University of Pennsylvania Press.

Duranti, Alessandro. 1997. *Linguistic Anthropology*. Cambridge: Cambridge University Press.

Foucault, Michel. 1973. *Madness and Civilization: A History of Insanity in the Age of Reason*. New York: Vintage.

Garfinkel, Harold. 1967. *Studies in Ethnomethodology*. Englewood Cliffs, NJ: Prentice-Hall.

Giddens, Anthony. 1984. *The Constitution of Society: Outline of the Theory of Structuration*. Cambridge: Basil Blackwell.

Good, Byron J. 1977. "The Heart of What's the Matter: The Semantics of Illness in Iran." *Culture, Medicine and Psychiatry* 1: 25–58.

———. 1994. *Medicine, Rationality, and Experience: An Anthropological Perspective*. New York: Cambridge University Press.

Goodwin, Charles. 1979. "The Interactive Construction of a Sentence in Natural Conversation." In G. Psathas, ed., pp. 97–121. *Everyday Language*. New York: Irvington.

Gottman, John M., Lynn Fainsilber Katz, and Carole Hooven. 1996. "Parental Meta-Emotion Philosophy and the Emotional Life of Families: Theoretical Models and Preliminary Data." *Journal of Family Psychology* 10(3): 243–68.

Jenkins, Janis Hunter. 1991. "The 1990 Stirling Award Essay. Anthropology, Expressed Emotion, and Schizophrenia." *Ethos* 19: 387–431.

Jenkins, Janis Hunter and Marvin Karno. 1992. "The Meaning of 'Expressed Emotion': Theoretical Issues Raised by Cross-Cultural Research." *American Journal Psychiatry* 149: 9–21.

Kakar, Sudhir. 1978. *The Inner World: A Psychoanalytic Study of Childhood and Society in India*. Oxford and New Delhi: Oxford University Press.

Karno, Marvin, Janis Hunter Jenkins, Aurora de la Selva, Felipe Santana, Cynthia Telles, Steve Lopez, and Jim Mintz. 1987. "Expressed Emotion and Schizophrenic Outcome among Mexican-American Families." *Journal of Nervous and Mental Disease* 175: 143–51.

Kleinman, Arthur. 1992. "Pain and Resistance: The Delegitimation and Relegitimation of Local Worlds." In M. J. Delvecchio Good, P. Brodwin, B. J. Good, and A. Kleinman, eds., pp. 169–97. *Pain as Human Experience: An Anthropological Perspective*. Berkeley: University of California Press.

Kopf, David. 1969. *British Orientalism and the Bengal Renaissance: The Dynamics of Indian Modernization, 1773–1835*. Berkeley and Los Angeles: University of California Press.

Kristeva, Julia. 1993. "The Speaking Subject is Not Innocent." In B. Johnson, ed., pp. 147–74. *Freedom and Interpretation* (The 1991 Oxford Amnesty Lectures). New York: Basic Books.

Kurtz, Stanley N. 1992. *All the Mothers are One: Hindu India and the Cultural Reshaping of Psychoanalysis*. New York: Columbia University Press.

McDaniel, June. 1989. *The Madness of the Saints: Ecstatic Religion in Bengal*. Chicago: University of Chicago Press.

Moerman, Michael. 1988. *Talking Culture: Ethnography and Conversation Analysis*. Philadelphia: University of Pennsylvania Press.

Nandy, Ashis. 1983. *The Intimate Enemy: Loss and Recovery of Self Under Colonialism*. Delhi: Oxford University Press.

Nasrin, Taslima. 1994. *Shame.* T. Gupta, trans. New Delhi, London, New York: Penguin Books.

Roland, Alan. 1988. *In Search of Self in India and Japan: Toward a Cross-cultural Psychology.* Princeton, NJ: Princeton University Press.

Sacks, Harvey, Emmanuel A. Schegloff, and Gail Jefferson. 1974. "A Simplest Systematics for the Organization of Turn-taking for Conversation." *Language* 50: 696–735.

Scheflen, Albert E. 1973. *Communicational Structure: Analysis of a Psychotherapy Transaction.* Bloomington: Indiana University Press.

Schieffelin, Bambi B., Kathryn A. Woolard, and Paul Kroskrity, eds. 1998. *Language Ideologies: Practice and Theory.* New York: Oxford University Press.

Schutz, Alfred. 1970. *On Phenomenology and Social Relations.* H. Wagner, trans. Chicago and London: University of Chicago Press.

———. 1976a. "Don Quixote and the Problem of Reality." In A. Brodersen, ed., pp. 135–57. *Collected Papers: II Studies in Social Theory.* The Hague: Martinus Nijhoff.

———. 1976b. "Making Music Together: A Study in Social Relationship." In A. Brodersen, ed., pp. 159–78. *Collected Papers: II Studies in Social Theory.* The Hague: Martinus Nijhoff.

Sullivan, Bruce. 2000. Personal communication.

VanGinneken, Jerune. 1996. Personal communication.

Waitzkin, Howard. 1991. *The Politics of Medical Encounters.* New Haven, CT: Yale University Press.

Wilce, James M. 1998. *Eloquence in Trouble: The Poetics and Politics of Complaining in Bangladesh.* New York: Oxford University Press.

———. 2002. "Tunes Rising From the Soul and Other Narcissistic Prayers: Contested Realms in Bangladesh." In D. Mines and S. Lamb, eds., pp. 289–302. *Everyday Life in South Asia.* Bloomington: Indiana University Press.

Wittgenstein, Ludwig. 1958. *Philosophical Investigations.* G. E. M. Anscombe and R. Rhees, trans. Oxford: Blackwell.

8 Innovative Care for the Homeless Mentally Ill in Bogota, Colombia

Esperanza Diaz, Alberto Fergusson,
and *John S. Strauss**

While it is not easy to describe or define recovery in mental illness, looking at patients' lives and listening to their stories of change provide access to the experiential dimension of recovery. A series of interviews conducted for a program evaluation in Santafe de Bogota, Colombia provided us with the opportunity to learn about this experiential dimension with an imprint of Colombian culture.

Colombian culture may be seen in terms of a powerful Spanish influence upon the culture of the indigenous Indians, intermixed with the culture of Africans who were forced into slavery by the Spaniards. Colombians speak Spanish, are mostly Catholics, and while they see themselves as morally conservative there is a thread of liberalism running through Colombian society that influences many aspects of everyday life. Colombia is described by Gomez (1994) as a country where violence, insecurity, economic insecurity, and social tension are endemic. The country has suffered from persistent violence ever since independence from Spain. From the very beginning this violence revolved around class and stemmed from extreme disparities in wealth. Guerrillas who originally based their operations in the jungles slowly infiltrated the urban population. "Drug lords," flourishing since the 1950s, convinced organized guerrilla movements to support marijuana and cocaine crops in exchange for money and arms. The drug lords have now emerged as a new class that has taken its place among the few who have plenty. Needless to say, they have not solved the poverty of the many. It is from the most afflicted of the homeless poor that the mentally ill served by the program described in this chapter are drawn.

The Colombian government has limited funds to serve the mentally ill poor. Large public institutions, struggling to provide services of any quality at all, serve the chronic mentally ill mainly through a custodial model. With deinstitutionalization, there have been reports of increased numbers of mentally ill patients living on the streets of Colombia's larger cities. A private foundation, the Colombian Assistance Foundation, is staffed by diverse professionals in health services, banking (Republic

Bank, the primary bank in Colombia) law, administration, and education, who, along with economists, businessmen, and politicians determine various social needs. This is determined on the basis of evaluation of information from government reports, the office of welfare and public health, along with independent evaluations sponsored by the same foundation. When the foundation targeted the health sector, they identified the elderly, the handicapped, and the mentally ill. To address problems of the homeless mentally ill in Santafe de Bogota, the Fundacion Granja Taller (FUNGRATA) was established.

FUNGRATA, founded in 1982 and developed by Alberto Fergusson M.D. with a team of other health professionals, pioneered an approach for the homeless mentally ill that aimed to address the person and his or her individual characteristics and needs. Its main purpose was the rehabilitation of the homeless mentally ill under conditions of respect and equality. FUNGRATA's goal is the rehabilitation of the homeless mentally ill through a therapeutic program developed within sheltered work. The program philosophy centers around several elements as crucial to the recovery process: work and creative activities, psychotherapy, and pharmacotherapy. FUNGRATA is premised upon the idea that the mentally ill have had a "developmental arrest" across different areas of human growth, and thus are in need of rehabilitation in a variety of areas. They also consider rehabilitation to be closely associated with such culturally specific ethnopsychological domains as "independence" and "autonomy." All activities are intended to foster movement toward personal "independence." This striving for independence and autonomy are central to the program, and this reflects the program's location within an ideology of individualism and achievement that pervade many Western societies, no less in Colombia.

The program identifies seven developmental steps toward rehabilitation: identification (finding mentally ill on the street), engagement (rapport building by staff with people on the street, taking days, months, or even years), entry into the program (familiarization upon arrival with staff and routines with a goal of moving toward participation in work and educational activities), recuperation (psychosocial awareness of the healing process), followed by three phases of progressive "integration" into the community through participation in wage-earning work while living independently. The patients are given frequent feedback on their progress. The level of rehabilitation has some influence on changes in living arrangements; the higher the level, the more ready patients are for independence.

In 1994, the first author went to Bogota to visit and interview the staff and patients of FUNGRATA, which by then had been in existence for twelve years and had requested an evaluation. This chapter draws on data gathered in the process of evaluation and focuses on the life experiences of patients within the program.

Fundacion Granja Taller (FUNGRATA)

The FUNGRATA staff includes a graduate nurse, a rehabilitation therapist, a psychologist, a psychiatrist, a technician for each of the workshops, three mental health workers, and ten psychology students who rotate through the program every year. The program has a director and a board of directors. It has two sites, one urban and one rural, in which eighty to eighty-five people can be accommodated.

The urban site in Bogota, the capital of Colombia and a city of eight million, is called *microempresa* (small business). The *microempresa* has a laundry, a bakery, a coffee shop, and a messenger service. Those accepted here work in one of these shops. Approximately ten blocks away is a house, referred to as the "intermediate house," with a capacity for ten to fifteen patients; it serves as residence for those who work in the city. Those who have reached a certain level of education and independence can move from the country site to the intermediate house and work in the *microempresa*. Some of them find employment independently of the *microempresa* but continue their follow-up and support with the program.

Patients eventually become independent to the extent that they live on their own. The site in the city provides a place where they can continue to work. It also provides accommodation. The city housing sponsored by the program is available, but patients can move to their own place in rented apartments while continuing the connection with the program indefinitely. Patients receive a small stipend for their work. Training is conducted by a multidisciplinary team of technicians who lead the workshops and therapists who teach each person about mental disorders and rehabilitation. Initially a patient might not be able to participate in any workshops at all, but slowly he or she is introduced into an activity that is intended to be "work-oriented," and, with peer encouragement, they often become engaged in this process.

The rural site – *La Granja*, or "the farm" – is located thirty kilometers to the north of Bogota in a small picturesque town. The flat surrounding countryside is suitable for dairy farming and crops such as potatoes, corn, fruits, and vegetables. A cluster of buildings houses the dining area and kitchen, the library, the theater or meeting hall, and consulting rooms for psychotherapy and medical attention. The pottery, the bakery, and the laundry shops are in separate one-story buildings. Workshops offered at the farm include vegetable production, small-scale dairy farming, pottery, laundry, bakery, art and drama, sport and physical fitness, recreation, and handyman services (carpentry, painting, and window washing). *La Granja* houses up to seventy people, who may stay there indefinitely. At the time of the evaluation, some had been at *La Granja* since the beginning of the program.

It also serves as the admission facility for new arrivals who are either identified on the streets or brought by relatives who are seeking help. The criteria for admission to the FUNGRATA program are that the person: 1) be between eighteen and fifty-five years old; 2) have been diagnosed as suffering from a chronic major mental disorder excluding substance abuse and disorders caused by a medical condition; 3) have been homeless; and 4) have an interest in participating in the program and agree to participate in one or more of the workshops offered.

The recruitment of patients is done by a small team from FUNGRATA that goes to the city streets and nearby towns to identify potential new patients. As noted previously, the recruitment process may take anywhere from days to years to accomplish. One member of the team initiates contact with a possible candidate to invite him or her to join the program. The team typically comprises two or three staff members and a patient at an advanced level of rehabilitation who is crucial in the process of engagement, giving the team credibility and conveying confidence to the person being approached. The team as a whole tries to understand the homeless person by learning about his or her activities and habits, in order to develop forms of engagement that are in keeping with the individual's lifestyle. The development of extensive outreach capabilities, and of multiple creative and flexible opportunities for the homeless have been demonstrated to be effective (Berman, Barilich, Rosenheck, and Koerber 1993), and the longer the outreach the better the engagement (Rosenheck and Lam 1997). About 20 percent of the homeless approached by the team refuse to participate.

The program is intended to function more or less like a flexible therapeutic community, with sharing of responsibilities, benefits, privileges, and government. Fostering responsibility and respecting independence are thought to be critical. When they are ready, patients are assigned to a therapist, with whom they meet several times a week for the purpose of becoming an "expert on his or her own mind," using a method called "*auto rehabilitacion acompanada*" (accompanied auto rehabilitation) developed by Fergusson (1997). The method involves learning about mental disorders and developing a closed therapeutic relationship with a therapist whose orientation is psychoanalytic but who is also trained in rehabilitation approaches for return to the community. While the literature on the psychoanalytic psychotherapy of schizophrenia shows mixed results

(Gunderson and Frank 1985), the importance of psychotherapy in psychosis is well documented (Coursey 1989; Harding and Zahniser 1994; McGlashan 1994; Coursey, Keller, and Farrell 1995; Gabbard, Lazar, Hornberger, and Spiegel 1997).

Instead of regarding homelessness as entirely negative, FUNGRATA's approach is to view it as conferring some advantages on individuals because, in the experience of clinicians involved in the program, being homeless can lead to the acquisition of skills that may prove helpful in the recovery from mental illness. Fear of the police, independence, resourcefulness, and inability to commit to traditional types of mental health treatment are some characteristics of homeless people. By way of contrast, the extant literature tends to convey a pervasively negative view of homelessness. It is regarded as a painful consequence of severe mental disorder in the absence of adequate treatment resources, poverty, shortages of residential housing options, a pervasive sense of pessimism, and a lack of follow-up with aftercare plans (Cohen, Putnam, and Sullivan 1984; Fleck 1986; Gelberg and Linn 1988; Shaner 1989).

FUNGRATA's flexibility in their program goals and therapeutic process, in relation to individual differences, was salient. It provides a farmlike environment and a city site offering different subsistence-type and creative work for the residents. This model of care is in sharp contrast to the asylum model of most Colombian hospitals. Residents of FUNGRATA are free to leave when they wish, unless staff have reason to be concerned for their (or others') safety.

Patients' Experiences: The Homeless Come Home

Part of our evaluation included interviews with patients in which we elicited life stories from them with the goal of understanding the changes that had occurred in their lives in the context of the program. The interviews were influenced by the explanatory model approach introduced by Kleinman (1980), in which patients' understandings of cause, course, treatment, and expected outcome are seen as critical to the understanding of illness experience. The people whose experiences are described below had a DSM-IV axis I diagnosis excluding substance-induced disorders and mental disorders due to medical conditions. All had been homeless and had been at the program for at least a year. The Brief Psychiatric Rating Scale (BPRS) was rated at the time of interview. The symptoms described on admission were taken from records. The scale for each symptom ranges from 1 (absent) to 7 (extreme). Six of the ten interviews completed during the evaluation process are reported here (Table 8.1). The initials are fictitious.

Table 8.1. *Summary description of interviewees with length of homelessness and length of stay*

Story	Gender	Age	Homelessness length	Residential stay
Maurading Viking to Security Guard	male	40	20 years	12 years
The Potion	male	33	1 year	12 years
The Walking Woman	female	44	3 years	9 years
I Love Begging	female	46	9 months	7 years
The Spell	male	37	1 year	12 years
Superman of the Volcano	male	27	1 year	5 years

From Marauding Viking to Security Guard (BQ)

At the time of the research interview, BQ was a forty-year-old single man living in a transitional house in the city. He worked as a security guard and messenger. Previously, he had been homeless for twenty years. According to case records, at the time of admission to the program, twelve years previously, his symptoms included grandiose and religious delusions, auditory hallucinations, paranoid ideation, loosening of associations, and insomnia. It was noted that he wore peculiar head attire. By the time of our interview, the Brief Psychiatric Rating Scale showed mild anxiety, moderate emotional withdrawal, mild feelings of guilt, and mild grandiosity.

On the streets of Bogota, he was called the Viking because of his headgear. He had lived on the streets from the age of eight, constantly moving around with the *galladas de gamines,* a small band of children who live on the streets stealing and hiding from the police with an ingenuity that extends to stowing away in airplanes. He washed cars, cleaned windshields at the traffic lights, did errands, and stole. He said he was a "delinquent" in order to survive. He also used drugs. He experienced a change when he went from delinquent to beggar saying that he lost interest in fending for himself and just begged for food, money, and cigarettes. He became fearful of people, believing that they were going to go after him to make him pay for what they had given him.

This is my home. I never had a home. My parents threw me out to the streets because I was a nuisance to them. On the streets, I learned to fight and defend myself. I was in *la picota* (city jail) for being a thief. I stole to eat and forced locks of empty houses to spend time in a nice home. I was a delinquent first, then a beggar when I got tired of running from the police. As a beggar, I was expected to pay back. When they asked me (after entering the program) to be the security guard for a business in Bogota, I realized the big change. I was not a thief anymore. I was watching a huge building with all those electric appliances and valuables. I did not steal, not even an egg. In the beginning, I was afraid. Once, the thieves came to steal and I defended the property. I scared them away. Quite a change! When the program first asked me to move to the city as a security guard, I became sad because I thought it was a demotion. . . . Then I realized the big change. I do not live on the streets. I do not have to return anything to anybody except with my work. Now what I want is to study. I would (not) be surprised if I get a girlfriend. I want to save money to buy more clothes, to fix my teeth, and for school.

When we interviewed him, he was dressed in a three-piece suit and talked with pride about his job as a security guard. In this case, the staff worked with him for six years on the streets trying to invite him to come for a visit before he started with the program. Initially he could not believe that they were offering him a job and shelter. It took a long time to trust them, but eventually he decided to accept the invitation. Slowly, he got into the activities of the program and as time went on, and he decided to meet with the doctor who prescribed medicines, which he took. He now expressed a wish to stop them soon because he felt he did not need them anymore.

What he found helpful was that the program expected him to pay for the services when he became able to provide for himself. For him, this signaled that he was no longer a beggar. He found it subjectively satisfying that he was able to work, earn some money, and live independently, not owing anything to anybody. He also wanted the program to continue to offer education only, as opposed to other services because in his experience, education was what made the change.

One might think that a child living on the streets of a city would experience this solely in terms of suffering, but BQ's narrative had the tone of adventure and mastery of difficult circumstances. As a consequence, he developed remarkable skills to survive on the city streets. By DSM-IV criteria, his behavior might be considered antisocial, but is it? A critical turning point was when BQ was not able to run away from the police any longer. He felt unable to cope, and this was, perhaps, the beginning of his mental disorder. He was unable to use his street survival skills any longer.

As a thief he had to take from others; this was a violation. As a beggar the money was voluntarily given to him. Perhaps that felt more comfortable but it placed him in a position of being unable to reciprocate. Work and pay gave him the opportunity to purchase shelter, services, and training, and no longer feel indebted. The shift from beggar to worker took place in a supportive environment, one that provided ample time for the substantial changes within him that this entailed. Finally, he was well aware of the irony of the transition from thief to security guard, which he described with a sense of mischievous pleasure.

The Potion (KR)

KR was a thirty-three-year-old, single man who lived in the city, shared an apartment with a roommate, and worked in a bakery. Before entering the program twelve years previously, he had been homeless for one year. At that time, his recorded symptoms included auditory hallucinations, persecutory delusions, manic behavior, psychomotor agitation, assaultiveness, suicidal ideation, and insomnia. The BPRS, at the time of our interview, showed anxiety, conceptual disorganization, tension, suspiciousness, and unusual thought content, all of them rated as mild. He believed he was sick due to a potion (*bebedizo*) given to him by his mother-in-law. He left home to walk from town to town. After a year, his brother found him wandering and took him to get help. His memory of his illness was that his "mind went blank," he lost energy, and could not work. KR described his belief in a force "pushing him" and described the ground under him trembling as he walked. He remembered hearing voices when nobody was around and said that he could hear his thoughts aloud. He understood these experiences as coming from witchcraft.

My life has changed. I live in an apartment that I share with a roommate. They asked me to move out of the transitional house because I bothered the girls. Now that I live alone I fix radios and other small appliances. Two months ago they changed my medicine and now I feel more energy to work. The medicine does not let me hear voices. The witches used to give me sucking bites since that time when my girlfriend's mother gave me that potion. Sometimes I thought of hanging myself but I was a coward and I could not. With the medicine, suddenly I did not hear the voices anymore and slept better. The medicine helps a lot. The bakery helps, too.... Now it is different. I live independently, I am clean, and I work. I had a girlfriend but she asked me for a child and I refused. She wanted me to share the rent and food. I never returned. I do not want to have children.

He did not find psychotherapy useful and he refused it. But he rediscovered that he could fix radios and small electric appliances, a skill he had been known for in the neighborhood where he lived. He liked being occupied; the bakery during the day, fixing radios at night. In the program, he said he recalled that he had a feeling of being powerful, after which time he reports that the voices stopped. But even though he said that the medicines were helpful, he was not happy about them. He remembered starting to dislike the medicines when he felt sluggish from them, reminiscent of the loss of drive when he was sick. When he discontinued his medication and the symptoms returned, he blamed the staff and the medicines for this. He saw the medicines as punishment from witchcraft and felt that somehow the staff members were responsible for this. On the other hand, he believed that if he again stopped the medicine the witchcraft would become worse.

KR explained the illness in terms of witchcraft, as a powerful force taking control. The principal change in his life, for him, was related to obtaining skills that allowed him to work, which altered his sense of self in a way that he experienced as healing. From being controlled by witchcraft, he moved toward feeling in control of his life primarily through work activities.

The Walking Woman (NQ)

NQ was a forty-four-year-old, single woman who lived at the country site. Before entering the program some nine years previously, she had been homeless for three years, following dismissal from a job as a maid after her behavior had become intolerable to her employer. Her symptoms on admission were those of auditory hallucinations, persecutory delusions related to the law and the state, somatic delusions, fearfulness, and thought disorganization. Her BPRS at the research interview showed mild anxiety, moderate conceptual disorganization, mild tension, moderate hostility, moderate suspicion, moderately severe hallucinatory behavior, mild psychomotor retardation, and moderately severe unusual thought content.

NQ had a sturdy build, a dark complexion from exposure to the sun, and hands hardened by work in the fields. Her appearance was remarkable on two counts. First, she wore an *escapulario*, a religious necklace with the *Virgin del Carmen* image, made out of a brown cotton material. This was worn over her blouse, unusual in that it is typically worn beneath the clothing. Secondly, she wore light-colored rubber boots. NQ called herself a "wanderer" and told how she initially had a very difficult time staying in the program, so she would continually leave and come back until at last she found some comfort in FUNGRATA. She felt her mind was controlled, and that she was being told to work hard or to walk away. The desire to walk continuously had gradually diminished, allowing her to stay at the program, but she still believed that wandering was her destiny. She also said that she did not have the right shoes to keep on walking so she stayed at the program.

When I was a little girl, I was crazy. My craziness was that I was going to say one thing but then I said something else. I used to think that one is born crazy, but now I know that the craziness starts with the life problems and the misery. I used to work as a maid. They made fun of me and suddenly they let me go. Then I started to beg. I got food from restaurants and I lived dirty. I wanted to walk and walk, but I ran out of shoes. My feet got blisters. I placed a formal complaint because they did not let me work anymore. In 1983, they took me to the hospital and they killed me. The law made me suffer hunger to kill me. The law is that way. They took me to a hospital, they injected me with poison, and I fell asleep. When I woke up again my body was gone. They killed all the families I worked with. They told me I suffered from "schizophrenias" which is arrogance, bad temper and fury. I was dead. But dead people also have a problem. The sickness of the dead is the "delayed hunger" and the constant walking. Here in the program I work in agriculture. We harvest carrots, cauliflower, and cabbage. I take care of some cows but I do not know how to milk them. I do not like too much what I do but I do not want to do anything else. I do not live on the street anymore. That is good. The medicine they give me is for the "delayed hunger." My soul is not dead yet.

In the program, she said she worked hard and pushed herself to produce. She loved walking by herself in the fields. She preferred to be alone, and working in the fields allowed her time to herself. She missed the streets but was afraid to leave the program because she feared being picked up by the police again and taken to a program that she would not like.

NQ believed that she was dead, an expression perhaps of the loss of her former self, or maybe of the idea that death is the end of all suffering. Yet within death, as she explained it, there was room for awareness of her current problems, since she believed in the sickness of death: the constant walking and the "delayed hunger." At one level, she may have been referring to the hunger she suffered on the streets, at another level, she explained her illness in terms of a lack of nourishment. It is a common belief in Colombia that food is the solution for a range of health problems. The program, she felt, had been treating her "delayed hunger" with medication, so "delayed hunger" was the explanation that justified her taking medicine. Note that NQ took four years to accept any medication at all; she needed strong reasons to accept something she initially associated with having been killed. It was only when she was able to see the medicine in terms of caring and nourishment that she could bring herself to take it. Even so, she was still ambivalent about it, for she missed the "fury" that would allow her to work better.

There was a hopeful element in NQ's narrative. She believed that her soul, in distinction to her body, was not dead. Hence, the importance of the *escapulario* that had the image of the *Virgin del Carmen* saving souls from purgatory. The *escapulario* was her protection but also a sign of hope. In NQ's psychosis, the themes of life after death and protection from the saints were strongly represented. The "kindness" of the program may have been seen by her as a protective sign from a higher power.

I Love Begging (NN)

NN was a forty-six-year-old woman who lived at the country site and worked in the bakery. She had previously lived on the streets for several months and had been at the program, on and off, for seven years. The case notes recorded religious and persecutory delusions (delusions of dogs after her), auditory hallucinations, ideas of reference, hostility, and assaultiveness. The BPRS at the time of our interview showed very mild anxiety, mild conceptual disorganization, mild guilt feelings, mild tension, mild depressive mood, moderate hallucinatory behavior, and moderate unusual thought content. She kept begging even at the program thus the title of this section came from this behavior.

NN married at a young age and had five children. Her husband was an "alcoholic" who beat her. He eventually left her and the children, and she started to work as a maid. She first consulted a mental health professional at the age of twenty-seven. In our interview, she looked submissive and was soft spoken. She said that the voices she heard initially told her to wander and then she got into the "habit" of begging. She was brought to the program by her sister because she was homeless and had "assaulted a man and threatened a dog." She had been in the program several times. In prior admissions, she had made great progress, but shortly after discharge from the program, she returned to living on the streets again.

The farm has helped. I do not have tremors anymore and I do not hear the voices. The program gives us shelter and teaches us to work. Who is going to do that for free? The voices used to tell me to walk and walk. The medicines take away the wish to walk. They advanced me to the house in the city but when I lived there I got a terrible sadness. I started to believe that the children were not well and I had to return to the farm. I do not want to go back to the city. I work in the bakery. I know how to bake bread. (Here she recited the recipe.) Being busy is good for me. My sister said that I am behaving because of the program but I miss the wandering. My doctor said that begging is ugly but my friends go out begging and they bring me potatoes.

NN was dissatisfied with the amount of money she was getting from her work and her attendance was erratic. The activity kept her busy and helped her forget about her tremor and the voices, but begging still held an important place in her mind. She said that begging was a bad "habit" but she still liked it. Begging was an important skill for her, a way to get money. At times, she tried hard to comply with the program's prohibition against begging but at others she protested passively, going along with the program up to a certain point and then either switching to a different workshop or decreasing her attendance.

NN's symptoms may be interpreted within the framework of gendered submissiveness that culturally characterizes Colombian womanhood. In a situation of physical abuse, this culturally prescribed submissiveness became dangerous, and for NN, rebellion was the only way. Her symptoms encouraged her to defy her family, allowed her to become aggressive, and enabled her to escape from her abusive husband. In this sense, her symptoms may be seen, in part, as a form of self-protection. She said that the main change within her occurred when she began to "behave" in the program. The program became, for her, a safe and protected environment, as her sister had said it would. The medication, she said, took away the wish to walk and helped her to be compliant, for she believed that the goal of her treatment was being obedient and compliant. This brought her back within the fold of Colombian cultural norms of respect for authority. The rebellion against her husband did not, therefore, entail a generalized rejection of female submissiveness

Begging was a skill, but also a behavior that her family and the clinicians in the program saw as inappropriate. For her, it had become a symbol of independence and freedom. She started to beg as a means of survival when she was not wanted anymore in her family's house. In the program, she remained conflicted in her attitude to begging, so she found a friend to beg for her, thereby enabling her to satisfy her desire to beg vicariously.

The Spell (IF)

IF was a thirty-seven-year-old, single man, who lived in an apartment in the city, where he worked in the laundry. He had been homeless for two months and had since stayed at the program for twelve years. His symptoms, on admission, were religious and persecutory delusions, somatic and auditory hallucinations, insomnia, hostility, irritability, psychomotor agitation, and loosening of associations. The BPRS during the period the research interviews were conducted showed very mild grandiosity, moderate suspiciousness, and moderate hallucinatory behavior. This person believed he was under a "spell," which he tried to get rid of in a variety of ways.

When he was first encountered on the streets of Bogota, he had come to the attention of the police because he liked to sleep in the entrances of buildings. He said he suffered from an "illness to the head." He believed there was a force that produced rain if he would do a ritual with a crucifix, a mirror, and salt. He said at times he felt angry and wanted to "break everything." His mother had become fearful of him after he beat her up, and so he could not return to live with her. The parish priest took him to a psychiatric hospital and, on discharge, he started living on the streets. There he tried several methods of treating the "spell." He consulted a vegetarian group that gave him the picture of a yogi to carry around and prescribed a vegetarian diet, which was difficult for him to keep up. Fruit and vegetables were expensive, so he modified the diet to milk and bread, which did not work. At the time of the interview, he was wearing a "magnetic cross of great power," its purpose to keep the bad spirits away. "When I take it off I am nobody."

The voices wanted me to go crazy. I used to believe in the spell. The spell is the combination of a crucifix, a mirror, and salt. I became violent. I beat my mother. I thought I was a saint and she was a devil. They took me to the hospital. I got better with medicine. I went back to work in construction and I stopped the medicine. Then I had an accident at work. I fell from a scaffold and fractured my arm. While in the hospital I started with the insomnia and got sick again thinking about the spell. I took to the streets. I walked for two months. I slept in entrances of buildings. They told me that the farm could help me. It was true I learned a lot. The noise does not allow me to hear the voices. When I am alone I hear them more.

He continued to believe, at times, that the technician in the laundry had spiritual powers to communicate with the workers there. He still heard voices, which the noise in the laundry helped to drown out, though they had become softer with the medicine. The great change, for him, was related to his ability to work in spite of his illness, and the ability to question his beliefs. He had a job, was proud of earning his own money, and lived independently in a rented room. A nurse taught IF to give injections, enabling him to help other members of the program.

IF explained his illness in terms of powerful external forces that had taken over his body. He felt he had to become "saintly" to fight those forces and this was aided by rituals, diets, and amulets. Religious groups of many kinds are frequently consulted by people with poor financial re-sources because they are cheaper than formal medical care and directly address beliefs in supernatural causes. The original explanation of his illness remained intact, but the spiritual component became modified from a socially visible ritual to wearing an amulet. This was more accept-able, but still gave him the protection he felt he needed. This, and being helpful as a nurse's assistant in the treatment of his fellow patients, were empowering for him.

Superman of the Volcano (EQ)

EQ was a twenty-seven-year-old, single man who lived in the city in his own apartment. He worked as a parking lot attendant in one of the city hospitals. He had been homeless for about a year and had been at the program for five years. His symptoms on admission were described as manic behavior, psychomotor agitation, assaultiveness, grandiose and persecutory delusions, auditory hallucinations, flight of ideas, and loosening of associations. The BPRS at our research interview showed only very mild tension, and all of the other symptoms were absent.

Particularly striking in EQ's case had been grandiose delusions of being "Superman." It is ironic that he was one of the few survivors of a volcanic eruption that killed about twenty thousand people, annihilating an entire town under a river of lava, mud, and stones. At the time EQ was in the psychiatric hospital (where he had been admitted twice previously with voices and ideas of being Superman). He had planned to hold out inside the hospital but when a wall fell down he decided to throw himself into a river of mud, which carried him miles away to another town. There, the Red Cross rescued him and he was admitted to a hospital in a nearby city.

EQ later went back to his family for a while, but eventually took to the streets and the parks. He was then admitted to the program, where he stayed for nine months before leaving to live again on the streets. There he had a motor vehicle accident when he walked in front of traffic, in the belief that he was Superman, sustaining a fracture in his left femur. He returned to the program a month later.

His only prior work experience had been in the cotton fields as a picker, and in the city, he found himself with no relevant skills. The program offered him training.

I had these strange "raptures." I started to have funny beliefs about being Superman and Bruce Lee. I thought it was because I stayed in bed for too long, doing nothing. I thought I needed action. I was in the hospital several times. . . . The volcano exploded while I was there. The river took me out. I got to the next town. There I was rescued. The water saved me. They put me in hospital again. I left to walk for about ten months. I was found wandering and somebody invited me to the program. Work was important for the change, the medicines too. I do not hear the voices anymore. They paid me once a month. The work helped a lot. They said that if your mind is occupied you get better. I have money to buy my own things. I have money to pay for my surgery. I do not have much left, but I feel happy.

Initially he worked in the farm bakery, then in the city bakery, and at the time of the interview he was working independently as a parking lot attendant, living on his own. He felt proud of being able to pay for his own living and medical expenses. He said that slowly his "health" improved. The main change occurred when the wish to work came back. He started to do things again. The beginning of purposeful activity may have been especially significant for EQ, who felt that it was inactivity that had led to his "raptures" in the first place. Now he looked genuinely content and laughed several times as he thought of these "raptures," now so far away. Of all those we interviewed, he was the one who was best able to achieve real distance from the problem and see that it was part of an illness.

We were struck by how little emphasis he placed on his escape from the volcano. His description was remarkably nonchalant. It was a miracle that this man was alive: He was one of the volcano survivors, but he did not seem excited about it. Perhaps it seemed small, to him, in comparison to his "raptures." Perhaps the grandiosity of his illness led him to think that his survival was a natural part of his world at that time.

Conclusion: The Subjective Experience of Change

In many instances, symptoms were construed by patients as playing a protective role. A good example of this was the woman who believed that the "fury" gave her energy when she was unable to work. A man believed he was a saint, and this belief allowed him to dominate the "forces" controlling his mind. Explanations of the illness by supernatural causes were frequent. Themes of life after death were part of the explanations. The *Virgin del Carmen* was the protector of a woman's soul. For one man, becoming a saint to attack demons was more comfortable than having a mental disorder.

As the explanations of the illness changed, acceptance of help became possible. Improvement was accompanied by a slow change in the explanations the person provided to him or herself. When the person found an explanation that was compatible with what the staff was proposing as help, there was a chance of acceptance of treatment. Why was it important for one woman to label her past misery as "delayed hunger"? It was a change that allowed her to view the problem as treatable and hopeful. Understanding this part of recovery becomes crucial for mental health professionals who hope to design appropriate interventions, ones that include and respect the patient's own developed solutions and acquired skills.

Perhaps most compelling of all was the diversity of street survival skills improvised by these patients to cope with homelessness. They included begging, stealing, scouting for food, and adopting a guarded manner. A "guarded manner" was parlayed by one person into a job as a security guard. As with the homeless struggle between dependence and independence, captured in the program's philosophy, many behaviors that might seem aberrant become part of the program. Wandering is one of those. Wandering and walking were part of being homeless, but they were also a frequently cited way of coping with the illness itself. Wandering was a way of leaving an uncomfortable situation, dealing with side effects from the medicine, and keeping distance from treatments that they were not willing to accept. Wandering is possible on the extensive grounds of the program thereby providing a setting for this struggle to play out.

Delusions sometimes served to decrease the fear. Further symptoms in themselves, they nonetheless were attempts to solve problems as well. Examples of these included: delayed hunger, eagerness for activity, the magnetic cross of great power, the protector of the souls, and vicarious begging. It is important to understand this type of self "cure" so as not to disrupt the patient while treatment is offered. On the street, they acquired survival skills to meet their basic needs. These street skills were used later on in the process of improvement.

The patients came from impoverished backgrounds, but this was assumed as a feature of their lives and not mentioned as a stressor. Like lack of safety on the streets, poverty was an unquestioned fact of life. In several accounts, begging was described in positive tones, only to become problematic when it was felt to be inappropriate rather than a skill. But begging was problematic in other accounts. Begging implied getting something for "free," which they would eventually have to pay back. Paid work, in this context, offers relief with a sense of independence.

The return to work was one of the most critical turning points in getting better. According to the patients, it kept the mind occupied, produced money, and reinforced independence. Work produced noise that distracted the voices, was a proof of agency and competence, put the person in contact with others leaving the isolation behind, and helped diminish fear. Being paid for, the activity increased their sense of self worth: that they did not owe everything to the program appeared particularly important for the men in whose cultural background the idea of *machismo* loomed large, with its implications that the man is a protector and a provider (Lewis-Fernandez and Kleinman 1994). Awareness of such cultural orientation is crucial, particularly with regard to types of therapeutic interventions that might increase shame, such as giving something for free, or being generous with a patient who does not have the possibility to pay back.

The corresponding example in relation to women had to do with submissiveness. Without awareness that submissiveness in the face of conflicting desires is a strongly gendered phenomenon in Colombia, it can easily be mistaken for a less-complicated compliance. If such issues are not taken into consideration, clinicians might easily be misled into thinking that women patients are listening and understanding when in fact they are not. The patient might feel obliged to follow submissively the treatment prescribed, unable refuse what is proposed, since independent thinking and exercise of a free will would seem ungrateful. Passivity becomes the rule.

Learning was very important for most; the acquisition of skills was, in itself, therapeutic. Medication was cited as important for improvement but for most it was seen as secondary to work. Medicines had many problems including cost, the investment of time in taking them, and the side effects. Yet even so, the medication was accepted by most, even those who did not believe they had an illness.

Religious frameworks of understanding were advanced by many of the patients and we found it important to be aware of the distinctively Colombian aspects of these explanations. If we had not been conversant with the *Virgin del Carmen,* and had not heard the patient say that her soul was still alive, we would not have understood that in this account of death there was hope. Her soul was still alive and she believed fervently in the protector of souls.

The FUNGRATA program, as opposed to other Colombian programs, does not focus on diagnosis because the main emphasis is on psychotherapy and working skills. The program's philosophy seems to incorporate ideological elements that foster individualism and community participation achievement. Then within the program, the struggle is between the dependency on the program's opportunities for permanent work and permanent residence and the independence and autonomy they can reach outside of the program. It is clear that whatever independence and autonomy are achieved by these patients, it is done on the basis that they have the opportunity for permanent work and permanent residence if they so desire, permanent protection one might say, for some even through sustained, if not permanent, dependence on the program. That is to say, there is a tension between cultural ideology of independence and the actual conditions of ongoing dependence that enable whatever autonomy that can be achieved to be achieved.

The program attempts to understand each person's unique way of coping and then helps to increase their effectiveness in gaining independence. Paul Koegel (1992) observed that the homeless mentally ill live their lives in ways that are best understood as meaning making. It seems to us that FUNGRATA's primary therapeutic goal is precisely this: the construction of personal meaning within an organized community setting. Its purpose is to understand each person's life and the meaning they have given to it. Homelessness was understood by the clinicians in part as conferring certain advantages that provided skills crucial for recovery. Knowledge about a mental disorder is important from the clinician's side but arguably even more important from the patient's point of view. FUNGRATA's approach strives to understand the person and the behaviors to then create interventions that are unique for each person. This process is neither brief nor simple.

NOTE

* The authors would like to express thanks to Dr. Tom Csordas and Dr. Janis Jenkins for their helpful editorial work.

REFERENCES

Berman, Steven S., John E. Barilich, Robert Rosenheck, and Gay Koerber. 1993. "The VA's First Comprehensive Homeless Center: A Catalyst for Public and Private Partnerships." *Hospital and Community Psychiatry* 44(12): 1183–4.

Cohen, Neal L., Jane F. Putnam, and Ann M. Sullivan. 1984. "The Mentally Ill Homeless: Isolation and Adaptation." *Hospital and Community Psychiatry* 35: 922–4.

Coursey, Robert D. 1989. "Psychotherapy with Persons Suffering from Schizophrenia: The Need for a New Agenda." *Schizophrenia Bulletin* 15(3): 349–53.

Coursey, Robert D., Andrew B. Keller, and Elizabeth W. Farrell. 1995. "Individual Psychotherapy and Persons with Serious Mental Illness: The Clients' Perspective." *Schizophrenia Bulletin* 21(2): 283–301.

Fergusson, Alberto. 1997. "Accompanied Autoanalysis and the Theory of Psychosis as Psychological Destruction and Decomposition." *Revista de la Sociedad Colombiana de Psicoanalisis* 22(2): 6–17.

Fleck, Stephen. 1986. "Psychosocial Approaches to the Treatment and Management of Schizophrenics." *Connecticut Medicine* 50(4): 243–50.

Gabbard, Glen O., Susan G. Lazar, John Hornberger, and David Spiegel. 1997. "The Economic Impact of Psychotherapy: A Review." *American Journal of Psychiatry* 154(2): 147–55.

Gelberg, Lillian and Lawrence S. Linn. 1988. "Social and Physical Health of Homeless Adults Previously Treated for Mental Health Problems." *Hospital and Community Psychiatry* 39: 510–16.

Gomez, Carlos. 1994. "La Psiquiatria en Colombia Situacion actual y Perspectivas." *Revista Colombiana de Psiquiatria* XXIII(3): 212–23.

Gunderson, John G. and Arlene F. Frank. 1985. "Effects of Psychotherapy in Schizophrenia." *Yale Journal of Biology and Medicine* 58(4): 373–81.

Harding, Courtenay M. and James H. Zahniser. 1994. "Empirical Correction of Seven Myths about Schizophrenia with Implications for Treatment." *Acta Psychiatrica Scandinavica* 90 (suppl. 384): 140–6.

Kleinman, Arthur. 1980. *Patients and Healers in the Context of Culture.* Berkeley: University of California Press.

Koegel, Paul. 1992. "Through a Different Lens: An Anthropological Perspective on the Homeless Mentally Ill." *Culture, Medicine and Psychiatry* 16(1): 1–22.

Lewis-Fernandez, Roberto and Arthur Kleinman. 1994. "Culture, Personality, and Psychopathology." *Journal of Abnormal Psychology* 103(1): 67–71.

McGlashan, Thomas H. 1994. "What Has Become of the Psychotherapy of Schizophrenia?" *Acta Psychiatrica Scandinavica* 90 (suppl. 384): 147–52.

Rosenheck, Robert and Julie A. Lam. 1997. "Client and Site Characteristics as Barriers to Service Use by Homeless Persons with Serious Mental Illness." *Psychiatric Services* 48(3): 387–90.

Shaner, Andrew. 1989. "Asylums, Asphalt, and Ethics." *Hospital and Community Psychiatry* 40(8): 785–6.

9 Symptoms of Colonialism: Content and Context of Delusion in Southwest Nigeria, 1945–1960

Jonathan Sadowsky*

One of the major achievements of African historical scholarship in the postcolonial period has been to show that ethnic identities, such as Yoruba, were socially shaped, processually unfolding entities, rather than static remnants of a primordial past. Over the same period a considerable scholarly and scientific literature developed about mental illness in southwest Nigeria, which focused on the Yoruba, the region's predominant ethnic group (Leighton, Lambo, Hughes, Leighton, Murphy, and Macklin 1963; WHO 1979; Westley 1993). Like Yoruba identity, which must be defined processually, groups and categories such as "the schizophrenias" are not primordial or unchanging entities. Much of the antipsychiatric literature that flourished in the 1960s erred in concluding that these categories were "only" myths, or therefore not "real" illnesses. To show that these categories are "in motion" is not to deny their reality or force for patients and caregivers, any more than to emphasize the historically formed character of ethnicities and national identities negates their subjective power.

A central proposition of many cross-cultural studies of mental disorders is that the illnesses are homogeneous but that the content varies in different cultural settings (Leighton et al. 1963). This tenet emerges from the important and rigorous task of forging a globally usable nosology and overturning a naïve form of cultural relativism. But one effect of this proposition has been to push considerations of content into the background. This chapter seeks to historicize and instantiate the reasons why content and context matter in the case of southwest Nigeria. It is fitting that the relationship between content and context be explored on the basis of material from this area, for it was T. Adeoye Lambo (1955), the Nigerian pioneer of cross-cultural psychiatry, who observed vast differences in presentation between hospitalized patients and those cared for traditionally.

The material for this chapter is derived from over a year of research conducted in Nigeria while based at the University of Ibadan and is thus part of a broader study of colonial processes and mental institutions. The

238

evidence is mainly drawn from the Nigerian National Archives in Ibadan and from case records of the Aro Mental Hospital in Abeokuta, to which the hospital graciously allowed me access. The chapter is adapted from my monograph (Sadowsky 1999) that analyzes the development of colonial Nigerian asylum policy, patient records from the Nigerian asylums, and the discourse of colonial psychiatry, at greater length. In this chapter, I focus on letters written by two Nigerian asylum inmates, chosen because the richness of the letters illustrates the possibilities of textual analysis of these kinds of sources. In particular, the chapter proposes to contribute to the literature on the political construction of delusion (Fisher 1985; Glass 1985).

Historians attempting to retrieve subjective representations of the experience of mental illness often face obstacles that anthropologists and clinicians, who work with living people, do not. Historians usually cannot generate their own database and have to work with whatever fragmentary records have been recorded or preserved. Recording and preserving the voices of people considered insane has rarely been a high priority in any society and is still less so in a situation of colonial domination. What might look to an anthropologist or clinician like incomplete evidence can, therefore, be treasure for a historian. I am not, in any event, making generalizable claims about the content of the materials I examine, but I am trying to show how such sources can be interpreted by using supporting evidence to place them in historical context. The method consists of a combination of internal textual analysis, reference to other contemporary materials (including missionary records, newspapers, government documents, and court records), and use of insights from comparative studies.

Background to Colonial Nigeria's Asylum Policies

Early in the twentieth century, the colonial government in southern Nigeria perceived a growing swarm of vagrant "lunatics" in the urban centers and responded by founding asylums for their confinement. These institutions pose the question, "by what standards were the inmates mad?" How did British-administered institutions determine "lunacy" across the cultural frontiers that separated them from Africans? I explore these questions with reference to two institutions in southwest Nigeria, the Yaba Lunatic Asylum and Abeokuta's Aro Mental Hospital. For most of the colonial period, Yaba Lunatic Asylum in Lagos, and other asylums in the country, were mainly custodial institutions that made little attempt to cure the inmates. Yaba was transformed into a curative mental hospital concurrently with Nigeria's transition to independence. Late in the colonial

period, the Aro Mental Hospital, famous because of T. A. Lambo's inno-
vations in outpatient care and syncretic therapy, began treating significant
numbers of patients (Lambo 1964; Asuni 1967, 1979).

Most of the research published so far about colonial psychiatry in Africa
has focused on the ways colonial psychiatry, for all its ostensible interest in African minds, represented a projection of *European* anxieties and
concerns and thus provides a rich field for the study of colonial mentality (Vaughan 1983, 1991; Dubow 1993; McCulloch 1995). This is a
compelling line of inquiry, but what follows puts more emphasis on the
self-representations of so-called Nigerian "lunatics." While the historiog-
raphy of disease, healing, and medical institutions in African history has
grown considerably in recent years, patients are relatively absent from
literature. This absence probably reflects source limitations more than
the priorities of researchers, but that is all the more reason to pay careful
attention to what sources are available.

Most asylum inmates in the southwest were ethnically Yoruba. The
main Yoruba word translated as "madness" or "madman" is *were*. It is syn-
onymous with "foolish or silly person." Yoruba healing for *were* is an empirical practice, not a closed "belief system" (Hallen and Sodipo 1986).
One consequence of this empirical approach is that it is also a changing
system, so it is hazardous to assume that current practices are identical to
those of several generations ago. The ethnographic work on the subject
nevertheless provides guides to knowledge and practices with some
antiquity (Prince 1964).

Yoruba healers have used a combination of herbal remedies, dramatic
ritual, and a form of divination based on the *Ifa* oral tradition (Abimbola
1976). Healers that rely mainly on herbs are referred to as *onisegun*. The
Ifa divination system is especially complex; its practitioners – *babalawos* –
learn a vast number of verses that are consulted at critical life junctures.
The healing occupations in Yoruba societies are professionalized, in the
sense that the practitioners belong to societies that attest to the compe-
tency of their members. Medical knowledge and practice is also often
passed on within families. Although there seems to be no question that
Yoruba nosologies have traditionally made a distinction between madness
and other ailments, Yoruba conceptions of health and illness are holistic
in the sense that well-being is considered to refer to both mental and
bodily state (Gbadegesin 1991). Many Yoruba are also pluralistic, seeking help in distress from Muslim and Christian healers, as well as from
those working in local traditions, as is common in many African settings
(Janzen 1978; Mullings 1984; Feierman 1985).

Yoruba healers recognize organic and physical problems, bewitchment,
and the actions of deities as possible causes of insanity (Prince 1964).

With regard to the last, Yoruba religions recognize a number of *orisa*, or deities, and the breach of a taboo associated with a deity or other offence may lead the *orisa* to inflict madness. Segun Gbadegesin (1991) also notes that Yoruba healers recognize both organic and extraorganic etiologies. Healers treat psychiatric ailments through a combination of ritual, consultations with the family members, and herbal medicines, especially the plant Rauwolfia, which is administered in a liquid and has a powerful sedative effect.

Some precolonial depictions of insanity in the region appear in missionary records from the nineteenth century. What is most striking about these records (which were written by both African and European missionaries) is the absence of any mention of differences between European and African patients with regard to insanity in Nigeria. This does not show that there were no differences, but it is significant that what differences there may have been were not deemed worthy of report. Nineteenth-century missionary records mention insanity without any apparent concern that the condition was especially prevalent. A number of newspaper articles from the last decade of the nineteenth century show, however, that by the 1890s, the colony's growing urban centers confronted significant social control problems due to mad people on the streets (Sadowsky 1999). By the early twentieth century, the fledgling colonial government concluded that it needed to provide some kind of facility for their confinement.

The colonial period began in Nigeria in the late nineteenth century and ended when Nigeria gained independence in 1960. The first asylums were established in 1906, and for the first two decades, the asylums were used as purely custodial institutions, with colonial officials having no higher aspiration for them. By the late 1920s, calls were begun for a reformed, curative hospital, calls that were received with scorn from most in the government at first, but with more sympathy starting in the mid-1930s. Once the government determined that a hospital would be desirable, though, inertia carried the day, until near the end of the Second World War. Development of therapeutic facilities proceeded in the mid-1950s, as Nigerian psychiatrists began to staff the institutions, which were then renamed hospitals. But most colonial officials before the 1950s considered anything more than custodial care for the insane an extravagance. Officials considered asylums "inappropriate" to the African way of life and provided them as a grudging admission that the government had some responsibility for the problem of vagrant lunatics in urban areas. Colonial policies caused massive changes in economy, law, education, and infrastructure, even as colonial ideology maintained that the government should avoid making impositions. One result of this contradiction was, as Vaughan (1983) has observed for the Nyasaland case, that there were no African equivalents for what Foucault called the "great confinement" in Europe (Foucault 1965). Whereas asylums underwent a massive expansion in the first half of the nineteenth century in Europe and North America, they were developed in much more limited ways in colonial Africa. But the numbers of people confined did grow at a rate that confounded contemporary observers, and because very modest resources were devoted to them, they were overwhelmed and overcrowded rapidly. The incarcerated insane numbered in the hundreds by the end of the colonial period; this was a small number compared to the total population, but far larger than government plans anticipated. There are also references to the much larger number of people turned away from the asylums due to overcrowding.

Few people, whether patients, their families, or government officials, seemed to want to use the lunatic asylums. Most Nigerians preferred to care for insane relatives at home or with traditional healers. Some inferences about the process of commitment and discharge can be made from letters written by family members to colonial administrators seeking to have patients admitted to asylums, as well as letters – by far more common – requesting that the patient be allowed to come home. Few of the requests for release overtly deny that the patient is insane. It is striking how many inmates were people who, because of their florid behavior, Europeans and Africans could agree were insane. This agreement may be seen as an anticipation in everyday practice of the scientific development of a globally usable nosology. Most of the petitions for release emphasize that the patient could be treated by a local healer, and in most cases, administrators agreed that the patient should be released to the care of a healer.

Reading Patients' Writing

Of the little evidence about individual patients in the colonial asylums that survive, most was written by administrators or clinicians. There are a few cases, though, where self-reports by patients have been preserved. What most strongly connects these reports is their highly political content.

The diagnosis "schizophrenia" was rarely used in the Nigerian asylums, but many of the patients showed behaviors that we can usefully describe as having "family resemblances" with schizophrenia. Indeed, their patterns of delusional thought and their language will strike a chord of recognition among people who have worked with patients with a diagnosis of schizophrenia.

A twenty-eight-year-old clerk admitted to Aro in August 1959 described his path to the hospital during the year before Nigeria's independence in this elliptical but captivating account:

I was well till 26/8/59. Suddenly, I took my notebook & started writing 'nonsense' in it like: 'I am the new money with 5 heads. All the world shall use it.' '*Awolowo* + *Awolowo* = *Double Awolowo. Double Awolowo* = *Double Victory.*'

I drew a flag showing where the boundary of the Western Region should be, i.e., the River Niger. Then I wrote, 'We are wonderful.' Then I packed my clothes, bible, ruler & prayer garment (I am an Aladura), my wristwatch my shorthand fountain pen. I gave them to my brother. I was displacing everything, so I was brought here. When I got to Abeokuta I heard the voice of a spirit, which asked me to say 'Irapada' [redemption], so I shouted 'Irapada.'

When I got here, I did not take food, in obedience to the spirit, which asked me not to take food. It said 'Have you not taken food before?' Later I thought that I was in the House of Representatives.

Since then I have known that we are not in the House of Representatives. We are in the Hospital. . . . The day I received my salary, I had another attack.

Such accounts can be difficult to interpret. How much of the language can be understood in terms of a psychotic process, how much in terms of a man writing in a language that is not his mother tongue (does he mean displacing or misplacing)? It is certainly beyond the scope of this chapter to comment on what appear in this text to be examples of a highly emotive symbolic logic, delusions of grandiose hue, profound misinterpretations of his immediate environment, command auditory hallucinations, perhaps an elevated mood, and subsequent insight into what he now recognizes to be "nonsense." But as Emily Dickinson wrote, "Much madness is divinest sense," an attitude implied in the quotation marks around the word nonsense. While the patient was "displacing everything," he also wrote with splintered eloquence about the themes of Nigeria's imminent independence. In this, and in many of the preserved accounts that I examined, the analysis of the language of the confined shows their subjective experience to be saturated with political and religious meanings. The identification with Obafemi Awolowo (the most prominent Yoruba politician of this period, founder of the Action Group political party, and premier of the Western Region at the time of the patient's writing) reflects brewing anxieties about ethnic conflicts – as does the concern with the boundary of the Western region. The cry of '*Irapada!*" possibly expresses a redemptive elation associated with the end of colonial rule, while the confusion of the hospital with "the House of Representatives" conveys a sense of the hospital as a political institution – perhaps also expressing a sense of the "Westernness" of the institution. Indeed, it is striking that prior to his admission the patient was divesting himself of items associated with his Western education – wristwatch, fountain pen, and bible – in a purging process anticipating redemption.

None of these interpretations has significance if we regard his words as *simply* the "raving" of a madman, or in clinical parlance, as symptomatic expressions of the loosening of associations and delusional thinking typical of a major psychotic process. From that perspective, what the lunatics *said* is not so important as what they had – a view that should be questioned not so much because it is wrong, but because it is incomplete. I propose instead to treat "raving" itself as a valid object of social analysis. The argument that these buried messages are worth excavating is developed in what follows. I am critical of the view that the content of psychotic speech is inconsequential, though I acknowledge that it is not always transparent. My approach presupposes that the "insane" do not differ from "normal" people in an absolute sense, but instead occupy a position on a spectrum containing the normal and the pathological (Jenkins 1994). I am not, though, attempting in this chapter to demonstrate this presupposition, which has long been a part of psychiatric thought, though a part that is less prominent in the most reductively biomedical psychiatry.

The content of the illness experience for many of the Nigerian patients was characterized by a political construction of delusion, similar to that noted for Barbados by Lawrence Fisher (1985). Of all the materials I examined, this was best illustrated by a remarkable set of letters written by a patient to the District Officer for Ijebu-Ode in 1943. Many years earlier, the patient had left Lagos, the colony's capital in the south, to study in Sierra Leone, and then to England to study law. There he was admitted to an English asylum in 1921. On return to Nigeria, he was treated by five healers. According to a case record entry, he was "reported to be irresponsible in his behaviour and dirty in his habits," and he was placed in Yaba Asylum. His letters read as a troubled prose poem on the partition of Africa:

The British government is now called the government of God. God, who is called Jehovah, great I am, is the author of the Ten Commandments and all the sacred Laws of the Holy England. The English are fighting for the government of God, whereas the Germans are fighting for a Nazi government, an invention made by Satan, the Devil.

Hitlerism must be destroyed. The man Herr Hitler, that German Devil, must pass away a mad man.

I am...a poor gentleman whom your worship sent to Lagos, Yaba Asylum for medical treatment. I am quite well and returned to Ijebu-Ode a discharged lunatic on Friday, April 19th 1943. All places inhabited by the black African race, in former times (before the First Great War) were governed by different powers from Europe, such as the English, the French, and the Germans. But now, by the justice of God, all these places are governed by the English. . . . All these places under the British government are collectively known as 'The Nigeria of God.'

God appeared to me, Solomon, King of Israel, in a dream by night, and said, 'Ask what I shall give thee.'

And I Solomon said, 'Thou hast made me king instead of my father David, and I am but a child. I know not how to conduct myself before thy chosen people. Give me an understanding heart, that I may distinguish between good and bad, judge thy people righteously.'

And God said to me, 'Because thou hast asked this, and not long life, or riches, or the life of thine enemies, I have given thee an understanding heart. And I have also given thee that which thou hast not asked, both riches and honour. . . .'

And I Solomon awoke; and behold it was a dream. Soon the time came when I had to put to the test the good gift of wisdom which I had received.

One day there came to Solomon two women, England and Germany, who lived in the same house, Europe. Each of them was the mother of a baby-boy, Nigeria; and the one infant, England's Nigeria (this is called the Nigeria of God) was only three days older than the other, Germany's Nigeria (the German Cameroons, etc.). But the one mother, Germany, had lain on her child by mistake in the night, and killed it. When she awoke and found that it was dead, she took it and laid it beside the other woman, England, while she slept, and carried off her living child. The other, England, soon found out the trick that had been played upon her. So a dispute arose between the two women, England and Germany. Each of them claimed the living Nigeria, and they came together to me Solomon to settle the matter.

I Solomon, having heard what each had to say, called for a sword, and bade one of my guards divide the living Nigeria in two, and give half to England, and half to Germany. Germany thought this was a good plan, but England exclaimed against it, saying, 'Oh my Lord, give Germany the living Nigeria, and on no account divide it.' (Nigerian National Archives 1921)

In this way the true parentage was discovered, and the living Nigeria was given to England. The letter seems to caricature the "paternalism" of colonialism, which was reflected in an imagery of parenthood that pervades colonial discourse. In May 1943, another letter, containing the following, was addressed to King George III at Buckingham Palace:

I am wisdom, the Conqueror of every foe of England. I am a Law Student, the 'Palace of Arts,' of the University of London, and the Founder of all British Universities and Schools. I am that I am.

The letters end, then, with the ultimate gesture of grandiosity, and a glorification of England. Some speculation about the letters' preservation in official records is warranted. It may have touched a nerve because the glorification of England is so extreme as to seem grotesque, as if lampooning the project of colonial hegemony. There may also be a subtle anticolonial message buried in this patient's letters. The last letter was directed to George III, Britain's monarch when the American colonies decided to rebel, launching a crucial sally in the gradual dissolution of Britain's first global empire. But these writings are more striking for the way they differ from the majority of records with political content, in which resentment toward the state is more or less overtly evident.

J. C. Carothers – a notoriously racist colonial psychiatrist best known for his work in Kenya – separated patients diagnosed with schizophrenia in a Kenyan asylum into those with persecutory delusions and those without, and maintained that Africans were especially prone to persecutory ones (Carothers 1951; Sadowsky 1999). How should we understand such an extraordinary focus on this particular symptom? "Persecutory delusions" are a commonly found symptom in mental patients anywhere. And in the case of Carothers, the emphasis on persecutory delusions is related to his colonial racism, which psychopathologized expressions of anticolonial sentiment. But in many of the Nigerian cases, judgments about psychopathology are inextricable from the political culture of colonialism. The diagnostic descriptor "persecutory delusions" was, for example, frequently applied to a number of "lunatic soldiers," men who had fought for Allied forces in World War II, and were judged to be insane on their return to Nigeria. We may well wonder about the "delusions" of a soldier fighting in the name of the free world in the service of a colonial government. The delusion may well echo the disillusionment the war occasioned for many soldiers who were not thought insane. Consider the example of a "lunatic soldier" who was diagnosed as having a "psychopathic personality," with a "history of erratic and violent behavior," and who was repatriated from Southeast Asia. His file contains a daily log of his rationality and aggressiveness, which shows a general tendency toward increasing irrationality. Soon after his admission to Aro, he was said to have developed a "persecutory complex against the British and became increasingly difficult to handle." Regardless of the criteria by which judgments were made about the presence or absence of symptoms, it is critical to the interpretation of the psychopathology recorded in these case files to recognize that resentment and aggression are predictable in a colonial society. In this case, for example, a man trained to fight for colonial superiors in a remote place, and then confined against his will might be expected to show rancor against the dominating power. Diagnosis was thus problematic not only because of "cross-cultural" differences, but also because of perceptions of appropriate social relations rooted in colonialism. While it is not possible within the confines of this chapter to convey the diverse range of delusional material recorded in colonial asylums in Nigeria, I was able to conclude, on the basis of a systematic review of these historical clinical data that the commonly noted symptom of "persecutory delusions" was overdetermined by the persecutory nature of colonialism itself (Sadowsky 1999).

Another way of looking at persecutory delusions is to posit that to the extent these inmates were mad, their madness allowed sentiments to flourish that might have otherwise been concealed. This perspective follows from psychoanalytic views of psychosis as entailing a free expression of unconscious wishes and drives (Arieti and Brody 1974). It may be naïve to believe that the mad are more properly regarded as seers or prophets. But it is a belief with origins in the observation that the mad can have an unsettling degree of insight into social inequities and existential dilemmas – even as they may not, from a clinician's point of view, show comparable insight into the nature of their illnesses.

The insane also sometimes identify with holders of power and prestige in uncomfortable ways, voicing common fantasies. A famous example in literature is the narrator of Nikolai Gogol's *Diary of a Madman*, who progresses toward his coronation as King of Spain, which for the reader is his forlorn admission to an asylum. Glass has proposed that this kind of identification forms a counterpart, or flipside, to paranoid delusion; by identifying with the powerful, one defends against the annihilation threatened by the persecution (Glass 1985). Consider the example of a patient who portrayed himself as a rival to one of the most famous black men in the world in the early 1950s – Ralph Bunche, whose efforts in the settlement in Palestine earned him a Nobel Prize. The patient, who was a convert from Islam to Christianity, reproduced his claim in triplicate:

I forward herewith one copy of an extract from my statement of policy, summary of actions since my stay in this land, an explanation of the issues involved in Korean War... one chart indicating my activities towards maintenance or attainment of peace in Korean field, and one baptismal certificate....

It would be seen that I possess an exclusive claim both to last year's award wrongly made to Ralph Bunche and this year's award yet to be made. A close scrutiny of my chart and religious qualifications will certainly justify the claims. Under the circumstances, kindly take step to make Bunche vomit what he has shrewdly swallowed. I am the owner.

In both cases, kindly remit me a sum of 16,000 [pounds], representing the 8,000 [pounds] last year, & 8,000 [pounds] for this year.

With regard to the Korean War] The conflict has been that of Democracy versus communism.... Xtianity stands for Democracy, Mohammedanism for communism. In Holy Koran, the regulation savours of communism, the rule being four wives to a man. In Xtianity, the order is one.... Christ's policy has been that of peace while Mohammed maintained a belligerent one.

In the mid-1960s, American psychoanalyst Helen Tartakoff, posited "a new nosological entity, the Nobel Prize complex" (Tartakoff 1966).

Tartakoff held that in postwar America, there was a strong discrepancy between a culture that idealized achievement and the institutional means it provided to attain it. This discrepancy caused pervasive distress for analysands of the time, with the Nobel Prize presenting a widely shared compensatory fantasy. As a discrete "nosological entity," the Nobel Prize complex has not gained wide currency. Yet Tartakoff may well have touched on an idea with wide significance. If contradiction between ambition and means of achievement was a key factor in the "Nobel Prize complex" in America at this time, in Nigeria such a contradiction was at least as likely, as the number of educated people was growing faster than the number of jobs commensurate with the skill level they had attained (Abernethy 1969).

Conclusion: Content and Context of Delusion

It would be misleading to ask if these patients were mad by "Yoruba" or "Western" standards. Such a line of inquiry, which is only recently waning in cross-cultural psychiatry, assumes boundedness and homogeneity in cultures. But these cultures – immensely complex and contested in themselves – were in a process of interaction. The insane in colonial Nigeria were insane according to the polysemic standards of a colonial society with many cultural values in interplay. An example is the patient who complained that he had been deprived of the Nobel Prize. His deviance was not uniquely "African" or "Yoruba," given mention in the 1960s of an American "Nobel Prize Complex." At the same time, there is a particularly Nigerian inflection to his letter, which combines an appropriation of Ralph Bunche's fame and honor with a discourse on conflict between Islam and Christianity. This does not mean that the "symptom repertoire" of lunatics was entirely new; the association of madness and nakedness, for example, has some antiquity among the Yoruba and continued into the colonial period. Asylums were sites of a kind of "creolization" of pathology, where what Vaughan has called the "idioms of madness" were not so much African, European, or universal, but specific to colonial Nigeria. Nor does this exhaust the issue of context; these patients, like those in the WHO studies, were hospital patients, a fact with epidemiological and experiential consequences.

Obeyesekere (1985) has commented on the way in which the constellation of symptoms that constitute depression became commonplace in Sri Lanka, despite the fact that it was incompatible with the Buddhism of that country to view suffering and depression as abnormal. Its introduction, he argues, was a testament to the power and prestige of the culture of Western medicine. Following Obeyesekere, we could say that the Nigerian asylum inmates were suffering syndromes "fused into conceptions" in Britain and the West, and then imported to Nigeria. But I would like to take Obeyesekere's argument a bit further. Obeyesekere also rightly draws attention to the power of Western medicine. But while brief vignettes illustrate his points about the cultural work that Buddhism prescribes, no examples are given of people in the hospitals. The specific content of their depression and the context of their diagnoses are omitted. Proponents of a universal psychiatric nosology concede that "content" of a disorder varies culturally. But this content *demands attention*; without it the patient is decontextualized, and the social dimension of affliction is obscured.

Historical specificity also allows us to reexamine some of the arguments for universalist views of insanity. Take, for example, Jane Murphy's article on psychiatric labeling – a classic, if controversial article in ethnopsychiatry (Murphy 1976). This article is a highly influential exposition of the antirelativist approach to mental illness. The article aims to dislodge a cornerstone of labeling theory, namely the belief that other cultures have radically different canons of deviance. Thomas Scheff and others argued that if very different cultures had radically different conceptions of mental illness, this would support the idea that "mental illness" was a social convention – and, by implication, not a "real" disease (though Scheff has abandoned an extreme formulation of this view [see Scheff 1984]). For example, it might be shown that the behavior the West considers madness was construed as shamanism or special insight in other cultures, and we would therefore have to reconsider our own understanding and treatment. Ruth Benedict and other ethnographers were cited to indicate that this was the case. Murphy conducted an empirical test.

Murphy's article was based on fieldwork among the Inuit and the Yoruba. She showed convincingly that among Inuit, where shamanism existed, the behavior of shamans was not identical to the mad, and that, in fact, those societies had *both* the categories of shamanism and madness – and that their categories of madness was not too dissimilar from Western ones. As for the Yoruba, Murphy argued that *"were"* was a fair translation of "madness," since it covered a similar range of behavioral abnormality. Murphy's blow to labeling theory was not decisive. Claims of cultural difference were never logically crucial to labeling theory. The most Murphy could claim to have proven was that similar labeling processes take place in different cultures. But the problems with Murphy's article run deeper. She shared with the labeling theorists the assumption that the Yoruba could fairly be used as an "Archimedean point" from which to assess Western psychiatric practice. In order for the Yoruba to fulfill this function they would ideally exist in remote isolation from Western practice. From a scientific point of view, one would not want to choose a part of Africa that had had eighty years of British-style asylums. This history, and indeed the asylums and mental hospitals generally, was entirely omitted in the article.

In a sense, it should not be terribly surprising that mental patients would draw their references from the political world surrounding them. But the point is worth stressing in light of the highly universalizing tendencies of biopsychiatry. It would be tempting to dismiss those tendencies as "positivistic," or to say they constitute "socially constructed knowledge" whose dominance we do not have to cede. Such a critique would be not so much untrue as truistic. Even if mental illness is a reality, even if those confined in the asylums were genuinely mentally ill, even if the symptoms of madness are partly caused by genetic or other organic factors, and even if these symptoms could be dispelled by medication, the specific content of the symptoms retains significance. The imposition of Western assumptions may lie not so much in the use of categories such as schizophrenia. Rather, the deeper cross-cultural problem may be the assumption, derived from a scientific culture that positively values reductionism, that biological lesions or genetic markers render questions of content and context irrelevant.

NOTE

* I am grateful for permission to republish, and all acknowledgments in my monograph, *Imperial Bedlam: Institutions of Madness and Colonialism in Southwest Nigeria*, apply to this chapter. The Social Science Research Council funded the research. For helpful comments on this version of the material, I would especially like to thank Sarah Adler, Robert Barrett, Conerly Casey, and Janis Jenkins.

This chapter is adapted from my monograph, *Imperial Bedlam: Institutions of Madness and Colonialism in Southwest Nigeria* (Sadowsky 1999), especially Chapter 4.

REFERENCES

Abernethy, David. 1969. *The Political Dilemma of Popular Education*. Stanford, CA: Stanford University.
Abimbola, Wande. 1976. *Ifa: An Exposition of Ifa Literary Corpus*. Ibadan: Caxton.
Arieti, Sylvano and Eugene B. Brody. 1974. *American Handbook of Psychiatry*, 2nd ed., vol. 3. New York: Basic Books.
Asuni, Tolani. 1979. "Therapeutic Communities of the Hospital and Villages in Aro Hospital." *African Journal of Psychiatry* 5: 35–42.
———. 1967. "Aro Hospital in Perspective." *American Journal of Psychiatry* 124 (6): 763–70.

Carothers, John Colin. 1951. "Frontal Lobe Function and the African." *Journal of Mental Science* 97(406): 12–48.

Dubow, Saul. 1993. "Wulf Sachs's *Black Hamlet*: A Case of Psychic Vivisection?" *African Affairs* 92(369): 519–56.

Feierman, Steven. 1985. "Struggles for Control: The Social Roots of Health and Healing in Modern Africa." *African Studies Review* 28 (2–3): 73–147.

Fisher, Lawrence. 1985. *Colonial Madness*. New Brunswick, NJ: Rutgers University Press.

Foucault, Michel. 1965. *Madness and Civilization: A History of Insanity in the Age of Reason*. New York: Vintage Books.

Gbadegesin, Segun. 1991. *African Philosophy: Traditional Yoruba Philosophy and Contemporary African Realities*. New York: Peter Lang.

Glass, James. 1985. *Delusion: Internal Dimensions of Political Life*. Chicago, IL: University of Chicago.

Hallen, Barry and J. Olubi Sodipo. 1986. *Knowledge, Belief, and Witchcraft: Analytic Experiments in African Philosophy*. London: Ethnographica.

Janzen, John. 1978. *The Quest for Therapy in Lower Zaire*. Berkeley: University of California Press.

Jenkins, Janis Hunter. 1994. "Emotion and Mental Disorder." In P. K. Bock, ed., pp. 97–120. *Handbook of Psychological Anthropology*. Westport, CT: Greenwood.

Lambo, T. Adeoye. 1955. "The Role of Cultural Factors in Paranoid Psychoses Among the Yoruba Tribe of Nigeria." *Journal of Mental Science* 101(423): 239–66.

———. 1964. "The Village of Aro." *Lancet* 2: 513–14.

Leighton, Alexander, T. Adeoye Lambo, Charles C. Hughes, Dorothea C. Leighton, Jane M. Murphy, and David B. Macklin. 1963. *Psychiatric Disorder among the Yoruba*. Ithaca, NY: Cornell University Press.

McCulloch, Jock. 1995. *Colonial Psychiatry and the African Mind*. Cambridge: Cambridge University Press.

Mullings, Leith. 1984. *Therapy, Ideology, and Social Change: Mental Healing in Urban Ghana*. Berkeley: University of California Press.

Murphy, Jane. 1976. "Psychiatric Labeling in Cross-Cultural Perspective." *Science* 191(4231): 1019–28.

Nigerian National Archives. 1921. Ibadan, CSO 19/9 N.290.

Obeyesekere, Gananath. 1985. "Buddhism, Depression, and the Work of Culture in Sri Lanka." In A. Kleinman and B. Good, eds., pp. 134–52. *Culture and Depression*. Berkeley: University of California Press.

Prince, Raymond. 1964. "Indigenous Yoruba Psychiatry." In A. Kiev, ed., pp. 84–119. *Magic Faith, and Healing*. New York: The Free Press of Glencoe.

Sadowsky, Jonathan. 1999. *Imperial Bedlam: Institutions of Madness and Colonialism in Southwest Nigeria*. Berkeley: The Regents of the University of California.

Scheff, Thomas. 1984. *Being Mentally Ill: A Sociological Theory*, 2nd ed. Chicago, IL: Aldine de Gruyter.

Tartakoff, Helen. 1966. "The Normal Personality in our Culture and the Nobel Prize Complex." In R. M. Loewenstein, K. R. Eissler, eds., pp. 222–52. *Psychoanalysis: A General Psychology*. New York: International Universities.

Vaughan, Megan. 1983. "Idioms of Madness: Zomba Lunatic Asylum, Nyasaland, in the Colonial Period." *Journal of Southern African Studies* 9(2): 218–38.

———. 1991. *Curing Their Ills: Colonial Power and African Illness.* Stanford, CA: Stanford University.

Westley, David. 1993. *Mental Health and Psychiatry in Africa: An Annotated Bibliography.* London: Hans Zell.

World Health Organization. 1979. *Schizophrenia: An International Follow-Up Study.* Chichester: John Wiley & Sons.

Part 3

Subjectivity and Emotion

10 Madness in Zanzibar: An Exploration of Lived Experience

Juli H. McGruder

It is clear that the outcome for schizophrenia is better in developing than in industrialized countries (see Hopper this volume) yet attempts to account for this difference have been speculative and elaborated in "a virtual ethnographic vacuum" (Hopper 1992:95). It is also clear that family predictors of relapse – hostility, criticism, and emotional overinvolvement expressed by relatives toward the ill family member – have proved robust when tested cross-culturally (Jenkins and Karno 1992). Jenkins (1991) has urged attention to the cultural salience and meaning of these predictors of relapse. Ethnographic study of particular families in the developing world coping with psychotic illness in the household is recommended to explain how social and emotional factors might moderate prognosis (Corin 1990; Sartorius 1992; Lucas and Barrett 1995).

Hostility in familial interactions is identified when criticism is generalized or pervasive (for example, "he's a failure at everything he does") or rejection ("he can live on the streets for all I care"). Criticism is defined in terms of a negative affective response (usually anger) to rule violation observed in language content and paralinguistic features of speech (Vaughn and Leff 1976). It is necessary both to identify cultural rules and to appreciate the range of familial and community responses to rule violation in order to understand criticism and hostility. Emotional overinvolvement must be understood in terms of kin relations and notions of the self. Overinvolvement and altered self/other boundaries may be presented in a variety of culture-specific idioms, whereas appropriate involvement with kin may be judged only by local standards (Jenkins 1991). Social withdrawal is a strategy by which people with schizophrenia buffer emotionally intense social interaction (Brown, Birley, and Wing 1972; Corin 1990).

This study examines three families that included five people diagnosed with schizophrenia and develops an understanding of illness, course, and impact on the family emotional environment that is grounded in a knowledge of cultural norms and social processes, including political upheaval and ethnic conflict. It is drawn from a more extensive study conducted in

255

Zanzibar, Tanzania (McGruder 1999) that sought to develop an ethnographically grounded approach to the study of schizophrenia. The study examines culture-specific notions of self and the spaces between self and significant others and takes into account cultural ideas about agency, accountability, and the appropriate handling of emotion.

Methods and Participants

Zanzibar is a semiautonomous island state in the republic of Tanzania, where traditional medical practice is legal and various forms of it are used. Biomedical psychiatric care was introduced there by British colonial authorities with the building of the first lunatic asylum at the turn of the last century (McGruder 1999). In 1988, I was an occupational therapist at Zanzibar's Kidongo Chekundu Mental Hospital. During that year, I interviewed twenty-three patients diagnosed with schizophrenia about their uses of traditional medicine and their illness explanatory models (Kleinman 1980). In 1994, I interviewed and observed traditional healers identified by the mental hospital's community outreach nurse as those involved in care of the mentally ill. In 1996–97 I conducted the study I report on here.

Thirty-two patients were nominated for the study by hospital staff. All met both ICD-10 and DSM-IV diagnostic criteria for schizophrenia and were recently discharged or ready for discharge. On forms I prepared, staff members recorded their impressions of patients' functional levels and living situations. I calculated a rough measure of illness severity for each by dividing the summed inpatient lengths of stay by the time elapsed since diagnosis. From the thirty-two nominated, I selected seven patients to get a mix of both genders and a range of ages, functional levels, illness severities, lengths of psychiatric history, and family constellations. The three families I report on here were the first I selected and those with whom I spent the most time. Two university human subjects protection boards and the medical research committee of the Zanzibar Ministry of Health approved the study methods and informed consent procedures.

During the eleven-month period of the study I visited families at home twice each week on average and they visited me. Social norms in Muslim Zanzibar allowed me to spend more time with female family members than with males. I accompanied families on visits to kin in the countryside and in town, attended weddings and memorial services, cooked with the women, went on picnics, and celebrated the end of Ramadhan with them. I accompanied four of the five patients on their follow-up visits to the mental hospital. None were inpatients during the study. All but one were taking medication through the outpatient department. My research assistant, Ahmed A. Salim, a local psychiatric nurse, and I conducted one taped interview with each family midway through the study year.

In addition to this prolonged engagement with the three identified families, I held two gender-segregated focus groups to discuss familial norms for expression of emotion, criticism, correction, and discipline. Some participants in the focus groups were mental hospital personnel; none were family members in my study. I talked with other community members about notions of self, madness, spirits, and Islam. Dr. A. I. Abdulwakil, a psychiatrist born in Zanzibar and educated in Tanzania, Germany, England, and Nigeria, has provided valuable consultation periodically during the decade I have spent learning about Zanzibar.

Families, Self, and Emotion in the Swahili Culture of Zanzibar

Marriage is nearly universal in Zanzibar and only 2.5 percent of Zanzibari women remain childless; the average desired number of children is 6.5 (Garssen 1988). Divorce is common. The values of modesty, concern for the rights of others, respect, shame, and privacy guide behavior in Swahili societies (Swartz 1991). Kin are portrayed in proverbs as more reliable and dependable than nonkin, but also potentially more irritating given their closeness. Offspring who contravene parental desires and lose their parents' blessing risk the loss of heaven. Child rearing is shared across the extended family.

Ninety-eight percent of Zanzibar residents are Muslims, and of those, 90 percent are Sunni Shafi'ites (Garssen and Haji 1989). Islamic ideology shapes daily rhythms and lifecycle marker events, informs moral choices, and provides succor for dealing with illness and adversity. Local Islamic scholars accept Al-Bukhari's collection of *hadith* as the body of writing that documents the acts of the Prophet Mohammed and thereby provides a guide to living. These *hadith* include accounts of healing by the Prophet, of his dealing with witchcraft, and advice about the *Jinn*. The Qur'an and *hadith* convey that Allah will not put upon humans more than they can bear, that suffering expiates sin, that one must bend to Allah's will, and that a heavenly reward awaits those who embrace with gratitude the tribulations that Allah sends them. They also endorse the idea that spirits are active in the everyday experience of humans.

Spirits are widely held to be a cause of madness. In 72 percent of cases of psychosis identified in an epidemiological survey in Zanzibar, families used both hospital and traditional forms of treatment (Bondestam, Garssen, and Abdulwakil 1990). Traditional treatment includes botanical remedies, therapeutic uses of the Qur'an, and spirit ritual.

The self in Swahili culture, while individuated, remains permeable to the presence of other beings. Spirits are more powerful than humans and can bring illness, bad luck, infertility, and other problems. Anger and violent feelings provoked in human interactions may be deflected into and expressed in interactions between humans and spirits (Caplan 1992). The spirits' willingness to act impulsively and unashamedly on desire marks them as "other." The spirits, whose ethnicity may be Arab, European, Malagasy, Ethiopian, or of a variety of mainland tribes, are troublesome like foreigners who intrude but do not greet (Giles 1995). Spirits may also be Swahili. But even Swahili spirits are autonomous, rude, selfish, and not given to controlling or concealing their emotions, unlike their (idealized) human counterparts who strive to live up to high standards of courteous behavior. Spirits may be sent purposely to harm, inherited from deceased ancestors, or attracted by one's desirability.

Neither the body and the soul, nor the body and mind are opposed concepts or spaces. Rather *mwili* (body) and *maumbile* (God-created nature) encompass *nafsi* (individual essence or vitality), *roho* (soul), *moyo* (heart), and *akili* (mind, intelligence, or reason). Both humans and other animals have *nafsi* and *roho*, so the vitality and soul concepts here are different from those of Christianity. Nonhuman animals do not have *akili*. A psychiatric nurse friend compared *nafsi* to the id and both *roho* and *moyo* to the ego. Statements of emotional or bodily feeling and self may use *nafsi*, particularly when emphasizing an individual point of view, but more often use *roho* and *moyo* (Johnson 1939).

Moyo is heart, both anatomically and figuratively. Things that one keeps to oneself are hidden in the heart, a private internal space. One woman participant in this study was distressed when hearing male voices (hallucinations, we would say), because hearing the men meant that they could see "even into [her] heart," a shameful experience. The heart may be broken, but this does not connote the degree of desolate unhappiness it does in English. It means something akin to disappointment. Hate (*chuki*), love (*upendo*), and happiness or joy (*furaha*) are felt in the *roho* or *moyo*, as are other emotions and sensations. Like many in the developing world, Swahili persons are said to construct individual identity in terms of social group membership (Swartz 1991; Middleton 1992). Yet my observations resonate with Kleinman's (1980) assertion that developing world people can define themselves in ways that accord much importance to the social group and yet be ruggedly individualistic. Although much social intercourse and action is tied to group goals and wants, the individuated self is recognized in a number of Kiswahili proverbs that remind us that:

Akili ni nywele, kila mtu ana zake.	Reason (intellect) is (like) hair, each person has her own.
Kizuri kwake, kibaya na mwenzake.	(What is) good to her (may be) bad to her companion/friend.
Penye wengi, pana mengi.	In a place having many people, there are many (points of view).

The first of these proverbs is so common in ordinary talk that Kiswahili speakers truncate it: *Akili, nywele.* Many verbs in Kiswahili make use of a reflexive particle and the ease of its incorporation even in borrowed verbs is more evidence of an individuated reflexive concept of self.

At focus group meetings I explained that some doctors believed getting better after mental illness is less likely if there are strong emotions expressed in the family. In order to appreciate whether families of patients were unusual in this regard, I needed help understanding how emotion was usually expressed in Zanzibar families. I asked participants to mention words for emotions that were part of family life, indicating that I assumed some conflict to be universal. In both men's and women's groups, love (*upendo*) and hatred (*chuki, uchukivu*) were mentioned first. The two groups' lists also included anger (*hasira*), grief (*msiba*), sadness or sorrow (*huzuni*), and joy or happiness (*furaha*). Beyond these terms, women's and men's responses diverged.

Next I asked participants to tell which emotions generally ought to be hidden and which ones might be shown freely; which emotions can be suppressed or controlled and which are impossible to control. Concealment of certain emotions and thoughts is important in Swahili society (Swartz 1991; Yahya-Othman 1994). Men and women agreed on the importance of hiding *chuki* (hate). Hatred should be held in the heart and allowed to dissipate. Keeping a pleasant exterior and greeting the object of one's hatred would gradually diminish hate – an example given by two women was of greeting one's cowife despite hatred and jealousy (*wivu*). Enacting courtesy or kindness was said to produce a prosocial feeling, called *mazoezi* (accustomedness) (confer Swartz 1991).

Participants agreed that anger (*hasira*) should be controlled or hidden and proverbs attest to the importance of doing so.

Hasira ni hasara.	Anger is loss.
Hasira ya mkizi ni faida ya mvuvi.	The anger of the cuttlefish is the profit of the fisherman.

In explaining the first proverb, people told stories of loss of temper leading a parent to strike a son or daughter – their grown offspring in the examples I heard – causing severe injury or death. The second proverb was explained in terms of the demonstration of anger leading to the loss of some desired result in interpersonal interaction such as social loss of face or destruction of friendship.

One woman offered the metaphor, "Anger is soda." Being used to our hydraulic metaphors of suppressed emotion, I took this to mean that, if unreleased, anger might explode. "No," she explained, "if you shake a soda and it bubbles up, you can only let it out a little at a time, not all at once. But better still you can also leave it be and it will calm down again."

When asked what emotions could be shown freely, women told of the dangers of all strong emotion, even joy (*furaha*). In an animated and lengthy discussion several told stories, some taken from Indian film, in which expression of joy was followed by death or grief (*msiba*). Although men discussed the control of anger and hatred, they could not think of an example in which joy must be hidden or suppressed. When I shared some of the women's stories of expressed joy turning to grief, the men scoffed. It seems that while women are thought less capable of controlling emotion, they themselves evince more wariness than men do of any strongly expressed emotion, even joy.

Both groups discussed self-control during grieving. It is considered a shameful thing for an adult to cry. An adage reinforces this: *Mtu mzima kulia ni aibu.* Grief is an emotion one cannot manage alone. During *matanga*, the social gathering of kin and friends following a death, the bereaved is never alone so that grief may be communally managed. It is not a shame to cry alone or to admit that you cried alone. To cry quietly is expected. Too noisy a show of grief is seen as an impertinent questioning of Allah's will.

Children are admonished not to cry. Boys are told *jikaze* (shore yourself up) and don't be like a girl. Girls are told *jikaze* or you will not get a suitor. Adults also described teaching emotional self-control through the example of adult behavior. One woman who worked in a household with American children expressed distaste for how much crying they did. "Any child old enough to speak, to tell you what is wrong, should not be crying so much."

On the topic of love (*upendo*) men and women differed again. Men said it is often necessary to hide love; women said that it is impossible to do so. I asked the women if it were (hypothetically) possible to hide love, would this be a good thing to try to do. They would not entertain the hypothetical but shouted me down saying, "You can't! You can't!" They reminded me of the wrap garment I was once given as a gift and the saying on it: *Mapenzi ni kikohozi hayawezi kufichika*: Love is (like) a cough, it cannot be hidden. Several pantomimed trying to suppress a cough that burst forth anyway. Men and women agreed that it would be a rare thing to express love verbally, but men said more emphatically that this is a matter of *aibu* (shame).

The preferred interaction style in Zanzibar is not very outgoing and intrusive especially between adults. The valued social demeanor is one of calm reserve. The lack of what we call assertiveness is not a sign of low self-esteem. Rather it appears to be a hallmark of healthy self-respect. One who offers unsolicited opinions, advice, or correction to other adults who are not one's children is considered ill bred or uncouth. Inside families, criticism is indirect as a rule. Disapproval, especially between adults, should be expressed through an intermediary. Both men and women stated that always with elders, generally with age peers, and often with their own and other people's children (depending on the specifics of the situation), it is best to take a complaint to a third party in the family and ask him or her to intervene. When having a problem with an elder, one looks for someone even higher in age and esteem. This avoidance of direct confrontation or criticism is not at all a laissez-faire principle of noninterference. Rather, it is a way to bring pressure to bear without being direct or causing the other to suffer shame. Participants agreed that one's children are not free to do as they like until after they are married, and even then should heed parental advice. The valorization of elders' authority, of emotional reserve in interpersonal social space, and of indirectness in disapproval, establishes an important context for observations of emotion and involvement in the families of persons with schizophrenia.

Despite his command of English and my provision of explanations and examples (taken in part from Jenkins [1991]) Ahmed, my research assistant, had great difficulty helping me to translate "emotional overinvolvement." At first he suggested we use *kudekeza* (to spoil). It was not until he saw a negative example of overinvolvement in a family that he grew certain that *kudekeza* did not cover it. There was no easy translation. For the purposes of the focus group meetings, Ahmed settled on a long construction for overinvolvement that would be glossed: "If one family member and the ill person are like a whole world unto themselves, or for example, if the family member loves the ill person too much or alternatively doesn't give him or her sufficient freedom or time/space, or pries very intently into private matters pertaining to that person." Focus group members agreed that one may carefully watch a disturbed family member but should do so in unobtrusive ways so that the person does not feel "pried into."

The Household of Amina, Hemed, and Kimwana

Amina, the head of the household, was the wife of Hemed and mother of Kimwana, both diagnosed with schizophrenia.[1] Hemed had spent 32 percent of his time as an inpatient since first diagnosed in 1961, all of that before 1979. With the exception of a brief period in 1991, Hemed had not taken psychotropic medicine since 1979. Kimwana was diagnosed at age twenty in 1983, but had never been an inpatient. She attended the outpatient clinic at the mental hospital and took neuroleptics most of the time. Amina divorced Hemed in 1970, but after he had a stroke and had no other relatives on the island, she took him back into their home to care for him.

During 1996–97 the household included (in addition to the three afore-mentiond): Amina's mother, two married daughters and their children, one unmarried daughter who was away at university most of the time, one unmarried son studying at Islamic teacher's college, Hemed's half brother who is deaf-mute, and Hemed's adopted sister and her children. Two infants were born to the household during the study year. Amina also had siblings in town and matrilineal kin in rural central Zanzibar. Kimwana visited them only rarely, when compelled to do so. Hemed did not leave the house.

The interactions and discourse I observed in this family support Jenkins' suggestion that cultural conceptions of the causes and mean-ing of mental illness can mediate the creation of social-moral status for ill family members that inhibits criticism and hostility (Jenkins 1991). When asked, Amina labeled family illnesses as tests from Allah. She ac-cepted the problems in her family with graceful acquiescence to Allah's will as I shall illustrate.[2] While Amina saw the ultimate cause for illnesses in the family as the Almighty, spirits were sometimes seen as more prox-imate causes. Hemed first became ill during his involvement in racially charged preindependence politics. According to Amina, he would go to political meetings and then come home upset and talking in ways she did not understand. He would speak, as if to someone else, on the where-abouts of political figures. He would threaten his children and beat his mother at times. I thought that the stresses of these meetings and the po-litical nature of Hemed's work at the time contributed to the onset of his illness. Amina said, however, that they believed it was related to a spirit he inherited from his father.

When Kimwana first had an incident of disturbed behavior (going outside one Sunday night and pleading in a loud voice for forgiveness from her deceased maternal relatives and her coworkers) Amina and her mother assumed the problem to be spirit possession. Perhaps a spirit from the maternal side of the family piqued at not having been duly recognized for protecting the child through her long years of schooling and into her government employment; perhaps a spirit sent by a jealous coworker via witchcraft; these were the older women's first ideas about the problem. When they could not get the spirit to say what it wanted, nor to calm down, they wondered if Kimwana might have cerebral malaria. They took her to the general hospital where she was admitted, eventually diagnosed with schizophrenia, and discharged on medication. For a time, Amina and her mother thought the white tablets were antimalarial pills. Eventually Amina learned that this was *ugonjwa wa akili* (illness of reason), a term used at the mental hospital but not an indigenous concept in Kiswahili. Amina considered traditional treatment for Kimwana and did consult a traditional practitioner at one time. For both Kimwana and Hemed, the family had used primarily "hospital medicine" and Qur'an reading.

Kimwana concerned her mother and sisters most when she was reclusive, or refused food, or to bathe, or do her hair. She heard the voices of men who worked in front of their home repairing bicycles say cruel and critical things to her. She told me that those who tormented her were there every day. Some days she did not hear them, but they were always there.

During our 1988 interviews, Amina often deferred to Kimwana or sought her input in narrating the story of her illness. In Amina's telling, Kimwana's illness was related to her work outside the house but now she nearly always stayed home. Amina seemed to withhold judgment, however, on whether Kimwana should be working or going out. She consistently refrained from anything like criticism or hostility when speaking about her daughter, whether Kimwana was present or not. Her tone in narration was neutral and matter-of-fact, never angry, although at times adamant or excited. She calmly remarked that Kimwana felt that the "bicycle repair men concern themselves with her affairs." Her tone conveyed no scorn, just a lack of agreement with this perception. She reported that sometimes Kimwana complained about having to take the medicine and she would reply, "Yes, my daughter, just rest from swallowing those tablets if you like." Amina believed that being without the medicine for too long would bring a recurrence of problems but she did not force the issue. She could be direct with Hemed when she felt it necessary.

Hemed still responded to the voices of unseen others, but was no longer difficult to manage. "The strokes have broken his anger," said Amina, and with his anger gone, she no longer saw his illness in the way that led her to divorce him. Once when Ahmed went to interview the family in 1988, Hemed came in from his place on the porch to see who the visiting stranger was. Amina told Hemed, "Say, these are matters for the doctor here. Don't stay here. Go out. He wants the opportunity to talk with us alone. Don't just say things." Hemed left without argument. Amina was at that time rather dismissive and possibly hostile toward Hemed. Later, after his second stroke and subsequent greater disability, I observed only her kindness, concern, and patience with him. But a complex multigeneration household like this has other members to consider.

When I visited in 1994, Faki (a younger brother) mentioned to me that Kimwana's maternal grandmother sometimes scolded her. During that time, Kimwana was often laughing to herself during prayers and during meals. "Grandmother becomes quite angry with her and tells her to stop," Faki said. I asked how the rest of the family responded. He shrugged. "We are accustomed. We say nothing. We know she is ill, but grandmother is not used to it. She doesn't think it is an illness."

I once observed Grandmother scold Kimwana rather fiercely for a small mistake. I had been offered a second cup of coffee but had declined. It was too late; Kimwana was already pouring. "Why have you poured?" Grandmother demanded fiercely, "she doesn't want it! Pour it back. Pour it back!" She went on for a bit scolding Kimwana. Ahmed, my research assistant, intervened by asking for the already poured cup. Later, he commented that he was surprised by the vehemence of the grandmother's response. Her show of irritability was a bit outside the valued emotional reserve and certainly different from other family members' manner with Kimwana.

When I met Bimkubwa, Kimwana's younger sister, in 1994, one of the first things she said to me was that her father was also mad and that so many people in the house was a problem. Europeans have much smaller families in comparison, she asserted; "There are too many of us and this place is too noisy." By 1996, Bimkubwa had married and seemed more calm, exuding a quiet strength and an aura of controlled determination. She was pregnant and had recently moved back home while her husband was studying overseas. She attempted to be direct with Kimwana but was not generally successful. For example, she told me that she would require Kimwana to come along when the other women came to visit me. When Kimwana said she could not, Bimkubwa did not argue with her but did not acquiesce to the situation with grace.

Sibling relationships are ones of hierarchical authority. One is generally bound to obey one's senior brothers and sisters. But in 1996, Bimkubwa was an adult, having achieved adulthood through marriage. She had more education than most, worked and contributed to family finances, and came to be in charge of her older sister Kimwana's treatment. She was more forceful than her mother about encouraging Kimwana to take the hospital medication and did not accept Kimwana's refusals as readily as Amina did. She took control of the storage and dispensing of medication after Kimwana threw all the tablets down the toilet once. Bimkubwa was the one who had intervened in 1991, when Hemed was disturbing the neighbors with his shouting, by going to the mental hospital and bringing him some haloperidol and benztropine.

I accompanied Kimwana on eight of her outpatient clinic visits, six of those with Bimkubwa along. Bimkubwa brought along the fluphenazine her brothers sent from England for Kimwana's use. She complained to the doctor that Kimwana now did nothing to help at home where before she had been very helpful. In 1994, their brother, Faki, had expressed concern to me that Kimwana did too much. The psychiatrist inquired during one office visit if Kimwana had opportunities to socialize at home. Was the family isolated? Were there other young women? Did they invite her to sit with them? Bimkubwa replied, "We are thirteen of us there in a small house and we are together." Bimkubwa listed herself and two other women as close to Kimwana's age and said:

We do invite Kimwana (to socialize). Most times, she refuses, or if she comes, after a bit she gets up and goes her own way. The television is in the room where Kimwana sleeps and we all gather there to watch it. But even then she withdraws. She doesn't like to watch and lies close to the wall, facing it.

September 1996 was a particularly difficult month for this family. On the first of September, Kimwana took an overdose of malaria medication. She was released from the general hospital after about twenty-four hours. Later she would tell me that she had wanted to die because her psychotropic medication made her feel so miserable. In mid-September, the flu or a bad cold went through the whole household, and Amina commented that they were too poor even to buy aspirin. Kimwana was asking not to be given her psychotropic medication and her mother was not forcing the issue.

By September 28, all had recovered from the virus and I spent a Saturday cooking with them. Kimwana was nowhere to be seen when I arrived. We began cooking and no one commented on her absence. Our cooking was interrupted by the arrival of some men from the extended family who brought additional things to cook. They pulled Amina aside to discuss the grandchildren's school fees. There was much confusion with children coming and going in two shifts from Qur'an school. Some were sent to the market for the coconuts now needed to prepare the eggplant the men had provided. In all the confusion we allowed a huge vat of tea to spoil when the milk in it curdled. One of the grandsons and I asked Amina whether the tea might be saved by straining it. She was a bit sharp

with us, repeating, "It has curdled. It is spoiled." Grandmother began
to grate coconuts. She always insisted on grating the coconuts herself,
despite her complaints about arthritic knees and ankles and the flexed
posture one must assume for this task. Amina made a new pot of tea.
Later while we had lunch we could hear Hemed across the hall shouting
"Lies! Lies!" Kimwana had not joined us during this entire time, neither
cooking nor eating. I asked Amina whether it was better to go see her
and greet her or just leave her alone. Amina thought a minute and said
to leave her alone.

Responsibility for feeding so many people when cooking plans change,
and things do not go smoothly, made it a very difficult day for Amina.
Her tone was sharp with two of her irritants, for a second or two. The
economic pressures of having two younger male breadwinners away with
no work and three disabled people in the household seemed to be mounting up. Amina became very sad in recounting her troubles. I thought for
a moment that she was going to cry. She said that life is hard; then, "In
Kiswahili we say, this is just a test. I am just waiting patiently [for relief,
implied]. I am resigned." The implication here was that such tests come
from Allah.

Throughout this difficult day, when both Hemed and Kimwana were
more disturbed than usual, there was still an air of permissiveness and
tolerance. They were allowed to withdraw from face-to-face contact with
others and Amina maintained their space by discouraging others from interfering with them. Later, Kimwana said this about her need to be alone:

I do like being on my own. I feel like calming myself, just silently. Just quiet and
silent. Being with people I feel like I am just tangled with them. I know I am sick
and I like to be on my own without getting harassment from people.

I also noted Amina's use of the interogative *mbona* in correcting the
children on the difficult day described previously. *Mbona* is employed in
statements more rhetorical than directly interrogatory, such as "Don't
you see that it is..." (Johnson 1939:269). This linguistic form is less
direct than an accusatory statement starting with "you." In Amina's
descriptions of Hemed's accusations when he first went mad, she did
not recount what he actually said to his elder female relative or to his son
when he "abused" them, just that he began "You, you, you..." This is
enough to differentiate his aggressive communication from her reserved
style and speaks to the cultural valorization of indirectness. I noted this
indirectness many times in intrafamilial communication and in messages
directed at me, as when Amina encouraged me to fast without saying I
should, or when Kimwana corrected my way of juicing lemons, by saying,
"We generally do it like this."

Despite a variety of interaction styles in this multigeneration household, Swahili cultural norms for communication and emotional expression and Islamic beliefs about the acceptance of adversity support a low-expressed emotion environment that appears to have benefited both Kimwana and Hemed. Sometimes their behavior tried their kin sorely, yet there was apparently very little criticism or hostility directed toward either of them. During the hottest months of the year, Kimwana slept beneath the only fan in the house. Hemed was afforded care when he became dependent and despite a legal Islamic divorce was taken back into the household. Moreover, while family members held different opinions about the nature of the illness and the appropriate treatment for it, there was little attempt to control Kimwana or Hemed or portray them as sources of problems for others. That is, there was little evidence of emotional overinvolvement.

The Household of Khadija and Yusuf

The next family I describe is like the first in several important ways: a two generation history of schizophrenia; a younger generation member who helps manage her sibling's illness; spirit-related explanatory models accepted alongside that of "hospital medicine"; and a worldview, supported by Islamic faith, that expects and acquiesces to adversity, particularly in the older generation. The odd beliefs of the younger patient are not criticized. Disapproval was voiced rarely and in indirect and reserved ways. There are important differences between the families as well. The younger generation patient (Yusuf) had acted out aggressively during periods of psychosis, had been hospitalized frequently, and had different strategies available to him for social withdrawal. Each patient's history and illness ideas are presented first, followed by examples of family interactions.

Of all of the people with a diagnosis of schizophrenia in my study, Khadija had the highest level of social functioning. Her oldest son, Yusuf, was more seriously ill. They lived in a small house in town, owned by the extended family, in order to be close to the hospital should an emergency arise. Khadija was the head of the household, cooked for nine or ten people daily, visited kin in rural areas to collect food and fuel, and sold handicrafts her sisters made. During the study period the household also included Khadija's two youngest sons, her young half brother (a child), her granddaughter, three children of friends from rural areas who wanted their children schooled in town, and, for a short time, one of Khadija's young grandsons. Ruweya, Khadija's older divorced daughter, lived across town in a private apartment in a female friend's home.

In 1957, soon after her marriage at age fourteen, Khadija's first child was stillborn and she became restless and anxious. This problem was diagnosed as spirit related and successfully treated by a traditional healer. In 1958, she miscarried. Eventually she had two daughters and then Yusuf. In 1964, her first husband was killed during the Zanzibar revolution. She and the children were imprisoned briefly. In 1969, she married again. Shortly after the birth of her fourth child in 1970, her second husband left. Khadija became very restless and cried for three days. She ran from her home, was picked up by police, and taken to the mental hospital. This was her first hospitalization. Her parents recounted to nurses the similar illness Khadija had experienced after the stillborn child. Khadija was given the diagnosis "schizophrenia, postpartum psychosis." In all, Khadija married three times and had three daughters and five sons. At least one more of these births, in 1972, initiated a period of restlessness and confusion for which she was treated on an outpatient basis. In addition to obstetrical events, her onset of symptoms often coincided with periods of hot weather and with the laborious rice harvest. Between 1970 and mid-1997, Khadija was admitted to the hospital for eleven brief stays, spending 3 percent of her time as an inpatient. She had attended the outpatient department with increasing regularity, obtaining medication every six to eight weeks and occasionally staying away for a few months.

Khadija could not recall the name of the disorder for which she received traditional treatment after her first child's stillbirth or anything else about her treatment, except that it gave her relief. She described herself as recently having gotten better as a result of help from the hospital. She seemed reluctant to speak directly about her illness or other troubles in life. Like many elders who avoided discussions of difficult times past, she expressed satisfaction that she could not remember. "Praise Allah, I have been fortunate to forget that time." We asked Khadija to tell us about the best and worst times of her life. She replied:

Troubles? I didn't have many. I had my family, my relatives there, and we were many. And therefore once I got problems there is a place to rest and there is comfort. I didn't have much difficulty in life.... There were, as I said, only those problems of politics [refers to her first husband's murder during the revolution] but, in general there weren't problems. I was nicely brought up by my parents. I was married; gave birth. No problems to grieve.

Khadija often evidenced an attitude of acquiescence to adversity. One day she and I were sitting in her kitchen as she prepared lunch. Khadija said that life *is* changes. First, you get pregnant, then you give birth, then you nurse the baby – all changes. Then you carry the child on your back and raise it – still more changes. She followed this with another example from women's lives listing role changes from child to big sister, wife, mother, and then grandmother. "Life," she repeated, "is all changes." Later we were talking about the revolution and she told me that a neighboring family lost two men, one in the June 1961 election riots, and another at the time of the revolution itself. "A shame," I said. "No," she corrected me, "it is just change again: happenings, events." She said that all events are already written. If such things happened again it would also be because they are written; because Allah wills it.

During Yusuf's first three admissions to the mental hospital he was given no medication. His provisional diagnosis at age twenty-five was acute confusional state secondary to marijuana abuse. On his fourth admission, seven months after his first discharge, he began receiving chlorpromazine and his problem was viewed as psychosis, later specified as schizophrenia. Between 1988 and 1997, Yusuf was admitted to the hospital twenty-nine times, spending 34 percent of his time as an inpatient.

When asked about the best and worst times of his life, Yusuf replied, "I enjoyed life before I got this *Jini*." Yusuf said he had at least one *Jini* (Jinn) and several angels that used his body. He could hear them but not see their faces. Sometimes they spoke through his mouth and this was a miracle. He felt like he was together with many other beings, Jinn and Angels who talked and whose presence he could feel. He once threw himself from a building and broke his leg during an episode in which "Many voices came out; different ones were coming out from my mouth." A voice commanded him to jump. Some of the voices "do still command me to do bad deeds but I no longer follow them. I know they are enemies."

Although he had frequently run away from it, Yusuf had also occasionally brought himself to the mental hospital. He was well liked there and did not mind going to the ward to nap after his outpatient occupational therapy group. Despite his potential identification with the institution or the people he found there, he resisted the label of madman or a mentally ill person. He externalized this opinion to others – an aunt he lived with once, nameless others who made this comment as he passed. He experienced his difference as a miracle, although at times a troublesome one. Although some of the beings who inhabited him were enemies and he must "forget what they say," others were helpful in reminding him to say his prayers and in keeping him slim.

Yusuf's discourse was often centered on issues related to Islam; some of it orthodox, some of it unusual. He desired a deeper immersion in

Islam. He was skilled at reciting Qur'an and had worked as an assistant to a Qur'anic healer. Yusuf had been treated with a variety of traditional treatments – botanical, spirit related, and Qur'anic – and his opinion of traditional treatment was positive. Yusuf, his mother, sister, and maternal great aunt agreed that he often improved with traditional treatment. Once Yusuf had taken hospital-issued medicines and the herbal preparations of a local healer together, until the man directed him to quit taking the hospital tablets. Yusuf complied and enjoyed a period of three months in which "his condition was very good, he calmed down so much" according to his sister. But that was followed by an abrupt and severe attack of psychosis, and Yusuf quit traditional treatment. He took fluphenazine injections at the time of the study, paid for by his sister. She was a believer in Islam, traditional botanicals, and biotechnology.

Khadija accepted spiritual explanations of illness but also saw to it that Yusuf took his injections. Yusuf's hospital file describes a time when he struck Khadija and other times when he reported to hospital staff that he felt as though he wanted to strike or kill someone. He was generally courteous and mild mannered, however. Khadija would voice concern to Ahmed or others at the hospital if she saw that Yusuf was "talking all alone" or "laughing just with himself." She directed him to attend the outpatient clinic if he did not initiate this, but did not make other demands of him. On learning that Ahmed and I were returning a young male patient to his father, Khadija advised us: "The father should be helped to understand that the young man must rest, that he can't take much heat, and that his soul (*roho*) should not be made too sharp" – an idiomatic way of saying he should not be angered or irritated. She spoke of her own rural extended family of rice, clove, and coconut cultivators as affording her the opportunity to rest as needed because they were many. Extended family size and financial networking seemed integral to removing the pressure for productivity from ill individuals. Yusuf's symptoms and hospitalization periods were markedly reduced in the year following Ruweya's return to Zanzibar from England when she undertook economic support of her mother and brother.

One day Khadija, Ruweya, Yusuf, and my assistant Ahmed came to our house for lunch. Khadija brought up the topic of how much Yusuf smoked and slept. She gently contradicted Yusuf's claim of smoking ten a day, saying that his consumption was going up and up and was more like twenty. She said, "He does forget how many he smokes," and reiterated that he just smokes and sleeps, all in a matter-of-fact tone while avoiding direct eye contact with him.

On another occasion during a conversation that was more formal, an audiotaped interview, Ruweya showed mild irritation with Yusuf's talk of miracles and wonders. He was telling about the time he and his sister had been in India and Oman. He got excited, speaking rapidly and said:

It was sunny and I thought, "I'm in Paradise" and there was a place that was so cold and I thought it was Heaven. Then I went to India and I was shown hell fire and heaven, alternately for six months and so then I thought it was not a place to stay. Then I returned to Zanzibar. The weather is fine here and I decided to stay.

Ruweya frowned and commented quietly that she did not like it when he spoke nonsense. Yusuf was voluble during this interview and much of what he said was metaphorical and hard to understand. Both Khadija and her paternal aunt Raya were present and neither reacted to this statement about heaven and hell or other fantastic things Yusuf said. Later, Ruweya told me that she thought Yusuf was trying to tell, in talking about heaven and hell, about the time they went from sea level heat to the cold of very high elevations in India.

Ruweya despaired of Yusuf's ever getting better. She worried about his future, and perhaps having to take care of him. She was instrumental in getting him involved in an outpatient group at the hospital, and washing his own clothes again, but she accomplished this by going through an intermediary at the hospital. Although Ruweya remarked that it is difficult when a young man, apparently fit, could not work, she did accept it. She felt much affection for her younger brother, and struggled to maintain her patience when he verbalized fantastic ideas.[3]

Yusuf walked about a lot and his roaming was solitary. No one in the family tried to restrict his movement. While his family's respect for his preference for being alone is similar to that of Kimwana's family, the gendered advantage that Yusuf had was obvious. As a male he could move about without violation of gendered social norms. While Kimwana's family allowed her to seek solitude inside the house, they became anxious when, during a period of restlessness, she wanted to go outside. They locked the doors. Generally, Kimwana saw herself as unable to go out and only did so once each month to keep her appointment at the mental hospital. Thus, they had cause for alarm. Part of their concern had to do with Kimwana's status as an unmarried female. Yusuf's maleness afforded him an additional strategy for withdrawal from social contact. Despite this gender difference, both families discussed thus far present a picture of a culture in which adversity is expected and embracing it without complaint is sanctified, and where indirectness, reserve, and tolerance in human interactions are highly valued. The last family I describe presents a picture, not of cultural variation so much as, of the distance between cultural ideals and lived human behavior.

Shazrin's Extended Family

The al-Mitende family is part of an Omani Arab clan that has practiced cousin marriage for several generations. The household I studied included the identified patient, forty-three-year-old Shazrin, and five other adults. Shazrin is in the care of her half brother, Abdulridha, who had the same mother. Their shared mother and Abdulridha's father were double cousins. Moreover, Abdulridha's father was Shazrin's second cousin. Abdulridha is married to Ruhaida, who was raised in the home of other extended family relatives. They have a developmentally disabled daughter, Azlina. Rohaizat is Abdulridha's other half sister, but via his father. She is married to their cousin, Amour. Amour and Rohaizat have ten children in the household, including one daughter who is also developmentally disabled. Rukia is the oldest adult in the household. She is Rohaizat's and Abdulridha's paternal aunt by blood. She is Amour's mother. She is Shazrin's and Abdutridha's mother's cousin.

Shazrin's problems began when she was just thirteen years old on the night of the new moon at the end of Ramadan. While applying henna with other female relatives, she saw a black cat enter and walk across the room, then disappear. The next day after visiting kin and feasting she felt unwell, complained of being hot, and of feeling as if she were going mad. She lay down to rest. Her mother told her to take off her new dress and her bracelets first and tried to help her to do so, but Shazrin began screaming. Her behavior was similarly disturbed over the next few days. Because of her report of seeing a black cat, she was thought to be suffering spirit possession via witchcraft. She was treated with traditional medicine by several practitioners with little or no improvement for the better part of a year. Then the family's neighbor and friend, a young medical doctor recently appointed to the mental hospital, persuaded them to take her there. The next time Shazrin became disturbed and hard to control, the police were called to take her to the mental hospital. She was admitted on an urgency order, a frightened child on a ward of grown women. She was diagnosed as a case of childhood schizophrenia by a visiting American psychiatric consultant. She remembered him as "very fierce." At age fourteen, according to letters in her medical record, Shazrin was already considered "chronic."

Since that time, she had divided her time between the mental hospital and the household of her half brother, Abdulridha, and that of her mother's sister, Asha. During most of the period of my study, Shazrin ate and slept at the home of her half brother. One wing of the home included the sitting room and bedrooms of Rohaizat and Amour's family. Abdulridha, Ruhaida, and their daughter, Azlina, had a bedroom and a sitting room upstairs in the other wing. Shazrin slept in their sitting room. Downstairs was the living space of Rukia, their aunt. There were some common rooms where the two wings met and a shared kitchen building in the courtyard below.

Shazrin had continued with traditional treatment intermittently throughout her thirty-year psychiatric history. She had been taken for a wide variety of treatments up and down the Swahili coast. Her half brother continued with a scalp treatment based on Arabic humoral medicine "to cool Shazrin's mind," using the recipe of a cousin who was a healer. Abdulridha disavowed all earlier traditional treatment and consistently aligned his views with hospital medicine in our discussions. Shazrin had spent approximately 19 percent of her time as an inpatient at the mental hospital since she was first diagnosed, and was admitted there fifty-six times. She was also briefly admitted to psychiatric units at two mainland hospitals. From 1988 until 1993, the family relied most heavily on the mental hospital for Shazrin's care. She resided there about one-third of the time. After a dysentery outbreak on the female ward in 1993, Abdulridha took Shazrin out of the hospital and vowed never to send her back again. He collected medicines through outpatient services at the hospital for both Shazrin and his daughter. Sometimes they attended these appointments.

Bodily discomforts, painful menstruation, and insomnia had been prominent symptoms throughout Shazrin's history. In the past she was talkative, sometimes hostile and aggressive. Her problematic symptoms during the period of the study were crying, not sleeping, and daytime inactivity. She occasionally kept the household awake by crying loudly most of the night. She had taken a variety of medicines over her thirty-year history of treatment, including up to fifty milligrams of fluphenazine every two weeks (a very large dose). In 1978, she had a course of electroconvulsive therapy. During the period of this study her medication was changed from haloperidol to thioridazine. Her psychiatrist hoped this more "activating" dopamine blocker would alleviate Shazrin's crying. Abdulridha had been complaining about Shazrin's crying to me for five months before he brought it to her psychiatrist's attention. Inspired by a radio program on depression from the Voice of America, Abdulridha came to see that there "is a medicine for this crying." He frequently admonished Shazrin not to cry with the adage that it is shameful for adults to do so.

Shazrin had often run away from home and had asked to be admitted to the mental hospital or had demanded that the family bring her there. Other times the family initiated admission. Hospital staff noted a difference between her behavior on the ward and that described at home. She often settled very quickly, even before medication was administered.

Sometimes the family refused to take Shazrin home when doctors recommended discharge. One doctor asked the social worker to explain to the family that Shazrin's problems were an illness for which she should not be punished. The narrative that follows was elicited by a diplomatically worded question about the doctor's suspicions that Shazrin's problems were exacerbated by familial relationships and that she was sent to the hospital as punishment. As Shazrin sat beside him looking fretful and distressed, Abdulridha narrated a series of incidents: one in which Shazrin attempted to beat her mother and in which he intervened, one in which Shazrin ran from home while others were preparing to break the fast during Ramadan and went on her own to the mental hospital, and one in which Shazrin toppled a large clothing cabinet inside a small room, effectively trapping their mother there. Although her brother believed Shazrin had longer periods of remission of symptoms in those days, she was "worse" when ill because she was young and strong. He said:

My control [of her] helped a bit, because she stopped some of those things, like [when] she used to strike people. She had energy because she was young. She is a coward now; her energy is lost. I have the ability to hold (stop, stabilize) her the way I want.

The male nurse who nominated Shazrin for inclusion in the study considered Abdulridha an exemplary caretaker. From our very first meeting (for informed consent) I noted Abdulridha's dramatic account of self-sacrifice to undertake the care of his sister. I also thought it odd that he was so aware of her menstrual cycle and could recount for me in this first meeting and on many subsequent visits exactly when she began and ceased to bleed. This information was shared enthusiastically and sometimes in public spaces, which struck me as strange in this culture where privacy and concealment are valorized. I worked to set aside my inferences about the nature of Abdulridha's involvement with Shazrin, even as observations accumulated, because hospital workers, including my research assistant Ahmed, saw Abdulridha as nothing other than a good brother. Eventually I learned that Abdulridha knew the length of Shazrin's menses because he washed the blood from her clothing. I found it incongruous that he would wash menstrual blood from her clothing when he proudly asserted that he had cured her incontinence by making her wash the soil from her own sheets and garments. Ahmed also found it most unusual, but it did not shake his impression that Abdulridha was a good and concerned caretaker.

It was many months later, after a tape-recorded interview with the family, that Ahmed's opinion changed. On the evening of the interview, Shazrin was unable to answer most of the questions directed to her and she became visibly uncomfortable with the situation. After a few attempts we gave up questioning her and concentrated just on the portions of the interview directed to other family members. After about an hour, Shazrin rose from her chair to go get some water. Abdulridha demanded to know where she was going and then chuckled at her, telling us that she was not actually in her usual state of mind. Ruhaida counseled us to try our questions with Shazrin at another time, speaking with her alone. While Shazrin was out of the room, I tried to persuade Abdulridha that our questions, even those directed to him, might be making her uncomfortable and that she need not be present for the rest of them. He disagreed, denied it was a problem for her to sit through this recounting of her illness history, and accused Shazrin of blaming others for her problems. He raised his voice to summon her back to the sitting room. When she returned I tried to reassure her that we did not wish to upset her. Abdulridha and Ruhaida began to tease her, saying that they would send her back to America with me. They laughed at her. She neither made eye contact with anyone nor responded to any of this. Abdulridha said, "She is not here at all now; she has been covered completely.... This indeed is the problem. I told you that you would see it." She sat silent as we proceeded a bit longer with the interview. Then she rose again and left the room. Abdulridha shouted for her to leave the door open. Ruhaida and Rohaizat began to laugh. Again Ahmed and I tried to persuade Abdulridha to release Shazrin from this interview. Again he refused, saying that she just wanted to lie down and that she could wait. He called her. She returned. He insisted that she stay. "Wait a while. You just don't want to listen," he said to her in a harsh and accusing tone. He prompted us to proceed. Although we ceased directing questions to Shazrin, he occasionally teased her with them. We hurried through the remaining questions and left.

On the way home, I restrained myself from telling Ahmed what I thought of these interactions because I wanted to hear his opinion before giving mine. He said he felt bad to be part of this tormenting of Shazrin and said we must only try to interview her alone on a day when she seemed better, perhaps at my house. In written notes Ahmed observed that Shazrin was turned into a laughingstock, and Abdulridha made matters worse when he forced her to speak. Ahmed concluded that in spite of being brother and sister, their relationship was more that of slave and master, with Shazrin extremely fearful before Abdulridha and his markedly critical and ridiculing tone of voice.

Jenkins has written about cultural dimensions of "emotional overinvolvement" as the "loss of family orientation" as the caretaker "adopts a nearly exclusive dyadic orientation with the patient" (Jenkins 1991:407). Abdulridha remained unmarried for five years between his divorce and his marriage to Ruhaida, odd given the resources at his disposal to secure another bride. When he returned from work, Abdulridha was in Shazrin's company. He directed her morning and evening hygiene and grooming. He was rarely in the company of his brother-in-law/cousin Amour, despite their residing in the same house. He did not sit at the mosque or the coffee seller's corner, like other men his age in the neighborhood. Jenkins also noted reports by overinvolved relatives that focus on the caretaker's extraordinary suffering because of the identified patient's illness. Abdulridha seemed to take Shazrin's crying as a personal affront:

I tell her, 'I do everything for you. You should stop all those behaviors in order to give me some encouragement but if you misbehave you will discourage me/ break my heart.' She would say, 'I am not crying' but all the same she keeps on.

After I had been with the family for six months, others inside and outside it began to share their opinions that Abdulridha's behavior toward Shazrin was not good for her or was contributing to her problems. "He tries to control her too much," one said. "He pushes her." "It is shameful the way he takes care of her bathing and her menstruation, with all those women in the house who could do that," said another. In addition to this intrusive overinvolvement and criticism from Abdulridha, Shazrin was the object of criticism and ridicule from some other family members. Although Abdulridha had vowed never to return Shazrin to the mental hospital, I heard Ruhaida threaten her with permanent placement there more than once. Eventually, I no longer tried to put off my inference that this was a family marked by negative expressed emotion and overinvolvement. I grew uncomfortable around them and began to dread my visits there. I felt like I was colluding in the process of troubling Shazrin somehow, although I maintained a supportive stance toward her. On a couple of occasions, Abdulridha tried to recruit me to join in disapproving of Shazrin's behavior. I resisted but he often twisted whatever I said and used it to get at her.

During an exercise in which the family was participating in preparing a kinship diagram, I saw how overinvolvement produced the very symptom that Abdulridha said troubled him most: Shazrin's loud crying. When we finished mapping Abdulridha's "dynasty," we turned our attention briefly to Shazrin's father's side. (Recall that Abdulridha had a different father.) Shazrin helped by naming her father's three wives. Abdulridha filled in some other details until it became clear that the old man had married his own grandchild. I recorded it without comment. Shazrin looked tense.

When I returned for the next visit, I began with my usual list of questions for clarification and ended by confirming that Shazrin's father's second wife was indeed his granddaughter. During all this Shazrin became progressively more restless on the floor, flipping over from side to side to prone, jiggling her legs, and rubbing her face in an odd repetitive way. Abdulridha and Ruhaida noticed this and ascribed it to her medicine no longer working. Abdulridha imperiously summoned Rukia (their aunt) from downstairs to help us with the older generations of the genealogy he could not do. Although she was busy cooking and did not want to participate, Abdulridha commanded her to stay. As the tension mounted, Shazrin stood up abruptly and walked from the room. Abdulridha commanded her to come back and sit down. She did but was physically even more restless. Abdulridha continued his questioning of Rukia and would not be dissuaded. Shazrin stood to leave again and Abdulridha ordered her to sit again. As she approached the door and said that she was leaving to go to her aunt's place, Abdulridha caught her arm and ordered her to stay. As she turned back she burst into very loud crying and screaming. Abdulridha called to me over the din, "You will now see everything of her illness, how it is." He called to Shazrin raising his voice to break through her loud screams, "Today you are showing your doctor your shame." "Let her go," I urged Abdulridha, practically begging, for this emotional display was powerful and difficult to watch. "I must control her here," he said. "I am afraid to let her go." "What do you think she will do?" I queried. "I do not know but I must control her here. She can't go out." I learned later he gave her a cold shower to "calm" her that night.

I left dumbfounded that Abdulridha and Ruhaida could casually discuss this emotional display as a symptom of Shazrin's illness and not admit to a connection between Abdulridha's control of her and this frustrated outburst, or between the shame at exposure of her grandfather's incest and her restlessness. Her crying did serve the instrumental purpose for Shazrin of carving out some space around her. Within minutes, her crying had cleared the small sitting room of more than half the adults assembled there. Several months earlier I had heard about another incident of Shazrin "crying the whole night" from Ruhaida as I sat with both women. Ruhaida said Shazrin cried because she was angry, but Shazrin hotly denied anger. I cannot say whether Abdulridha's self-confessed need to control Shazrin bodily can be justified by her past behavior. I feel certain that without Abdulridha's controlling overinvolvement and the harsh scolding, threats, and ridicule Shazrin experienced, she would have been a higher functioning person and less miserable. I saw glimpses of this person when Abdulridha was not around, when Shazrin visited my home with other women, and when she made small jokes to me when we were alone.

Conclusion

This chapter shows two contrasting emotional styles in families of patients with schizophrenia in Zanzibar. In the families of Hemed and Kimwana, and Khadija and Yusuf, indirectness in conflict resolution was valued and tolerance for the individual (even idiosyncratic) nature of family members was apparent. In this emotional style, notions of appropriate familial concern are entwined with the belief that all adversity is sent from Allah for a purpose one cannot know, and that preternatural spirits are active in producing deranged behavior. Recent research in the United States has shown that family members' beliefs about a patient's ability to control him or herself and perceptions of an internal locus of control for themselves support higher levels of negative expressed emotion (Hooley 1998; Lopez, Nelson, Snyder, and Mintz 1999). Norwegian researchers found guilt in family members to be a correlate, and perhaps a determinant, of high levels of criticism, hostility, and emotional overinvolvement (Bentson et al. 1998). In Zanzibar, it would appear that acquiescence to the external control of the Almighty undercuts guilt, exonerates patient and family, and sustains tolerance and acceptance of the patient. Swahili cultural notions of personhood, and the valuing of reticence and indirectness, also participate in this protective environment, which seems to mitigate against emotional overinvolvement even in large, close families living in comparatively small spaces.

The second style is evident in the case of Shazrin and Abdulridha. In this family, the idea that Shazrin's problems were sent by Allah was brought up only once, obliquely, when Ruhaida explained to an older generation male that I was with them to learn about their tests or trials. Shazrin and her patriline were often identified as the source of the problem. Blame swirled around her. Although this, too, is a religious Muslim family, whose ancestors built several mosques in Zanzibar, the notion of embracing adversity was not prominent. Perhaps it is their class status (for they are persons of the former ruling class now in reduced circumstances since the revolution) that energized Abdulridha's embrace of Western medical explanations for his sister's crying. It certainly seemed his allegiance to biological explanations obtained from psychiatrists and the Voice of America legitimated his interference with Shazrin in his own mind and allowed him to see himself as part of the "modern" world. He had given up his life, he said, to care for this medically marked and deficient person. Ruhaida looked from her own retarded daughter, to that of her sister-in-law, to Shazrin and sighed, "We have three like this we must care for in this house."

Finally, these cases support the argument that elements of "expressed emotion," particularly criticism and emotional overinvolvement, can be identified across cultural settings (Jenkins and Karno 1992). Indeed, it was after we observed the first incident in which Shazrin was ridiculed that Ahmed translated the concept of emotional overinvolvement in terms of the ill family member being interfered with and "pried into" too much, of having insufficient freedom, and of being part of a dyad that is like "a whole world" unto itself. That my method was ethnographic description rather than the standardized Camberwell Family Interview typically used in expressed emotion research made it possible to capture the contextual and interactive nuances that rendered these factors consequential for family members in a particular culturally inflected way. More studies in this vein can go further in answering Jenkins' (1991) call for an comparative understanding of "expressed emotion" that is grounded in an understanding of cultural definitions of self, agency, autonomy, and accountability.

NOTES

1 All names used are pseudonyms chosen by the families themselves. Kimwana chose her name, which means "small daughter," and gave her younger sister the name "Bimkubwa," which could be translated "Miss Boss Lady." I have known this family since 1988. Kimwana participated in another study with me at that time.

2 In describing Amina's care of her ill family members I do not mean to depict her as a long-suffering martyr. She talked of troubles rarely, and some of that only at my researching behest.

3 I continued to follow these families after the study year described previously. In 2000, one of Yusuf's younger half brothers joined the household and began to voice criticism of Yusuf. As Yusuf's symptoms increased, Ruweya used the newly formed family support group at the mental hospital to indirectly intervene with her half brother and persuade him to moderate his approach to Yusuf. This points up the limitations of one-time snapshots of family factors and illness profiles taken from one key informant that have been typical in expressed emotion research and World Health Organization schizophrenia outcome studies, respectively. An ethnographic approach allows consideration of changes in large and complex families over time.

REFERENCES

Bentson, H., T. H. Notland, O. G. Munkvold, B. Boye, I. Ulstein, H. Björge, G. Uren, A. B. Lersbryggen, K. H. Oskarsson, R. Berg-Larsen, O. Lingjaerde, and U. F. Malt. 1998. "Guilt Proneness and Expressed Emotion in Relatives of Patients with Schizophrenia or Related Psychoses." *British Journal of Medical Psychology* 71: 125–38.

Bondestam, Sixten, Joop Garssen, and Abdulwakil I. Abdulwakil. 1990. "Prevalence and Treatment of Mental Disorders and Epilepsy in Zanzibar." *Acta Psychiatrica Scandinavica* 81: 327–31.

Brown, George, J. L. T. Birley, and John Wing. 1972. "Influence of Family Life on the Course of Schizophrenic Disorders: A Replication." *British Journal of Psychiatry* 121: 241–58.

Caplan, Pat. 1992. "Spirits and Sex: A Swahili Informant and His Diary." In J. Oakley and H. Callaway, eds., pp. 64–81. *Anthropology and Autobiography*. London: Routledge.

Corin, Ellen. 1990. "Facts and Meaning in Psychiatry: An Anthropological Approach to the Lifeworld of Schizophrenics." *Culture, Medicine and Psychiatry* 4: 167–89.

Garssen, Joop. 1988. "Mortality, Fertility and Contraceptive Knowledge, Attitudes and Practices in Zanzibar." In *1988 Survey Provisional Results. Zanzibar: Report of the Statistical Unit*. Zanzibar Ministry of Health.

Garssen, Joop and Mohammed Haji Haji. 1989. "Statistical Tables for Health Planners and Administrators." *Zanzibar: Report of the Statistical Unit*. Zanzibar Ministry of Health.

Giles, Linda L. 1995. "Sociocultural Change and Spirit Possession on the Swahili Coast of East Africa." *Anthropological Quarterly* 68(2): 89–106.

Hooley, Jill. 1998. "Expressed Emotion and Locus of Control." *Journal of Nervous and Mental Disease* 186(2): 374–78.

Hopper, Kim. 1992. "Cervantes' Puzzle – A Commentary on Alex Cohen's 'Prognosis for Schizophrenia in the Third World: A Re-evaluation of Cross-cultural Research.'" *Culture, Medicine and Psychiatry* 16(1): 89–100.

Jenkins, Janis Hunter. 1991. "Anthropology, Expressed Emotion, and Schizophrenia." *Ethos* 19: 387–431.

Jenkins, Janis Hunter and Marvin Karno. 1992. "The Meaning of Expressed Emotion: Theoretical Issues Raised by Cross-cultural Research." *American Journal of Psychiatry* 149(1): 9–21.

Johnson, Frederick. 1939. *A Standard Swahili-English Dictionary*. Oxford: Oxford University Press.

Kleinman, Arthur. 1980. *Patients and Healers in the Context of Culture: An Exploration of the Borderland between Anthropology, Medicine and Psychiatry*. Berkeley: University of California Press.

Lopez, Steven R., Kathleen A. Nelson, Karen S. Snyder, and Jim Mintz. 1999. "Attributions and Affective Reactions of Family Members and Course of Schizophrenia." *Journal of Abnormal Psychology* 108(2): 307–14.

Lucas, Rod H. and Robert J. Barrett. 1995. "Interpreting Culture and Psychopathology: Primitivist Themes in Cross-cultural Debate." *Culture, Medicine and Psychiatry* 19: 287–326.

McGruder, Juli. 1999. *Madness in Zanzibar: "Schizophrenia" in Three Families in the "Developing" World*. Unpublished doctoral dissertation. Seattle: University of Washington.

Middleton, John. 1992. *The World of the Swahili: An African Mercantile Civilization*. New Haven: Yale University Press.

Sartorius, Norman. 1992. "Commentary on 'Prognosis for Schizophrenia in the Third World,' by Alex Cohen." *Culture, Medicine and Psychiatry* 16: 81–4.

Swartz, Marc J. 1991. *The Way the World Is: Cultural Processes and Social Relations among the Mombasa Swahili.* Berkeley: University of California Press.

Vaughn, Christine E. and Julian P. Leff. 1976. "The Influence of Family and Social Factors on the Course of Psychiatric Illness: A Comparison of Schizophrenic and Depressed Neurotic Patients." *British Journal of Psychiatry* 129: 125–37.

Yahya-Othman, Saida. 1994. "Covering One's Social Back: Politeness among the Swahili." *Text* 14(1): 141–61.

11 Subject/Subjectivities in Dispute: The Poetics, Politics, and Performance of First-Person Narratives of People with Schizophrenia

Sue E. Estroff

I've had my brain and what it has produced, admired in the past, then questioned before being invalidated, and ticked off as being the diseased organ of a "schizophrenic." It has been messed up with drugs and electroshocks, so called 'treatments' in which I had no say. It has suffered much that was unnecessary. Mainly, I've had to struggle alone with it in order to explore and conquer the inner and outer dimensions of my reality. Tomecek, in Susko 1991:267.

I have spent years of my life existing as a footnote, a case note, a clinical note, clinging to the understanding that I was a defective biological unit. Somehow time, matter, and the joke of genes and enzymes had exiled me to the sidelines of being. This may truly be a valuable perspective for those who observe mental illness, but for me, as subject, this tree bore only dry and tasteless fruit.

- I have a chemical imbalance; it wasn't really me that did those things.
- I have a chemical imbalance; I really didn't feel those things.
- I have a chemical imbalance; I didn't really experience those things.
- I have a chemical imbalance; I didn't really think those things.
- I am a chemical and I don't really think.

Here is an insight! The entire human drama of love, suffering, ecstasy, and joy, just chemistry. Granger 1994.

In these excerpts, Granger and Tomecek, two very different people with schizophrenia, convey a less felicitous view of the "Decade of the Brain" than the neuropsychiatric research community and advocates such as the National Alliance for the Mentally Ill (NAMI), who laud the vocabulary and progress of this brain-besotted era. Tomecek juxtaposes his lonely struggle, lack of autonomy and agency, and sense of damage via treatment with brain-based language. He is invalidated as a diseased organ, referring to his brain as "it." Granger, who had his first experience with schizophrenia during his first (and last) year of medical school at Harvard, is similarly unrepresented by his identity as a defective biological unit – a dry and tasteless fruit. He mocks the reduction of subjective experiences to chemistry.

These excerpts are but two of many written and spoken statements by consumer/survivor/ex-patients (c/s/x)[1] that work the same territory – sometimes mocking, angry, or despairing of the absence of themselves as recognizable subjects in the current neuropsychiatric renaissance. These narrations epitomize the competing dualities that make up what I abbreviate as the subject/subjectivity problem in schizophrenia. First, there are disagreements about the subject-as-person. C/s/x experience themselves as reduced to diseased brains and essentialized into chemicals rather than acknowledged as the perhaps enigmatic, but nonetheless sentient, persons they know themselves to be. Second, there is disagreement about the subject-as-topic. That is, c/s/x may hold entirely different views of what schizophrenia is than many who diagnose, treat, and study them, and thus also are at odds about what, if anything, afflicts them, and what should be done in response. There is then, disagreement about the subject (as topic) at hand, schizophrenia, and the subject (as person) – whether one has it and who defines what *it* is. The lack of common ground and understandings, of intersubjectivity, extends to the subject (the person and schizophrenia) and their subjectivities – their experiences with and understandings of schizophrenia and its treatment.

Scientific formulations of schizophrenia do not account for, indeed often exclude the illness experiences of many people so diagnosed. C/s/x narratives of schizophrenia protest this absence, representing experiential scenarios that cannot be accommodated within the prevailing paradigms of clinicians and researchers. What is at stake here is authority and authenticity concerning identity, definition, meaning, and experience in schizophrenia – and ultimately what happens to and about people with schizophrenia. This is the ricocheting, synergistic fulcrum that I explore in this chapter.

To this end, I engage in an analysis of recent, first-person narrations of the experiences of schizophrenia against the backdrop of and in contrast to third-person narratives and representations. First-person narratives, like the previous two, are produced by individuals diagnosed with schizophrenia – these are sometimes spoken or performed in a witnessing mode at public gatherings, lately are published in venues like *Schizophrenia Bulletin*, and surface regularly in the fugitive press of advocacy (for example, *Dendron*), in collections published by small presses or organizations, and treatment program newsletters, often as poetry (for example, Krawiec 1993). Second-person narratives are produced by family members and others intimately involved with the diagnosed person, and are exemplified by Jay Neugeboren's (1997) recent book, *Imagining Robert*. These stories are often told by relatives in a witnessing mode similar to that of the first-person narratives – in public forums such as legislative hearings and in support-group meetings. Third-person narratives are those produced by researchers, clinicians, reporters, and others, such as advocates, whose primary relationship with the individual with schizophrenia is based on the presence of the illness, hardship, or other credential of difference (see, for example, Kleinman 1988; Sheehan 1995).

The points of contrast, contestation, and convergence of these narratives have received insufficient attention from the various scholarly communities engaged in the study of schizophrenia. One goal of this chapter is to place these overlooked narratives in a scholarly landscape in a deliberately remedial move. A second goal is to locate these disputes within the contexts of current debates, or "representational wars," about the production of knowledge in sociocultural studies and medicine, with particular reference to schizophrenia.

Schizophrenia in and as Dispute

People diagnosed with schizophrenia talk back to experts, relatives, the public, and advocates who write about, treat, and otherwise represent them – and have done so for centuries (Peterson 1982; Porter 1988; Sommer, Clifford, and Norcross 1998). As perhaps the prototype of psychiatric disorder, schizophrenia has been a protean site for disputes of various kinds (Foucault 1965). Disagreement and contestation about meaning, reality, and identity may represent the quintessence of schizophrenia. Narratives of protest, and in milder form what we have called normalizing talk (Estroff, Lachicotte, Illingworth, and Johnston 1991), dispute the presence of psychosis, symptoms, or disease (Granger 1994), decry cruelty and injustice at the hands of others (Chamberlin 1978), propose alternative scenarios to dominant professional models and family explanations (Clay 1994), and convey compelling, wrenching portraits of anger, anguish, and triumph (for example, Vonnegut 1975; Susko 1991). More numerous, less lyrical perhaps, and decidedly less widely available, are the experiential narrations spoken aloud at local and national mental health gatherings, and found in treatment program newsletters, self-advocacy publications, and collections of "self stories" published by various private sources (for example, Still Surviving 1991–93; Spaniol and Koehler 1994; Gibbons 1995).

What place do these often unruly expressions of grief, these sometimes quiet voices of reasoned despair, these stories of uncelebrated but extraordinary lives have in the scientific/scholarly discourse about and understandings of schizophrenia? Is it possible or even beneficial to include the quintessence of unreason in our reasoned discourse about unreason? I do not suppose here that these disparate versions of subject and subjectivity *should* be joined. Yet in the name of empirical rigor, accuracy, and multidimensionality, it seems to me that the scholarly enterprise around and of schizophrenia must take some account of the enduring and now explosive body of commentary and reporting, of basic data, if you will, that derive from c/s/x.

At present, *Schizophrenia Bulletin* devotes one to three pages per issue to a well-edited first-person account. Occasionally, clinicians and researchers write forewords to collections of narratives, or mention them in footnotes. It is emblematic of the problem that the mainstream academic press of psychiatry publishes bibliographies of "patient autobiographies" (for example, Sommer and Osmond 1983; Sommer et al. 1998), but not the accounts themselves. The existence of the accounts is acknowledged, but their content is not included.

Most in absence from the scientific/scholarly discourse are the chronicles of unrecognition, fear, danger, capture, sensate torture, annihilation, and indignant anger that pervade c/s/x narratives. These are the accounts of trauma, persistence, and courage of people with schizophrenia – and some of those who care for them (for example, Gennari 1995; Wasow 1995). They are the voices of survival, healing, gratitude, reconstitution, and everyday life of people who struggle with symptoms of treatment as well as symptoms of illness. Some of the language is frankly political, often dramatic, and intensely personal. These are themes and voices that we explore in this analysis.

Posing the previous questions, and those thereby provoked, about these topics, visits trodden and none-too-inviting turf. My intentions are not to critique and criticize individual clinicians and scholars, nor to rehearse doctor bashing and antipsychiatry rhetoric. It is perhaps inevitable that a frequent response to the strong sentiments expressed in these narratives is to frame them as denial, lack of insight, transference, or evidence in direct contradiction to the narrator's claim of validity. (On the other hand, one might characterize these responses as countertransference.) The effort in this chapter is to turn down the noise from all sides a bit so that the experiences of people with schizophrenia are less peripheral to the enterprise of understanding and treating schizophrenia. Poetry and other forms of narration and performance by c/s/x constitute the primary data for the analysis.

Domains of Dispute

To be sure, patients with many illnesses other than schizophrenia complain about their care (for example, Dickey 1970; Frank and Foote 1991), contrasting their desires, sensations, and sentiments with clinical practice and scientific representations. James Dickey writes in his rebellious lament, *Diabetes*:

> All right! Physicians, witness! I will shoot my veins
> Full of insulin. Let the needle burn
> In . . .
> You know, I had just as soon crush
> This doomed syringe
> Between two mountain rocks, and bury this needle in needles
> Of trees. Companion, open that beer.
> How the body works   how hard it works
> For its medical books is not
> Everything: everything is how
> Much glory is in it: . . .

What matters to Dickey is the glory and a cold beer on a hot summer day. He is weary of his regimen of moderation, lettuce, and exercise – youthful doctors and their medical knowledge are a world apart from him.

You Don't Get It – You Can't Get It

Much of the mutual unintelligibility about schizophrenia between c/s/x and third-person narrators may be accounted for by a paradigm held, ironically, in common by the two groups. This paradigm can be summed up as: You don't get it. You can't get it. From the c/s/x perspective, clinicians and researchers **don't** understand schizophrenia – **don't** listen, care, comprehend, have all the information. At the same time, clinicians and researchers **can't** understand because they have not experienced first-hand schizophrenia or psychosis, or treatments such as neuroleptics and their side effects, hospitalization, or forced treatment. There is a failure of both will and ability.

From the clinician/scholar perspective, c/s/x **don't** get it because THEY do not want to acknowledge that they have a psychiatric disorder and because they do not see the world and understand the rules and meanings adhered to by clinicians/scholars. Simultaneously, the contention is that c/s/x **can't** understand *because* they have schizophrenia, which limits their ability to comprehend the technical information, and/or they lack insight and are in denial. Again, there are failures of ability and will, of motivation and capacity. In my view, the impasse created by this reciprocally held paradigm impoverishes the scholarship of schizophrenia and embitters the experiences of c/s/x.

Scientifically authorized representations of schizophrenia differ enormously – ranging from neuroimaging to viral theories to clinical trials of new medications to health services outcomes to ethnographies. The variation among the scholarly discourses requires a facility akin to multilingualism in order to grasp the range of approaches and findings. The discrepancies between these sometimes mutually unintelligible vocabularies mirrors the gap between them and the lived narrations of first- and second-person accounts. What differs between the first- and second- versus third-person representations is not confined to *how* schizophrenia is talked and written about, but includes *what* is discussed as well. It is not just vocabulary or tone that are in dispute, though these, too, are at odds, perhaps most understandably. The topics and persons and experiences and meanings hover in disagreement and disarray – intersubjectivity about the subjects is lacking.

Another dimension of miscommunication and absent understanding between c/s/x and others stems from what we call "symptoms of treatment." We use this term to refer to medication and ECT side effects, experiences in inpatient and outpatient treatment settings, and the sensate and emotional responses of c/s/x to mental health professionals, police, fellow patients, and family members. The term derived from our examination of illness accounts and self-labeling among people with severe, persistent, psychiatric disorders (Estroff et al. 1991). When we asked research participants to describe their illnesses or problems, they did not make a distinction between DSM-IV symptoms of schizophrenia and their responses to medication, or experiences in treatment settings, or in relation to their families and others. For the people with schizophrenia in our study, the "symptoms of treatment" are of one experiential piece with the symptoms of illness. Scholarly and scientific separations of these two domains – treatment and illness – and the failure to recognize their essential entanglement, contributes to an enduring absence of agreement, not to mention accurate empathy, with c/s/x.

Treatment as sensate torture is familiar to people undergoing chemotherapy and surgery for cancer and has a substantial presence in the clinical enterprise and research literature (Cassell 1982; Quill 1991). Yet this dimension of schizophrenia has a shadowy place outside of first-person narratives. That this is so makes a strong case for the **don't/can't get it** claims of c/s/x about scholars and practitioners.

Authority Begets Authenticity/Authenticity Begets Authority

Another dimension of the **don't/can't get it** argument concerns the arena of professional dominance of the knowledge production and reproduction enterprise. If researchers and clinicians do not know what having and living with schizophrenia is like, and thereby lack sufficient knowledge to really understand or to provide effective treatment, their authority to write about schizophrenia and to dictate treatment is fundamentally challenged. Sally Clay (1994:2) writes, "Those of us who have had the experience called 'mental illness' know in our hearts that something profound is missing in these diagnoses. They do not take into account what we have actually endured. Even if the 'bad' chemical or the 'defective' gene is someday found, madness has its own reality that demands attention." In a similar vein, a c/s/x/ author observes to the psychiatrist: Schizophrenia is nothing more than a word to her (from *The Lighthouse*, a c/s/x/ newsletter published in Madison, Wisconsin).

In a sense, the c/s/x community views second- and third-person accounts as unauthorized biographies. This claim replicates the biography versus autobiography dispute – whose version of a life should be privileged? The c/s/x counter move is to claim authority via authenticity for their autobiographical accounts, and to grant authority to their experiences. Thus, the Self-Help Empowerment Center in Boston, an organization run by c/s/x with a variety of medical, professional, and "life" degrees, now offers training conferences for mental health professionals called pointedly, Learning From Us.

At stake here is who has the authority and the warrant to represent whom, upon what this authority rests, and what criteria are salient in the assessment of the divergent representations. Also at issue is access to the knowledge-producing landscape – that is, funding for services and research, professional journals, and the print and other media. The following excerpted exchange illustrates this problematic. This communication represents a direct critique of the knowledge production enterprise by a c/s/x to a "researcher," the authenticity/authority dispute, and the broader politics of professions and involuntary treatment.

(January 6, 1995 via e-mail)
Dear Dr. Estroff,
I had occasion to report on the July issue of Hospital and Community Psychiatry and made very disparaging references to your research contribution, "The Influence of Social Networks and Social Support on Violence by Persons With Serious Mental Illness" pp. 669–678.

I was shocked when [ ] and [ ] both immediately came to your defense citing the fact that you had spent time living with the homeless and had both a sensitivity and compassion for the plight of people labeled "mentally ill." Quite frankly I did not get that impression from your article. It pointed to the mothers of schizophrenic daughters as the main target for violence and appearing in this journal it was just one more brick in the wall of a justification for "forced treatment" and community out-patient commitment proceedings. I realize that your receiving publishing credits in a professional journal may represent job security under the university policy of publish or perish ruling, however, I hope that you would take under advisement the fact that your research was very sorely used by this publication . . . . . . it is the psychiatric profession itself that has an uncontrollable propensity toward violence and not the unfortunates who come under its control. In your article you very cleverly avoid the most obvious conclusion that the "mentally ill" may have excellent reasons (aside from the fact of their supposed "mental illness") not to feel safe in their own homes. I really do wish that your investigation would have dwelt on the patient's definition of the larger "family problem" that these people were the designated symptom for.

With this introduction, I truthfully would not expect you to reply. I have not accepted at face value the testimony of [ ] that you are a kind and loving person. I see you instead through the pages of this yellow rag journalism as putting your foot squarely on the necks of the poor and hurt and wounded people who mistakenly look to psychiatry for an answer and receive instead a chemical boot to the brain. Until convinced otherwise, I shall remain a very irate and disagreeable critic of your published research who is in need of some assurance that beneath the sheep's cloak you apparently wear (that at least convinces intelligent women of your pastoral intent) there is not lurking the talons and teeth of a vicious wolf ready to tear helpless people even further apart with your ministrations of "intensive case management" and removal to "places of residence" other than their home.

(January 8, 1995 via e-mail)
Dear Dr. Estroff,
I will respond with all due civility. If you do not like unkind words, then you will find my point of view un-manageable and simply delete my response instead of forming a continuing dialogue.

Your point of view in the research that I read appearing in the journal that you chose, suggests a lack of concern about whether the resultant labels further disable and isolate the people in our society who are hurt and disabled – some by choice of the role of being mentally ill in their own family so that others may appear well in comparison.

. . . I do not welcome a conversation with someone who pretends to follow a path of enlightenment. I want to know that someone in the field of medicine or research is looking at the possibility of healing rather than only social control. Now possibly you have those views privately and felt that the journal you were writing for would not let you express them. I simply do not know. I only know that when I was the cover of that issue, I was dumb struck. I saw your research was sponsored by a grant by NIMH and I know that it must have taken years of pre-planning to set up all of the research grants that culminated in an issue of the H&CP Journal that had such a devastatingly one sided portrayal of violence. I am sure that when you wanted to find research money you were told that the topic of violence was of concern to the grant funders. I wonder if it occurred to you that you were perhaps being used in a nefarious system of saving the Asylum system and medical model of "forced treatment" in America.[2]

This critique ranges from the very personal to the broadly political. American society, the profession of psychiatry, NIMH, and the media are

implicated as doing violence to mentally ill people. Perhaps the most difficult aspect of responding to this communication was countering the desire
to frame it as pathological in some way, to see it and the author as attacking
irrationally. What I found most unnerving were his repeated challenges to
my personal and professional motives and politics. My benevolence was
in question, and what I took to be enduring moral, intellectual political
commitments to the welfare of c/s/x were under harsh scrutiny. Could he
be right? My work was thinly veiled ambition and a monumental charade.
More importantly, the battle for authority in print, and of intention and
consequence, was joined over my work, not in the abstract or over drug
trials or brain-imaging research.

One clue to the interlocutor's outrage was the line, "I only know when
I was the cover of that issue, I was dumb struck" [emphasis mine]. While
the story in question was not written about this particular person, it
was, for him, exquisitely *about him*. For me, the journal article was a
publication; for him, it was *his* identity, *his* life, a liability of and for people
like him. Schizophrenia is a word to me. I don't get it.

Schizophrenia: What, Who, and How to Respond

At the heart of many first-person accounts are a series of linked assertions
about what schizophrenia is, whether the person has it, and what kind of
treatment or response would be helpful or harmful – in view of answers to
the first two questions. The following excerpt illustrates one perspective
echoed often among c/s/x:

What is compelling about madness is the tantalizing hint that it holds the secrets of
consciousness, of healing, and of spiritual power.... For me, becoming 'mentally
ill' was always a spiritual crisis, and finding a spiritual model of recovery was a
question of life or death.... I plunged into a hell of darkness and despair. When I
did not eat or sleep or talk to my friends, the college called the ambulance to pick
me up. The attendants gave me a shot of Thorazine, put me in a straight jacket, and
carried me off. At the mental hospital I was diagnosed with schizophrenia, locked
in seclusion for several weeks, and drugged with 1200 mg. a day of Thorazine.
Later the doctor told me that my entire experience with spiritual ecstasy and
darkness was sick and irrational, and had no meaning whatsoever. Shamed, I
stayed in the hospital for five months.... I was defeated. I considered myself
a complete and utter failure for the rest of my life. God was gone.... I have
been given just about every psychiatric drug in the med room.... Few of these
'treatments' helped me at all, and most of them damaged me badly. They left
me debilitated and desperate. One might wonder why I am still standing at all.
I certainly owe no thanks to the mental health system. The faith in my inner
experience always returned to strengthen me, it is only this spiritual outlook that
enabled me to go on. (Clay 1994:3–4)

Clay is damaged by the violence done to her body and to her search for meaning in her madness. The resulting shame, defeat, and despair are of much more concern to her than primary symptoms. In her experience, the symptoms of treatment override the symptoms of illness. Clay's view is but one of many expressed by c/s/x that diverges fundamentally from current neuropsychiatric paradigms of schizophrenia as a brain disease, evidenced by cognitive deficits arising from brain anomalies, resulting in social deficits, requiring medication, and confinement when necessary.

Symptoms and Sequelae of Treatment

The view of treatment for schizophrenia as punitive, dangerous, and often ineffective is the area of perhaps most agreement between first- and second-person accounts. Writing about his brother, Robert, who has schizophrenia, Neugeboren (1997:22) observes:

Medication and research are fine, I think, but meanwhile, back on Robert's ward, he has to sneak out of his room to telephone me, and his doctors rarely call me to inform or confer, and the only link to the outside world for thirty or so acutely psychotic patients is a single pay phone.... Meanwhile, back on the ward, important messages don't get through (thus, when Robert, for the first time in his life threatened suicide, and I informed one of the nurses, and I called back a few days later to speak to Robert's doctor, I discovered that the doctor had never been told of Robert's threat). Meanwhile, back on the ward when Robert breaks a tooth, it takes more than three months for him to get his dentures back, during which time he must eat with his gums....

When Neugeboren asks Robert why he is restless and angry, he replies, "I'm angry because I'm being treated like a second-class citizen – like a subpatient – and always told to wait. I'm treated like a sub*moron*! Like the most important thing in the world is their lunch hours!" (Neugeboren 1997:38).

The author's formulation of schizophrenia in the following poem conveys a complacency-shattering image of treatment as punishment/imprisonment; treatment as dangerous, a beast – the conformity monster – as opposed to safety and care.

The Unhinged Mind

SOME YEARS AGO
I was told
that I had unhinged my mind
I found
that they had decided

that I had unhinged my mind
in a paranoid-schizophrenic sort of way
I learned
that the punishment
for unhinging your mind
in a paranoid-schizophrenic sort of way
was anything up to
life imprisonment
in a "mental hospital"
while your mind was drugged to a dead stop
RECENTLY
I saw on TV
a snake who had unhinged his jaw
to swallow a huge rat
I worried about that snake
I hope he realized
how vulnerable he was
lying there with his jaw unhinged
I was afraid that some huge beast
which the snake had never even known existed
would come along and swallow up that snake
while he lay there with his jaw unhinged
NEXT TIME
I unhinge my mind
to absorb
a concept too big to be easily swallowed
I am going to try to find
a safe place
to hide
where the conformity monster won't get me.
(Bill Nordahl, in *Altered State*, Volume 3, Issue 1, March 1994)

The following poem invokes a similar sense of danger and damage, but is more explicit about the sensate dimensions of inpatient psychiatric treatment experiences. The author contrasts intentions (help) and outcomes (harm), marking the discrepancy between our intentions versus her experience. The title asserts that these experiences constitute her life, her accomplishment, her biography – a moving and grotesque irony:

Resume

Stripped or bound
Knocked around
Drugged or shocked
The doors all locked
The windows grated
But we are hated

They ridicule our meditation
Rather give us medication
Confine us in those fishbowl rooms
Trains us early for our tombs
Blinding lights, stare in the glass
While they inject us in the ass
Surly, angry male attendants
Dignity a tattered remnant
Hold us down and bruise our arms
They call it help but we are harmed.
(Gail X, from a consumer support group newsletter from Maine)

The Personal Politics of Treatment: Who Makes the Rules and Roles

The poems excerpted in this section revisit the experiences of psychiatric treatment as harmful, but focus particularly on treatment relationships and the micropolitics of treatment settings. The imbalances in power between inmates and their guardians qua guards – particularly in psychiatric confinement – are familiar, thanks to Goffman (1963), Foucault (1965), and more recent scholars too numerous to inventory. Unchallenged control and surveillance – first within and now outside the walls of psychiatric institutions – set the stage for the degradation, humiliation, and outrage that are expressed.

In the poetry that follows, there are expressions of pleading, and of need for and desires for help from others. The narrators spin tales of hopes unmet, of common humanity, and they repeatedly call for recognition, understanding, and even tenderness from those who provide treatment. Startling contrasts appear between the inner longings of the authors and the harsh and unresponsive human landscape that each describes. Each poem speaks to "you" and of "we." Each represents an explicit communication – messages set sail in empty medication bottles – sent to unnamed but ever so vividly recollected others. It is difficult to ignore the poignancy of continued longing in the wake of such toxic neglect and abuse:

To The System; The Mental Health Worker

How come talking to you
When I most need it,
When I'm trying to prevent
Bad happenings,
High-wired mind crashes;
How come at these times,

When I'm paying for your services,
Paying to be trapped
In your mazes of contradicting webs;
How come talking to you
At these times
Is talking
To the all-powerful
Invisible wall
And all that seems to happen
Is that my "weird" words
and frightening thoughts
Get bounced back
In my face
And then it is
Goodbye,
Time's up,
...And when I am tied down
And shot up again
With your fake caring
And distance,

It could be you
Neglected, strapped to a stretcher,
Lying in a dirty hallway,
With mind-altering drugs
Plowing through your veins,
Causing nightmares, daymares,
Numbness, isolated, paralyzed,
Body and soul
That I didn't have before
Until you gave it to me...
You are the one
With all your mild-mannered ways,
Subtle indifference,
Blatant hostility,
That could change things,
But you are too busy
Protecting your own little world,
Keeping your safe "therapeutic"
Distance from us,
Just like I'm trying to protect
My little world from your abuse,
Soft and reassuring as it may
Sometimes be...
Between the numbers of you
That held me down, sat on me,
Injected me, made me nothing
But a wrong statistic...

And it's only a matter of time
Before you could be one of us.
(Anonymous, from a c/s/x newsletter published in Philadelphia,
    Pennsylvania)

Too Deep for a Bandaide

I have fallen from grace in your eyes,
How uncooperative of me not to be well.
My sadness is an affront to your skill
As I dare to remain enmeshed in pain.
Do not be insulted by this bit of news,
But you have not touched me and it doesn't matter
One way or the other. It is my failure, not yours.
I hide the ugly truth within me so well,
Sometimes with humor, often with silence.
Of course then you cannot see the inner war
That threatens to break my will and my heart.
Forgive my anger at your lack of understanding.
It isolates me, causes fear which inspires anger,
And I know you do not care enough to know me.

But you are correct in your flippant judgment
I have not applied the bandaides on schedule.
Perhaps it is because the wound is deep,
It will not heal by covering it with thin defenses.
This gaping hole in my being may fester
If it is not cleansed and opened to the light,
And it must be done tenderly or it may be fatal.
(Maria Kathleen King, from *The Lighthouse*, a newsletter from
    consumers in Madison, Wisconsin)

It is perhaps all the more remarkable in the face of such hurt and anger,
that calls for help, for healing, and for relationships, endure. In contrast
to the image of the treatment-refusing, isolated, and defiant person with
schizophrenia often portrayed in the literature (for example, Satel 1995),
the author of the poem entitled, *Help* (Lowry Geary, from the Portland
Coalition Advocate, Volume 6, Number 1, Summer 1989), pleads more
pointedly for shared solace:

    ... This anxious day
    can we at least together
    share dismay
    at what has taken place here?
    ... can i lay down beside you a fleece
    for a sign
    that there is a purpose here

and then tomorrow
can you help me to forbear it?
can you help me. . . .

Part of what may fuel the exile of reports such as these from the discourses of schizophrenia treatment, policy, and experience is a kind of paralysis in response to the enormity of the suffering and the wounded fury of the authors. Administrators sigh and launch into a treatise of pragmatics – tight budgets, accreditation standards, statutes, and lack of alternatives. Clinicians abdicate organizational control to the administrators and rush to "cover" too many patients in too little time. The staff is underpaid, hard to hire or hard to fire. It is always someone else's fault or responsibility. Mental health services researchers want to know how large the sample is and how shame and suffering are measured. Each of the previous selections implicates the rules and roles of treatment and organizations as obstacles to the humane recognition and healing that are sought. The question to consider here is whether the rules and roles of scholars and researchers of schizophrenia will cause us to join, or break, from these ranks.

Politics, Policy, and Outrage

Performing the Struggle

The scene: a meeting of seasoned mental health administrators and researchers – people whose credentials as "getting it," as sympathetic to c/s/x concerns and experiences were established (are they ever?) – and seasoned c/s/x leaders – people whose credentials as "knowing it," as willing to work with providers' constraints and limits were established (are they ever?).

The setting: a conference room in a New York hotel. A core group has been meeting for over a year to improve communications between clinicians, administrators, relatives, and c/s/x. This meeting is funded by a national association of mental health providers and is intended to lay the groundwork for a national implementation agenda, a strategy for spreading the discussion and its benefits to other locales. The first hour or so goes well enough. There are the usual introductions, self-presentations, and the like. We take a break. The c/s/x group gathers separately in the lobby ostensibly to have a smoke.

When we reconvene, they let us know in unambiguous terms that the "agenda" is not theirs, but ours. We should listen to them, not vice versa. It is time for us to be quiet and listen. Several people in the room were shocked, some angered, and some were bewildered. After recovering from my surprise, it seemed a reasonable critique, not a personal attack, and I offer to leave the meeting, and so do some others. This is not greeted with approval by the c/s/x group. They want us to stay. They wanted to and did take control of the meeting and the agenda, but we had to remain engaged to make the power shift meaningful and authentic.

The scene: a radio talk show in New York City. I am a guest along with a well-known psychiatrist whose fondness for involuntary medication and confinement as a solution to nearly every problem is legendary. The topic at hand is what to do about people with severe psychiatric disorders who commit acts of violence toward others. This topic is of current interest (in the fall of 1998) due to the recent shooting of two guards in the Capitol in Washington, D.C. by a person identified as having schizophrenia, and the recent fatal stabbing in New York by another person with schizophrenia. The psychiatrist has used these incidents to further his forced-treatment agenda and has written op-ed pieces for the *Wall Street Journal* and *New York Times*. At one juncture in the discussion, I objected to his "fear mongering" and "spectacle making" about violence and psychiatric disorder because of the resultant harm to and stigmatization of the vast majority of c/s/x who are not violent. The talk show host then silenced me with this comment:

If you had to choose between funding the mental health system based on fear of crazy people or not funding it at all, which would you choose? People are not going to fund the system because of altruism – they barely fund education and they actually get something from schools. But fear and need for their own protection – that they'll pay for.

He went on to express sympathy with my position, but repeated his assertion of political pragmatics. In my head were the sensibilities of the c/s/x at the meeting described previously, and the indignation of my e-mail critic. How to communicate the legitimacy of their views and experiences and retain credibility? That it seems such a conundrum at this and other moments is the problem. That there is a choice between credibility, authority, and legitimacy and representing the experiences of c/s/x described here *is* the problem.

Writing the Rage

The following poem is full of anger and outrage, and is baldly political in imagery and thrust. The language is harsh, mocking, and threatening. It seems most important to consider why the author might have felt moved to write in this way. Why is her anger so raw, so personal, and her desire for revenge so keen? The challenge is to read this selection as political rather than pathological, and to seek the origins and fuel of these passions rather than to judge their expression as problematic:

Comrades

What will it take
to find me on my knees
in the Coalition's office chapel
with my brothers?
The story of my people,
a grave-studded testament
to the un-remembered dead.
Mostly agnostics, mostly suicides
lying in religious tombs
much as they lived,
with no rights,
not possessed of so much
as one's own damn body.
My fallen brothers rest not easy
In lie-bought graves to please the neighbors.
I must apologize.
I go on; I have passed.
Oreo mentality;
Tardive dyskinesia affects my tongue only.
No one sees.
No more tremors,
No more drugs,
No more side effects.
And my ex-therapist
(sort of like an ex-husband, only more so)
told me I need to
leave my brothers behind
cleanse them even from my mind
so that I may get well.
I am healthy already
and getting stronger every day.
Your oblivious normalcy turns my gut.
WE ARE REVOLUTIONARIES,
and *there will* be a reckoning.
(Gail X, from a consumer support group newsletter from Maine)

Concluding Thoughts

Some sort of reckoning, well short of revolution, can arise from the territory explored in this chapter. The range and reach of the disputes conveyed herein are substantial. But perhaps by identifying more precisely their particulars, we may make some progress. It seems to me that there are two interlocking sets of conundrums that require attention and that constitute the current impasse. The first concerns the c/s/x claim that we both don't and can't get it. Authenticity of experience is theirs alone, yet the inability of others to offer them authentic empathy and recognition is a source of substantial suffering, humiliation, and outrage. If we do not, by choice, and cannot, by insufficiency understand, know, and recognize, then what are we to do?

The second conundrum revolves around the claims and frames of second and third parties to schizophrenia that c/s/x complaints, rebuttals, and indictments are primarily symptoms of illness – pathological and not validly experiential in origin. Or, if not invalid or symptoms of illness, these experiences lie within the realm of policy, administration, and implementation of treatment, and are not essential to the nature and understanding of schizophrenia.

These reciprocal, mutually negating propositions generate and maintain much of the anguish and anger expressed in the previous narratives. Like creationism versus evolutionism – this may be an irresolvable dispute. The grounding assumptions of the parties may be so incompatible that a common discourse is impossible. Yet short of resolution (or revolution) there are some moves that may enrich the scholarly discourse and perhaps assuage some of the passions that fuel the c/s/x experience.

The inclusion of c/s/x experiences as legitimate subjects and subjectivities worthy of study, serious examination, and inclusion in the science of schizophrenia would challenge brain-based paradigms, but is not of necessity incompatible. What raises the ire and crushes the spirits of many c/s/x is their invalidation by and invisibility to those who have authority, but lack authenticity. But all this is so much easier said than done. First, there are problems with the methods and means to expanding schizophrenia paradigms to include contradiction, complication, and paradox. Sentiments and sensibilities, the poetics of experience, are not quantifiable and thus will not easily survive the skepticism of science. The power of prose images, of performed resistance, will not compete well with statistical power. How many people feel this way? What are the diagnoses of those who respond in this way to treatment? Is this a representative sample? On which axis of DSM-IV would these signs and symptoms and experiences belong? How much did their treatment cost? Were they taking their medications?

A further complication arises because of disputes about agency and schizophrenia.[3] On the one hand are brain-based conceptions of schizophrenia that strip individuals of any modicum of willful, autonomous, and reasoned perception and experience. This is Granger's complaint at the beginning of the chapter. On the other hand are claims of near absolute agency made by an interesting collection of c/s/x rights activists, clinicians such as Jay Haley (1986), civil libertarian and disability rights advocates, and many c/s/x in their daily lives. A popular slogan in the disability rights movement asserts, "Nothing About Me Without Me." Ironically, exaggerated claims of agency may pose as many problems as erasure of agency for people with schizophrenia – and both are probably inaccurate. Endless accusations and counteraccusations of "othering" from both camps may be useful politically, but beyond prompting analyses such as this one, may contribute little to furthering scholarly progress. Public views, statutory language, and scientific knowledge are murky, incomplete, and in conflict about how much and what kind of agency and self-control to expect, demand, or recognize from the person with schizophrenia. These uncertainties contribute to the precariousness of making one's way through the terrain of schizophrenia.

There are politically based reasons for resisting sharing of authority between first-, second-, and third-person narrators of schizophrenia. Fear and loathing of involuntary treatment, particularly inpatient confinement and forced medication, is as widespread among c/s/x as is its endorsement among clinicians and relatives/caregivers. None of the latter would claim coercion and force are desirable or preferable, but rather necessary. For some c/s/x there can be no compromise, for others, robust due process protections are acceptable. The divide on this issue is so impassioned and substantial it creates barriers to alliances and common ground on other fronts. The brain-disease model bears the weight of most of the rationale for involuntary treatment, and this further taints the science of schizophrenia for many c/s/x. Making progress toward incremental increases in shared understandings will require that the often irreparable humiliation of forced treatment be at least acknowledged in the calculus of necessity advanced by the relevant authorities.

Granger (1994:11) warns, "Don't let your treatment interfere with your recovery." Taking the full measure of why he warns, and of what he warns, represents an alluring call for future scholarship of schizophrenia.

NOTES

1 I use the term *consumer/survivor/expatient*, and the acronym *c/s/x*, because it is the term of choice of most of the people with serious psychiatric disorders with whom I work, from whom I learn, and about whom I read. There are ongoing debates among people who have been diagnosed with and treated for schizophrenia about what to call themselves, as well as controversy with some others about these designations (Estroff 1997). It is emblematic of the problematic nature of the present paper that the name of this group, and their social and political identities, are areas of such contestation.

2 The person who wrote this message died in September 1998, but I use this correspondence with his permission based on our mutual agreement that others might learn from our encounter. After the first e-mail message, I wrote back, telling the writer that I would be willing to engage in a discussion with him, but that his apparent anger made it difficult for me to respond. Thus, his reference to civility in the second message. At the time I received this critique, I was teaching a seminar on research ethics and moral quandaries in producing knowledge. When the class read the critique, their first question to me was what I wanted from my critic. Absolution? Recognition? Agreement about my good intentions? I am still not certain. I was particularly taken aback by this critique because it was my intention in the article to challenge the notion that violence was attributable solely to people with schizophrenia. The qualitative and quantitative findings supported strongly the view that *mutual* threat pervaded relationships where violence occurred between the patients and family members in the study.

3 I am indebted to Louis Sass' discussion of the original paper for this analytical frame.

REFERENCES

Cassell, Eric J. 1982. "The Nature of Suffering and the Goals of Medicine." *New England Journal of Medicine* 306(11): 639–45.

Chamberlin, J. 1978. *On Our Own: Patient Controlled Alternatives to the Mental Health System.* New York: McGraw-Hill.

Clay, S. 1994. *The Wounded Prophet.* Paper presented at the First National Forum on Recovery from Mental Illness sponsored by the National Institute of Mental Health.

Dickey, James. 1970. "Diabetes." In *The Eye-Beaters, Blood, Victory, Madness, Buckhead, and Mercy.* New York: Doubleday.

Estroff, Sue E. 1997. "What's in a Name? Plenty." *Journal of the American Psychiatric Nurses Association* 3(4): 1–2.

Estroff, Sue E., in collaboration with William Lachicotte, Linda Illingworth, and Anna Johnston. 1991. "Everybody's Got a Little Mental Illness: Accounts of Illness and Self Among Persons with Severe, Persistent Mental Illnesses." *Medical Anthropology Quarterly* 5(4): 331–69.

Estroff, Sue E., C. R. Zimmer, W. S. Lachicotte, and J. Benoit. 1994. "The Influence of Social Networks and Social Support on Violence by Persons with Serious Mental Illness." *Hospital and Community Psychiatry* 45(7): 669–79.

Foucault, Michel. 1965. *Madness and Civilization.* New York: Vintage Books.

Frank, Arthur and C. E. Foote. 1991. *At the Will of the Body.* New York: Houghton Mifflin.

Gennari, E. C. 1995. *Beyond the Labels: A Mother's Story.* Rumford, RI: Karma Publishing.

Gibbons, Kaye. 1995. *Frost and Flower: My Life with Manic Depression So Far.* Decatur, GA: Wisteria Press.

Goffman, Erving. 1963. *Behavior in Public Places: Notes on the Social Organization of Gatherings.* New York: Free Press of Glencoe.

Granger, D. 1994. *Recovery from Mental Illness: A First Person Perspective of An Emerging Paradigm*. Paper presented at the First National Forum on Recovery from Mental Illness sponsored by the National Institute of Mental Health and the Ohio Department of Mental Health. April 1994. Unpublished ms. 16pp.

Haley, Jay. 1986. "The Art of Being Schizophrenic." In pp. 55–80. *The Power Tactics of Jesus Christ*. Rockville, MD: The Triangle Press.

Kleinman, Arthur. 1988. *The Illness Narratives*. New York: Basic Books.

Krawiec, Richard and Marianne Clayter, eds. 1993. *In Our Own Words: Writings from People in Shelters*. Raleigh, NC: Voices Community Press.

Neugeboren, Jay. 1997. *Imagining Robert: My Brother, Madness, and Survival*. New York: William Morrow.

Peterson, Dale. 1982. *A Mad People's History of Madness*. Pittsburgh, PA: University of Pittsburgh Press.

Porter, Roy, ed. 1988. *A Social History of Madness: The World Through the Eyes of the Insane*. New York: Weidenfeld & Nicholson.

Quill, Timothy E. 1991. "Death and Dignity: A Case of Individual Decision Making." *New England Journal of Medicine* 324(10): 691–4.

Satel, S. 1995. "When Disability Benefits Make Patients Sicker." *New England Journal of Medicine* 333(12): 794–6.

Sheehan, S. 1995. "The Last Days of Sylvia Frumkin." *The New Yorker*, February 20, 27: 200–11.

Sommer, Robert, Jennifer S. Clifford, and John C. Norcross. 1998. "A Bibliography of Mental Patients' Autobiographies: An Update and Classification System." *American Journal of Psychiatry* 155(9): 1261–4.

Sommer, Robert and Osmond, H. 1983. "A Bibliography of Mental Patients' Autobiographies, 1960–1982." *American Journal of Psychiatry* 140(8): 1051–4.

Spaniol, LeRoy and Martin Koehler. 1994. *The Experience of Recovery*. Boston: Boston University Center for Psychiatric Rehabilitation.

Still Surviving Essay Contest: *Mental Health Consumers/Psychiatric Survivors Tell Their Stories, 1991–1993*. Wisconsin Coalition for Advocacy, Bureau of Mental Health–Wisconsin, and Wisconsin Community Fund.

Susko, Michael A., ed. 1991. *Cry of the Invisible: Writings from the Homeless and Survivors of Psychiatric Hospitals*. Baltimore, MD: Conservatory Press.

Vonnegut, Mark. 1975. *The Eden Express: A Personal Account of Schizophrenia*. New York: Praeger Publishers.

Wasow, Mona. 1995. *The Skipping Stone: Ripple Effects of Mental Illness on the Family*. Palo Alto, CA: Science and Behavior Books.

12 "Negative Symptoms," Commonsense, and Cultural Disembedding in the Modern Age

Louis A. Sass

Introduction

Psychiatric attention in the last decade or more has focused increasingly on the so-called "negative symptoms" of schizophrenia – symptoms defined by diminishment of normal forms of behavior or expression. The symptoms in question include flatness of affective expression, paucity of speech, a lack of socially directed behavior, and an apparent apathy and lack of sustained attentiveness particularly to people or the environment. For various reasons, both the subjective and the cultural dimensions of these symptoms have been neglected or even denied.

It is sometimes claimed that the concept of "negative symptoms" is perfectly atheoretical, merely a convenient way of classifying symptoms. Often, however, negative symptoms have been understood to represent a fundamental diminishment of psychological activity or subjective life, especially of the higher mental processes involving volition, self-awareness, reasoning, abstraction, and complex emotional response. This is congruent with the original conceptualization of negative versus positive symptoms that was offered toward the end of the nineteenth century by Hughlings Jackson and his followers: "In every insanity," wrote Jackson (1932:411, quoted in Foucault 1987:19), "more or less of the highest cerebral centers is out of function, temporarily or permanently, from some pathological process." Wrote Jackson's disciple, Charles Mercier, "The affection of function is always in the direction of loss, of deficit, or diminution . . . degradation of action to a lower plane" (Clark 1981:284). In the traditional Jacksonian view, such positive symptoms as hallucinations and delusions are but secondary phenomena, emanations from primitive levels of neural organization that are released or disinhibited due to the primary deficit of higher, inhibitory processes.[1]

In recent years, the negative symptoms have come to be more central to the diagnosis of schizophrenia, and they are increasingly considered to have etiologic or pathogenetic priority. There are good empirical and theoretical reasons for some of these developments. Unlike positive symptoms, the negative symptoms occur in all or nearly all cases of schizophrenia; and they appear to be especially prominent in the earliest (as well as in the residual) phases of the development of the schizophrenic condition (McGlashan and Fenton 1992). What is problematic, however, is the often unreflected-upon ways in which the underlying nature and experience of these symptoms are being conceptualized, and in which their pathogenic role is being conceived (see Sass 2000).

Both the traditional and contemporary understanding of this constellation of symptoms manifest what one might call the two main tenets of neurobiological reductionism. The negative symptoms are understood as a direct psychological manifestation of a "basic defect" or "deficiency" in schizophrenia that is assumed to be, first, a relatively unmediated manifestation of an abnormality of the brain and, second, to result in a loss of the higher or more self-aware forms of conscious life. The assumption of biological determinism, of an exclusively brain-to-mind direction of causality, implies that cultural or social factors can be of no more than merely "pathoplastic" importance (see Kleinman 1987; Sass 1992:358); while the assumption of lowered mental level implies that the subjectivity of such patients lacks real complexity and can readily be described in quantitative and pure deficit terms: as a mere dimming or diminishment of higher or more reflective forms of conscious life.

Too often, psychiatric discussion of schizophrenia and culture has taken place in a kind of phenomenological and theoretical vacuum – without careful consideration of the qualitative specificity of schizophrenic experience or a sufficiently focused and coordinated appreciation of the relevant aspects of the sociocultural order. Here I shall attempt to avoid both these pitfalls. I shall argue that, far from indicating a lowering or shutting-down of conscious awareness, many negative-symptom experiences in schizophrenia actually involve forms of "hyperreflexivity" and alienation. There is an exacerbation of various kinds of self-consciousness, often involving disengagement from the grounding frameworks, assumptions, and bodily dispositions or tendencies that normally serve as the taken-for-granted foundation of organized action and experience. Usually this is accompanied by a diminishment not of mental life, but of the instinctive energies and dynamic connectedness crucial to what psychiatrist Eugene Minkowski (1927, 1987) termed "vital contact" with reality.

Many of the frameworks and dispositions from which the patient becomes disengaged are strongly cultural (and possibly universal) in origin. Their smooth functioning is a precondition of normal social existence. We shall also see that these core features of schizophrenia, if properly understood, show remarkable resemblances to some key aspects of modern culture and society – that is itself marked by a "wholesale reflexivity" and associated forms of detachment from commonsense reality (Giddens 1990:39, 176). After discussing these affinities, I shall speculate about some ways in which modernity might contribute to or exacerbate certain characteristics of schizophrenia or schizotypical conditions and might also be especially problematic for a person endowed with this style of being.

The condition of schizophrenia deserves to be of special interest both to cognitive anthropologists and cultural psychologists. The person with schizophrenia is an anomalous yet exemplary figure: a person who fails to adopt the social practices or internalize the cultural frameworks that are essential to normal social life, yet whose failure to do so can illuminate these very frameworks and processes of internalization, while at the same time typifying some of the most distinctive features of the modern age.

Loss of Natural Self-Evidence

Perhaps the most profound analysis specifically devoted to the subjective side of the so-called negative symptoms is to be found in a recent classic of German phenomenological psychiatry: Wolfgang Blankenburg's (1991) book, *The Loss of Natural Self-Evidence: A Contribution to the Psychopathology of Symptom-Poor Schizophrenics*. The original title is *Der Verlust der Naturlichen Selbstverstaendlichkeit*.[2] In his book, Blankenburg focuses on patients of the subtypes hebephrenic and simple schizophrenia. He offers a phenomenological description of the "basic disturbance" or "basic disorder" (German: *Grunstoerung*; French: *trouble fondamental*) that, in his view, is central to the pathology of all individuals with schizophrenia but that is often obscured by the presence of positive symptoms. Blankenburg is well aware of the difficulty of capturing the "specificity of what appears non-specific" (1991:30, 6)[3] in schizophrenic experience. He thinks, however, that the subjective dimension of the basic disturbance can best be described as a loss of the usual commonsense orientation to reality, with its unquestioned sense of obviousness and its unproblematic background quality, which allows a person to take for granted so many of the elements and dimensions of our shared world. To describe this subtle, but distinctive alteration of the lived world of schizophrenia, Blankenburg borrows a phrase from a patient, Anne, his primary case example: "loss of natural self-evidence." Blankenburg cautions against understanding this loss as a pure privation. Rather, it involves a kind of dialectical negation, a process that must be understood as constituting not so much a deficient as a *different* manner of being-in-the-world (1991:29, 100; 6, 58). See also Parnas and Bovet (1991).

Empirical studies show that although people with schizophrenia often do well on many intellectual tasks that require abstract or logical thought, their difficulties emerge most dramatically when they are asked to engage in more practical modes of thought, especially when these call upon judgment about the social world (see Cutting and Murphy 1988, 1990). Blankenburg's patient, Anne, describes herself as lacking something banal yet truly fundamental, something that in normal experience, she says, is "always already" assumed and "comes before" everything that people notice (see Blankenburg 1991:131, 133; *83, 84*). Anne also speaks of losing the "evidence of feelings" (1991:77; *42*) and of lacking the sense of repose that is inherent in having a "stable position" or "point of view" (*Standpunkt*) on life and its challenges (1991:80, 72; *45, 38*). "What am I missing, really?" she asks. "Something small, funny, [strange?; *komisch*], something important, but without which one cannot live.... To exist is to have confidence in one's way of being.... I need support in the most simple everyday matters.... It is certainly the natural evidence [*die naturliche Selbstverstaendlichkeit*] which I lack" (1991:77; *42*).

Anne constantly has the sense of starting anew. She experiences a mood of quasi-surrealist alienation-cum-fascination in which everything strikes her as somehow "strange," "funny," or novel (Blankenburg 1991:138–40; *89–91*). Blankenburg compares this to the "amazement concerning all that is most obvious," which, according to Husserl's disciple, Eugen Fink, is the essence of the phenomenological philosopher's querying of the "axioms of the everyday" (1991:111, 112; *66–67*). Anne feels outside, beside, or detached (1991:78, 171, 181–2; *43, 116, 123–4*) – as if, she says, "I was regarding from somewhere outside the whole movement of the world [*als ob ich das ganze Weltgetriebe so von aussen anschaue*]" (1991:113; *68*). This makes it difficult for her to carry out many of the actions of daily life in a fluid and efficient manner. Instead she is hesitant, awkward, and uncertain. She lacks self-confidence, spontaneity, and good practical judgment. Traditional assumptions about madness and delusion have portrayed the person with schizophrenia as someone who is too prone to belief (this is inherent in the notion of "poor reality-testing" that grounds many definitions of "psychosis" and "delusion"). It can be argued, however, that it is actually *the loss* of a more normal rootedness in a common web of belief that plays a more central role in the pathology and even, in fact, in processes of delusion-formation (see Blankenburg 1991:31; *7* re. Matussek; Sass 1992:269–78).

As Blankenburg (1991) recognizes, this loss of self-evidence is closely bound up with self-consciousness of various kinds, with what I would call "hyperreflexive" tendencies to become explicitly aware of issues that would normally be so taken-for-granted as to remain unnoticed. Anne herself speaks of being "hung up" (*haengen bleibe*) on obvious questions and problems that healthy persons simply pass by (1991:79; *44*). Whereas other people effortlessly develop and depend on a habitual "way, a manner of thinking" that orients and channels their action and thought, Anne explains that, for her, "everything is an *object* of thought" [*Bei mir is das alles nur angedacht*] (1991:126–7; *79*). She is, in fact, unable to stop thinking and questioning the most commonplace facts or axioms of daily life, and finds herself posing questions that she herself recognizes as pointless or banal (1991:79–82, 91; *44–7, 52*). In *La Schizophrenie* (1927), the phenomenological psychiatrist Eugene Minkowski describes such a man with schizophrenia who "wanted to know what difference there was between putting one's hands straight into a normal jacket pocket and putting them into the sloping pockets of an overcoat" (quoted in Cutting 1991:294). A similar patient whom I knew seemed to have floated free of all sense of practical or realistic context, and would find herself wondering about the oddest things, such as why people walked on the treads rather than the risers of staircases.

"Basic Disturbance" and "Basic Symptoms"

Blankenburg (1991) describes "loss of natural self-evidence" as a "*basic disturbance*" or "*basic disorder*" (*Grundstoerung*). He states, however, that this is not meant to impute to it either temporal priority or causal primacy in the development of the condition (1991:27; *4*). The concept is meant to capture essence not cause; to describe the overall tenor or the fundamental conditions of possibility of the schizophrenic lifeworld. Blankenburg expresses considerable skepticism about the possibility of describing any *single* fundamental disorder that could gracefully encompass all the different aspects of schizophrenia (1991:28; *4*). Still, he does give a certain priority to his favored notion, "loss of natural self-evidence."

Consider, for instance, Blankenburg's treatment of the hyperreflexive tendencies that so often accompany the loss of commonsense reality in schizophrenia. Blankenburg (1991) tends to conceive of them as *secondary* phenomena that develop in some kind of compensation for the more fundamental disorder, which is the loss of natural self-evidence itself (1991:92–4; *53–5*).[4] While recognizing that this compensatory hyperreflexivity can have the effect of *further* eroding the complacency of natural self-evidence, Blankenburg does not conceive of hyperreflexivity as playing a primary role in this erosion. He is also inclined to interpret another important feature of schizophrenia – the weakening of the ego's sense of autonomy and vitality – as a consequence of the loss of self-evidence, which supposedly undermines the very foundations of vigorous or effective action (1991:149; *98*). And Blankenburg interprets the sense of fatigue that people with schizophrenia often report as a tertiary effect – a consequence of the effortful hyperreflexive struggles that develop in compensation for, or as consequences of, the loss of self-evidence (1991:132–3, 156; *84–5, 103*). One might ask whether it is necessary to give "loss of natural self-evidence" quite the priority that it is accorded in his book. Might not other factors have an equal claim to playing a central role in both a thematic and an etiological sense?

One theorist who places the energetic or dynamic aspect of schizophrenia at the center is Eugene Minkowski. In Minkowski's (1987, 1999) view, the *"trouble generateur"* of the schizophrenic condition is the "loss" or "rupture" of "vital contact with reality" and the corresponding diminishment of vital impulse or force. It is not difficult to imagine how such a diminishment could generate such phenomena as hyperreflexivity and the loss of self-evidence.[5] Vital impulse might be thought of as an amalgam of appetite and energy. It is what motivates human actions and what organizes our experiential world in accordance with needs and wishes, thereby giving to objects what the psychologist J. J. Gibson called their "affordances," their significance for us as obstacles, tools, objects of desire, and the like. In the absence of this impulse and the orientations it generates, the very structure of action and of the act of awareness will be altered. For then there can no longer be any clear differentiation of means from goal, no reason for *certain* objects to show up in the focus of attention while others recede, no reason for attention to be directed outward toward the world rather than inward toward one's own body or processes of thought. The world will be stripped of all the affordances by which the fabric of commonsense reality is knitted together into a meaningful whole.[6]

But similar arguments could be made for the primacy of hyperreflexivity. It seems obvious that the emergence of the normally tacit into the focus of awareness could itself have the effect of undermining the normal sense of natural self-evidence – the latter, after all, clearly depends on retaining a sense of the taken-for-granted background that is incompatible with such awareness. Hyperreflexivity will also disorganize the normal goal-oriented quality of experience, and this seems likely not only to cause fatigue, but also to detach a person from the normal sources of emotional and instinctual engagement with the world.

It is true that the more intellectually introspective forms of hyperreflexivity on which Blankenburg focuses may not be basic enough to play a truly primary role in the etiology of the illness. Hyperreflexivity, however, includes not merely actively directed or *reflective* forms of self-consciousness, but also a host of other, more passive or automatic ways in which an agent or subject comes to focus on itself or features of its own functioning. These "operative" forms of hyperreflexivity, as we might call them,[7] can include, for example, experiences in which the person comes to feel removed from his body and emotions through a focal awareness of proprioceptive sensations. Many of the experiences that people with schizophrenia or schizotypal disorder describe do, in fact, involve a tendency to feel consciously aware of, and therefore removed from, psychological phenomena that would normally be experienced tacitly while conscious attention focused elsewhere. Of particular interest here is the careful research on the subjective dimensions of premorbid and prodromal phases of schizophrenia carried out by the German psychiatrists G. Huber, J. Klosterkoetter, and their colleagues on what they call the "basic symptoms." The "basic symptoms" are on a continuum with Bleuler's fundamental symptoms or the negative symptoms of contemporary psychiatry (as Klosterkoetter notes [1992:31]), but they are studied from the *patient's* point of view and with a focus on early stages in the illness.

Using the Present State Examination and the Bonn Scale for the Assessment of Basic Symptoms, Klosterkoetter and colleagues (Klosterkoetter 1992; Klosterkoetter et al. 1997) studied patients who were at risk for, but had not yet developed, schizophrenia. They uncovered a panoply of relatively mild, nonpsychotic anomalies affecting various domains. One cluster of symptoms involves alterations of perception and interaction with the surrounding world that are reminiscent of Blankenburg's loss of natural self-evidence. In this hyperalert state, the patient experiences mutations of the perceptual world whose effect is to give an altered look and irritating complexity to the things, sounds, voices, faces, gestures, and patterns of behavior that the patient perceives around him – that now come to seem estranged as well as affectively stirring in some peculiar way (Klosterkoetter 1992:33). Often this is combined with a loss of automatic skills and with various forms of interference with the smooth flow of motor activity.[8]

Another cluster of the early-stage "basic symptoms" studied by Klosterkoetter includes cenesthesias of various kinds: sensations of movement or of pulling or pressure inside the body or on its surfaces; electric or migrating sensations; awareness of kinesthetic, vestibular, or thermic sensations; and sensations of diminution or enlargement, of heaviness or lightness, of sinking or emptiness, or of numbness or stiffness of the body or its parts. These cenesthetic experiences appear to involve hyperreflexive awareness of bodily sensations that would not normally be attended to in any sustained fashion. The hyperreflexivity in question can have a more automatic or a more active quality (operative or reflective hyperreflexivity). It has been shown that these strange bodily sensations so often experienced by people with schizophrenia are remarkably similar to the experiences reported by normal subjects who, in psychological experiments, have been encouraged to adopt a detached, introspective stance toward their own bodies (see Angyal 1936; Hunt 1985:248; Sass 1994a:90–7, 159–61).

Bringing Blankenburg together with Huber and Klosterkoetter enables us to describe both sides of what can seem a contradictory aspect of schizophrenia: namely, the simultaneously abstract and concrete qualities of their cognitive/perceptual orientation. Whereas Blankenburg primarily draws our attention to abstract preoccupations that can give schizophrenic thought and speech a quasi-philosophical quality, the Huber/Klosterkoetter studies document the ways in which larger units of experience and action tend to be broken down due to preoccupation with the sensory particulars that constitute what they term the forms of "basal irritation."

The "Intentional Arc" and the "Tacit Dimension"

Both of these developments can be illuminated by using some concepts and terminology from two philosophers with complementary views: the phenomenologist, Maurice Merleau-Ponty, and the chemist and philosopher of science, Michael Polanyi. Merleau-Ponty speaks of what he calls the "intentional arc," which forms the fundamental dynamic structuring of our field of awareness and lived world, and which he compares to a "mobile vector, active in all directions... through which we can orient ourselves towards anything outside and inside us, and have an attitude to that object," and which "endows experience with its degree of vitality and fruitfulness" (Merleau-Ponty 1945:158, 184; 1962:135–6, 157, translation altered).

Polanyi (1964, 1967) describes the basic structure of this intentional arc as a continuum between what is objectified or focally known (the object of awareness) and what is known in a tacit or implicit manner, which includes the background or context as well as the structures and processes of the embodied knowing self. One might contrast these two ways of knowing one's own body by distinguishing the body representation from the bodily or corporeal subject – the first referring to an objectifiable image (conscious or unconscious) that one has *of* one's own body; the second referring to the body as a sensori-motor subject that grounds and constitutes the world of our perceptual awareness (Merleau-Ponty 1962:90–106 and *passim*, for example, p. 106 re: the body as "the potentiality of a certain world"; also Gallagher and Meltzoff 1996).

Polanyi (1967:x, 17) uses the term "indwelling" to describe the kind of relationship that one normally has to one's own body: a condition in which tacitly experienced bodily sensations serve as the proximal term in the "from-to" structure that is the essence of the intentionality of consciousness. But indwelling is not restricted to the body alone. By using a cane in the service of exploring the world, for example, "we incorporate the cane in our body – or extend our body to include it – so that we come to dwell in it" (Polanyi 1964:55; see also Merleau-Ponty 1962:152). From an experiential standpoint, it is as if our very nerves had actually migrated down through the cane, allowing us to move the cane with the spontaneous familiarity and immediacy of our hand and to feel what the tip of the cane touches (the "distal" term) in almost as intense and unmediated a way as if the cane were our fingertip itself. Imagine, however, what can happen if one ceases to be so interested in what lies out there in the world, or if one desists from adopting an active, exploratory posture. Then, gradually, the tendrils of selfhood pull backward: The cane comes again to be an object rather than an extension of one's arm; the plane of hypersensitivity that is felt boundary between self and world, migrates backward up the cane to locate itself again at the tips of one's actual fingers. What can happen in schizophrenia, I will argue, is that this backward migration travels further still, until what might have been thought to be inalienable aspects of the self come to seem separate or detached.

A fascinating account of the experiences that can occur under these circumstances is provided by Antonin Artaud, a writer, actor, and general man of the theater who was diagnosed with schizophrenia and who spent the last ten years of his life as an asylum patient. Artaud's writings have been recognized as one of the rare sources that offer a detailed account of the subjective side of the so-called negative symptoms (Selten, Van Den Bosch, and Sijben 1998; see also Sass 1996, 2000). In the two passages I shall quote, Artaud describes what seem to be experiences of his own face, not as it might appear in a mirror or as seen by another person, but as it must have felt from within. The passages are particularly interesting given that one's own face is the part of one's physical being with which one is most likely to feel identified – which would normally be experienced, not as an object, but as the very medium of one's intentionality.

To understand the first passage, one needs to recognize that a person's face can indeed be an active emptiness. It is experienced as the locus of one's intentionality, of that sense of being a conscious, object-directed subjectivity that Sartre aptly compares to a kind of "nothingness" (Sartre 1956). As such, the lived face is also the point of orientation for all our knowing of objects, and in this sense it does somehow attract and orient – in a metaphorical sense, "magnetize" – all that passes in front of it. In this passage from a letter written in 1932, Artaud seems, then, to be describing "sensations" that are in some respects reasonably normal, even though in other respects these sensations are also transformed – reified and externalized – by the fact of being brought into focal awareness:

There is a certain sensation of emptiness in the facial nerves, but an active emptiness, so to speak, which physically took the form of a kind of vertiginous magnetization of the front of the face. These are not images and this should be taken almost literally. For this physical vertigo was horribly distressing and this sensation that I am describing reached its climax two or three years after the onset of my disease. (Artaud 1976:289)

In the second, more disconcerting passage (from "The Nerve Meter" of 1925), we encounter grotesque forms of self-alienation that can occur under conditions of prolonged withdrawal and hyperreflexive contemplation. Here Artaud imagines a time, "ten years from now" when, as he puts it, "the plays of my soul will be deciphered" and "the geometry of the void understood." In this surreal utopia of which he dreams, all people will be privy to the hyperreflexive visions that Artaud knows so well, thereby overcoming his sense of isolation and sparing him the struggle to communicate. Of particular interest here is Artaud's powerful description of certain strange transformations of facial self-awareness that occur when experiences that would normally be tacit and inner are subjected to the light of hyperreflexive awareness. This causes the fulminating sensations and squirming patterns of facial experience to become so objectified that his face actually seems to lift up off his head like a membrane:

Then . . . arborescent bouquets of mind's eyes will crystallize in glossaries [and] people will learn what the configuration of the mind is, and they will understand how I lost my mind. Then they will understand why my mind is not all here; then they will see all languages go dry, all minds parched, all tongues shriveled up, the human face flattened out, deflated as if sucked up by shriveling leeches. And this lubricating membrane will go on floating in the air, this caustic lubricating membrane, this double membrane of multiple degrees and a million little fissures, this melancholic and vitreous membrane, but so sensitive and also pertinent, so capable of multiplying, splitting apart, turning inside out with its glistening little cracks, its dimensions, its narcotic highs, its penetrating and toxic injections, and all this then will be found to be all right, and I will have no further need to speak. (Artaud 1965:39–40)

Both aspects of these paradoxical descriptions – their phantasmatic as well as their hyperspecific or hyperconcrete qualities – are reminiscent of the experiences described by subjects in the introspectionist experiments previously mentioned. Both aspects can be understood as bound up with a hyperreflexive gaze: as being, at least in part, products of a focused, introspective awareness that derealizes sensations by detaching them from the unnoticed background while simultaneously subjecting these sensations to processes of externalization and reification.

A person who has these sorts of experiences will not feel fully at one with his bodily movement or speech, or for that matter, with his feelings or thoughts. Blankenburg's patient, Anne, who had some manneristic qualities, spoke of not being really "present" or of being "strange to myself" (Blankenburg 1991:77, 94; *42, 54*). It is easy to imagine how such experiences of self-alienation might be conducive to various features of the negative-symptom syndrome – to forms of inactivity and withdrawal and to a sense of effortfulness. We might consider as well its effect on emotional experience and expression.

Affective experience generally seems to be rooted in experiences of bodily states – in "representations" or "images of the body" that have come to be associated as "somatic markers" with particular contexts or stimulus situations (Damasio 1994). It seems likely, however, that normal emotional experience would involve, for the most part, not representations of the objectified body *image* so much as implicitly felt experiences involving the body *subject*. These would-be experiences in which the somatic markers, patterns, or tension-states are experienced as the tacitly inhabited medium of an attitude – such as fear, desire, or disgust – that is directed toward some object in the world. (Such experiences could be described as the subjective correlates of the emotional affordances of the world.) When experiences normally in the tacit dimension come to be the objects of a more focal and objectifying awareness, as happens with Artaud, one would expect profound transformations in the felt quality of the affective life. Rather than serving as an attitude *toward* the world, certain emotional configurations would instead be experienced at a subjective distance, almost as objects in themselves, while others might simply fail to coalesce at all. The normal fluidity and flow of both affective experience and affective expression would be disrupted, leading to a sense of awkwardness, artificiality, and distance, in the patient's affective experience as well as in the expression visible to others.[10]

It is not surprising that a person having such experiences will not fall readily into conventional or habitual ways of behaving, talking, or thinking. Such a person is likely to hold herself back – thereby to become aware of, and, at the same time, detached from habits of bodily being and affective response as well as cognitive framework assumptions that might otherwise function invisibly.[11] Loss of natural self-evidence, withdrawal, disruption of graceful, spontaneous movement: These may all be rooted in the sense of hyperreflexive detachment that is inherent in the "basic symptoms."

I do not mean to argue here for the priority of hyperreflexivity *over* loss of self-evidence or diminished vital contact, but, rather, to emphasize the essentially complementary nature of these several themes or factors emphasized by Blankenburg, Minkowski, and myself. It is possible to construct pathogenic models that treat one or another of these factors as the prior abnormality or "defect" that gives rise to the other two.[12] It seems likely, however, that these three processes (along with other factors as well) are locked into a more intimate complementarity on the causal plane, and that any straightforward linear model would be overly simplistic. Research on "basic symptoms" in premorbid stages of schizophrenia has, in any case, identified early experiential anomalies that are consistent with all three of these facets. Phenomenological investigation might suggest that the seeming distinctness of the factors is only illusory: that loss of self-evidence, hyperreflexivity, and loss of vital contact are actually aspects of a single whole that we happen to be describing from several different angles of vision.

Cultural Frameworks

I have been speaking of guiding frameworks and assumptions and of habits of bodily activity and response. These, of course, will be affected by, and may in fact largely derive from, the particular sociocultural environment in which the person lives. Cultural forms and practices can be understood as "patterns of meanings embodied in symbols" and as sets of control mechanisms guiding experience and behavior (Geertz 1973:89, 44). As such, they tend to stabilize and legitimate a pervasive set of moods and motivations that lend a certain tone, sense of reality, and bias to our living. (I am speaking of cultural contexts with a reasonable degree of cohesion and coherence, and of relatively nonmarginalized persons. The exceptional status of both modernity and schizophrenia will be discussed later in this chapter.) Religious symbols and meanings, for example, provide not merely consolation but orientation. They do this by "inducing in the worshipper a certain distinctive set of dispositions (tendencies, capacities, propensities, skills, habits, liabilities, pronenesses) which lend a chronic character to the flow of his activity and the quality of his experience" (Geertz 1973:95).

The loss of natural self-evidence we have been examining will necessarily unhinge one from, and put one at odds with, the cultural surround – not only from mythic and religious meanings, but also from the habits and tacit framework assumptions that normally guide our everyday cognitive activity and ways of behaving. Such an unhinging necessarily makes it more difficult to feel a sense of solidarity with or trust in others, or to speak, think, and gesture with that easy synthesis of spontaneity and convention that identifies one as a member of a given social group. It is not difficult to see how this might lead to the forms of behavioral withdrawal and inaction of the negative-symptom syndrome. Somewhat less obvious, perhaps, is the disconcerting impact that such developments may have on everyday cognitive functioning.

In a recent book on cognitive anthropology, Bradd Shore (1996) describes the iterative processes of embedding that are necessary for the acculturation of ways of thinking, judging, and perceiving. Cultural knowledge, he notes, is distributed among different kinds of knowing that are "always layered as different kinds of knowledge, at different degrees of distance from focal awareness." It is the "tacit integration of deeper levels" that "makes possible the focal attention to levels of play closer to the surface" (Shore 1996:313). For a person afflicted with hyperreflexive tendencies, the initial internalization of cultural frames will be more difficult, and, once achieved, less likely to become stabilized and to persist. This can affect the long-term developmental processes involved in the inculcation of bodily, emotional, and cognitive ways of being and interacting (such as Bourdieu's *habitus*) over the course of maturation. This is what Blankenburg's patient Anne seems to be referring to when she describes other people as having effortlessly developed a habitual "way" or "manner of thinking," whereas for her everything seems to be an "*object* of thought" (see previous discussion). The failure of embedding may also disrupt the development of more short-lived patterns, such as the shared understanding of what can be presupposed and what needs to be more explicitly stated in the course of a developing conversation (as described in the work of the ethnomethodologists; Sacks 1992). Studies of schizophrenic language indicate that abnormalities are not a matter of syntax or semantics but of the pragmatic dimension – and involve, in large measure, the subtle and shifting patterns of tacit and explicit, of what can be presupposed as background versus what needs to be asserted in the course of a conversation (Schwartz 1982).

When there are failures of embedding, when the tacit becomes explicit, this should not be understood in purely quantitative terms – that is, as a surfeit of input, a flooding into consciousness that overloads some kind of limited-capacity processing mechanism. The effect of such a disembedding is also to prevent these framework assumptions from performing the organizing, world-stabilizing role that is so crucial for guiding the normal flow of activity and experience. A simple but suggestive confirmation of some of the consequences of this can be found in some research studies described in Roy D'Andrade's recent book, *The Development of Cognitive Anthropology* (1995:212–16).[13] These results suggest that adherence to group norms may have the advantage of encouraging a certain stability over time in one's conceptualizing of the world. D'Andrade (1995) speaks of the role of the social milieu in maintaining our "internal guidance systems," noting that goals are inclined to lose their force without social support (D'Andrade 1995:243). It appears, then, that there may be some intrinsic link between two of the most distinctive features of mental states associated with schizophrenia: the sheer eccentricity and the sometimes kaleidoscopic fluidity or slippage that are characteristic of their conceptual or cognitive style (see Holzman, Shenton, and Solovay, 1986; Sass 1992:124–34).

The way in which normally tacit or background assumptions can intrude into conscious awareness, thereby disrupting ongoing processes of thought and action, is vividly described in an autobiographical passage from a letter by Antonin Artaud. In the letter, Artaud describes his thinking as a "violent flow" of mutually interfering thoughts and as a "prolific and above all unstable and shifting juxtaposition" (Artaud 1965:293). But he immediately goes on to deny the sense of plenitude or vital excess this might seem to imply. Artaud's account shows that the violent flow and consequent disorganization is really a kind of hyperreflexive cascade – a proliferation of meta-perspectives involving a tendency to experience his own mind almost as if from an external standpoint. "The brain," he writes:

sees the whole thought at once with all its circumstances, and it also sees all the points of view it could take and all the forms with which it could invest them, a vast juxtaposition of concepts, each of which seems more necessary and also more dubious than the others, which all the complexities of syntax would never suffice to express and expound. (Artaud 1965:293)

Artaud describes himself as "losing contact *with*" but, at the same time, becoming focally aware *of* "all those first assumptions which are at the foundation of thought" (1965:290). Explicit awareness of the *conditions* of thought serves to undermine his capacity for sustained and focused thinking.

... this slackening, this confusion, this fragility ... correspond to an infinite number of new impressions and sensations, the most characteristic of which is a kind of disappearance or disintegration or collapse of first assumptions which even causes me to wonder why, for example, red (the color) is considered red and affects me as red, why a judgment affects me as a judgment and not as a pain, why I feel a pain, and why this particular pain, which I feel without understanding it ... (Artaud 1965:294)

This slippage of viewpoints seems to be the counterpart of a decline in the vital reactivity and spontaneous directedness that normally gives bias, direction, and a kind of organization to one's thinking. As Artaud explains with his characteristic precision:

in every [normal] state of consciousness there is always a dominant theme, and if the mind has not 'automatically' decided on a dominant theme it is through weakness and because at that moment nothing dominated, nothing presented itself with enough force or continuity in the field of consciousness to be recorded . . . in the absence of some precise thought that was able to develop, there was slackening, confusion, fragility. (Artaud 1965:293)

The anthropologist Shore (1996:107) also draws our attention to one potentiality that the embedding of cultural assumptions allows: the possibility of a paradoxical form of "marginal play" whereby a person draws attention to a cultural frame by defying it or otherwise calling it into question. Most societies have their quasi-ritualized, often carnivalesque ways of doing this, their institutionalized meta-moments when standard hierarchies are overturned and the usually unspoken comes to be said aloud. People with schizophrenia have a particularly fraught relationship to marginal play. Their alienation and hyperreflexivity can sometimes give them a kind of special insight into the arbitrariness and consequent absurdity of social conventions, and they often have a natural affinity for the marginalized and self-marginalizing edges of society. Often they seem to adopt what seems, in any particular society, to be the "path of most resistance" (Schooler and Caudill 1964:177), and they may adopt a stance of hyperautonomy and contrarianism that may be experienced as the epitome of willful defiance (Sass 1992:108–15). This contrarianism may involve, at least in part, an active identification with an outsider role that is also being imposed upon them by an ostracizing society. There is also a sense in which their cognitive eccentricities are more affliction than act – less a matter of being motivated to hear the beat of a different drummer than of simple inability to stay in step. Further, the meta-moves and frame breaking in which they so readily engage may also be rather beyond their control – not so much a game at which they play as a kind of uncontrolled slippage that plagues them. Whereas the phenomenologist, even in his armchair, must make a concerted effort to achieve this bracketing of everyday assumptions and the unnatural illumination that accompanies it, for the person with schizophrenia, the unnatural falling away happens all too easily, even in the midst of attempts at practical action (Blankenburg 1991:115–16; 70–1).

I have been talking about the relationship between schizophrenia and culture in general. But what if we consider *modern* culture or society in particular? Does modernity, or modernism, have any special relevance for schizophrenia? Elsewhere I have reviewed cross-cultural and transhistorical research, which indicates that schizophrenia seems to be more chronic and perhaps more severe in modern westernized societies, and which, in far more tentative fashion, may indicate that at least the withdrawn, autistic, flat-affect, or bizarre forms of schizophrenia may also have a higher incidence and prevalence in such societies (Sass 1992:355–74, 1994b, 1997; see also Beiser and Iacono 1990). Here I should like to focus more directly on the less dramatic experiences that are associated with the negative or fundamental symptoms. As we shall see, many central features of modern society described in canonical works of sociology seem almost identical to our portrait of schizophrenia. After discussing these affinities, I will speculate about the possible causal role that modernity might play in exacerbating or prolonging schizophrenia, and perhaps even in the etiology of some types or aspects of this condition.

Modernity

Perhaps the key feature of modernity, given our present concerns, is the attenuation of the unquestioned sense of inevitability or objective groundedness of prevailing cultural frameworks and assumptions. The sociologists Helmut Schelsky and Arnold Gehlen (Zijderveld 1986) describe the loss of a sense of intuitive ease and unproblematic accessibility and an accompanying subjectivism that occurs when individuals realize, at some level of awareness, that the values and grounding assumptions by which they live are, in some (not fully conscious) sense, chosen by them and then imposed on the world. Historians writing on the "history of mentalities" – such as Norbert Elias – have described a shift from extraverted traditional societies in which emotional life, organized through myth and ritual, is at the center, to the more introverted modern societies in which intellectual processes are far more dominant (Hutton 1981:243, 249). Peter Berger (1980:xi) describes this development as a shrinking of the background of human life, the domain of the taken-for-granted and the unnoticed, along with a concurrent expanding of the foreground, the realm of phenomena toward which we are likely to direct focal or analytic forms of attention and about which we might entertain doubt. By way of contrast, we might consider Evans-Pritchard's (1937) description of the tight web of belief he encountered among the Azande in the 1920s – where "every strand depends on every other strand, and a Zande cannot get out of its meshes because this is the only world he knows." The Zande does not experience this web as an "external structure in which he is enclosed. It is the texture of his thought and he cannot think that his thought is wrong" (Evans-Pritchard 1937:194–5).

Recent anthropology has thoroughly criticized the myth of the pure and internally coherent "primitive" or "tribal" society. Yet it remains true that in most tribal, traditional, or premodern cultures, skepticism is both rare and, when present, rather limited in scope. In *The Problem of Unbelief in the 16th Century*, Lucien Febvre (1982) describes how restricted and shallow the forms of unbelief were in that era, even in the case of a (for his time) avant-garde skeptic such as Rabelais. Certainly we do not find the "wholesale reflexivity," the "thoroughgoing, *constitutive* reflexivity," or "institutionalization of doubt" that Anthony Giddens (1990:39, 52, 176) discerns in the modern age.

The roots of these tendencies toward introspection and loss of commonsense certitude are often traced to Descartes (for example, Arendt 1958). But Descartes must be understood as merging into larger currents of sociopsychological development that transformed the very structures of selfhood. Panopticism and normalization (Foucault 1979); the literary journey into the interior that began in the eighteenth century (Heller 1976); the increasing preoccupation with the internal perception of our own bodies (*cenesthesia*) that marks the modern sensibility (Starobinski 1982); even the rise of the social or human sciences themselves: These and many other factors helped to foster a moral and social order that, in Charles Taylor's (1988:310) words, enjoins human beings "to turn inward and become aware of our own activity and of the processes that form us," to "stop simply living in the body or within our traditions and habits, and by making them objects for us, subject them to radical scrutiny and remaking."

One of the consequences of this self-detachment and accompanying relativism is what the poet Louis Aragon called "the vertigo of the modern" (quoted in Callinicos 1990:29), a condition clearly exemplified by Ulrich, the antihero protagonist of Robert Musil's great modernist novel, *The Man Without Qualities* (1965). Ulrich is a "possibilitarian" who has lived since childhood in a "subjunctive mood." It is difficult for him to make decisions; he too readily sees the arguments for all possible choices. In fact, Ulrich can hardly summon up any sense of reality at all; he experiences "only a world going in and out, aspects of the world falling into shape inside a head" (Musil 1965:7, 15, 71, 129). As a result, he is prone to contemplation and doubt rather than to strong emotions or impulses to act.

To understand the potential impact of the modern condition on at least one type of individual with schizophrenia, it is necessary to consider the impact of this kind of cultural setting on a person prone not only to withdrawal, detachment, and self-consciousness – *schizoid* tendencies or defenses – but to certain attentional disturbances as well – that is, to *schizotypal* disturbances that may make it difficult to hold stable a given framework or figure/ground orientation. The following statements by several patients capture the destabilizing cognitive slippage that is found in schizophrenic as well as schizotypal conditions: "Everything I think of always gets away from me." "Everything in me is changing continually." "My thoughts are so confused, everything is wavering, nothing is fixed – one cannot hold fast to anything" (Goldstein 1964:31). A person prone to this sort of slippage and loss of grounding is likely to suffer a diminished sense of vitality, motivation, or even legitimacy as a perspective on the world. One consequence of the loss of normal embeddedness in a framework is that the person must devote energy and a kind of active, conscious effort and control to processes that would normally take place automatically. The very constitution of self and world – a "transcendental operation" that normally occurs in a largely passive fashion (Blankenburg 1971:84) – may require an almost *physical* effort that uses up available resources. This may account, at least in part, for the lack of energy and the general sense of exhaustion so characteristic of the negative-symptom syndrome in schizophrenia (see Blankenburg 1971:132–3, 153–6, regarding schizophrenic "asthenia").

A person prone to this sort of slippage and hyperreflexivity will probably have difficulties in *any* society. His or her problems are, however, likely to be multiplied in a society with the *same* tendencies, for such a society will encourage tendencies (toward hyperreflexivity and alienation) that are already problematic for persons predisposed in this direction. This may help to account for the fact that schizophrenia seems to be a more chronic and severe condition in modernized than in more traditional cultural settings (Jablensky 1987). After all, it is not as if, in a modern, relativistic society, it is any less necessary to find assumptions and frameworks that are capable of organizing one's experience and guiding one's actions. To the contrary. Drawing a horizon around oneself may be more difficult in a relativistic culture lacking entrenched rituals and institutions, but it is also more necessary in an individualistic culture that combines relativistic trends with intense demands for efficiency and conformity of various kinds (see Gellner 1988:262). Nietzsche (1980:10) described as the basic condition of *all* life the need to live, much of the time, within a *single* perspective: "And this is a general law: every living thing can become healthy, strong and fruitful only within a horizon; if it is incapable of drawing a horizon around itself or, on the other hand, too selfish to restrict its vision to the limits of a horizon drawn by another, it will wither away feebly or overhastily to its early demise."

Traditionally, there have been two, rather different ways of conceiving how a person in a relativistic context can orient him- or herself within a perspective or horizon. One possibility is a kind of passive falling back, a lapsing into the most familiar and conventional habits of the average human being – into what Heidegger (1962:167) calls the condition of *das Man*. A second possibility is that of the Nietzschean superman – the person who actively creates an idiosyncratic or even unique orientation and style of being. Unfortunately, neither alternative seems very viable for a person with the fundamental or basic symptoms of schizophrenia.

One does at times have the sense that a person with schizophrenia is trying desperately hard to fit in with convention. Usually, however, there will be an awkward, stiff, or exaggerated quality that betrays something overly willful, disengaged, or self-conscious about the behavior. Alternatively, a person with schizophrenia (perhaps the *same* person at a different time) may also seem bent on inventing a completely original way of life almost out of thin air (see Binswanger 1987; Sass 1992:97–115). I knew one young man diagnosed as having schizophrenia who would spend hours inventing ways of dancing on one foot, or playing the piano without benefit of training or conventional knowledge of any kind. The reactionary, often somewhat exhibitionistic, quality of such behavior gives some indication of the effort it takes to sustain it. Truly to live with*in* such an orientation can hardly be easy for a person who must make a constant (and almost necessarily self-undermining) effort to *prevent* himself from lapsing into self-consciousness and detachment of various kinds.

Conclusion

In closing, I would like to say a word about the special interest that the study of schizophrenia and subjectivity holds for those working at the interdisciplinary border between the study of culture and of the individual psyche, normal or abnormal.

With the recent resurgence of cognitive anthropology and cultural psychology, scholars are taking considerable interest in developmental processes whereby cultural schemas mold the psyche as well as in dynamic processes whereby these schemas organize ongoing action. In this context, schizophrenia is of interest both for what such persons come to notice and for what they fail to do. Through their hyperreflexivity and loss of natural self-evidence, such persons can bring to light various assumptions and frameworks that might otherwise go unnoticed. Also, their tendency toward a rather unnatural kind of illumination makes us aware of the crucial role that the tacit dimension plays in normal processes of experience and acculturation. It helps us appreciate how frameworks can fail to be internalized or to maintain the tacit status that is necessary for them to play their organizing, world-constituting role.

People with schizophrenia are of special interest for a second reason as well, one that has to do with basic notions about the relationship of illness and society.

The relationship between psychopathology and social norms has often been understood as conforming to one of two opposite patterns. According to a view endorsed by Ruth Benedict, what counts as illness or pathology in a given social context will sometimes be propensities that *deviate* from the norms the culture endorses as the essence or ideal of human nature (Benedict 1934/1964; Foucault 1987:61); she refers to such persons as "abnormals of conflict." If individualism is exalted among the Kwakiutl and suppressed among the Zuni, it follows that extreme autonomy will seem healthy in the first context, but pathological in the second. But psychopathology may also involve an *exaggeration* of the norm – an exacerbation of widely distributed and favored propensities, which, however, are normally tempered by conflicting characteristics or a healthy inclination toward moderation. Benedict spoke here of the "abnormals of extreme fulfillment of the cultural type." Here one might think of Christopher Lasch's conception of narcissistic disorders or, closer to our present concerns, of George Devereux's (1980) understanding of schizophrenia as "the typical ethnic psychosis of complex civilized societies" (quoted in Jablensky 1987:163), an exaggeration of the "basically schizoid" character of the modern human being. Schizophrenia, at least as I have been characterizing it here, seems to have a peculiar status, for there is a sense in which it fits into both of these abstract possibilities.

The loss of commonsense obviously involves deviation from the norm. It is, in fact, a sort of *quintessential*, or perhaps one should say, a kind of *meta*-deviation – one that results not from some tendency to develop traits that just *happen* to be devalued in a particular society but from an incapacity for, or refusal of, acculturation as such.[14] But as I hope was established here, there is also a clear sense in which schizophrenia typifies some of the most characteristic features of modernity. Nietzsche (1980:7, 50) might easily have been thinking of schizophrenia (at least as we find it in modernized societies) when he described "fragmentation and fraying of all foundations" as among the "remarkable symptoms of our age."

We might say, then, that schizophrenia is really a kind of *meta*-pathology – and in both a psychological and a social sense. As a mode of individual experience, it is often characterized by a kind of disconcerting meta-consciousness, a hyperreflexive awareness that can bring the patient face-to-face with abstract dimensions as well as concrete particulars of experience that usually recede into the background of awareness. But it is also a kind of meta-deviation on the social plane – a condition whose anomalous and alienated/alienating status is not accidental but essential to its very nature. Let us recall, in closing, that modernity is, in certain crucial respects, *also* a meta-phenomenon – a kind of *meta*-culture or *meta*-society. I do not mean to imply that modern society somehow manages to be all embracing, to transcend all the idiosyncrasy or narrowness of perspective characteristic of all other societies. I do, however, wish to call attention to the special affinity modernity has for self-consciousness and meta-awareness – that is, to its preoccupation with its own underlying assumptions and rules as well as with personal and cultural counterfactuals of all sorts. Here, then, we discover what is perhaps the deepest affinity between schizophrenia and modern society: Each is defined by forms of hyperreflexivity that lie at the core of its decentered, ever self-decentering soul.

NOTES

1 On Jackson and his influence, see Stengel (1963); Clark (1981); Berrios (1985).
2 A translation of a key Blankenburg article (Blankenburg 1969) will appear in a future issue of the journal *Philosophy, Psychiatry, Psychology*.
3 Page numbers given second and in italics are from the German edition.
4 In Blankenburg's view, it is *because* the patient has already lost the self-evidence of normal frameworks of meaning that he is now forced to notice these frameworks, and to struggle to construct, in a deliberate and conscious manner, new frameworks by which to live.
5 Research on the basic symptoms shows that decline in dynamic aspects are to be found among the earliest symptoms. Klosterkoetter and colleagues (1997) describe, for example, a cluster of basic symptoms involving disturbances of concentration, of immediate recall, and of thought initiative or "thought energy," as well as a retardation and impediment of thought processes.
6 At times, schizophrenics appear to experience something akin to *Heideggerian Angst*: the anxiety born of registering the arbitrariness of any particular way of looking at life and the vertigo this can engender. At other times, they experience the more nihilistic anxiety described in Sartre's *Nausea*: the sense of living in a world in which pure matter, devoid of all human meaning or purpose, looms forth as the only realm that truly exists (Sass 1992:49, 139).
7 I take the term "operative" from Merleau-Ponty (1962:xviii). For discussion of the distinction between operative and reflective hyperreflexivity, see Sass (2000).
8 The combination of loss of natural self-evidence and of diminished vital contact is nicely illustrated in "The Street," a short prose piece by Robert Walser, a writer who suffered from schizophrenia (1982:123–5).
9 The term "intentional" has an everyday as well as a technical meaning: It refers both to the volitional or willful quality of a given action and to the object directedness of the act of consciousness. Polanyi's account shows how tightly linked these two aspects really are; for it implies that the structure of awareness – for example, what is a focal and what a subsidiary element of awareness – is bound up with the nature of one's practical orientation and goal directedness.

10 We now know that emotion-related, spontaneous movement sequences and deliberate or voluntary actions are actually triggered in two different parts of the brain (Damasio 1994). The facial expressions of a person who relies on deliberation and volitional control will, therefore, look awkward, artificial, and unconvincing – as often seems the case in schizophrenia. As an illustration, consider the strangely off-putting self-portraits by Messerschmidt, a psychotic sculptor of the eighteenth century (Kris 1964).

11 On habits of bodily being, see Bourdieu's (1990) notion of the *habitus*. On cognitive framework assumptions, see Foucault's (1994) notion of the *episteme*.

12 Constructing such models can be useful for generating etiological hypotheses – for example, for suggesting how we might understand the experiential implications of certain neurocognitive abnormalities or sociocultural factors, and how any given factor might give rise to different aspects of schizophrenic experience. The possible pathogenic or pathoplastic significance of certain aspects of the modern social order is discussed in the text. It is interesting to speculate about the possible correspondences between particular neurocognitive abnormalities and particular abnormalities on the experiential plane. The hypothesis of defective working memory, for example, might seem most directly to implicate the issue of natural self-evidence, for it is working memory that supplies the frameworks of expectation that constitute our sense of existing within familiar horizons. The notion of a (hippocampus-based) dysfunction of the "comparator-system" seems to point most directly to the issue of hyperreflexivity, since in the absence of this normal function, what is usually presupposed (for example, tacit sensations of body awareness) are likely to emerge into focal awareness. Abnormalities in feedback of willed intention (so-called "efferent feedback") might be closest to the notion of loss of vital contact, since such a condition implies a passive, merely observational experience of one's own action and thinking.

13 D'Andrade describes a study in which the anthropologist James Bolster examined the use of semantic categories pertaining to different types of manioc plants in the folk botany of the Jivaro people. Bolster found a striking correlation between the *conventionality* and the *reliability* over time of a given Jivaro informant's semantic categories. Those Jivaro individuals whose choice of semantic labels correlated most highly with that of the group, were also the ones who tended to call a particular type of manioc plant by the same name when shown it on a later occasion. D'Andrade (1995:214) relates this to a word association study that found a correlation between the commonality or conventionality of an individual's word association responses and the tendency for that individual to give the same associations to a given stimulus word when the word was repeated on a later occasion (Moran, Mefferd, and Kimble 1964). A sample of individuals diagnosed with schizophrenia was included in the word association study, and, interestingly enough, those with schizophrenia produced fewer modal or conventional responses and were also less consistent or reliable over time in the associations they gave.

14 It is interesting that individuals with a schizophrenic diagnosis, when studied cross-culturally, often seem to go against, or to pervert, *whatever* the most important norms are in a given culture, as if they nearly always managed to

avoid, reject, or distort what matters most. (Their deviance is not necessarily rejection; it may sometimes involve parodylike exaggeration of conventional behavior; see Laing [1965:102]; Binswanger [1987].) The fact that schizophrenic behavior may be remarkably heterogeneous on a literal level does not necessarily argue against its existence as a real entity, as is sometimes claimed (for example, Barrett 1998). As I suggest in this chapter, these heterogeneous behaviors do share the more abstract quality of (society-relative) deviation, and this quality may itself stem from some common psychological or even neurocognitive characteristics.

REFERENCES

Angyal, Andras. 1936. "The Experience of the Body-self in Schizophrenia." *Archives of Neurological Psychiatry* 35: 1029–53.

Arendt, Hannah. 1958. *The Human Condition*. Chicago, IL: University of Chicago Press.

Artaud, Antonin. 1965. *Antonin Artaud Anthology*. J. Hirschman, ed. San Francisco, CA: City Lights Books.

———. 1976. *Antonin Artaud: Selected Writings*. S. Sontag, ed., H. Weaver, trans. New York: Farrar, Straus, and Giroux.

Barrett, Robert. 1998. "The 'Schizophrenic' and the Liminal *Persona* in Modern Society" (review of Sass, *Madness and Modernism*). *Culture, Medicine and Psychiatry* 22: 465–94.

Beiser, Morton and W. G. Iacono. 1990. "An Update on the Epidemiology of Schizophrenia." *Canadian Journal of Psychiatry* 35: 657–68.

Benedict, Ruth. 1934/1964. "Anthropology and the Abnormal." In D. Haring, ed. *Personal Character and Cultural Milieu*. Syracuse, NY: Syracuse University Press.

Berger, Peter. 1980. "Foreword." In A. Gehlen, ed., P. Lipscomb, trans., pp. vii–xvi. *Man in the Age of Technology*. New York: Columbia University Press.

Berrios, German E. 1985. "Positive and Negative Symptoms and Jackson: A Conceptual History." *Archives of General Psychiatry* 42: 95–7.

Binswanger, L. 1987. "Extravagance, Perverseness, Manneristic Behavior and Schizophrenia." In J. Cutting and M. Shepherd, eds., pp. 83–8. *The Clinical Roots of the Schizophrenia Concept*. Cambridge, UK: Cambridge University Press.

Blankenburg, Wolfgang. 1969. "Ansatze zu einer Psychopathologie des 'Common Sense.'" *Confinia Psychiatrica* 12: 144–63.

Blankenburg, Wolfgang. 1991. *La Perte de L'Evidence Naturelle: Une Contribution a la Psychopathologie des Schizophrenies Pauci-Symptomatiques*. J. M. Azorin and Y. Totoyan, trans. Paris: Presses Universitaires de France. (Originally appeared in German in 1971: *Der Verlust der Naturlichen Selbstverstaendlichkeit: Ein Beitrag zur Psychopathologie Symptomarmer Schizophrenien*. Stuttgart: Ferdinand Enke Verlag.)

Bourdieu, Pierre. 1990. *The Logic of Practice*. R. Nice, trans. Stanford, CA: Stanford University Press.

Callinicos, Alex. 1990. *Against Postmodernism*. New York: St. Martin's Press.

Clark, Michael J. 1981. "The Rejection of Psychological Approaches to Mental Disorder in Late Nineteenth-century British Psychiatry." In A. Scull, ed., pp. 271–312. *Madhouses, Mad Doctors, and Madmen: The Social History of Psychiatry in the Victorian Era.* Philadelphia: University of Pennsylvania Press.

Cutting, J. 1991. "Books Reconsidered: *La Schizophrenie*: E. Minkowski." *British Journal of Psychiatry* 158: 293–5.

Cutting, J. and D. Murphy. 1988. "Schizophrenic Thought Disorder: A Psychological and Organic Interpretation." *British Journal of Psychiatry* 152: 310–19.

_____. 1990. "Impaired Ability of Schizophrenics, Relative to Manics or Depressives, to Appreciate Social Knowledge about Their Culture." *British Journal of Psychiatry* 157: 355–8.

Damasio, Antonio. 1994. *Descartes' Error: Emotion, Reason, and the Human Brain.* New York: Avon Books.

D'Andrade, Roy. 1995. *The Development of Cognitive Anthropology.* Cambridge, UK: Cambridge University Press.

Devereux, George. 1980. *Basic Problems of Ethnopsychiatry.* Chicago, IL: University of Chicago Press.

Evans-Pritchard, E. E. 1937. *Witchcraft, Oracles, and Magic Among the Azande.* Oxford: Oxford University Press.

Febvre, Lucien. 1982. *The Problem of Unbelief in the 16th Century.* B. Gottlieb, trans. Cambridge, MA and London: Harvard University Press.

Foucault, Michel. 1979. *Discipline and Punish: The Birth of the Prison.* A. Sheridan, trans. New York: Vintage Books.

_____. 1987. *Mental Illness and Psychology.* A. Sheridan, trans. Berkeley: University of California Press.

_____. 1994. *The Order of Things: An Archaeology of the Human Sciences.* New York: Vintage Books.

Gallagher, Shaun and Andrew Meltzoff. 1996. "The Earliest Sense of Self and Others: Merleau-Ponty and Recent Developmental Studies." *Philosophical Psychology* 9: 211–33.

Geertz, Clifford. 1973. *The Interpretation of Cultures.* New York: Basic Books.

Gellner, Ernest. 1988. *Plough, Sword, and Book.* London: Collins Harvill.

Giddens, Athony. 1990. *The Consequences of Modernity.* Stanford, CA: Stanford University Press.

Goldstein, Kurt. 1964. "Methodological Approach to the Study of Schizophrenic Thought Disorder." In J. S. Kasanin, ed., pp. 17–40. *Language and Thought in Schizophrenia.* New York: Norton.

Heidegger, Martin. 1962. *Being and Time.* J. Macquarrie and E. Robinson, trans. New York: Harper and Row.

Heller, Erich. 1976. *The Artist's Journey into the Interior and Other Essays.* San Diego, CA: Harcourt, Brace, Jovanovich.

Holzman, Philip S., Martha E. Shenton, and Margie R. Solovay. 1986. "Quality of Thought Disorder in Differential Diagnosis." *Schizophrenia Bulletin* 12: 360–72.

Hunt, Harry. 1985. "Cognition and States of Consciousness." *Perceptual and Motor Skills* 60: 239–82.

Hutton, Patrick. 1981. "The History of Mentalities: The New Map of Cultural History." *History and Theory* 20: 237–59.

Jablensky, Assen. 1987. "Multicultural Studies and the Nature of Schizophrenia: A Review." *Journal of the Royal Society of Medicine* 80: 162–7.

Jackson, John Hughlings. 1932. "The Factors of Insanities." In J. Taylor, ed. *Selected Writings of John Hughlings Jackson*, vol. II. London: Hodder and Stoughton.

Kleinman, Arthur. 1987. "Anthropology and Psychiatry: The Role of Culture in Cross-cultural Research on Illness." *British Journal of Psychiatry* 151: 447–54.

Klosterkoetter, J. 1992. "The Meaning of Basic Symptoms for the Development of Schizophrenic Psychoses." *Neurology, Psychiatry, and Brain Research* 1: 30–41.

Klosterkoetter, J., G. Gross, G. Huber, A. Wieneke, E. M. Steinmeyer, and F. Schultze-Lutter. 1997. "Evaluation of the 'Bonn Scale for the Assessment of Basic Symptoms-BSABS' as an Instrument for the Assessment of Schizophrenia Proneness: A Review of Recent Findings." *Neurology, Psychiatry, and Brain Research* 5: 137–50.

Kris, Ernst. 1964. *Psychoanalytic Explorations in Art*. New York: Schocken.

Laing, Ronald David. 1965. *The Divided Self*. Harmondsworth, UK: Penguin.

McGlashan, T. H. and W. S. Fenton. 1992. "The Positive-negative Distinction in Schizophrenia: Review of Natural History Validators." *Archives of General Psychiatry* 49: 63–72.

Merleau-Ponty, Maurice. 1945. *Phénoménologie de la perception*. Paris: Gallimard.

——. 1962. *The Phenomenology of Perception*. C. Smith, trans. London: Routledge and Kegan Paul.

Minkowski, Eugène. 1927. *La Schizophrenie*. Paris: Payot.

——. 1987. "The Essential Disorder Underlying Schizophrenia and Schizophrenic Thought." In J. Cutting and M. Shepherd, eds., pp. 188–212. *The Clinical Roots of the Schizophrenia Concept*. Cambridge, UK: Cambridge University Press.

——. 1999 [1966]. *Traite de Psychopathologie*. Paris: Synthelab.

Moran, L. J., R. B. Mefferd, and J. P. Kimble. 1964. "Idiosyncratic Sets in Word Association." *Psychology Monographs: General and Applied* 78: 1–22.

Musil, Robert. 1965. *The Man Without Qualities*. New York: Perigee.

Nietzsche, Friedrich. 1980. *On the Advantage and Disadvantage of History for Life*. P. Preuss, trans. Indianapolis, IN: Hackett.

Parnas, Joseph and Pierre Bovet. 1991. "Autism in Schizophrenia Revisited." *Comprehensive Psychiatry* 32: 7–21.

Polanyi, Michael. 1964. *Personal Knowledge: Toward a Post-Critical Philosophy*. New York: Harper Torchbooks.

——. 1967. *The Tacit Dimension*. Garden City, NY: Anchor Books.

Sacks, Harvey. 1992. *Lectures on Conversation*. Oxford: Blackwell.

Sartre, Jean-Paul. 1956. *Being and Nothingness*. H. E. Barnes, trans. New York: Philosophical Library.

Sass, Louis. 1992. *Madness and Modernism: Insanity in the Light of Modern Art, Literature, and Thought*. New York: Basic Books.

——. 1994a. *The Paradoxes of Delusion: Wittgenstein, Schreber, and the Schizophrenic Mind*. Ithaca, NY and London: Cornell University Press.

_____. 1994b. "Civilized Madness: Schizophrenia, Self-consciousness, and the Modern Mind." *History of the Human Sciences* (special issue on "Identity, Self, and Subject) 7: 83–120.

_____. 1996 " 'The Catastrophes of Heaven': Modernism, Primitivism, and the Madness of Antonin Artaud." *Modernism/Modernity* 3: 73–91.

_____. 1997. "The Consciousness Machine: Self and Subjectivity in Schizophrenia and Modern Culture." In U. Neisser and D. Jopling, eds., pp. 203–32. *The Conceptual Self in Context: Culture, Experience, Self-Understanding.* Cambridge, UK and New York: Cambridge University Press.

_____. 2000. "Schizophrenia, Self-experience, and the So-called 'Negative Symptoms.'" In D. Zahavi, ed., pp. 149–82. *Exploring the Self: Philosophical and Psychopathological Perspectives on Self-Experience.* Amsterdam: John Benjamins Publishing Co.

Schooler, Carmi and William Caudill. 1964. "Symptomatology in Japanese and American Schizophrenics." *Ethnology* 3: 172–8.

Schwartz, Steven. 1982. "Is There a Schizophrenic Language?" *Behavioral and Brain Sciences* 5: 579–88.

Selten, John-Paul, Robert J. Van Den Bosch, and A. E. S. Sijben. 1998. "The Subjective Experience of Negative Symptoms." In X. F. Amador and A. S. David, eds., pp. 78–90. *Insight and Psychosis.* Oxford and New York: Oxford University Press.

Shore, Bradd. 1996. *Culture in Mind: Cognition, Culture, and the Problem of Meaning.* New York: Oxford University Press.

Starobinski, J. 1982. "A Short History of Body Consciousness." S. Matthews, trans. *Humanities in Society* 1: 22–39.

Stengel, E. 1963. "Hughlings Jackson's Influence in Psychiatry." *British Journal of Psychiatry* 109: 348–55.

Taylor, Charles. 1988. "The Moral Topography of the Self." In S. Messer, L. Sass, and R. Woolfolk, eds., pp. 298–320. *Hermeneutics and Psychological Theory.* New Brunswick, NJ: Rutgers University Press

Walser, Robert. 1982. *Selected Stories.* C. Middleton et al., trans. New York: Farrar, Straus, and Giroux.

Zijderveld, Anton C. 1986. "The Challenges of Modernity." In J. D. Hunter and S. C. Ainlay, eds., pp. 57–75. *Making Sense of Modern Times.* London: Routledge and Kegan Paul.

13 Subjective Experience of Emotion in Schizophrenia

Ann M. Kring and *Marja K. Germans**

... [I]t has appeared both from crude observation and from detailed study of the facial expression that the alleged indifference, apathy, and emotional disharmony of the schizophrenic is more a matter of impression than correct evaluation of the inner experience of such a patient. It has followed that the study of such inner affective experiences by positive objective means seems urgently indicated if the nature of the schizophrenic processes is to be elucidated. Harry Stack Sullivan 1927.

The notion that schizophrenia patients' subjective experience of emotion might not match their facial expressions is not new. Indeed, early theorists, including Sullivan and Bleuler, among others, commented on an apparent discrepancy between what schizophrenia patients reported feeling and what they outwardly expressed to others. Moreover, family members have noted that their ill relatives often report experiencing strong emotions. For example, Bouricius (1989) presented samples of her son's diary writings, which articulated the experience of clear and complex emotions. Nonetheless, psychological research into the emotional features of schizophrenia has lagged behind the astute observations of the early theorists and family members.

In this chapter, we will concentrate on one aspect of the subjective experience of schizophrenia, namely the subjective experience of emotion. In our view, which is shared by a number of psychological researchers, emotions are complex, multichannel systems that have developed through the course of human evolutionary history to help us deal with problems, challenges, and other events and stimuli in our environment. An emotional response consists of at least three components, including a behavioral or expressive component, a subjective or experiential component, and a physiological component. A number of researchers, particularly in psychology, have demonstrated that the coordinated engagement of these emotion components subserves both intra- and interpersonal functions in nondisordered individuals. For example, emotions motivate goal-directed behavior (for example, Nesse 1990; Frijda 1994), and they influence attention toward relevant events in the environment (for example, Frijda 1994; Levenson 1994). However, emotions also serve a number of social or interpersonal functions, including the ways in which emotions are embedded within ongoing social interactions (for example, Averill 1982; Campos, Campos, and Barrett 1989; Lutz and Abu-Lughod 1990). For example, emotional expressions promote social communication by providing information about the social environment and by evoking emotions in others with whom we interact (Keltner and Kring 1998). As we will articulate, the various emotion components are not often coordinated in schizophrenia, and thus a number of the important functions that emotions subserve are not fully realized (Keltner and Kring 1998; Kring and Bachorowski 1999). Indeed, the very nature of these emotion disturbances in schizophrenia contributes to the difficulty inherent in understanding the experience of schizophrenia. Moreover, the interpersonal consequences of emotion disturbances in schizophrenia may constitute a great impediment to intersubjectivity.

We will first review findings on the subjective experience of emotion in schizophrenia, focusing on historical writings and theories, the description and measurement of emotion-related symptomatology, and more recent psychological research on the nature of emotion disturbance in schizophrenia. In the course of the review, we will distinguish studies that examine schizophrenia patients' feelings in response to emotional situations and stimuli from studies that examine patients' feelings about their illness. In addition, we will argue that these emotion disturbances contribute to difficulties in interpersonal interactions and relationships. Next, we will highlight important gaps in our knowledge about the subjective experience of emotion in schizophrenia with an eye toward directions for additional research. Finally, we will discuss the implications of the findings on emotion in schizophrenia for the assessment and treatment of the disorder.

Historical Perspectives and Emotional Symptoms of Schizophrenia

As noted previously, early theorists wrote extensively about emotional disturbances in schizophrenia. For example, Bleuler wrote:

Occasionally, a patient will maintain that he has a marked and powerful affect, whereas the observer can note none or another type of affect than that which the patient professes to feel. (Bleuler 1950:51)

Here we see the suggestion that there may be a dissociation between what patients seemed to *experience* emotionally compared to what they *display* outwardly. In contrast to this description of "powerful feeling," both Bleuler (1950) and Kraeplin (1971) also wrote that patients often appeared to be emotionally indifferent or that they experienced little pleasurable emotion, a deficit state better known as anhedonia. Interestingly, Rado (1956) hypothesized that schizophrenia patients' anhedonia contributed to an increase in the experience of negative emotions, since hedonic experience may serve to buffer against the experience of negative emotions.

Despite these rich clinical descriptions of the emotional features of schizophrenia, systematic research on these features was not conducted until fairly recently. The attenuated expressivity and hedonic deficit described by these early theorists are most often referred to today as the symptoms of flat affect and anhedonia. Contemporary research on the emotional features of schizophrenia in general and these two symptoms in particular has been greatly aided by the development of reliable symptom rating scales. These include the Scale for the Assessment of Negative Symptoms (SANS); (see Andreasen [1982]) and the Schedule for the Deficit Syndrome (SDS); (see Kirkpatrick, Buchanan, McKinney, Alphs, and Carpenter [1989]). For a review, see Earnst and Kring 1997). According to clinical rating scales such as these, flat affect is typically defined by diminished outward expression of emotion. Patients with this symptom may speak in a monotone voice, have poor eye contact, use few gestures, and display a blank and unchanging facial expression. Anhedonia, on the other hand, is defined as an inability to experience pleasure. Patients with this symptom may report experiencing little or no pleasure in response to purportedly pleasurable events, such as eating, sexual activity, or engaging in social interaction. Although perhaps obvious, it is nonetheless important to note that ratings of flat affect are made based upon an interviewer's *observation* of the patient's behavior. By contrast, ratings of anhedonia are based upon the patient's report of their *subjective* states.

Both flat affect and anhedonia are fairly common symptoms of schizophrenia. By one analysis, flat affect is observed in as many as two-thirds of patients with schizophrenia (WHO 1973), although there is also evidence that prevalence of flat affect is likely to vary by culture, and that there are unresolved methodological problems with the assessment of flat affect across cultures (Jenkins 1994). Moreover, flat affect may be relatively chronic (Knight, Roff, Barnett, and Moss 1979); stable across time (Pfohl and Winokur 1982; Kring and Earnst 1999; but see Keefe, Lobel, Mohs, Silverman, Harvey, Davidson, Losonczy, and Davis 1991); related to a poor prognosis (Carpenter, Bartko, Strauss, and Hawk 1978; Knight and Roff 1985; Fenton and McGlashan 1991); and more common in schizophrenia than in depression (Andreasen 1979).

Anhedonia appears to be as prevalent as flat affect in schizophrenia. For example, of a sample of 187 schizophrenia patients, 76 percent showed at least some hedonic deficit and 23 percent showed severe anhedonia (Fenton and McGlashan 1991). Anhedonia appears to be related to poorer premorbid functioning (Katsanis, Iacono, Beiser, and Lacey 1992; Rey, Bailer, Brauer, Handel, Lauberstein, and Stein 1994); is stable across time and clinical state (Keefe et al.1991; Lewine 1991; Blanchard, Mueser, and Bellack 1998); and although anhedonia seems to be present throughout the course of the disorder, it appears to be more severe in chronic schizophrenia (Harrow, Grinker, Holzman, Kayton 1977; Keefe et al. 1991).

Psychological Research on Emotion in Schizophrenia

Perhaps one of the more well-replicated findings in the literature on emotion in schizophrenia is that schizophrenia patients are less expressive (both facially and vocally) than nonpatients in response to a variety of contexts and stimuli, including emotionally evocative films (Berenbaum and Oltmanns 1992; Kring, Kerr, Smith, and Neale 1993; Mattes, Schneider, Heimann, and Birbaumer 1995; Kring and Earnst 2003; Kring and Neale 1996), cartoons (Dworkin, Clark, Amador, and Gorman 1996), and social interactions (Borod, Alpert, Brozgold, Martin, Welkowitz, Diller, Peselow, Angrist, and Lieberman 1989; Krause, Steimer, Sanger-Alt, and Wagner 1989; Martin, Borod, Alpert, Brozgold, and Welkowitz 1990; Kring, Alpert, Neale, and Harvey 1994; Mattes et al. 1995). Moreover, schizophrenia patients' pattern of facial and vocal expression have been distinguished from other patient groups with symptoms that bear resemblance to flat affect, including depression, Parkinson's Disease, and patients with right hemisphere brain damage (Levin, Hall, Knight, and Alpert 1985; Borod et al. 1989; Martin et al. 1990; Berenbaum and Oltmanns 1992). Using a variety of measures of emotional expression, these findings corroborate clinical ratings of flat affect.

However, what makes these findings all the more interesting, is that despite their diminished expressive behavior, schizophrenia patients reported experiencing similar, and in some cases, greater amounts of emotion compared to nonpatients. In our own work, we have found the same basic pattern in four different studies. Namely, schizophrenia patients report experiencing about the same amount of positive emotion in response to positive film clips, and they report experiencing more negative emotion in response to both positive and negative film clips. This pattern is illustrated in Figure 13.1. These data support Bleuler's early observation that schizophrenia patients' outward display of emotion does

Positive Emotion

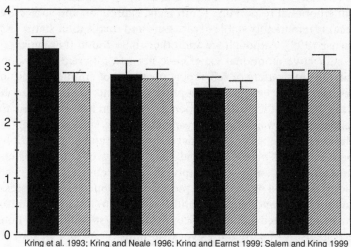

Kring et al. 1993; Kring and Neale 1996; Kring and Earnst 1999; Salem and Kring 1999

Negative Emotion

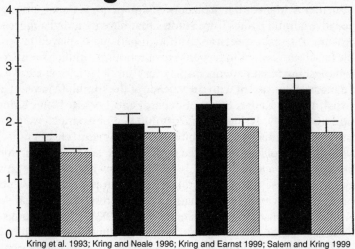

Kring et al. 1993; Kring and Neale 1996; Kring and Earnst 1999; Salem and Kring 1999

Figure 13.1.

333

not provide an accurate representation of their subjective experience of emotion.

It is important to point out that we and others have found this same pattern both when patients were on medication (Berenbaum and Oltmanns 1992), and when they were off medication (Kring et al. 1993; Kring and Neale 1996; Kring and Earnst 2003). Moreover, we have found that emotional responding (both facial expression and subjective experience) is remarkably stable across time and medication status (Kring and Earnst 1999). Although we and others have found that patients' reports of subjective emotional experience are not different from nonpatients using a wide variety of self-report measures of emotion, it has nonetheless been suggested that schizophrenia patients cannot report how they actually feel but instead are reporting based on how they think the investigators might want them to respond (that is, response bias). However, additional evidence of emotional responding renders the possibility of response bias less plausible. Recall that our view of emotion posits at least three emotion components: expression, subjective experience, and physiology. Adding a physiological measure of emotion to their assessment of emotional responding, Kring and Neale (1996) found that schizophrenia patients exhibited greater skin conductance responding than nonpatients in response to emotionally evocative films, even though they displayed very few observable facial expressions. This finding is consistent with now classic research by Venables who demonstrated that schizophrenia patients with flat affect exhibited greater skin conductance responding than patients without flat affect (Venables and Wing 1962).

Further evidence that schizophrenia patients respond emotionally to evocative stimuli comes from studies that have included a more sensitive measure of facial expression. Although patients displayed fewer observable facial expressions in response to emotional stimuli, a number of studies have shown that patients display very subtle, microexpressive displays in a manner consistent with the valence of the stimuli (Mattes et al. 1995; Earnst, Kring, Kadar, Salem, Shepard, and Loosen 1996; Kring, Kerr, and Earnst 1999; Kring and Earnst 2003). For example, we have shown that schizophrenia patients exhibit more zygomatic (cheek) muscle activity, which is typically associated with positive emotion, than corrugator (brow) muscle activity, which is typically associated with negative emotion, in response to positive stimuli. By contrast, patients exhibit more corrugator activity than zygomatic activity in response to negative stimuli (Kring and Earnst 1999; Kring and Earnst 2003). These findings of more subtle facial muscle activity in response to emotional stimuli bolster the conclusion that schizophrenia patients are responding emotionally.

Although schizophrenia patients may exhibit subtle facial expressions, these displays are not observable to others, and this relative inexpression has a number of interpersonal consequences. For example, spouses of schizophrenia patients with negative symptoms, including flat affect, reported greater marital dissatisfaction (Hooley, Richters, Weintraub, and Neale 1987). Healthy individuals reported experiencing more fear and sadness and were themselves less expressive when they interacted with a schizophrenia patient than when they interacted with another healthy individual (Krause, Steiner-Krause, and Hufnagel 1992). Using symptom rating scales to measure diminished expressivity, Bellack, Morrison, Wixtead, and Mueser (1990) found that patients who were least expressive had poorer interpersonal relationships and poorer adjustment at home and in other social domains. Without the benefit of overt signs of emotion, others may misinterpret the ongoing emotional state of a patient with schizophrenia. Moreover, there is some evidence indicating that schizophrenia patients may not be aware of how unexpressive they are (Kring 1991). Thus, patients may not understand others' reactions in ongoing interactions, and they may not take alternate measures to make their internal emotional state known.

One initially puzzling finding from our studies of emotional responding in schizophrenia was that patients' reports of positive emotion were not dampened, which might be expected given the prevalence of anhedonia in schizophrenia. Before reconciling this finding with other findings on anhedonia, it is first necessary to briefly review the relevant literature on anhedonia in schizophrenia.

Anhedonia in Schizophrenia

In addition to clinical rating scales, perhaps the most widely used measures of anhedonia are scales that were developed by Chapman and colleagues (Chapman, Chapman, and Raulin 1976) based on the theories of Meehl (1962, 1973) and Rado (1956). Chapman and colleagues developed the Scales for Physical and Social Anhedonia to measure stable individual differences in the capacity to experience sensual and social-interpersonal pleasure, respectively. The Scale for Physical Anhedonia consists of sixty-one true/false items describing various purportedly pleasurable experiences involving eating, touching, feeling, sex, movement, smell, and sound, with higher scores indicating greater anhedonia. The Scale for Social Anhedonia, on the other hand, purportedly taps the nonphysical pleasures of being with other people: socializing, talking, competing, and interacting with people in other ways.

As part of the development and validation of these scales, Chapman et al. (1976) found that schizophrenia patients (all medicated, all male) scored higher than nonpatient controls on both the Physical Anhedonia (PAS) and the Social Anhedonia (SAS) scales. Other studies have since replicated the finding that schizophrenia patients score higher than non-patients on one or both of these scales (Clementz, Grove, Katsanis, and Iacono 1991; Grove, Lebow, Clementz, Cerri, Medus, and Iacono 1991; Berenbaum and Oltmanns 1992; Blanchard, Bellack, and Mueser 1994; Schlenker, Cohen, and Hopmann 1995; Blanchard, Mueser, and Bellack 1998).

Only a small number of studies have examined the relationship between clinical rating scale measures of anhedonia and the Chapman scales. Lewine (1991) found that the PAS was significantly related to the SANS ratings of anhedonia while patients were both on and off medication. By contrast, Blanchard et al. (1994) found that interviewer ratings of SANS anhedonia-asociality were not significantly correlated with either the PAS or SAS. Blanchard and colleagues argued that the failure to find a significant correlation between these two measures was due largely to a difference in the time period on which the measures were based. That is, the SANS measure of anhedonia referred to the time spent in the hospital, where patients were exposed to limited sources of pleasure, whereas the Chapman scales presumably tapped a larger domain of experience.

Although many schizophrenia patients are more anhedonic than non-patients, it remains unclear whether schizophrenia patients differ from other psychiatric patients. Blanchard et al. (1994) found that schizophrenia patients scored higher than bipolar patients on both scales. However, other studies have failed to find differences between schizophrenia patients and other psychiatric groups on these scales. Schuck, Leventhal, Rothstein, and Irizarry (1984) found that schizophrenia patients' scores on the PAS did not significantly differ from psychiatric controls' scores. Similarly, schizophrenia patients with blunted affect did not differ from depressed patients on either the PAS or the SAS (Berenbaum and Oltmanns 1992). The failure to find group differences on these scales could simply reflect the fact that not all schizophrenia patients have anhedonia. Indeed, in their intial study, Chapman et al. (1976) observed a bimodal distribution of scores on the PAS indicating that some patients' scores were very similar to nonpatients, whereas other patients had significantly higher scores. More recently, Kirkpatrick and Buchanan (1989) found that schizophrenia patients who met the criteria for the deficit syndrome (stable, enduring negative symptoms not attributable to secondary sources such as depression or medication side effects) scored higher on both scales than patients who did not meet the deficit syndrome criteria. Taken together, these findings further support the contention that anhedonia is not universal among schizophrenia patients.

More recently, researchers have examined the relationship between anhedonia measures (Chapman scales or clinical rating scale measures) and reports of subjective emotional experience in response to emotional stimuli. For example, Schneider, Gur, Gur, and Shtasel (1995) found that schizophrenia patients reported experiencing less happiness following a happy mood induction, although their reports of experienced emotion were not significantly correlated with clinical ratings of anhedonia. Two studies that have examined the relationship between responses to emotionally evocative films and anhedonia found different results. Blanchard et al. (1994) found that schizophrenia patients' PAS scores were negatively correlated with their reports of positive emotion after both positive and negative emotion-eliciting film clips. That is, the higher the patients scored on the anhedonia measure, the less positive emotion they reported feeling after viewing emotionally evocative stimuli. By contrast, Berenbaum and Oltmanns (1992) found that blunted schizophrenia patients did *not* differ from nonpatients in their reported emotional experience to emotional film clips even though they scored higher on both the PAS and SAS. Blanchard et al. (1994) argued that sample differences (inpatients versus outpatients) and measurement differences (standardized measures versus single adjective ratings) were likely responsible for the different findings across the two studies.

Do Schizophrenia Patients Experience Less Positive Emotion?

An apparent discrepancy emerges in the studies reviewed thus far. With few exceptions, studies that present emotionally evocative stimuli to schizophrenia patients find that patients report experiencing the same amount of positive emotion as nonpatients. Yet, other studies find that schizophrenia patients score higher on clinical rating scales of anhedonia and the Chapman scales, indicating that they would likely experience less positive emotion, particularly pleasure, than nonpatients. How can these findings be reconciled? This pattern of finding suggests to us that the nature of hedonic deficit in schizophrenia may be more circumscribed. Specifically, we have argued (Kring 1999; Germans and Kring 2000) that while schizophrenia patients may not report a pleasure deficit when positive stimuli are presented to them, they may manifest an impaired ability to anticipate the hedonic value of forthcoming pleasurable experiences. Hedonic experience can be considered as comprising appetitive (anticipatory) and consummatory components (for example, Klein 1987). In other words, the pleasure one derives from the imagining or expectancy of a rewarding or pleasurable experience (appetitive pleasure) leads to the pursuit and engagement in the pleasurable activity, which results in consummatory pleasure. The research previously described suggests that when presented with emotional material, patients can and do experience positive emotion. However, when asked more generally about whether they find circumstances pleasurable, they are likely to report experiencing less positive emotion.

Other evidence supports this claim. For example, Myin-Germeys, Delespaul, and DeVries (2000) had schizophrenia patients complete self-reports of emotional experience at random, daily time intervals over a two-week period, and found that they reported experiencing less positive emotion and more negative emotion than nonpatient controls. Myin-Germeys et al. concluded that the hedonic deficit evident in these patients' self-reports might be linked to the decreased frequency with which these patients participated in pleasurable activities and social interactions, perhaps because they could not anticipate that such activities would be pleasurable. Evidence from studies of nonpatients indicates that social activities are linked with positive emotion, whereas sedentary activities are emotionally neutral (Clark and Watson 1988; McIntyre, Watson, Clark, and Cross 1991). Interestingly, Delespaul (1995) found that when asked to report their daily activities, schizophrenia patients described themselves as "doing nothing" (versus engaging in hobbies, sports, social activities, or watching television) five times more frequently than nonpatient controls. Thus, on a daily basis, schizophrenia patients may not report experiencing pleasure, particularly pleasure linked with social interaction, because they are not participating in pleasurable activities. Although these findings support the notion that anhedonia is linked to a failure to engage in pleasurable activities, it is difficult to determine whether patients' diminished engagement in rewarding pastimes is a cause or a consequence of hedonic deficit.

Schizophrenia Patients' Emotions about their Illness

Although there are relatively few systematic studies into the nature of emotion disturbance in schizophrenia, there are even fewer examinations of patients' reports of their feelings *about* their illness. This is unfortunate, because as Strauss and others (for example, Strauss 1989, 1994; Corin 1990) have more clearly and eloquently articulated, we cannot begin to fully appreciate the nature of schizophrenia, nor adequately conceptualize treatments, without a meaningful consideration of the patients' feelings about their illness.

Cutting and Dunne (1989) asked schizophrenia patients about any changes in their emotions following the time when the patient experienced a change in "the way things were" (Cutting and Dunne 1989:218) using an open-ended, narrative approach. In their original sample, 75 percent of the patients reported a change in their emotions. In a second sample, they asked more specific questions about particular emotions, including depression, fear, elation, anxiety, and numbness. Schizophrenia and depressed patients didn't differ in their reports of these emotions; all reported experiencing negative emotions following their initial episode. It is nonetheless interesting to note that nearly all (19/20) of the schizophrenia patients reported experiencing fear, and over two-thirds of the patients reported experiencing depression and anxiety. A quarter of the sample reported experiencing numbness, and just 4/20 patients reported elation. Thus, these findings indicate that the onset of schizophrenia is accompanied by several negative emotions.

From an anthropological perspective, Corin (1990) asked patients about their interpersonal interactions, social roles, and family dynamics. Patients who had a better outcome (operationalized as fewer rehospitalizations) had a stronger social support network of family and friends that offered emotional support. Yet, these patients often sought to distance themselves from others, perhaps as Corin argued, to protect themselves from stressors potentially associated with relapse. Indeed, the tendency to limit one's social contacts may serve as a form of emotion regulation. Social interactions are replete with emotions, both positive and negative; patients may thus seek to regulate their emotional experience, in part, by limiting and choosing their social interactions (see Strauss [1989] for a similar argument). It is interesting to note that although the patients with fewer rehospitalizations in Corin's study were more actively detached from social interactions and social roles, they did not report experiencing this as negative. By contrast, patients who had a poorer outcome reported feelings of rejection, loneliness, and isolation, and these feelings were congruent with their relatively fewer social roles and contacts. Related to this finding, Gerstein, Bates, and Reindl (1987) found that outpatient schizophrenia patients reported as much loneliness as self-identified lonely, but not psychiatrically ill, individuals. Moreover, the schizophrenia patients in this study reported experiencing more isolation and dejection than did the lonely nonpatient controls. In a study that examined mental illness, including schizophrenia across two different cultures, Jenkins (1997) found that among those patients who did not describe their lives in terms of mental illness, 66.7 percent of Euro-American schizophrenia patients and 57.1 percent of Latino schizophrenia patients described their experience in affective terms (typically related to distress), suggesting that the emotional features are indeed salient when patients describe their illness.

Often, consideration of patients' emotions about the illness are studied in the context of insight or awareness of illness (for example, McEvoy,

Schooler, Friedman, Steingard, and Allen 1993; Amador, Flaum, Andreasen, Strauss, Yale, Clark, and Gorman 1994; Selten, Gernaat, Nolen, Wiersma, and van den Bosch 1998). In a study by Selten and colleagues (Selten et al. 1998), schizophrenia patients' reports of their subjective experience of symptoms, including flat affect and anhedonia, were compared with psychiatrists' ratings of these symptoms. If a patient failed to report a symptom that a psychiatrist rated as present, it was labeled a "false negative." Although the authors noted that the psychiatrist rating was not necessarily "perfectly valid" (Selten et al. 1998:352), this type of mismatch between psychiatrist and patient report was nonetheless considered a "less realistic" (Selten et al. 1998:353) assessment on the part of the patient. Deciding about the accuracy of two discrepant reports is never an easy task. But might it not be the case that a patient's failure to concur with a psychiatrist's rating reflects something other than lack of insight or limited self-awareness? For example, as previously noted, patients' reports of how they generally feel often do not match their reports of how they feel in an emotional situation. Thus, asking a patient whether or not they generally experience pleasure (or even to describe what kinds of things they find pleasurable) might lead to a different response compared to asking a patient if he or she derived pleasure following the consumption of a favorite meal. This is not to say that patients' failure to report a symptom is unimportant or that clinical rating scales are uninformative. Rather, our point is to suggest that the context in which questions about symptoms are asked can lead to different responses. Moreover and perhaps more importantly, the tendency to consider a mismatch between patient and psychiatrist reports as inaccurate on the part of the patient seems to convey the message that the patient's subjective report is therefore not meaningful.

In summary, studies that have sought to ask what patients feel about their illness generally find that patients feel distressed, lonely, rejected, isolated, fearful, and anxious. In short, patients feel a number of negative emotions and few positive emotions. These findings bear striking resemblance to the findings reviewed here: Both in emotional situations and in daily life, schizophrenia patients report experiencing more negative emotions than nonpatients.

Unresolved Issues

To briefly summarize, a number of studies have empirically supported the early writings of Bleuler and others: Schizophrenia patients often report experiencing strong emotions yet do not display them outwardly. Further consideration of the subjective experience of emotion in schizophrenia suggests that patients may experience more negative emotion than non-patients, both in response to emotionally evocative material and in daily life. Moreover, schizophrenia patients may experience less positive emotion than nonpatients, particularly in daily life, and this may be related to patients' limited ability to anticipate that available activities will provide them pleasure. However, patients may more actively choose to avoid social interactions in order to regulate emotion (both positive and negative). Corin (1990) found that patients did not experience having more limited social contact negatively; however, it is unclear whether they viewed this more limited social environment as positive.

Despite this progress in our understanding of emotional features in schizophrenia, a number of unanswered questions remain. For example, it remains unclear if this pattern of emotional responding (that is, limited expression despite strong experience of emotion) is equally prevalent among women with schizophrenia. Almost none of the studies above included women patients in their sample. Studies that did include women did not look for gender differences. Yet we know that there are substantial differences in emotional expression between nonpatient men and women (see, for example, Brody and Hall 1993; Kring and Gordon 1998). In a study of adult schizophrenia patients' childhood movies, Walker, Grimes, Davis, and Smith (1993) found that preschizophrenia girls displayed *fewer* expressions of joy from infancy to adolescence compared to their healthy siblings, but more negative expressions in adolescence. Although the literature on emotion in nonpatients suggests fewer differences in the subjective experience of emotion between men and women, it is nonetheless important to examine gender in studies of emotion and schizophrenia, particularly given that there are a number of gender differences in schizophrenia (for a review, see Salem and Kring 1998).

It also remains unclear whether this pattern of emotional responding in schizophrenia is found across cultures. For example, Ramirez, Johnson, and Opler (1992) found that Puerto Rican schizophrenia patients manifested fewer negative symptoms, including flat affect and anhedonia than Anglo-American patients. Dassori, Miller, and Saldana (1995) found that Mexican-American schizophrenia patients exhibited more withdrawal than Anglo-American patients, but these groups did not differ on other measures of negative symptoms. Thus, negative symptoms may not be as prevalent in other cultures. Perhaps more importantly, however, the meaning of these symptoms across cultures may vary dramatically. Jenkins (1988) found that various manifestations of mental illness (including schizophrenia, but also including depression and anxiety) were characterized as *nervios* rather than (or in addition to) mental illness by Mexican-American families. When these family members were given the opportunity to describe what *nervios* was like, their descriptions were categorized in emotional terms: easily angered, anxious, and sad or depressed. This finding suggests that emotional features of schizophrenia may be among the more salient characteristics of the disorder among Mexican-Americans (yet these features are not necessarily considered part of a mental illness).

Conclusions, Clinical Implications, and Future Directions

Recent advances in psychological research have led to more systematic examinations of emotional responding in schizophrenia. Moreover, the adoption of paradigms and methods from the emotion research literature has allowed us to more precisely study schizophrenia patients' pattern of emotional responding. We now know that although schizophrenia patients display few outwardly observable expressions of emotion, they nonetheless report experiencing a wide range of both positive and negative emotions. In addition, patients' emotional responding is stable across time and does not appear to be strongly affected by more traditional neuroleptic medications (Kring and Earnst 1999). What remains to be seen, however, is whether some of the newer, "atypical" medications might impact emotional responding, particularly flat affect. Recent research on the atypical neuroleptics such as clozapine suggests that these agents may be more effective in treating negative symptoms including flat affect (for example, Kane, Honigfeld, Singer, and Meltzer 1988; Meltzer 1991; Miller, Perry, Cadoret, and Andreasen 1994; Umbricht and Kane 1995).

The findings previously reviewed also have important implications for the assessment of emotional features in schizophrenia. In particular, laboratory-based measures of emotional responding can provide important information that is not easily accessed with clinical rating scales. For example, ratings of flat affect might be misinterpreted to mean that a schizophrenia patient is without feeling. Indeed, studies that rely solely on clinical rating scales that typically assess only one component of emotion may fail to adequately capture the essence of the emotional disturbance in schizophrenia, which appears to be the lack of coordinated engagement of emotion response components. Although the experimental control offered by a laboratory manipulation of emotion answers important questions, its generalizability is limited. However, results from these laboratory studies can then suggest a number of hypotheses that can then be tested in a more ecologically valid (but less-well-controlled) setting. For example, examining emotional response tendencies in contexts such as social interaction with family members is a direction that deserves further empirical attention. In addition, psychologists would do well to adapt methods, such as ethnographies and narrative analyses used by other disciplines, including anthropology, linguistics, and sociology in order to more adequately capture the subjective experience of emotion in daily life among schizophrenia patients (Corin 1990; Kleinman 1995). A combination of laboratory and field methods would be an ideal marriage in order to study, for example, the social consequences of diminished emotional expression and inability to describe one's feelings to others (Keltner and Kring 1998). In addition, narrative analyses would provide informative information on the contexts in which patients are likely to experience diminished pleasure and positive emotion. Such a methodological approach can also provide important information about the meaning of emotional symptoms both within and across cultures (Jenkins 1997) as well as a more complete account of a patient's description of their own subjective emotional experience.

NOTE

* During the preparation of this article, Ann M. Kring was supported, in part, by a grant from NARSAD.

REFERENCES

Amador, Xavier F., Michael Flaum, Nancy C. Andreasen, David H. Strauss, Scott A. Yale, S. C. Clark, and Jack M. Gorman. 1994. "Awareness of Illness in Schizophrenia and Schizoaffective and Mood Disorders." *Archives of General Psychiatry* 51: 826–36.

Andreasen, Nancy. 1979. "Affective Flattening and the Criteria for Schizophrenia." *American Journal of Psychiatry* 34: 208–12.

———. 1982. "Negative Symptoms in Schizophrenia: Definition and Reliability." *Archives of General Psychiatry* 39: 784–8.

Averill, James R. 1982. *Anger and Aggression.* New York: Springer-Verlag.

Bellack, Alan S., Randall L. Morrison, John T. Wixtead, and Kim T. Mueser. 1990. "An Analysis of Social Competence in Schizophrenia." *British Journal of Psychiatry* 156: 809–18.

Berenbaum, Howard and Thomas F. Oltmanns. 1992. "Emotional Experience and Expression in Schizophrenia and Depression." *Journal of Abnormal Psychology* 101: 37–44.

Blanchard, Jack J., Alan S. Bellack, and Kim T. Mueser. 1994. "Affective and Social-behavioral Correlates of Physical and Social Anhedonia in Schizophrenia." *Journal of Abnormal Psychology* 103: 719–28.

Blanchard, Jack J., Kim T. Mueser, and Alan S. Bellack. 1998. "Anhedonia, Positive and Negative Affect, and Social Functioning in Schizophrenia." *Schizophrenia Bulletin* 24: 413–24.

Bleuler, Eugen. 1950 [1911]. *Dementia Praecox or the Group of Schizophrenias.* J. Zinkin, trans. New York: International Universities Press, Inc.

Borod, Joan C., Murray Alpert, Alizan Brozgold, Candace Martin, Joan Welkowitz, L. Diller, E. Peselow, B. Angrist, and A. Lieberman. 1989. "A Preliminary Comparison of Flat Affect Schizophrenics and Brain-damaged Patients on Measures of Affective Processing." *Journal of Communication Disorders* 22: 93–104.

Bouricius, Jean 1989. "Negative Symptoms and Emotions in Schizophrenia." *Schizophrenia Bulletin* 15: 201–8.

Brody, Leslie R. and Judith A. Hall. 1993. "Gender and Emotion." In Michael Lewis and Jeanette M. Haviland, eds., pp. 447–60. *Handbook of Emotions*. New York: Guilford Press.

Campos, Joseph J., Rosemary G. Campos, and Karen C. Barrett. 1989. "Emergent Themes in the Study of Emotional Development and Emotion Regulation." *Developmental Psychology* 25: 394–402.

Carpenter, William T., John J. Bartko, John S. Strauss, and Alan B. Hawk. 1978. "Signs and Symptoms as Predictors of Outcome: A Report from the International Pilot Study of Schizophrenia." *American Journal of Psychiatry* 135: 940–5.

Chapman, Loren J., Jean P. Chapman, and M. L. Raulin. 1976. "Scales for Physical and Social Anhedonia." *Journal of Abnormal Psychology* 85: 374–82.

Clark, Lee A. and David Watson. 1988. "Mood and the Mundane: Relations between Daily Life Events and Self-reported Mood." *Journal of Personality and Social Psychology* 54: 296–308.

Clementz, Brett, William M. Grove, J. Katsanis, and William G. Iacono. 1991. "Psychometric Detection of Schizotypy: Perceptual Abberation and Physical Anhedonia in Relatives of Schizophrenics." *Journal of Abnormal Psychology* 100: 607–12.

Corin, Ellen E. 1990. "Facts and Meaning in Psychiatry. An Anthropological Approach to the Lifeworld of Schizophrenics." *Culture, Medicine and Psychiatry* 14: 153–88.

Cutting, John and Francis Dunne. 1989. "Subjective Experience of Schizophrenia." *Schizophrenia Bulletin* 15: 217–31.

Dassori, Albana M., Alexander L. Miller, and Delia Saldana. 1995. "Schizophrenia among Hispanics: Epidemiology, Phenomenology, Course, and Outcome." *Schizophrenia Bulletin* 21(2): 303–12.

Delespaul, Philippe A. E. G. 1995. *Assessing Schizophrenia in Daily Life*. Maastricht, The Netherlands: Universitaire Pers Maastricht.

Dworkin, Robert H., Scott C. Clark, Xavier F. Amador, and Jack M. Gorman. 1996. "Does Affective Blunting Reflect Affective Deficit or Neuromotor Dysfunction?" *Schizophrenia Research* 20: 301–6.

Earnst, Kelly S. and Ann M. Kring. 1997. "Construct Validity of Negative Symptoms: An Empirical and Conceptual Review." *Clinical Psychology Review* 17: 167–89.

Earnst, Kelly S., Ann M. Kring, Michael A. Kadar, Jill E. Salem, David Shepard, and Peter T. Loosen. 1996. "Facial Expression in Schizophrenia." *Biological Psychiatry* 40: 556–8.

Fenton, Wayne S. and Thomas H. McGlashan. 1991. "Natural History of Schizophrenia Subtypes II: Positive and Negative Symptoms and Long-term Course." *Archives of General Psychiatry* 48: 978–86.

Frijda, Nico H. 1994. "Emotions are Functional Most of the Time." In Paul Ekman and Richard J. Davidson, eds., pp. 112–22. *The Nature of Emotion: Fundamental Questions*. New York: Oxford University Press.

Germans, Marja K. and Ann M. Kring. 2000. "Hedonic Deficit in Anhedonia: Support for the Role of Approach Motivation." *Personality and Individual Differences* 28: 659–72.

Gerstein, Lawrence H., Harry D. Bates, and Morey Reindl. 1987. "The Experience of Loneliness among Schizophrenic and Normal Persons." *Journal of Social Behavior and Personality* 2: 239–48.

Grove, William M., B. S. Lebow, Brett A.Clementz, Anna Cerri, C. Medus, and William G. Iacono. 1991. "Familial Prevalence and Coaggregation of Schizotypy Indicators: A Multitrait Family Study." *Journal of Abnormal Psychology* 100: 115–21.

Harrow, Martin, Roy R. Grinker, Philip S. Holzman, and Lawrence Kayton. 1977. "Anhedonia and Schizophrenia." *American Journal of Psychiatry* 134: 794–7.

Hooley, Jill M., John E. Richters, Sheldon Weintraub, and John M. Neale. 1987. "Psychopathology and Marital Distress: The Positive Side of Positive Symptoms." *Journal of Abnormal Psychology* 96: 27–33.

Jenkins, Janis Hunter. 1988. "Ethnopsychiatric Conceptions of Schizophrenic Illness: The Problem of *Nervios* within Mexican-American Families." *Culture, Medicine and Psychiatry* 12: 303–31.

———. 1994. "Culture, Emotion, and Psychopathology." In S. Katayama and H. Markus, eds., pp. 307–35. *Emotion and Culture: Empirical Studies of Mutual Influence*. Washington, DC: American Psychological Association Press.

———. 1997. "Subjective Experience of Persistent Schizophrenia and Depression among U.S. Latinos and Euro-Americans." *British Journal of Psychiatry* 171: 20–5.

Kane, John, Gilbert Honigfeld, Jack Singer, and Herbert Meltzer. 1988. "Clozapine for the Treatment-resistant Schizophrenic: A Double-blind Comparison with Chlorpromazine." *Archives of General Psychiatry* 45: 789–96.

Katsanis, Johanna, William G. Iacono, Morton Beiser, and Lizabeth Lacey. 1992. "Clinical Correlates of Anhedonia and Perceptual Aberration in First-episode Patients with Schizophrenia and Affective Disorder." *Journal of Abnormal Psychology* 101: 184–91.

Keefe, Richard S. E., Daniel S. Lobel, Richard C. Mohs, Jeremy M. Silverman, Philip D. Harvey, M. Davidson, M. F. Losonczy, and K. L. Davis. 1991. "Diagnostic Issues in Chronic Schizophrenia: Kraepelinian Schizophrenia, Undifferentiated Schizophrenia, and State-independent Negative Symptoms." *Schizophrenia Research* 4: 71–9.

Keltner, Dacher and Ann M. Kring. 1998. "Emotion, Social Function, and Psychopathology." *Review of General Psychology* 2: 320–42.

Kirkpatrick, Brian and Robert W. Buchanan. 1989. "Anhedonia and the Deficit Syndrome of Schizophrenia." *Psychiatry Research* 31: 25–30.

Kirkpatrick, Brian, Robert W. Buchanan, P. D. McKinney, L. D. Alphs, and W. T. Carpenter. 1989. "The Schedule for the Deficit Syndrome: An Instrument for Research in Schizophrenia." *Psychiatry Research* 30: 119–23.

Klein, D. 1987. "Depression and Anhedonia." In David C. Clark and Jan Fawcett, eds., pp. 1–14. *Anhedonia and Affect Deficit States*. New York: PMA Publishing.

Kleinman, Arthur. 1995. "Suffering and Its Professional Transformation." In Arthur Kleinman, ed., pp. 995–1119. *Writing at the Margin: Discourse between Anthropology and Medicine*. Berkeley: University of California Press.

Knight, Raymond A. and James D. Roff. 1985. "Affectivity in Schizophrenia." In Murray Alpert, ed., pp. 280–316. *Controversies in Schizophrenia: Change and Constancies*. New York: Guilford Press.

Knight, Raymond A., James D. Roff, J. Barnett, and J. L. Moss. 1979. "Concurrent and Predictive Validity of Thought Disorder and Affectivity: A 22 Year Follow-up of Acute Schizophrenics." *Journal of Abnormal Psychology* 88: 1–12.

Kraepelin, Emil. 1971 [1917]. *Dementia Praecox and Paraphrenia*. R. M. Bradley, trans. Huntington, NY: Robert E. Krieger Publishing Co.

Krause, Rainer, Evelyne Steimer, Cornella Saenger-Alt, and Guenter Wagner. 1989. "Facial Expressions of Schizophrenic Patients and Their Interaction Partners." *Psychiatry* 52: 1–12.

Krause, Rainer, Evelyne Steimer-Krause, and Hans Hufnagel. 1992. "Expression and Experience of Affects in Paranoid Schizophrenia." *Revue Européenne de Psychologie Appliquée* 42: 131–8.

Kring, Ann M. 1991. *The Relationship between Emotional Expression, Subjective Experience, and Autonomic Arousal in Schizophrenia*. Unpublished doctoral dissertation.

———. 1999. "Emotion in Schizophrenia: Old Mystery, New Understanding." *Current Directions in Psychological Science* 8: 160–3.

———. 2003. "Nonverbal Behavior in Schizophrenia." In P. Philippot, E. Coats, and R. S. Feldman, eds., *Nonverbal Behavior in Clinical Settings*. New York: Oxford University Press.

Kring, Ann M., Murray Alpert, John M. Neale, and Philip D. Harvey. 1994. "A Multichannel, Multimethod Assessment of Affective Flattening in Schizophrenia." *Psychiatry Research* 54: 211–22.

Kring, Ann M. and Jo-Anne A. Bachorowski. 1999. "Emotions and Psychopathology." *Cognition and Emotion* 13: 575–99.

Kring, Ann M. and Kelly S. Earnst. 1999. "Stability of Emotional Responding in Schizophrenia." *Behavior Therapy* 30: 373–88.

Kring, Ann M. and A. H. Gordon. 1998. "Sex Differences in Emotion: Expression, Experience, and Physiology." *Journal of Personality and Social Psychology* 74: 686–703.

Kring, Ann M., S. L. Kerr, and Kelly S. Earnst. 1999. "Schizophrenic Patients Show Facial Reactions to Emotional Facial Expressions." *Psychophysiology* 36: 186–92.

Kring, Ann M., S. Kerr, D. A. Smith, and J. M. Neale. 1993. "Flat Affect in Schizophrenia Does Not Reflect Diminished Subjective Experience of Emotion." *Journal of Abnormal Psychology* 104: 507–17.

Kring, Ann M. and J. M. Neale. 1996. "Do Schizophrenic Patients Show a Disjunctive Relationship among Expressive, Experiential, and Psychophysiological Components of Emotion?" *Journal of Abnormal Psychology* 105: 249–57.

Levenson, Robert W. 1994. "Human Emotion: A Functional View." In Paul Ekman and Richard J. Davidson, eds., pp. 123–6. *The Nature of Emotion: Fundamental Question*. New York: Oxford University Press.

Levin, Smadar, Judith A. Hall, Raymond A. Knight, and Murray Alpert. 1985. "Verbal and Nonverbal Expression of Affect in Speech of Schizophrenic and Depressed Patients." *Journal of Abnormal Psychology* 94: 487–97.

Lewine, Richard R. J. 1991. "Anhedonia and the Amotivational State of Schizophrenia." In A. Marneros, Nancy C. Andreasen, and Ming T. Tsuang, eds., pp. 79–85. *Negative vs. Positive Schizophrenia*. Berlin: Springer-Verlag.

Lutz, Catherine A. and Llla Abu-Lughod. 1990. *Language and the Politics of Emotion*. New York: Cambridge University Press.

Martin, Candace C., Joan C. Borod, Murray Alpert, Alizah Brozgold, and J. Welkowitz. 1990. "Spontaneous Expression of Facial Emotion in Schizophrenic and Right Brain-Damaged Patients." *Journal of Communication Disorders* 23: 287–301.

Mattes, R. M., F. Schneider, H. Heimann, and N. Birbaumer. 1995. "Reduced Emotional Response of Schizophrenic Patients in Remission during Social Interaction." *Schizophrenia Research* 17: 249–55.

McEvoy, Joseph P., Nina R. Schooler, Edward Friedman, Sandra Steingard, and M. Allen. 1993. "Use of Psychopathology Vignettes by Patients with Schizophrenia or Schizoaffective Disorder and by Mental Health Professionals to Judge Patients' Insight." *American Journal of Psychiatry* 150: 1649–53.

McIntyre, Curtis W., David Watson, Lee A. Clark, and Stephen A. Cross. 1991. "The Effect of Induced Social Interaction on Positive and Negative Affect." *Bulletin of the Psychonomic Society* 29: 67–70.

Meehl, P. E. 1962. "Schizotaxia, Schizotypy, Schizophrenia." *American Psychologist* 17: 827–38.

———. 1973. *Psychodiagnosis – Selected Papers*. Minneapolis: University of Minnesota Press.

Meltzer, Herbert Y. 1991. "Pharmacologic Treatment of Negative Symptoms." In John F. Greden and Rajiv Tandon, eds., pp. 217–31. *Negative Schizophrenic Symptoms: Pathophysiology and Clinical Implications*. Washington, DC: American Psychiatric Press.

Miller, Dell D., Paul J. Perry, Remi J. Cadoret, and Nancy C. Andreasen. 1994. "Clozapine's Effect on Negative Symptoms in Treatment-refractory Schizophrenics." *Comprehensive Psychiatry* 35: 8–15.

Myin-Germeys, Inez, P. A. Delespaul, and M. W. DeVries. 2000. "Schizophrenia Patients are More Emotionally Active than is Assumed Based on their Behavior." *Schizophrenia Bulletin* 26: 847–54.

Nesse, R. M. 1990. "Evolutionary Explanations of Emotions." *Human Nature* 1: 261–89.

Pfohl, Bruce and George Winokur. 1982. "The Evolution of Symptoms in Institutionalized Hebephrenic/Catatonic Schizophrenics." *British Journal of Psychiatry* 141: 567–72.

Rado, Sandor. 1956. *Psychoanalysis of Behavior: Collected Papers*. New York: Grune and Stratton.

Ramirez, P. M., P. B. Johnson, and L. A. Opler. 1992. *Ethnicity as a Modifier of Negative Symptoms*. Presented at the annual meeting of the American Psychiatric Association, Washington, DC.

Rey, E. R., J. Bailer, W. Brauer, M. Handel, D. Lauberstein, and A. Stein. 1994. "Stability Trends and Longitudinal Correlations of Negative and Positive Syndromes within a Three-year Follow-up of Initially Hospitalized Schizophrenics." *Acta Psychiatrica Scandinavica* 90: 405–12.

Salem, Jill E. and Ann M. Kring. 1998. "The Role of Gender Differences in the Reduction of Etiologic Heterogeneity in Schizophrenia." *Clinical Psychology Review* 18: 795–819.

———. 1999. "Flat Affect and Social Skills in Schizophrenia: Evidence for their Independence." *Psychiatry Research* 87: 159–67.

Selten, Jean-Paul, Hajo B. Gernaat, Willem A. Nolen, Durk Wiersma, and Robert J. van den Bosch. 1998. "Experience of Negative Symptoms: Comparison of Schizophrenic Patients to Patients with a Depressive Disorder and to Normal Subjects." *American Journal of Psychiatry* 155: 350–4.

Schlenker, Regine, Rudolf Cohen, and Gereon Hopmann. 1995. "Affective Modulation of the Startle Reflex in Schizophrenic Patients." *European Archives of Psychiatry and Clinical Neuroscience* 245: 309–18.

Schneider, Frank, Ruben C. Gur, Raquel E. Gur, and Derri L. Shtasel. 1995. "Emotional Processing in Schizophrenia: Neurobehavioral Probes in Relation to Psychopathology." *Schizophrenia Research* 17: 67–75.

Schuck, Jochen, D. Leventhal, H. Rothstein, and V. Irizarry. 1984. "Physical Anhedonia and Schizophrenia." *Journal of Abnormal Psychology* 93: 342–4.

Strauss, John S. 1989. "Subjective Experiences of Schizophrenia: Toward a New Dynamic Psychiatry-II." *Schizophrenia Bulletin* 15: 179–87.

———. 1994. "The Person with Schizophrenia as a Person II: Approaches to the Subjective and Complex." *British Journal of Psychiatry* 164(suppl. 23): 103–7.

Sullivan, Harry Stack. 1927. "Affective Experience in Early Schizophrenia." *American Journal of Psychiatry* 6: 467–83.

Umbricht, Daniel and J. M. Kane. 1995. "Risperidone: Efficacy and Safety." *Schizophrenia Bulletin* 21: 593–606.

Venables, P. and J. K. Wing. 1962. "Level of Arousal and the Subclassification of Schizophrenia." *Archives of General Psychiatry* 7: 62–7.

Walker, Elaine F., K. E. Grimes, D. M. Davis, and A. J. Smith. 1993. "Childhood Precursors of Schizophrenia: Facial Expressions of Emotion." *American Journal of Psychiatry* 150: 1654–60.

World Health Organization. 1973. *The International Pilot Study of Schizophrenia*. Geneva: World Health Organization.

Index

Other books in the series (*continued from page iii*)

8 Margaret Lock, Allan Young, and Alberto Cambrosio (eds.), *Living and Working with the New Medical Technologies: Intersection of Inquiry*

The series also includes a group of *theme books* that are designed as course material for advanced undergraduate and graduate students and that synthesize emerging scholarship from relatively new subfields or reinterpret the literature of older ones. Published theme books are

9 Daniel Moreman, *Meaning, Medicine and the "Placebo Effect"*
10 Susan Reynolds Whyte, Sjaak van der Geest and Anita Hardon, *The Social Lives of Medicines*

Future titles will include
James Trostle, *Epidemiology and Culture*
Andrea Wiley, *An Ecology of High-Altitude Infancy: A Biocultural Perspective*